LINKing Assessment
and Early Intervention

LINKing Assessment and Early Intervention

An Authentic Curriculum-Based Approach

by

Stephen J. Bagnato, Ed.D.
Children's Hospital of Pittsburgh
University of Pittsburgh

John T. Neisworth, Ph.D.
The Pennsylvania State University

and

Susan M. Munson, Ph.D.
Duquesne University

·P A U L·H·
BROOKES
PUBLISHING Co®

Baltimore • London • Sydney

·P A U L·H·
BROOKES
PUBLISHING C⁹ ®

Paul H. Brookes Publishing Co.
Post Office Box 10624
Baltimore, Maryland 21285-0624

www.brookespublishing.com

"Paul H. Brookes Publishing Co." is a registered trademark
of Paul H. Brookes Publishing Co., Inc.

Typeset by Brushwood Graphics, Inc., Baltimore, Maryland.
Manufactured in the United States of America by
Thomson-Shore, Inc., Dexter, Michigan.

The LINK vignettes that appear herein are composites representing the needs of many types
of children and families whom the authors have helped through collaborative interagency
assessment, intervention, and consultation services provided through both The Pennsylvania State University and the University of Pittsburgh in partnerships with community-
based early intervention programs. All names and identifying information, including specific functional needs and family circumstances, have been altered to ensure confidentiality.

Second printing, April 2000.
Third printing, June 2002.

Library of Congress Cataloging-in-Publication Data

Bagnato, Stephen J.
    Linking assessment and early intervention: an authentic curriculum-based approach /
    by Stephen J. Bagnato, John T. Neisworth, and Susan M. Munson.
        p.   cm.
    Includes bibliographical references and indexes.
    ISBN 1-55766-263-0
    1. Education, Preschool—Curricula.   2. Child development—Evaluation.   3. Special
education—Curricula.   I. Neisworth, John T.   II. Munson, Susan M.   III. Title.
    LB 1140.4.B33   1997
    371.9—DC20   96-43160
                                                                                          CIP

British Library Cataloguing in Publication data are available from the British Library.

Contents

About the Authors

Stephen J. Bagnato, Ed.D., NCSP, Developmental School Psychologist and Associate Professor of Pediatrics and Psychology, University of Pittsburgh School of Medicine, Child Development Unit, Rangos Research Center, Children's Hospital of Pittsburgh, 3705 Fifth Avenue, Pittsburgh, Pennsylvania 15213-2583

Stephen J. Bagnato is Associate Director of Developmental Psychology and Coordinator of both Early Childhood Diagnostic Services and Developmental Neuropsychology Services at Children's Hospital of Pittsburgh. Dr. Bagnato specializes in alternative team assessment and intervention strategies for infants and preschoolers with neurodevelopmental and neurobehavioral disorders as well as for their families. The recipient of a national brain injury research award in 1987, Dr. Bagnato has published more than 80 clinical research studies in early intervention, school psychology, developmental disabilities, and developmental neuropsychology. Dr. Bagnato is Principal Investigator for a 3-year school-linked research and program development grant from the U.S. Department of Education, Office of Special Education and Rehabilitative Services (OSERS), one of only four such grants awarded nationally. The program, Collaborative Health Interventions for Learners with Disabilities (Project CHILD), evaluates the efficacy of a transagency developmental health care model to meet the mental health and physical health needs of infants and preschoolers with developmental disabilities and their families. In addition, Dr. Bagnato is the director of psychology interdisciplinary training for a 3-year Maternal and Child Health Leadership Training Grant in Neurodevelopmental Disabilities at the University of Pittsburgh and Children's Hospital entitled The University, Community, Leaders, and Individuals with Disabilities (UCLID) Center. Dr. Bagnato is a fellow of the American Psychological Association in Division 16 and a member of the journal editorial boards of *School Psychology Quarterly, Journal of Psychoeducational Assessment, Journal of Early Intervention,* and *Topics in Early Childhood Special Education.* Along with Dr. Neisworth, in 1995, he received the American Psychological Association (Division 16) Best Research Article Award for "A National Study of the Treatment and Social Invalidity of Intelligence Testing for Early Intervention." He is the coauthor of professional "best practice" position statements on early childhood assessment for the National Association of School Psychologists and Division for Early Childhood of the Council for Exceptional Children as well as the coauthor of *Assessment for Early Intervention: Best Practices for Professionals* (Guilford Press, 1991), and *System to Plan Early Child-*

hood Services (American Guidance Service, 1990). Dr. Bagnato is in demand in 47 states as a consultant on early intervention practices.

John T. Neisworth, Ph.D., Professor of Special Education, Director, Early Intervention Training Program, The Pennsylvania State University, 226 A Moore Building, University Park, Pennsylvania 16802

John T. Neisworth has extensive research experience and expertise in early intervention curricula and assessment and has authored 12 texts in the areas of special education and early intervention. He is the coauthor of the highly regarded *HICOMP Preschool Curriculum* (Psychological Corporation, 1980), the widely used assessment text *Assessment for Early Intervention: Best Practices for Professionals* (Guilford Press, 1991), and *System to Plan Early Childhood Services* (American Guidance Service, 1990). Dr. Neisworth has directed numerous funded projects, including the federally funded Comprehensive Early Intervention master's program, and he co-directs the Collaborative Leadership Program to prepare Special Education/School Psychology interdisciplinary professionals for early intervention. He has written a chapter, "Recommended Practices in Assessment for Early Intervention," in *Early Intervention/Early Childhood–Special Education: Recommended Practices* (PRO-ED, 1996). Along with Dr. Bagnato, in 1995, he received the American Psychological Association (Division 16) Best Research Article Award for "A National Study of the Treatment and Social Invalidity of Intelligence Testing for Early Intervention." Dr. Neisworth is in demand in 47 states as a consultant on early intervention practices. Finally, Dr. Neisworth is cofounder of *Topics in Early Childhood Special Education.*

Susan M. Munson, Ph.D., Associate Professor, Special Education Program, School of Education, Duquesne University, 101B Canevin Hall, Pittsburgh, Pennsylvania 15282

Susan M. Munson is the coordinator of the Undergraduate Special Education Program. Dr. Munson specializes in educational assessment in special education and in the area of inclusive educational practices for students with mild disabilities. She is Project Coordinator for the Early Intervention Interdisciplinary Field Experience Program (EIIFE), which is funded through the Pennsylvania Department of Education Higher Education initiative. This program involves field-based training in interdisciplinary, team-based assessment for teams of students in preservice nursing, occupational therapy, and special education in cooperation with Duquesne University's School of Health Sciences and School of Nursing. This project's training focus expanded to include early intervention service providers and parents during the 1996–1997 academic year. Dr. Munson is also a co-coordinator of a 2-year grant from the Pennsylvania Developmental Disabilities Council to restructure the undergraduate teacher education curriculum to prepare future educators to teach students with diverse learning needs.

Preface

This volume represents the culmination of our model for linking assessment and early intervention; the LINK model had its genesis in *LINKING Developmental Assessment and Curricula: Prescriptions for Early Intervention* (Bagnato & Neisworth, 1981). The second edition, *LINKING Developmental Assessment and Early Intervention: Curriculum-Based Prescriptions* (Bagnato, Neisworth, & Munson, 1989), added the element of curriculum-embedded assessment to the LINK model. Now, we elaborate and extend that model, building on six standards that are described and operationalized herein, to demonstrate how it can be used to identify, customize, and implement an authentic approach to curriculum-based evaluation by using those combinations of curriculum-embedded and curriculum-compatible systems that best sample real-life capabilities and accommodate special needs.

The evolution of our approach is in response to fundamental changes in assessment for early intervention that have occurred since the first edition was published in 1981. Three phases in this rapid evolution can be noted: During the first phase, assessment for early intervention was largely "inherited" from materials and practices for use with school-age children, with traditional norm-referenced intelligence tests and developmental scales routinely being force fitted for use with infants, toddlers, and preschoolers. The second phase is characterized by field validation and the use of the first generation of criterion-referenced, or curriculum-based, systems influenced by the passage of PL 94-142, the Education for All Handicapped Children Act of 1975 (subsequently reauthorized as PL 101-476, the Individuals with Disabilities Education Act [IDEA] of 1990). The third and present phase of assessment involves the expanded development and predominant use of authentic curriculum-based assessment measures that directly relate to worthwhile, functional, and teachable objectives in response to the provisions of PL 99-457, the Education of the Handicapped Act Amendments of 1986, which was further amended by PL 102-119, the Individuals with Disabilities Education Act Amendments of 1991. The three volumes in which we have refined the LINKing approach have both chronicled and influenced these fundamental and progressive changes in assessment methods and practices.

When preschool education for children with special needs first became widespread in the early 1970s, professionals viewed assessment as being largely disconnected from intervention. In general, assessment involved the use by psychologists of traditional norm-referenced scales, most often early intelligence tests, such as the Gesell Developmental Schedules (Gesell, 1949), the Bayley Scales of Infant Development (Bayley, 1969), and the Cattell Infant Intelligence Scale (Cattell, 1966).

Teachers were forced to use their creativity to attempt to translate information from traditional scales into teachable goals and activities, most often with limited success; indeed, such assessment methods produced labels rather than plans for intervention. In the late 1970s and early 1980s, the numerous model demonstration programs funded by the U.S. Office of Special Education and Rehabilitative Services produced several field-validated materials that linked assessment to intervention for the first time. These materials included assessment instruments that contained the objectives of the curricula to which they were attached. These linked systems also had the advantage of uniting parents and professionals, because assessment items were now more specific and of clear interest to teachers and parents. The first edition of *LINKING* (Bagnato & Neisworth, 1981) promoted this trend by posing a clinical model to bridge the assessment/curriculum gap by linking information from traditional norm-referenced developmental scales to newly developed curricula, thus facilitating individualized curriculum goal planning. This first edition also offered a review of the few developmental curricula and assessment materials that were commercially available to accomplish assessment/intervention linkages. With the emergent predominance of curriculum-based methods in early intervention, the second edition of *LINKING* (Bagnato, et al., 1989) codified an assessment/curriculum linkage model, "LINK," and illustrated the use of the many newly developed linked curriculum-based developmental assessment/intervention/evaluation systems available to practitioners.

In a companion volume (Bagnato & Neisworth, 1991), we predicted the next wave of change in assessment for early intervention by discussing the basis for curriculum-based assessment within a convergent assessment model. The convergent model is based on our thesis that early childhood assessment is actually a complex collaborative decision-making process that synthesizes information from multiple sources, settings, occasions, and instruments.

This text advocates the use of linked curriculum-embedded assessment systems in early intervention, supplemented by only a few curriculum-compatible scales that meet certain standards of utility and acceptability. Moreover, we enthusiastically forecast another fundamental change in assessment for early intervention—that is, the use of curriculum-based assessment that relies on *authentic* sources and samples of behavior for worthwhile planning and evaluating of child and family goals and progress.

In this book, six standards are offered for use in evaluating assessment materials. These standards characterize assessment that is clearly useful for program planning and monitoring, deemed worthwhile by professionals, parents, and caregivers, and capable of making a difference—for teachers, therapists, and other professionals; for parents; and for the children themselves, who are, after all, the focus of our efforts.

REFERENCES

Bagnato, S.J., & Neisworth, J.T. (1981). *LINKING developmental assessment and curricula: Prescriptions for early intervention.* Rockville, MD: Aspen Publishers, Inc.

Bagnato, S.J., & Neisworth, J.T. (1991). *Assessment for early intervention: Best practices for professionals.* New York: Guilford Press.

Bagnato, S.J., Neisworth, J.T., & Munson, S.M. (1989). *LINKING developmental assessment and early intervention: Curriculum-based prescriptions* (2nd ed.). Rockville, MD: Aspen Publishers, Inc.

Bayley, N. (1969). *Bayley Scales of Infant Development.* San Antonio, TX: The Psychological Corporation.

Cattell, P. (1966). *The measurement of intelligence of infants and young children.* San Antonio, TX: The Psychological Corporation.

Education of the Handicapped Act Amendments of 1986, PL 99-457, 20 U.S.C. § 1400 *et seq.*

Education for All Handicapped Children Act of 1975, PL 94-142, 20 U.S.C. § 1400 *et seq.*

Gesell, A. (1949). *Gesell Developmental Schedules.* San Antonio, TX: The Psychological Corporation.

Individuals with Disabilities Education Act (IDEA) of 1990, PL 101-476, 20 U.S.C. §§ 1400 *et seq.*

Individuals with Disabilities Education Act Amendments of 1991, PL 102-119, 20 U.S.C. § 1400 *et seq.*

Acknowledgments

We owe much appreciation to Ms. Glenda Carelas, whose dedicated work and skill in word processing enabled us to produce a coherent and integrated manuscript. Ms. Carelas has been a committed member of our "publication team" since the early 1980s, when she also helped to produce the first edition of *LINKING*. At the Children's Hospital of Pittsburgh, Helen McElheny's commitment and diligence have also contributed immeasurably to the completion of this manuscript. We also acknowledge the many graduate students at The Pennsylvania State University, the University of Pittsburgh, and Duquesne University who formed our interuniversity team to help us with the research for this book. Special appreciation is extended to Jeannie Dougherty, Davi Kathiresan, Christina Coco, and Cherie Defenbaugh. We owe much to the numerous consultee groups in 40 states with whom we had the pleasure of collaborating for their honest and insightful appraisal of the problems and solutions in assessment for early intervention.

Our work was inspired by the experiences of our own preschoolers, both children and grandchildren—the two Michaels, Mark, and Samantha—whose own preschool experiences and special friends kept our work authentic.

We must also acknowledge that the research activities for this book were aided by the efforts of students, trainees, and faculty who are supported by the following federal and foundation grants: U.S. Department of Education, Office of Special Education and Rehabilitative Services, School-Linked Services Competition; Collaborative Health Interventions for Learners with Disabilities (Project CHILD)—The Developmental Healthcare Resource Partnership, H023D40013; Jewish Healthcare Foundation of Pittsburgh, Project Early CHILD: A Consultative Model for Developmental Healthcare Support in Early Intervention Programs; U.S. Department of Education, Office of Special Education Programs, Collaborative Leadership Training Program in Early Intervention; U.S. Department of Health and Human Services, Maternal and Child Health Bureau (MCHB) Interdisciplinary Leadership Education for Health Professionals Caring for Children with Neurodevelopmental and Related Disabilities (LEND); and the University, Community, Leaders, and Individuals with Disabilities (UCLID) Center at the University of Pittsburgh, MCJ 429414.

Foremost,
to the memories of
Stephen J. Bagnato, Sr., and Anne Neisworth,
cherished father and mother,
whose strong beliefs, self-reliance, and social consciences
indelibly shaped our personal and professional lives.

And
with special recognition
to the personal and professional life and memory of
Richard LeVan, D.Ed.,
a model husband and father,
a tireless advocate for families and children with disabilities,
a valued colleague,
and
a pioneering, nontraditional school psychologist.
We deeply miss his partnership,
but his legacy will endure
in our continuing commitment to early intervention.

1

Bridging the Assessment–
Early Intervention Gap

Tests don't make decisions—people do. Parents and professionals continually make at least tentative decisions on the basis of information derived from tests; sometimes such information is good and sometimes it is bad. When we are considering the educational and developmental fates of children, we need a solid basis for making decisions. Assessment materials and procedures should and could, but very often do not, provide good information.

The assessment process causes confusion and great anxiety for many people, in particular parents of children with special needs. These parents—and concerned professionals—understand that assessment is much more than a bureaucratic procedure that requires perfunctory paperwork; assessment is a pivotal and emotion-filled activity that plays a major role in determining the futures of children and their families.

A parent who suspects that his or her child may have a problem asks three basic questions: "What's wrong with my child?" "What will my child be like later?" and "What can be done to help my child?" As professionals, we know that providing answers to these questions is not easy. Each question requires a different set of considerations and assessment procedures and instruments.

"What's wrong with my child?" asks the professional to make a diagnosis: Into which syndrome or clinical category does the child best fit? Making such a diagnosis entails comparing the child's characteristics and performance with the typical or normative performance of children of the same age. This comparison is often required to determine eligibility for early intervention. Norm-based assessment, therefore, plays a primary role in diagnosing or categorizing childhood disorders; such assessment, given its standardized administration and cutoff scores, is often used inappropriately, resulting in the denial of services or premature and inaccurate diagnoses.

"What will my child be like later?" asks the professional to make a prognosis or prediction. Such a question has no definitive answer; developmental progress does not depend exclusively on diagnostic category or "what's wrong." To a great extent, a child's prognosis depends on the quality of his or her subsequent experiences and on the impact of intervention.

"What can be done to help my child?" asks the professional to plan and initiate an assessment program to guide intervention for each individual child. Providing answers to this question is the major mission of assessment for early intervention.

In this chapter, we discuss the gap that exists between assessment and early intervention; identify some of the traditional assessment practices and beliefs that have contributed to this gap; describe six prominent assessment models; examine recommended assessment practices that may bridge this gap; and introduce the six standards of good assessment materials and practices in early intervention.

THE ASSESSMENT–EARLY INTERVENTION GAP

A number of factors have contributed to the assessment–early intervention gap that exists when assessment fails to provide credible information for useful, worthwhile decision making. Two major factors are 1) confusion about or conflicts in assessment purpose and 2) the antagonistic features of conventional assessment materials and practices.

Assessment Purpose

To avoid confusion or conflicts, assessment specialists are in clear agreement that the *purpose* of conducting an assessment must be established before assessment materials are selected and used. The field of child development includes proponents of purpose: "Different decisions require different types of instruments and different types of assessment strategies. . . . It is the *purpose* and not the population that defines the instrument chosen" (Wachs & Sheehan, 1988, p. 401). Hayes, Nelson, and Jarrett (1987), members of the field of counseling and clinical psychology, also present a compelling case for evaluating assessment according to its *utility*, which hinges on how well it fulfills its purpose. It is critical to resolve any conflicts in or confusion about the purpose of an assessment if that assessment is to be useful. Articulating the purpose of assessment is so crucial, in fact, that we have made it the central theme in both a text (Bagnato & Neisworth, 1991a) and a chapter on recommended practices in assessment (Neisworth & Bagnato, 1996). It is also important to recognize that decisions based on assessment can have either low or high stakes (Meisels, 1989) and that the stakes of a decision should be considered when selecting assessment materials.

Antagonistic Features of Conventional Assessment

Planning a program and making recommendations for instruction and therapy place different demands on assessment and are the most important concerns of parents. Careful and sensible assessment can produce a blueprint or framework for an appropriate child development program. Traditional diagnostic assessment reports, however, usually lack practical program recommendations. Indeed, many diagnostic reports are "dead ends" that offer little more than scores, clinical labels, and (perhaps) vague recommendations for programming. This gap between assessment and programming need not exist. Unfortunately, prevailing policies often require professionals to use inappropriate materials and practices to satisfy funding requirements or to comply with federal, state, or health care reimbursement regulations.

Most conventional, norm-referenced, standardized materials developed through psychometric procedures do not meet standards for acceptable assessment in early intervention. In fact, traditional measures are most often at odds with the needs and missions of early intervention. We identify seven characteristics of conventional assessment that make it minimally useful, irrelevant, or actually antagonistic to the missions of early intervention. The seven antagonistic features are 1) use of global trait measures, 2) inappropriate use of normative scoring, 3) forcing standardized procedures to fit all children, 4) dependence on traditional validities, 5) instructional irrelevance of item content, 6) professional boundaries, and 7) low utility of assessment reports. These characteristics are examined within the context of the following section's discussion of more appropriate assessment measures.

FOUNDATIONS FOR LINKING ASSESSMENT AND INTERVENTION

The antagonistic features of conventional assessment cannot be circumvented by adept use or by performing the scoring adjustments that are often recommended by publishers. Materials and procedures that are compatible with the characteristics of young children and the missions of early childhood education have become available. In the following section, we identify nine features of recommended practices and contrast them with their antithetical features of conventional practices (several of which are the above-mentioned antagonistic characteristics); these nine features of recommended practices provide the foundation for linking assessment and intervention.

Assessment versus Testing

Testing and assessment are related, but not identical, activities. We all have had our capabilities tested in our school experience, but few of us have had our skills assessed. The critical differences between these two operations are magnified when they involve infants and preschoolers. The primary distinctions between testing and assessment concern the quality, scope, and usefulness of the information obtained (see Table 1.1). On the one hand, testing is merely quantitative: The child is described by a number. On the other hand, assessment integrates both quantitative and qualitative data that are translated into treatment-based terms. As Salvia and Ysseldyke (1995) noted

> *Testing*, then, means administrating a particular set of questions to an individual or group of individuals in order to obtain a score. That score is the end product of testing. Testing may be part of a larger process known as *assessment*; however, testing and assessment are not synonymous. Assessment in educational settings is a multifaceted process that involves far more than the administration of a test . . . Assessment is the process of collecting data for the purposes of making decisions about students. (p. 5)

Assessment must be a comprehensive process of collecting information about a child. Information that permits the analysis of a child's language, personal-social, motor, cognitive, and interactive skills must be gathered. Seldom are developmental problems "pure" and specific. For example, an infant with motor problems may not be able to move around the environment or initiate social interactions as much as another child. As a result of his or her restricted mobility, other areas of development (e.g., cognitive, language, social) may be affected. Assessment, accordingly, must include all areas of development to provide the whole picture of a child's functional development.

Comprehensive assessment is often prescriptive as well as descriptive; it describes a child's strengths and weaknesses with a practical result—the creation of an individualized education program (IEP) or an individualized family service plan (IFSP). Prescriptive assessment, unlike diagnostic (or descriptive) assessment, results in recommendations that focus intervention and promote progress. The school psychologist who conducts child assessments with a focus on attainable objectives and adheres to a functional, criterion-referenced orientation maintains credibility with early childhood educators, other team members, and parents. Such an approach en-

Table 1.1.   Model of a convergent assessment battery

Measure	Purpose of measure
Norm based	Determine degree of child's developmental impairment through comparison
Curriculum based	Identify curricular objectives, offer adaptations, and monitor child progress/program impact
Judgment based	Include parent and professional perceptions of child's status and progress
Ecological	Characterize the social and physical qualities of the child's environment

sures the appropriate match between scales and purpose and synchronizes the assessment-intervention-evaluation sequence.

Functional Orientation versus Categorical Orientation

Previous approaches to assessing children with special developmental needs emphasized a categorical or diagnostic orientation through the use of global trait measures of theorized traits or capacities (e.g., intelligence, aptitude, motivation). Such measures lack the relevance and the program or curricular specificity needed to identify objectives. The measurement of inferred conditions or traits is an attempt to describe what the child *has* (e.g., mental retardation, emotional disturbances, brain injury) rather than what the child *does* (e.g., gets along with peers, dresses and grooms self, recognizes letters). Such a diagnosis may be termed a *genotypic* appraisal, because it presumes to identify a general, underlying condition. There are two major limitations to the genotypic, diagnostic approach: 1) various symptoms are not distinct or pure, in that different groups share disability characteristics; and 2) identification of disability does not automatically suggest preferred individualized treatment. As a result of these limitations, the diagnostic approach cannot offer specifics to guide in determining what to teach (i.e., objectives), how to teach (i.e., methods, materials), or how to detect progress (i.e., evaluation).

Assignment to a clinical category (i.e., diagnostic assessment) is particularly difficult and unproductive when assessing very young children. The young exceptional child has not yet developed a stable repertoire of skills, undergoes rapid changes, and has not experienced the organizing and enhancing effects of structured play and therapy. A functional orientation is more practical and is clinically proven. A functional, or *phenotypic,* appraisal describes what a child does or does not do under specific conditions; it describes and operationally defines the observable skills and limitations that the child typically exhibits. Functional or phenotypic assessment provides a framework for goal planning; it conveys the view that progress is to be expected and that such progress can be charted and described so that goals can be revised.

Gone are the days when diagnostic specialists could "test" only intelligence and believe that a child's behavior and skills were sampled representatively. The young child's lack of differentiation or integration in developmental competencies makes this approach ludicrous. Nevertheless, many professionals, especially traditionally trained psychologists, continue to use a one-dimensional perspective and approach. They attempt to extend downward practices used with school-age children and apply them to preschoolers. This practice contributes to a significant antagonistic feature of traditional assessment (i.e., testing)—the nonspecific and low-utility information provided for reports. Assessment reports are often vague, confusing, and laden with jargon. These reports are usually test centered, and they organize results around each test to which a child

has been subjected rather than around developmental or referral needs (Bagnato & Neisworth, 1991a). In addition, little or no common content base exists between conventional assessment materials and early childhood education curricula. Even when norm-based instruments and curricula do share content (e.g., Gesell Developmental Schedules [Gesell, 1949] and developmental curricula), this compatibility is rarely utilized when professionals plan programs. In addition, in some cases, developmental milestone objectives may not be appropriate (e.g., for children with physical limitations).

Broad and integrated services can be delivered only when professionals target the multiple dimensions of a child and family's needs. Comprehensive assessment addresses the child's complex developmental and behavioral needs within and across several domains (e.g., cognitive, language, perceptual fine motor, social-emotional, gross motor, adaptive) and detects the impact of disabilities on development. In addition, various behavior response classes (e.g., self-regulation, reactivity, activity, normalcy, endurance, attention) are targeted.

Developmental Approach versus Psychometric Approach

When a developmental approach is used to assess young children, developmental theory provides the underlying research base, and developmental/behavioral strategies provide the content and methods. Clinical research clearly demonstrates that developmental sequences and expectancies offer a viable bridge between assessment and early intervention. Given this theoretical and practical underpinning, the content validity of assessment and treatment is unquestioned. Although typical developmental sequences may not apply strictly to children with disabilities, the functional sequence does provide a reference point for practical goal planning and for determining the degree of a child's impairment. The developmental approach to assessment is structured, yet it offers the advantage of a flexible clinical strategy for assessing young children.

Whereas developmental assessment examines a child's functional strengths and areas of concern, psychometric assessment measures psychological traits or alleged processes and expresses the results numerically. When the psychometric approach is used, intelligence, personality, motivation, creativity, and other traits are assessed with psychometric instruments to produce scores (e.g., IQs). These scores usually summarize how well a child performed and "how much" of the specified trait that child presumably has, usually relative to his or her peers. Note that the trait measures are not specific things that the child does or does not do; they are qualities that the child supposedly has or does not have.

In addition, the psychometric approach contains the antagonistic feature of forcing standardized procedures to fit all children. The same items and demands are used for all children, and alternative or adaptive strategies, such as altering the stimulus characteristics of tasks or permitting alternative response modes to enable a child to circumvent impairments and demonstrate intact skills, are not allowed. This approach violates the principle of equity, which is central to our notions of justice, professional ethics, and recommended practices. When applied to teaching, *equity* refers to using methods and materials for a given student that provide that child an equal opportunity to learn. For example, a child who has limited vision cannot, and should not be expected to, use the same printed materials as do his or her peers with typical vision; instead, we must provide large-print materials, magnifiers, audio supplements, and so forth. For this child, the use of *equal* methods and materials would not be *equitable*.

Most educators agree that students with special needs need special teaching and that enforcing the use of the same materials and methods for all students violates many rules of good teaching and good sense. Although equitable teaching may seem sensible to almost everyone, equitable assessment has been neither universally practiced nor universally recognized. Psychometric assessments can be characterized as equal because they are standardized (i.e., the same materials and administration procedures are used for all children), but they certainly cannot be characterized as equitable. Children with sensory, motor, social, or attention difficulties are unlikely to achieve valid cognitive scores when they are assessed by instruments that have been standardized and normed on children with typical characteristics.

Major early childhood professional organizations have published position statements that clearly draw the line in the sand and demand an end to conventional practices. Especially notable is the declaration of the Association for Childhood Education International (Perrone, 1991): "We now believe firmly that *no standardized testing should occur in the preschool and K–2 years*" (p. 137).

Criterion Referencing versus Norm Referencing

Norm-referenced assessment has traditionally been overused in the early intervention field (Bagnato & Neisworth, 1991a; Shonkoff, 1981). Although norm-based measures may be useful for comparing a child with a referent group, such measures do not yield prescriptions for action. Reliance on this method for prescriptive purposes and progress evaluation is an example of the antagonistic feature of inappropriate use of normative scoring. Furthermore, children with special needs or significant cultural differences cannot be compared with most normative groups; such comparisons are fraught with problems of credibility and often are contrary to common sense. This issue is an example of confused purpose. "Proving" that a child has mental retardation (i.e., meets standardized syndrome criteria) does not help a professional create an IEP. Diagnostic instruments (typically norm referenced) are seldom useful for program planning or monitoring. Moreover, norm-referenced assessment has led to insensitive measurement of child development in early intervention programs.

Another drawback of norm-referenced assessment is that it promotes the antagonistic trait of instructional irrelevance of item content. Instead of focusing on whether item content is relevant or valuable, the psychometric procedures used to determine item content for normative assessment focus on whether items strongly discriminate among age groups. Therefore, an item that is performed correctly by 80% of both 3- and 4-year-olds would not be considered a useful assessment item, whereas an item that is performed correctly by 80% of 4-year-olds but by only 30% of 3-year-olds would be considered an excellent example of an item having high age discrimination. Psychometric items that have high age discrimination frequently have little or no instructional utility. As a result, many curricular items that are based on psychometric milestones stressed by norm-referenced assessment (e.g., stringing beads, stacking blocks, standing on one foot) are not worth teaching.

Criterion-referenced assessment, in contrast, refers to the measurement of a performance relative to a stated standard. This method evaluates a child's attainment of developmental (i.e., curricular) objectives. *Attainment, mastery,* and *learning* must be qualified by the stated criteria. When has a child learned to print his or her name or to share his or her toys? Most objectives must be accompanied by known criteria to be considered accomplished. Hasty IEP writers often add, after each objective, "90% of the time." This criterion frequently makes no sense and simply cannot be verified. What does "prints his or her name correctly 90% of the time" really mean? Many teachers prefer to use a more discrete criterion, such as "correctly five consecutive times," or to specify maintenance and generalization, such as "correctly 9 of 10 times for the next week at home as well as at the center." Whatever standards are chosen, they should be clear enough to permit agreement among observers. Criteria should shift to higher standards as capabilities are refined. The use of reasonable criteria allows us to determine with relative certitude that children are indeed learning and using what they learn. The criteria should not be so cumbersome and time consuming that they are not used; sometimes a simple rating scale or parent report can verify that a child has mastered a set of objectives and is ready to move on.

Task Analysis and Training versus Ability Training

Special education and allied professions have a history of experimenting with ineffective therapeutic approaches (e.g., ability training). Since the mid-1980s, however, the fields of special education, in general, and early intervention, in particular, have demonstrated that combined developmental and behavioral approaches (e.g., task analysis and training) are most effective; despite this finding, outdated methods still abound in 1997. In particular, methods that purport to improve a child's abilities have received considerable attention, although they have no substantial record of success. For example, neuropsychological, cognitive retraining, and related approaches represent revamped versions of the ability-training faith.

Effective education for young children relies on research-based strategies built on developmental task analyses of skills and behavioral methods of instruction and treatment. In the place of nebulous abilities, task analysis focuses on the sequential breakdown of measurable skills, thereby allowing a child's current range of primitive-to-advanced capabilities to be assessed and framed as instructional objectives. An approach that uses task analytic methods naturally blends developmental and behavioral dimensions and adaptive and functional techniques and, therefore, links assessment and intervention.

Longitudinal Samples versus One-Time Samples

Young children with special needs require special considerations for both assessment and treatment. Infants, toddlers, and preschoolers with sensorimotor and social impairments have limited behavioral repertoires and variable patterns of arousal and responses because of their lack of experiences with their environment, their disabilities themselves, and their young ages. Given the special needs of these children, traditional approaches that emphasize single-session and single-source assessments, especially when used to make a diagnosis, are extremely inappropriate.

Serial assessments are the key to accurate description, prescription, and prediction in early intervention. School psychologists and other diagnostic specialists must advocate the use of longitudinal procedures to assess a child's status and outcome. Longitudinal techniques that use both norm- and criterion-referenced methods link assessment and intervention most effectively and offer valid strategies for monitoring progress and establishing accurate individual predictions of what a child's needs will be when he or she reaches school age. Longitudinal assessment–intervention strategies permit such analysis. The teacher, parent, school psychologist, and preschool administrator must arrange program priorities to allow for longitudinal procedures—not only is this recommended practice to do so, but it is also the law.

By instituting longitudinal procedures, we are able to blur the professional boundaries that constitute an antagonistic characteristic of traditional (i.e., one-time) assessment. The several professions concerned with early childhood have traditionally been separate and have played discrete roles. The division of labor among psychologist, therapist, and teacher has been distinct and even legalized. Teachers have not been permitted to administer and interpret the results of certain tests, and school psychologists have been prevented from offering treatment or consultation. Professional jargon has distanced psychologists from teachers, teachers from social workers, and everybody from parents. Such a professional Tower of Babel has hindered useful communication about designing and delivering education. Although children with and without special needs have been integrated through inclusion, professional integration seems much less pervasive. Professional isolation curtails the valuable cross-talk that can bring specialists together in a child and family's interest. Conventional assessment materials and practices do little to provide transdisciplinary materials that foster collaboration and have not been family friendly or engaging for parent participation. New materials and practices, in particular, curriculum-based assessment, deemphasize jargon, stress authentic behaviors, and invite collaborative decision making.

Program Planning Purposes versus Diagnostic Purposes

The distinction between diagnosis and prescription underscores the most important aspect of assessment: purpose. Testing, the attainment of a score or index for a child, is conducted primarily to categorize the child's problem and to apply a label. Assessment, in contrast, is conducted in a functional manner by combining both quantitative and qualitative information to determine a program for a child. Although this distinction may seem to involve superficial semantic play, the distinction is central to effective service delivery for preschool-age children, as discussed previously.

Ecological View versus Child-Only View

Traditional assessment has been focused almost exclusively on the child: After all, it is the child who develops or does not develop typically and who has problems, needs, and potential. It is the child for whom we design an IEP and plan a program on the basis of assessment findings. Assessment must, however, view a child in the context of his or her relevant settings and circumstances (i.e., from an ecological perspective). A child's home environment, the quality of parenting skills, and other domestic circumstances should be considered. In addition, the quality of the child's preschool, child care, or other program and/or the quality of caregiver interactions should be evaluated. Proper, albeit minimal, assessment of the child's ecosystem through family interview, judgments, ratings, and anecdotes, as well as other measures, permits better program placement, instructional prescriptions, parent participation, and progress monitoring across settings.

Assessment of the family itself, however, differs from assessment of the child within the context of the family. Instruments and procedures that permit families to identify their needs and priorities have begun to be developed (Bailey & Henderson, 1993; Dunst, Jenkins, & Trivette, 1984). Most of these instruments use family self-reporting because it is the family members' own perceptions, and not the judgments of an outside professional, that must be ascertained. This family-centered approach also avoids many of the concerns that professionals have about intruding into a family's affairs. An ecological approach enables us to assess the family's own estimate of strengths and concerns with regard to information, support, explanations to others, community services, and family functioning (Bailey & Simeonsson, 1988a).

New Concepts versus Traditional Concepts of Validity

Most of us are familiar with conventional validity constructs and definitions. We have all learned that *validity* refers to the degree to which an instrument measures that which it is purported to measure. Likewise, most of us have learned about predictive and construct validity. Newer concepts (i.e., convergent, treatment, and social validities), however, challenge and replace these traditional notions (i.e., construct, content, concurrent, and predictive validities) (Cronbach, 1988; Messick, 1988; Moss, 1992). In fact, dependence on traditional validities is one of the antagonistic traits of traditional assessment practices. These validities and other psychometric criteria, such as internal consistency and test–retest reliability, focus on the structure rather than the function or treatment utility of assessment (Hayes et al., 1987). When a teacher receives little or no help from the assessment tools, however, those tools are not valuable, regardless of whether they meet traditional criteria. For example, a child's height, weight, head circumference, and shoe size may be highly reliable and valid measures, but they are instructionally useless to a teacher. A discussion of three concepts of validity that support recommended practices follows.

Convergent Validity

Assessment validity refers to the quality of information provided to guide decision making. Validity, therefore, does not reside within an instrument; rather, validity depends on that instrument's use and contribution to the goodness of decisions made. Similarly, predictive validity cannot be inherent to a set of materials; eventual outcomes (predictions) depend on intervening events. *Convergent validity* captures the several new concepts of validity and pools estimates. The real validity concern is how well assessment materials and practices help us make informed, useful, and worthwhile decisions for children and families.

Treatment Validity

The primary role of assessment is to guide treatment, intervention, and education. *Treatment validity* is concerned with the degree to which assessment contributes to beneficial outcomes (Hayes et al., 1987). Assessment can make this contribution in at least three ways: 1) identifying goals and objectives to be reached, 2) determining methods and materials to help reach goals or objectives, and 3) detecting progress or change related to intervention and/or instructional efforts. When assessment performs one or more of these functions, it has treatment or use validity.

Social Validity

Just as assessment should be useful, it should be perceived as having *social validity* (i.e., being valuable and worthwhile) (Wolfe, 1978). An assessment tool (e.g., IQ test) may be useful for specifying certain objectives, but those objectives may not be judged as worth pursuing. Specific items found on IQ tests are typically neither useful nor worthwhile to teach. Social validity, like treatment validity, involves performing three functions: 1) generating worthwhile goals, 2) using assessment materials and practices that are considered acceptable, and 3) producing findings that have social significance. Demanding that assessment have social validity recognizes the importance of partnerships with parents. Collaborative selection and use of assessment in real-life contexts moves practice from clinical test scores to useful, valued information.

PROMINENT ASSESSMENT MODELS

We can build on the above-discussed foundations to link assessment and intervention by examining six prominent assessment models that possess many of the qualities we identify as supporting the mission of early intervention. These six models are criterion-referenced assessment, convergent assessment, functional/adaptive assessment, authentic/performance assessment, dynamic assessment, and play-based assessment. The primary model is criterion-referenced, or curriculum-based, assessment, and the five remaining models often are incorporated into this model to enhance and customize it.

Criterion-Referenced Assessment

Curriculum-based assessment (a type of criterion-referenced assessment) is, by far, the most prominent of the assessment models; it is used in all early intervention programs that link assessment, intervention, and evaluation (Bagnato & Hofkosh, 1990; Bagnato & Neisworth, 1980; Bagnato, Neisworth, & Capone, 1986; Bagnato, Neisworth, & Munson, 1989; Bricker, 1987). This model gained such prominence because it was developed by early intervention researchers throughout the United States to address the specific issues that surround the assessment and creation of programs for children with special needs. The objective was to design a method of assessment that was linked directly to intervention goals or expected outcomes.

We have operationally defined curriculum-based assessment as "a form of criterion-referenced measurement wherein curricular objectives act as the criteria for the identification of instructional targets and for the assessment of status and progress" (Bagnato & Neisworth, 1991a, p. 87). This type of assessment traces a child's progress along a continuum of objectives within a developmentally sequenced curriculum and exists in two forms: curriculum compatible and curriculum embedded. Curriculum-compatible assessment measures are instruments that stand alone (i.e., are not joined to a specific curriculum) and can be linked to any of a number of commercially available curricula through a process we have termed LINK (see Chapter 5). The most widely used of these instruments is the Battelle Developmental Inventory (Newborg, Stock, Wnek, Guidubaldi, & Svinicki, 1988). Curriculum-embedded assessment measures are developmental scales that exist within the hierarchical skill sequences of specific curricula and form the basis by which assessment, intervention, and evaluation are linked (i.e., the assessment scale and the curricular activities share the same objectives). The most widely used of these instruments is the HELP Curriculum: Hawaii Early Learning Profile (VORT Corporation, 1995).

Curriculum-based assessment fulfills the following five important purposes of early intervention:

- To analyze and profile developmental competencies
- To offer adaptations for use with children who have disabilities
- To target integrated IFSP goals
- To monitor incremental gains
- To facilitate teamwork

Curriculum-based assessment is built on a developmental sequence or task analysis of strengths and areas of concern that reflect the increasing complexity of a child's development. Each task or process in the sequence represents a developmental stage that serves as a "rung," or prerequisite, needed to reach the next skill. The sequence itself is the "ladder" that connects assessed skills, targeted goals and objectives, and benchmarks.

Many curriculum-based assessment tools organize the skill sequences into domains and subdomains (see Chapter 2). The most general level of curricular organization (i.e., major curricular domains) coincides with the central areas to be assessed according to

PL 99-457, the Education of the Handicapped Act Amendments of 1986 (subsequently reauthorized as PL 102-119, the Individuals with Disabilities Education Act Amendments of 1991). These domains are cognitive, language, social-emotional, perceptual/fine motor, gross motor, and adaptive skills. The middle level of curricular organization (i.e., common subdomains) is attention and memory, symbolic play, coping, receptive language, expressive language, gestural imitation, conversation skills, peer interaction, and nonverbal reasoning. In addition, many curricula and curriculum-compatible instruments cross-reference the developmental skills, so that they reflect natural or expected patterns of skill acquisition; this cross-referencing results in the most specific level of curricular organization (i.e., strands of related interdomain skills). Strands of skills recur across and within domains; for example, social skills recur in the language domain, cognitive skills recur in the play domain, and fine motor skills recur in the adaptive skills domain.

We have previously proposed that curriculum-based assessment is structured by a sequence of activities that proceed from general to specific and have outlined the increasingly fine-grain and linked, or interrelated, missions of assessment in early intervention (illustrated in Figure 1.1 as a sequence of wide- to narrow-angle sighting lenses). We call this process LINKing (Bagnato & Neisworth, 1979; Bagnato & Neisworth, 1980; Bagnato et al., 1989) to underscore the vital connection, or link, that must exist among the assessment, teaching, and evaluation of skills. Assessed and predicted behaviors also must be essentially similar to forge strong links between assessment and intervention and to ensure that evaluations reflect progress accurately (Newland, 1973).

Bricker (1987) operationalized a type of linked assessment-intervention-evaluation model and published the first commercially available system to link assessment to intervention. This system—Assessment, Evaluation, and Programming System (AEPS) for

LINKING ASSESSMENT—INTERVENTION GOALS

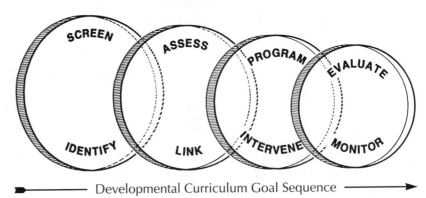

Figure 1.1.   The LINKing process is represented by a series of sighting lenses that become increasingly narrow throughout the process. (From Hassett, V.B., & Herson, M. [Eds.]. [1987]. *Psychological evaluation of the developmentally and physically disabled*, p. 183. New York: Plenum Press; reprinted by permission.)

Infants and Children—has four components (measurement [i.e., assessment] for children from birth to three, curriculum for children from birth to three, measurement for children from three to six, and curriculum for children from three to six) and both provides specific activities for performing initial assessment and helps parents and professionals ensure that children meet IEP/IFSP objectives through formative and summative progress evaluations (Bricker, 1993; Bricker & Pretti-Frontczak, 1996; Bricker & Waddell, 1996; Cripe, Slentz, & Bricker, 1993).

Another feature that is unique to curriculum-based assessment is the capacity to organize and facilitate team assessment activities. Two aspects of curriculum-based assessment foster teamwork: 1) the domain structure, which accommodates input from parents and various specialists; and 2) flexible procedures, which allow us to stage and administer tasks differently for individual children, to gather data primarily through observations and reports, and to use the style of team interaction that best fits each child and family. Figure 1.2 specifies the various people who may be involved in an assessment (i.e., parent, teacher, psychologist, occupational thera-

CURRICULAR DOMAINS & TEAMWORK

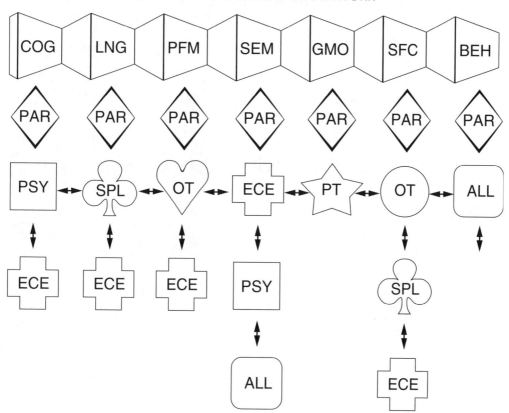

Figure 1.2.   Suggested roles of team members when assessing various domains. (*Domains:* COG = cognitive, LNG = language, PFM = perceptual/fine motor, SEM = social-emotional, GMO = gross motor, SFC = self-care, and BEH = behavior. *Teams:* PAR = parent, PSY = psychologist, SPL = speech-language pathologist, OT = occupational therapist, ECE = early childhood educator, PT = physical therapist, and ALL = whole team.)

pist, physical therapist, speech-language pathologist) and delineates the suggested roles that each person should play (i.e., primary or consultative responsibility, as determined when planning the assessment).

Curriculum-based models also enable parents and professionals to choose from among the three primary teamwork styles used in early intervention: multidisciplinary, interdisciplinary, and transdisciplinary. The multidisciplinary style of assessment (Figure 1.3) requires each professional to participate separately and by using the procedures and outlook unique to his or her discipline. We have argued that this form of "teamwork" masquerades as a team approach and, in reality, disregards the needs of young children and the expected patterns of behavior in young children, because it does not take into consideration the low endurance, short attention span, and lack of self-regulation that are nearly universal among young children (Bagnato & Neisworth, 1991b). In the interdisciplinary style of assessment, illustrated in Figure 1.4, each team member works either in tandem or in a dyad (e.g., physical therapist and speech-language pathologist) with the parents and other professionals to conduct the assessment. Continuous cross-talk and in situ collaboration are hallmarks of interdisciplinary assessment, which is often the most appropriate style. Figure 1.5 illustrates the transdiscipli-

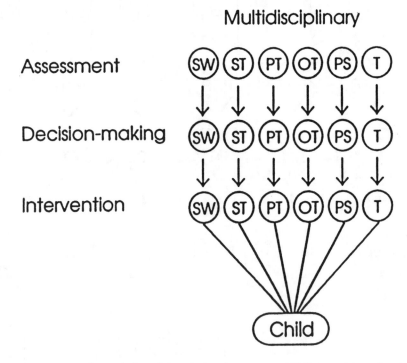

Figure 1.3. The multidisciplinary style of assessment. (SW = social worker, ST = speech therapist, PT = physical therapist, OT = occupational therapist, PS = psychologist, and T = teacher.) (From Woodruff, G., & Hanson, C. [1987]. *Project KAI.* Brighton, MA: Handicapped Children's Early Education Program; adapted by permission.)

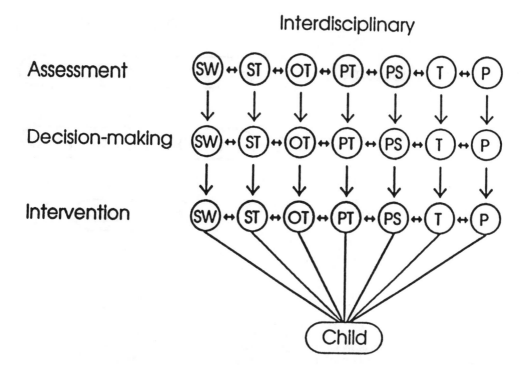

Figure 1.4.   The interdisciplinary style of assessment. (SW = social worker, ST = speech therapist, OT = occupational therapist, PT = physical therapist, PS = psychologist, T = teacher, and P = parent.) (From Woodruff, G., & Hanson, C. [1987]. *Project KAI.* Brighton, MA: Handicapped Children's Early Education Program; adapted by permission.)

nary style of assessment. In transdisciplinary assessment, parents and one professional conduct the entire assessment. The child is usually assessed through play, and all domains are surveyed; the other (nonprimary) professionals serve as consultants, usually in some variation of arena assessment. As noted, curriculum-based assessment can accommodate all three styles of team assessment.

Convergent Assessment Model

Many early intervention professionals and administrators continue to use a single criterion for early childhood assessment, despite the fact that so doing defies PL 99-457 and PL 102-119, common sense, and research results. Many professionals in specific disciplines (e.g., psychologists, speech-language pathologists, occupational therapists) depend on traditional norm-referenced assessment measures because they erroneously believe that such measures provide a reliable and valid assessment. In fact, such measures have been found to be inappropriate in form, function, and content for perhaps a majority of children with special needs. In addition, although curriculum-based assessment should be the foundation of all early intervention programs, many program administrators either fail to adopt a systematic curriculum package or implement a single curriculum for

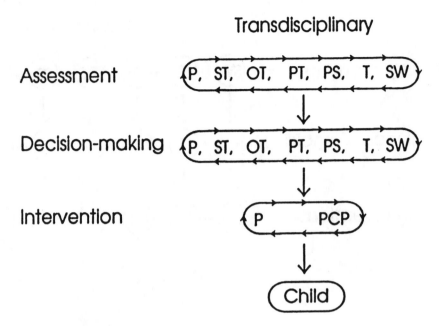

Figure 1.5.   The transdisciplinary style of assessment. (P = parent, ST = speech therapist, OT = occupational therapist, PT = physical therapist, PS = psychologist, T = teacher, SW = social worker, and PCP = primary care provider.) (From Woodruff, G., & Hanson, C. [1987]. *Project KAI.* Brighton, MA: Handicapped Children's Early Education Program; adapted by permission.)

all children. Moreover, many professionals disregard or fail to include family self-appraisal and reports of the child's environment.

In recognition of these realities of early intervention practices, we formalized the convergent assessment model (Bagnato & Neisworth, 1991a), a multidimensional perspective on early childhood assessment that built on our concepts and the views of many prominent experts in early intervention and related fields (Bailey & Simeonsson, 1988b; Bailey & Wolery, 1989; Hayes et al., 1987; Mott et al., 1986; Shonkoff, 1981; Simeonsson, Huntington, & Parse, 1980). This model is intended to guide professionals in generating richer assessments that are more sensible, valid, useful, and sensitive. In this context

> *Convergent assessment* refers to the synthesis of information gathered from several sources, instruments, settings, and occasions to produce the most valid appraisal of developmental status and to accomplish the related assessment purposes of identification, prescription, progress evaluation, and prediction. (Bagnato & Neisworth, 1991a, p. 57)

Convergent assessments are generated when a team of professionals and parents collaborates to construct and use an individualized assessment battery for a child. The resultant battery comprises several methods of assessment that blend qualitative and quantitative information about a child, his or her physical and social environment (e.g., home, preschool), and the family. The logic of this approach dictates that the early intervention team can determine with greater confidence the needs of a child and family when multiple sources provide similar or identical information. In a similar fashion, when multiple sources provide contradictory information, the team is alerted to a problem and can proceed to resolve differences through negotiation and collaborative decision making.

This assessment model challenges traditional assumptions of assessment, redefining it as a rich, human decision-making activity instead of as a discrete, clinical test-giving activity. In other words, the convergent assessment model assumes that

> Early childhood assessment is a flexible, collaborative decision-making process in which teams of parents and professionals repeatedly revise their judgments and reach consensus about the changing developmental, educational, medical, and mental health service needs of young children and their families. (Bagnato & Neisworth, 1991a, p. xi)

The convergent model of assessment is concerned with both the mechanics and the process of synthesizing diverse diagnostic information and, on the basis of that information, making important judgments and decisions in the form of practical intervention recommendations. Because it addresses issues of treatment, social, and convergent validities, convergent assessment offers two strong advantages for young children with developmental disabilities and their families: 1) a richer, wider, more natural sampling of the child's capabilities and the family's priorities (i.e., the mechanics) and 2) an integrated composite of the child's and family's strengths and areas of concern (i.e., the process) (Bagnato & Neisworth, 1990).

Assessment data derived from the convergent model can be summarized, synthesized, and applied in three ways: 1) by comparing and contrasting data from multiple sources, 2) by using the independent judgments of team members (including parents), and 3) by using a flexible process of collaboration and negotiation. Figure 1.6 illustrates the multidimensional character of convergent assessment and demonstrates the convergence of data derived from multiple sources, settings, domains, and occasions to be used for multiple purposes (i.e., the mechanics). The mechanics of the convergent assessment process are discussed in detail in the sections that follow.

Multiple Settings

Assessment for early intervention should occur in multiple settings. Information gathered from within several different environmental contexts is needed to gauge the extent to which a child can generalize his or her competencies across settings (e.g., home, playground, preschool). The ability to transfer skills learned in one setting to another setting offers the strongest evidence that a child is generalizing and, therefore, learning. Assessments from multiple settings also help parents and professionals determine the interactive effects of each environment's physical (e.g., room layout, types of toys available) and social (e.g., number of children involved in

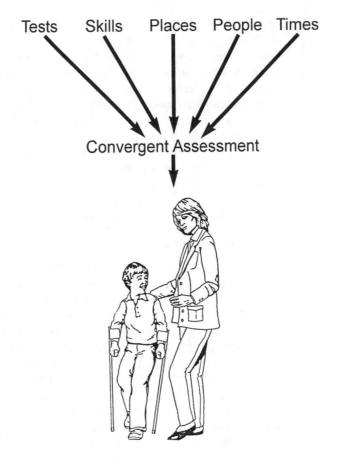

Figure 1.6. The multidimensional character of convergent assessment and the process of convergence.

group circle time) attributes and whether those attributes support or hinder a child's ability to learn.

Multiple Occasions

Assessments must occur on multiple occasions. Assessments conducted at different times of the day and on different days of the week enable us to determine the consistency of a child's behavior and the impact of factors, such as fatigue, endurance, and sleep requirements, on a child's ability to learn. Multiple-occasion assessment is important, in particular for infants and young children with ongoing medical conditions and special developmental needs.

Multiple Sources

Assessments should incorporate information from multiple sources. Various people can contribute information about a child's strengths and areas of concern and a family's priorities and resources. Early intervention professionals from several disciplines, family members, and other caregivers all can offer unique perspectives and provide valuable insights to make assessments accurate, complete, and relevant.

Multiple Measures

Assessments must include multiple measures (i.e., a battery of developmental scales) to determine a child and family's capabilities and needs. Research has demonstrated that accurate, prescriptive assessments are provided when the batteries used comprise several different measures (e.g., norm based, adaptive, curriculum based, judgment based, ecological) that examine various attributes of a child and his or her environment as well as the interactions among these attributes. Such batteries may include traditional cognitive skills; criterion-referenced instruments; and measures of play skills, information processing, attention, coping, and parent–child interaction.

Multiple Domains

Assessments must measure multiple domains. A comprehensive assessment of the developmental and behavioral areas that constitute a profile of the child is needed to determine a child's attainment of a number of developmental skills. This profile should include the traditional developmental domains (i.e., cognitive, language, perceptual/fine motor, social-emotional, gross motor, and adaptive skills). For very young children and those with disabilities, the profile should also include such areas as self-regulation, social competence, reactivity, habituation, emotional expression, endurance, self-stimulation, and so forth. In addition, the measurement of factors, such as the impact of chaotic settings, a parent's sensitivity to a child's behavioral cues, and child- versus parent-initiated activities, helps provide a more complete picture of a range of important developmental functions. It should be noted that all of the domains assessed are also teachable or supportable skills.

Multiple Purposes

Assessments must fulfill multiple purposes. The various assessment procedures and the purposes they address (i.e., screening/identification, comprehensive assessment/curriculum referencing, program planning/intervention, progress monitoring/program evaluation) should all be included and be connected to one another. Each procedure/purpose in this sequence serves as a prerequisite for the one it precedes, and, as the sequence proceeds, it becomes increasingly fine focused: Screening provides only a gross estimate of a child's status; children are assigned to one of two categories—those with problems that merit further examination and those without problems. Comprehensive assessment yields a finer, more detailed analysis. This level of assessment provides direction and items for tying assessment measures to curricula and for planning programs. Next, program planning guides the actual day-to-day content and methods of a program. Because planning is attached to comprehensive assessment, professionals are able to design goals and objectives that are feasible for use in a given program. Finally, a child's progress and a program's efficacy are evaluated on the basis of whether and to what extent developmental and behavioral goals are achieved. This assessment may be both formative and summative. To summarize, multiple-purpose assessment may be used to assess a child's development, place that child in an appropriate setting, plan a program, monitor the child's progress, and evaluate the program's impact.

To illustrate how the convergent assessment model incorporates the above-described factors, Table 1.1 presents a framework for developing an individualized convergent assessment for a child with special needs. Our research results indicate that an individualized assessment battery that comprises at least four central measures or procedures (i.e., norm based, curriculum based, judgment based, ecological) generates a neurodevelopmental profile and diagnostic outcomes that have greater representation, technical adequacy, and treatment and social validities (Bagnato & Neisworth, 1991a). As shown in Table 1.1, each measure offers a specific advantage in and fulfills a vital mission of the assessment process. Tables 1.2, 1.3, and 1.4, respectively, apply the framework by suggesting convergent assessment batteries for a child from birth to 24 months, a child who is at risk for or has a mild developmental disability from 2 to 6 years, and a child with autism/pervasive developmental disorder. All of these examples show measures that tie eligibility determination to curriculum planning and goal setting (as a result of the similarity between the content of the norm- and curriculum-based measures) and broaden assessment to include a child's developmental context and information from various people, settings, and domains.

The second advantage of convergent assessment—its process—is how it facilitates the converging, or synthesizing, of data and translates those data into practical decisions. The System to Plan Early Childhood Services (SPECS) (Bagnato & Neisworth, 1990) is an efficient, and arguably the only, example of a commercially available convergent assessment system. (SPECS and its three operational components are reviewed in Chapter 4.) The first component of SPECS is Developmental (D)–Specs, a generic functional rating scale that summarizes, profiles, and equates results from

Table 1.2. Early development (0–24 months)

Measure	Convergent battery
Norm based	Infant Psychological Development Scale (1980) or Kent Infant Development Scale (1985)
Curriculum based	Infant Learning (1981) or Carolina Curriculum for Infants and Toddlers with Special Needs (2nd ed.) (1991)
Judgment based	Early Coping Inventory (1988)
Ecological	Family Day Care Rating Scale (1989)

Table 1.3. At risk for or having mild developmental disability (2–6 years)

Measure	Convergent battery
Norm based	Battelle Developmental Inventory (1984)
Curriculum based	Battelle 2–6 Curriculum (1990) or Hawaii Early Learning Profile (1979)/Help for Special Preschoolers (1986)
Judgment based	System to Plan Early Childhood Services (1990) and Preschool and Kindergarten Behavior Scales (1994)
Ecological	Family Needs Survey (1985)

multiple measures and sources. The second component is Team (T)–Specs, a flexible process that is used to ensure that all team members (i.e., various professionals, parents) play equal roles in comparing and contrasting the results of D–Specs, resolving differences, and making decisions. The third and final component of SPECS is Program (P)–Specs. By using P–Specs and T–Specs in conjunction, team members can use the assessment results to make specific decisions about service delivery. P–Specs involves answering 45 questions in 10 early intervention program areas: early education; adaptive options; behavior, speech-language, occupational, and physical therapies; and vision, hearing, medical, and transition services. The team is able to create dual profiles of a child's functional capabilities (T–Specs profile) and program options of varying degrees of intensity (P–Specs profile). These profiles form the basis for evaluating a child's progress and a program's impact; T–Specs ratings fall between 1 (lowest) and 5 (highest), and P–Specs ratings range from 0% to 100% (see Figures 1.7 and 1.8).

The convergent assessment model and SPECS operationalize the definition of early assessment as a fundamentally flexible and human process of collaborative decision making about a child's strengths and areas of concerns rather than as a sterile process of test giving to categorize children and plan their futures (e.g., eligibility, continuation, diagnosis) on the basis of arbitrary cutoff scores.

Authentic/Performance Assessment Model

Numerous researchers have proposed alternatives to traditional norm-referenced assessment for children with disabilities. Alternatives that have gained the most acceptance, in particular for young children, are authentic and performance-based assessment (Cohen &

Table 1.4. Autism /pervasive developmental disorder

Measure	Convergent battery
Norm based	Battelle Developmental Inventory (1984)
Curriculum based	Individualized Assessment and Treatment for Autism (1979) and Psychoeducational Profile–Revised (1994)
Judgment based	Childhood Autism Rating Scale (1988) and System to Plan Early Childhood Services (1990)
Ecological	Parenting Stress Index (1986)

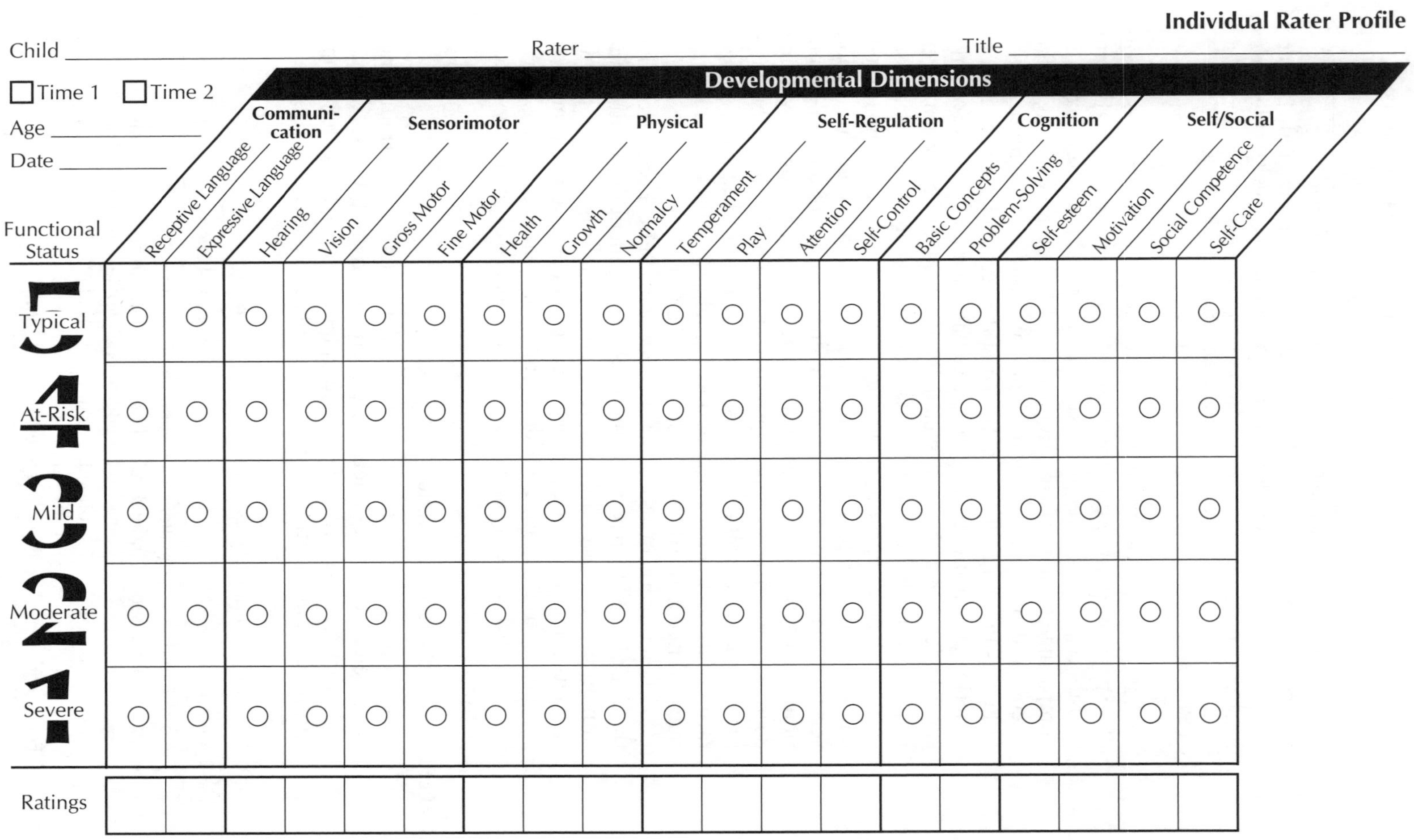

Individual Rater Profile

Child _____
☐ Time 1 ☐ Time 2
Age _____
Date _____

Rater _____
Title _____

Developmental Dimensions

Communi-cation		Sensorimotor			Physical			Self-Regulation			Cognition			Self/Social		
Receptive Language	Expressive Language	Hearing	Vision	Gross Motor	Fine Motor	Health	Growth	Normalcy	Temperament	Play	Attention	Self-Control	Basic Concepts	Problem-Solving	Self-esteem	Motivation	Social Competence	Self-Care

Functional Status

L̄ Typical
4 At-Risk
3 Mild
2 Moderate
1 Severe

Ratings

Figure 1.7. An example of an Individual Rater Profile from SPECS. (From Bagnato, S.J., & Neisworth, J.T. [1990]. *System to Plan Early Childhood Services [SPECS]*. Circle Pines, MN: American Guidance Service; reprinted by permission.)

INTENSITY RATINGS PROFILE

Child _____   ☐ Time 1 Age _____   ☐ Time 2 Age _____

Intensity	1.0 Early Education	2.0 Adaptive Services	3.0 Early Education	4.0 Speech-Language Therapy	5.0 Physical Therapy	6.0 Occupational Therapy	7.0 Vision Services	8.0 Hearing Services	9.0 Medical Services	Total Program Services (0-90)	10.0 Transition Services
100% High Intensity	23	18	42	15	15	15	13	13	21	180	55
95	27	17	40	14	14	14	12	12	20	171	52
90	25	16	39	13	13	13			19	162	50
85	24	15	36				11	11	18	153	47
80	22	14	34	12	12	12			17	144	45
										135	
75	21		32	11	11	11	10	10	15	126	42
70	20	13	29				9	9	14	117	39
65	18	12	27	10	10	10			13	108	37
60	17	11	25	9	9	9	8	8	12	99	34
55	15	10	23	8	8	8	7	7	11		32
										90	
50	14	9	21	7	7	7			10	82	29
45	13	8	19				6	6	9	73	26
40	11	7	17	6	6	6			8	64	24
35	10	6	15	5	5	5	5	5	7	55	21
30	8	5	13	4	4	4	4	4	6		19
										45	
25	7	4	11				3	3	5	37	16
20	6		8	3	3	3			4	28	13
15	4	3	6	2	2	2	2	2	3	19	12
10	3	2	4						2	10	8
5 Low Intensity	1	1	2	1	1	1	1	1	1	0	6
0% Low Intensity	0	0	0	0	0	0	0	0	0	0	0

Figure 1.8. An example of a completed Intensity Ratings Profile from T–Specs. (From Bagnato, S.J., & Neisworth, J.T. [1990]. *System to Plan Early Childhood Services [SPECS]*, p. 15. Circle Pines, MN: American Guidance Service; reprinted by permission.)

Spenciner, 1994; Coutinho & Malouf, 1992; Elliot, 1994; McLaughlin & Warren, 1995; Pike & Salend, 1995). Authentic assessment procedures are endorsed by the National Association for the Education of Young Children (NAEYC), which recommends the use of developmentally appropriate assessment techniques for all young children and advocates the abolition of standardized norm-referenced testing in early childhood education settings (Goodwin & Goodwin, 1995; NAEYC, 1996; Perrone, 1991). The Division for Early Childhood (DEC) of the Council for Exceptional Children also delineates recommended assessment practices that depart absolutely from psychometric, standardized practices (Neisworth & Bagnato, 1996). The DEC recommendations hinge on family-centered, authentic information gathered and shared by all team members. The effort exerted should be related to the social consequences of the decisions to be made. Finally, school psychologists, who are put in the position of determining eligibility for preschoolers, have also expressed concern with policies that require standardized, norm-referenced assessment of young children; they recommend more flexible, informative practices (National Association of School Psychologists, 1990). A strong and engaging argument for "testing without tests," written by a school psychologist (LeVan, 1990), is a pioneering benchmark for advocating useful, sensible assessment.

Coutinho and Malouf (1992) emphasized three major features of performance-based assessment: performance dimension, authentic dimension, and instructional linkage. The *performance* dimension is "a student's active generation of a response and highlights the fact that the response is observable either directly or indirectly via a permanent product" (Coutinho & Malouf, 1992, p. 63). The related *authentic* dimension emphasizes the real-life nature of a task and the natural context in which the assessment occurs or the observational data are gathered. Authenticity is essential for three reasons: 1) the more realistic or natural the task, the greater the motivation to the child and the more applicable the task to everyday events and situations; 2) authentic tasks and circumstances promote the importance of a competency-based approach to the education of young children with special needs and focus the assessment across all disciplines on complex sets of skills and processes and the generalization of learning across settings; and 3) authentic tasks or competencies require the assessor(s) to make no inferences about a child's capabilities, because the behavior sampled—and its natural effect on toys, activities, people, the environment, and so forth—is directly observable. The third feature, *instructional linkage*, emphasizes the extent to which the assessment tasks are "aligned with curriculum outcomes" (Coutinho & Malouf, 1992, p. 64) and the modifications needed to support a child's performance and learning. The authentic, or performance, assessment model has been labeled neobehavioral (Elliot, 1991) because it is more closely allied with a behavioral approach than with a norm-referenced, psychometric approach.

Proponents of authentic assessments for children with special needs advocate the design of individualized assessment strategies that receive high marks for being performance based, authentic, and connected to instruction. In practice, however, such strategies are often not used. For example, many early childhood educators assess the acquisition of language skills by children who are nonverbal by administering tests that use a flipcard format to measure receptive and expressive language skills and are conducted in an isolated setting with one adult tester. Such tests clearly are not performance based, authentic, or relevant for instruction and have low treatment and social validities. A more authentic assessment would assess a nonverbal child's social and communication skills by observing the child's ability both to initiate a social interaction with a peer through sounds, gestures, and other alternative forms of communication and to follow directions given by his or her parents at home or by his or her peers in the context of a cooperative game. Such assessment receives high marks for observable evidence of the skill, real-life relevance, and ties to curricular objectives accompanied by appropriate sensory/response modifications. It should be noted that natural assessment tasks emphasize areas of strength rather than areas of concern; skills that a child can exhibit to some degree are assessed, and required increases in fluency, consistency, complexity, and so forth are identified. Finally, such assessment procedures address both the process and the product of learning rather than focusing solely on the product.

Teachers, in particular, use observational methods to document behavior and behavior changes formally and informally. Teachers also note the effect of their interaction with a child on

that child's learning and, in so doing, discover which strategies the child uses to problem-solve, thereby determining which supports are needed to promote learning. In this respect, authentic assessment methods share features with curriculum-based and dynamic assessment strategies (Lidz, 1991).

We stress that curriculum-based and authentic assessment models are closely and fundamentally compatible. Future curriculum-based models must be designed to assess real-life developmental competencies (e.g., initiating a social interaction) rather than contrived and meaningless tasks (e.g., fitting pegs in a pegboard in a timed test). The circumstances for these assessments must be genuine activities that occur in the child's life to allow for the practice and generalization of learning.

Two exemplary authentic assessment systems are AEPS (Bricker, 1993) and the Work Sampling System (WSS) (Meisels et al., 1994). AEPS (discussed previously) is an excellent example of the curriculum-based assessment systems that have been developed with functional and authentic attributes as their primary distinguishing characteristics. The goals and tasks used in AEPS stress hierarchically sequenced competencies that are readily observable, measurable, and teachable contexts. Figure 1.9 shows examples of strands in the hierarchical sequence of prerequisite competencies needed to accomplish various social goals. Note that the acts and circumstances that are emphasized in these sequences reflect truly authentic skills that can be nurtured in an early intervention program that encompasses both home and preschool settings. WSS was developed in conjunction with NAEYC guidelines regarding developmentally appropriate practices in early childhood assessment. WSS stresses the use of direct, naturalistic observation of the children in early childhood settings and of portfolios containing samples of each child's actual work (e.g., drawings, photographs, speeches, songs, videotapes, stories) to determine that child's status, instructional needs, and progress. The emphases of WSS are on identifying strengths and creating nonrestrictive descriptions of areas of concern. Figure 1.10 shows a WSS domain that illustrates the system's genuine content.

Dynamic Assessment Model

The model of dynamic assessment is based on the work of Feuerstein (1979, 1980) and was modified for use with preschoolers with special needs by Lidz (1991). Dynamic assessment involves the use of a "test–teach–test" procedure to engage the child as an active learner in performing applied activities to assess the child's approach to problem solving. This type of assessment relies on an interactive exchange between the assessor and the child (i.e., a mediated learning experience). Feuerstein (1979) observed that a mediated learning experience "mediates the world to the child by framing, selecting, focusing, and feeding back environmental experiences in such a way as to produce appropriate learning sets and habits" (p. 71). Proponents of

Social Domain

Strand A: Interaction with adults

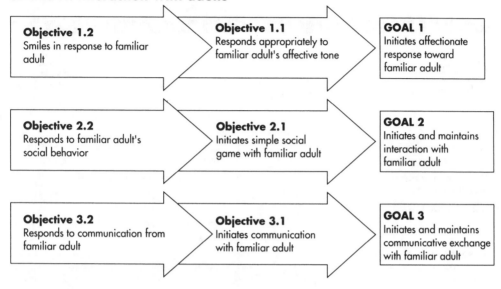

Strand B: Interaction with environment

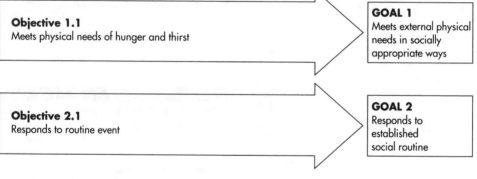

Strand C: Interaction with peers

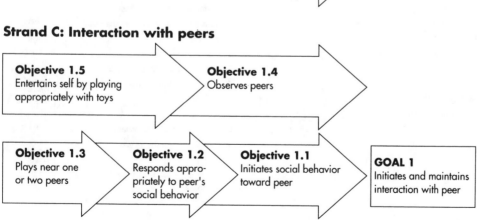

Figure 1.9. Strands in the hierarchical sequence of competencies needed to meet social goals in AEPS. (From Bricker, D. [Ed.]. [1993]. *Assessment, evaluation, and programming system for infants and children: Vol.1. AEPS measurement for birth to three years*, p. 335. Baltimore: Paul H. Brookes Publishing Co.; reprinted by permission.)

I | Personal and Social Development

A Self concept F W S

1 Begins to show comfort with self as someone growing in skills and abilities (p.1) — Not Yet / In Process / Proficient

2 Starts to show self-direction in actions (p.1) — Not Yet / In Process / Proficient

B Self control F W S

1 Follows classroom rules and routines (p.1) — Not Yet / In Process / Proficient

2 Uses classroom materials purposefully and respectfully (p.2) — Not Yet / In Process / Proficient

3 Manages transitions (p.2) — Not Yet / In Process / Proficient

C Approach to learning F W S

1 Shows eagerness and curiosity as a learner (p.2) — Not Yet / In Process / Proficient

2 Selects one activity from several suggested alternatives (p.2) — Not Yet / In Process / Proficient

3 Approaches tasks with flexibility and inventiveness (p.2) — Not Yet / In Process / Proficient

4 Seeks help when encountering a problem (p.3) — Not Yet / In Process / Proficient

D Interactions with others F W S

1 Interacts with one or more children (p.3) — Not Yet / In Process / Proficient

2 Interacts with familiar adults (p.3) — Not Yet / In Process / Proficient

3 Participates in the group life of the class (p.3) — Not Yet / In Process / Proficient

4 Participates and follows simple rules in group activities (p.3) — Not Yet / In Process / Proficient

5 Shows empathy and caring for others (p.4) — Not Yet / In Process / Proficient

E Conflict resolution F W S

1 Seeks adult help when needed to resolve conflicts (p.4) — Not Yet / In Process / Proficient

II | Language & Literacy

A Listening F W S

1 Listens with understanding to directions and conversations (p.5) — Not Yet / In Process / Proficient

2 Follows directions that involve a two-step sequence of actions (p.5) — Not Yet / In Process / Proficient

B Speaking F W S

1 Speaks clearly enough to be understood by most listeners (p.5) — Not Yet / In Process / Proficient

2 Uses language for a variety of purposes (p.6) — Not Yet / In Process / Proficient

C Literature and reading F W S

1 Listens with interest to stories read aloud (p.6) — Not Yet / In Process / Proficient

2 Shows interest in reading-related activities (p.6) — Not Yet / In Process / Proficient

D Writing F W S

1 Uses scribbles and unconventional shapes to "pretend" write (p.6) — Not Yet / In Process / Proficient

III | Mathematical Thinking

A Approach to mathematical thinking F W S

1 Shows interest in quantity and number (p.7) — Not Yet / In Process / Proficient

B Patterns and relationships F W S

1 Sorts objects into subgroups that vary by only one attribute (p.7) — Not Yet / In Process / Proficient

C Number concept and operations F W S

1 Shows curiosity and interest in counting and numbers (p.7) — Not Yet / In Process / Proficient

D Geometry and spatial relations F W S

1 Identifies several shapes (p.8) — Not Yet / In Process / Proficient

2 Shows understanding of several positional words (p.8) — Not Yet / In Process / Proficient

Figure 1.10. An example of the genuine content of WSS. (From Marsden, D.B., Meisels, S.J., Jablon, J.R., & Dichtelmiller, M.L. [1994]. *Work Sampling System: Kindergarten developmental guidelines*, p. 12. Ann Arbor, MI: Rebus Planning Associates; reprinted by permission.)

dynamic assessment maintain that these mediated learning experiences guide the professional in determining the extent to which the child benefits from instruction (i.e., potential) and the types of interactions and supports that foster learning. Dynamic assessment tasks can be taken directly from a curriculum or extrapolated from authentic activities that occur in real-life settings.

Lidz (1991) modified and conducted rigorous research on the use of mediated learning experiences with preschoolers by means of two devices: the Mediated Learning Experience (MLE) and Rating Scale and the Preschool Learning Potential Assessment Device (PLPAD). The MLE rating scale assesses the following several dimensions of child–assessor interactive behavior in learning: intentionality, meaning, transcendence, sharing (joint regard) of experience, task regulation or competence, competence with praise, competence/zone of challenge or proximal development, psychological differentiation, contingent responsivity, affective involvement, and change.

To summarize, the three central components of the dynamic assessment model are 1) active engagement of the child in the task, 2) emphasis on "learning-to-learn" strategies to foster independent problem solving, and 3) recommendations for arranging instructional techniques (based on assessment outcomes) that are tailored to a given child.

Functional/Adaptive Assessment Model

The functional model of assessment of young children, especially those with severe disabilities, identifies those clusters of behaviors that have the greatest likelihood of increasing a child's competence in interacting with people and objects in his or her environment. Dunst and McWilliam (1988) created OBSERVE, a system that enables interventionists to facilitate children's development of response-contingent skills by identifying each child's response capabilities and matching those capabilities with appropriate learning opportunities. The functional, or adaptive, model stresses the use of alternative sensory and response capabilities for children with sensory, neuromotor, linguistic, and affective-behavioral impairments. The use of appropriate learning materials, toys, and positioning arrangements is vital to this assessment process. Much like curriculum-based and dynamic assessment models, the functional model combines assessment and intervention as part of a continuous process that presents assessment activities as opportunities for learning on the part of the child and for identifying changes that are needed in the intervention strategies on the part of the assessor.

The Pediatric Evaluation of Disability Inventory (PEDI) (Haley, Coster, Ludlow, Haltiwanger, & Andrellos, 1992) is a system that exemplifies the functional, or adaptive, assessment model. PEDI concentrates on detecting functional competencies for intervention in three primary domains: adaptive skills, mobility, and social func-

tion. The assessment identifies a child's level of ability for each functional skill, determines the level of assistance the child requires to perform that skill, and provides a general categorization of the level of therapeutic intervention that is recommended. Figure 1.11 shows the PEDI Caregiver Assistance and Modification Scale, which incorporates these features of functional assessment.

Every Move Counts (Korsten, Dunn, Foss, & Francke, 1993) is a functional/adaptive curriculum for young children with disabilities; this curriculum fuses structured observational assessments and intervention activities. Every Move Counts identifies a child's physical capabilities and communication skills on continuums through the use of a functional matrix that allows the interventionist to tailor strategies to that child's limitations and to promote generalization through expansion strategies. All of the skills that are taught and assessed are functional and authentic in that they address true capabilities that are expressed in genuine daily activities. An intervention is planned on the basis of sensory response and communication assessments of a child's matrix of function capabilities; this intervention includes aspects such as positioning techniques, order of presentation of stimuli, reinforcement procedures, and expansion routines (Figure 1.12).

Parts II and III: Caregiver Assistance and Modification

Circle the appropriate score for Caregiver Assistance and Modification for each item.

	Caregiver Assistance Scale						Modification Scale			
	Independent	Supervision	Minimal	Moderate	Maximal	Total	None	Child	Rehab	Extensive
SELF-CARE DOMAIN	5	4	3	2	1	0	N	C	R	E
A. **Eating**: eating and drinking regular meal; do not include cutting steak, opening containers or serving food from serving dishes	5	4	3	2	1	0	N	C	R	E
B. **Grooming**: brushing teeth, brushing or combing hair and caring for nose	5	4	3	2	1	0	N	C	R	E
C. **Bathing**: washing and drying face and hands, taking a bath or shower; do not include getting in and out of a tub or shower, water preparation, or washing back or hair	5	4	3	2	1	0	N	C	R	E
D. **Dressing Upper Body**: all indoor clothes, not including back fasteners; include help putting on or taking off splint or artificial limb; do not include getting clothes from closet or drawers	5	4	3	2	1	0	N	C	R	E
E. **Dressing Lower Body**: all indoor clothes; include putting on or taking off brace or artificial limb; do not include getting clothes from closet or drawers	5	4	3	2	1	0	N	C	R	E
F. **Toileting**: clothes, toilet management or external device use, and hygiene; do not include toilet transfers, monitoring schedule, or cleaning up after accidents	5	4	3	2	1	0	N	C	R	E
G. **Bladder Management**: control of bladder day and night, clean-up after accidents, monitoring schedule	5	4	3	2	1	0	N	C	R	E
H. **Bowel Management**: control of bowel day and night, clean-up after accidents, monitoring schedule	5	4	3	2	1	0	N	C	R	E
Self-Care Totals	**SELF-CARE SUM** [ ]									Self-Care Modification Frequencies
MOBILITY DOMAIN										
A. **Chair/Toilet Transfers**: child's wheelchair, adult-sized chair, adult-sized toilet	5	4	3	2	1	0	N	C	R	E
B. **Car Transfers**: mobility within car/van, seat belt use, transfers, and opening and closing doors	5	4	3	2	1	0	N	C	R	E
C. **Bed Mobility/Transfers**: getting in and out and changing positions in child's own bed	5	4	3	2	1	0	N	C	R	E
D. **Tub Transfers**: getting in and out of adult-sized tub	5	4	3	2	1	0	N	C	R	E
E. **Indoor Locomotion**: 50 feet (3-4 rooms); do not include opening doors or carrying objects	5	4	3	2	1	0	N	C	R	E
F. **Outdoor Locomotion**: 150 feet (15 car lengths) on level surfaces; focus on physical ability to move outdoors (do not consider compliance or safety issues such as crossing streets)	5	4	3	2	1	0	N	C	R	E
G. **Stairs**: climb and descend a full flight of stairs (12-15 steps)	5	4	3	2	1	0	N	C	R	E
Mobility Totals	**MOBILITY SUM** [ ]									Mobility Modification Frequencies
SOCIAL FUNCTION DOMAIN										
A. **Functional Comprehension**: understanding of requests and instructions	5	4	3	2	1	0	N	C	R	E
B. **Functional Expression**: ability to provide information about own activities and make own needs known; include clarity of articulation	5	4	3	2	1	0	N	C	R	E
C. **Joint Problem Solving**: include communication of problem and working with caregiver or other adult to find a solution; include only ordinary problems occurring during daily activities; (for example, lost toy; conflict over clothing choices.)	5	4	3	2	1	0	N	C	R	E
D. **Peer Play**: ability to plan and carry out joint activities with a familiar peer	5	4	3	2	1	0	N	C	R	E
E. **Safety**: caution in routine daily safety situations, including stairs, sharp or hot objects and traffic	5	4	3	2	1	0	N	C	R	E
Social Function Totals	**SOCIAL FUNCTION SUM** [ ]									Social Function Modification Frequencies

PEDI — 5

Figure 1.11.   PEDI Caregiver Assistance and Modification Scale. (From Haley, S.M., et al. [1992]. *Pediatric Evaluation of Disability Inventory [PEDI]: Development, standardization, and administration manual*, p. 5. Boston: PEDI Research Group and New England Medical Center Hospital; reprinted by permission.)

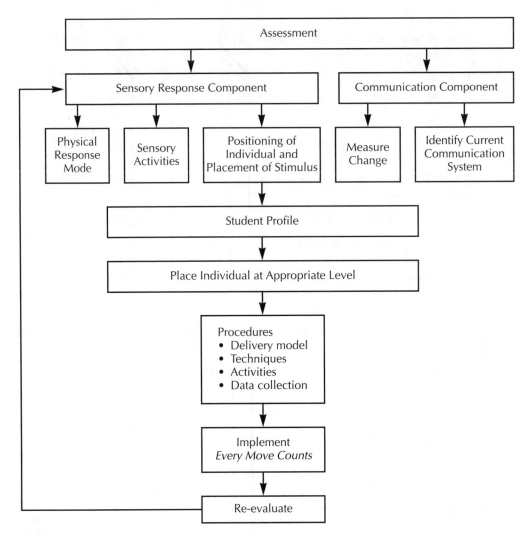

Figure 1.12. The assessment process based on a child's functional matrix. (From Korsten, J.E., et al. [1993]. *Every Move Counts*, p. 31. San Antonio, TX: Therapy Skill Builders/The Psychological Corporation.)

Play–Based Assessment Model

Since the mid-1990s, play-based assessment models have gained wide acceptance in early intervention programs. Play-based strategies are considered the most natural and developmentally appropriate assessment framework for young children for several reasons: Play-based assessment methods match expected early childhood styles of behavior, involve parents and professionals in the play session, use the child's own toys, provide a natural setting for observing the child's typical play skills, and allow flexible accommodations to be made to situations and materials to better suit each child's unique functional limitations and temperament.

One of the most widely used play-based systems is the Transdisciplinary Play-Based Assessment (TPBA) and Transdisciplinary

Play-Based Intervention (TPBI) system (Linder, 1993a, 1993b). Although TPBA and TPBI are discrete instruments, they are linked closely to one another. Figure 1.13 shows an example of the Social-Emotional Observation Worksheet from TPBA (Linder, 1993a).

RECOMMENDED ASSESSMENT PRACTICES

Given the importance of assessment for making diagnoses, determining service eligibility, making programming decisions, and tracking progress, it is imperative to make assessment *decisions* that are accurate, useful, and worthwhile. Our focus must be on the quality of decisions and not on the scores, per se. To aid in this decision-making process, we provide a summary of recommendations for assessment practices in early intervention. These recommendations reflect the new paradigm of assessment as decision making on the basis of inclusive information and with an emphasis on parent participation. (For an expanded discussion of recommended practices, see Neisworth & Bagnato, 1996.) These recommended practices incorporate facets of the prominent assessment models discussed in the previous section. (The five recommended practices discussed in this chapter are addressed in greater detail in Chapter 5.)

1. Use multiple perspectives.   The newer concepts of validity (Cronbach, 1988; Messick, 1989; Moss, 1992) emphasize the importance of including several informants and, as a result, several perspectives in the assessment process. Parents, in particular, are valuable partners in offering information and perspectives that are not otherwise available to professionals. Much has been written concerning parent–professional agreement or congruence of information (Suen, Lu, Neisworth, & Bagnato, 1993). Researchers have apparently sought agreement or high correspondence between parents and professionals within a conventional psychometric paradigm. Indeed, some researchers have provided training for parents to teach them to see their children in much the same way as do professionals, thereby achieving agreement or correspondence. This insistence on agreement, however, results in redundant information and actually obviates the richness of information available by including another perspective (Suen, Logan, Neisworth, & Bagnato, 1995). The issue should not be who is right or more accurate; multiple observers contribute perspectives from within multiple contexts to provide a more complete picture of a child's status. The use of multiple perspectives acknowledges that a child's behavior can vary considerably as a function of the situation. "Clinic behavior" rarely resembles at-home performance at all, and it is the variability or cross-situationality of behavior that must be captured. Hyperactive behavior, for example, must be demonstrated across situations for the diagnosis of hyperactivity to be made.

2. Use multiple techniques.   Assessment instruments include observation formats, checklists, structured interview proto-

Social-Emotional Observation Worksheet

Name of child: _____ Date of birth: _____ Age: _____

Name of observer: _____ Discipline or job title: _____ Date of assessment: _____

On the following pages, note specific behaviors that document the child's abilities in the social-emotional categories. Qualitative comments should also be made. The format provided here follows that of the Observation Guidelines for Social-Emotional Development in **Transdisciplinary Play-Based Assessment.** *It may be helpful to refer to the guidelines while completing this form.*

I. Temperament

A. Activity level

   1. Motor activity:

   2. Specific times that are particularly active

      a. Beginning, middle, or end:

      b. During specific activities:

B. Adaptability

   1. Initial response to

      a. Persons:

      b. Situations:

      c. Toys:

   2. Demonstration o

      a. Smiling, verbalizing, touching

      b. Crying, ignoring or moving away, seeking security

   3. Adjustment time:

   4. Adjustment time after initially shy or fearful response *(circle one)*:

      a. Self-initiation   b. Adult as base of security   c. Resists; stays uninvolved

C. Reactivity

   1. Intensity of stimuli for discernible response:

   2. Type of stimulation needed to interest child *(circle those that apply)*:

      a. Visual, vocal, tactile, combination

      b. Object, social

   3. Level of affect and energy:

   4. Common response mode:

   5. Response to frustration:

TPBA ꞊Play-Based꞊ TPBI

Figure 1.13.   First page of an eight-page TPBA Social-Emotional Observation Worksheet. (From Linder, T.W. [1993a]. *Transdisciplinary Play-Based Assessment: A functional approach to working with young children* [Rev. ed.], p. 153. Baltimore: Paul H. Brookes Publishing Co.; reprinted by permission.)

cols, standardized test sequences, and so forth. Norm-referenced, curriculum-based, and ecological surveys are just some of the materials available to professionals and parents (see Neisworth & Bagnato, 1988). A high-quality assessment includes the use of several types of instruments and methods, such as formal and informal testing, observation, and interviews, to characterize a child's functioning. *Formal testing*, which has standardized content and procedures, is one widely used conventional strategy. Although we emphasize its limitations, norm referencing does have clear strengths, and it is often informative to compare a child with his or her peers. The problems associated with "sensible standardized assessment," however, often mean that valid comparisons cannot be made among children with and children without special needs (Bagnato, Neisworth, & Munson, 1993; Fuchs, Fuchs, Benowitz, & Barringer, 1987). *Informal testing* is another technique that can be quite valuable; it includes those procedures that are related to ecological surveys, checklists, and other less-structured means of ascertaining a child's attainment.

There is no substitute for *observations* in real-life situations (Lincoln & Guba, 1985; Odom & Shuster, 1986). As mentioned previously, performance is situational, and observation in a child's usual settings offers perhaps the best information. Authentic assessment (Wiggins, 1989) focuses on purposeful behavior in children's actual circumstances and clearly is preferred over "tabletop testing."

In addition, *interviews* of family members, educational assistants, and others who are familiar with a child can be most helpful. These interviews can guide us toward more focused assessment, raise questions, and help resolve discrepancies among findings (Diamond & Squires, 1993). Finding out from a parent, for example, that a preschooler plays happily with others for hours on end at home counterbalances the possible concern raised by a professional who is trying to work with a so-called oppositional, noncompliant, or defiant child (what preschooler is *not* sometimes oppositional or defiant?). It is also important to be aware of parent concerns and to value parent appraisals (Glascoe, MacLean, & Stone, 1991). Parents can and do provide biased information, but their input can complement and challenge professional bias.

3. *Assess on multiple occasions.* Longitudinal, serial assessment is essential. Not only may a child be "out of sorts" on a particular day, but early development itself is characterized by spurts, reversals, and oscillations (Ausubel & Sullivan, 1970; Cole & Cole, 1989). Repeated assessment documents the stability of findings and detects changes. Professionals are advised to distribute their assessment efforts with a given child over time and varied settings. The single-session, brief encounter assessment approach cannot be justified and, in fact, is out of compliance with PL 99-457 and PL 102-119. Collecting appraisals across multiple settings and occasions

from parents and professionals provides a convergence of information. The wider the information base available, the greater the credibility or validity of assessment for decision making (Bagnato & Neisworth, 1991b).

4. *Use authentic item content.* It is important to note that the various assessment techniques—testing, observing, and interviewing—are associated with different types of instruments (e.g., curriculum based, play based, functional). Equally important is the nature of the item content. There are at least three bases for item content: developmental milestones, functional competence, and the presence of atypical behavior. Each of these may or may not be appropriate for assessing a particular child and may or may not center on real-life behavior expressed in natural situations.

The idea of *developmental milestones,* the most familiar content, was made prominent by the landmark contributions of Gesell (1949) and refers to item content that assesses attainment of developmentally significant abilities. Developmental schedules are widely used and clearly helpful in detecting delays and difficulties. It should be noted, however, that many of the milestone behaviors were identified through the use of psychometric procedures. Psychometrically selected behaviors separate age groups but are not necessarily critical themselves; some examples are stacking four blocks, standing on one foot, and drawing a circle. Furthermore, numerous developmental milestones that are important, per se, may never be reached by a child with certain sensorimotor disabilities. Walking by age 1 (or any age), using single words, and finding a hidden object (visually) are examples of items that are tied to standard sensorimotor functioning. Imposing such standard milestones on children with special needs may serve to penalize them, even when they may be able to exhibit an equivalent skill through other means (Coster & Haley, 1992). "Walking across the room" may not be possible for a given child, but "getting across the room" may be done with facility. It is important to realize that a child who gets across the room by a means other than walking has not achieved the standard developmental milestone, per se, but may well be functionally "on schedule" in his or her development (see the paragraph that follows for a discussion of the difference).

Functional competence refers to item content that assesses attainment of functions rather than requirements for demonstrating attainment by performing a particular (standard) task (Arndorfer & Miltenberger, 1993). Eating (not necessarily using a spoon), communicating (not necessarily verbally), and finding a hidden object (not necessarily visually) indicate a child's functional competence. Many children with physical disabilities must be assessed by using functional content items rather than typical developmental milestones (Snell, 1987).

The *presence of atypical behaviors* refers to item content that assesses problems that may not result from a developmental delay or impairment but rather from behaviors, such as self-injury, excessive rocking, hyper- or hypoactivity, and so forth. These behaviors may act to block subsequent development, although the child may not, when the behaviors are present, manifest sufficient delays to qualify for early intervention according to the usual criteria. Children with neurodevelopmental problems, prenatal exposure to drugs, acquired brain injury, and autism exhibit atypical behaviors that are not addressed in the content of conventional assessment instruments (Neisworth, Bagnato, & Salvia, 1995).

We must turn to nonconventional materials to find *authentic item content* (Greenspan & Meisels, 1994). Real behavior in real contexts should be the most critical focus of assessment. Practical versus "paper" intelligence, after all, is what matters in life (Sternberg, Wagner, Williams, & Horvath, 1995). Decontextualized, psychometrically derived, norm-referenced items administered in a standardized fashion must be replaced by alternative materials based on authentic objectives taught and assessed in natural contexts. *The higher the stakes of decisions, the more authentic (i.e., less inferential) the assessment on which those decisions are based should be.* It is important to consider the inverse relationship between stakes and level of inference. When important decisions are to be made (e.g., eligibility for services), authentic, low-inference information must be used.

5. *Make collaborative decisions.* We emphasize that several people, especially parents, must contribute information to provide a wide base for decisions. But who makes the decisions? Just as professionals and parents collaborate to gather information, so too must parents and professionals collaborate to make decisions on the basis of that information. Convergent assessment (Neisworth & Bagnato, 1996) and collaborative decision making produce a strong basis for determining eligibility and reaching programming decisions (Bagnato & Neisworth, 1990; Slentz & Bricker, 1992). When a true partnership is formed, professionals and parents can work together rather than square off as adversaries (Dunst, 1991).

STANDARDS FOR ASSESSMENT MATERIALS

The recommended practices endorsed by professional organizations include certain standards; early childhood education and intervention researchers have provided data and/or theory-based arguments to support several of these standards as desirable qualities of assessment instruments. In the section that follows, we present six standards (found in the foundations for linking assessment and intervention, prominent assessment models, and recommended practices discussed previously) for developmentally appropriate assessment materials and practices; these standards are used by LINK to connect assessment, intervention, and evaluation and to evaluate the materials reviewed in Chapter 4.

The six standards of assessment materials for use with young children are

1. *Authenticity:* Does the assessment focus on actual child behavior in real settings?
2. *Convergence:* Does it rely on more than one source of information?
3. *Collaboration:* Does it involve cooperation and sharing, especially with parents?
4. *Equity:* Does it accommodate special sensory, motor, cultural, or other needs rather than penalize children who have such needs?
5. *Sensitivity:* Does it include sufficient items for planning lessons and detecting changes?
6. *Congruence:* Was it developed and field tested with children similar to those being assessed?

Other characteristics, such as cost, ease of use, durability, training needed, and so forth, may also be important. These six standards, however, provide a criterion-based system (i.e., LINK) for professionals and parents to use when choosing assessment materials. These six standards are also used to choose curricula (see Chapter 2).

CONCLUSIONS

By its very nature and purpose, assessment is a social enterprise. From start to finish, social decision-making is involved during the assessment process. As professionals, we develop assessment materials based on social norms or expected standards; use judgment in selecting materials to use with a child; decide when and where to administer standardized or informal instruments; and interpret information obtained through testing, interviews, and observation. Indeed, in all phases of assessment, professionals make judgments and decisions that help change and form the outcomes.

The psychometric movement in psychology, education, and child development was an attempt to shift testing from the "subjective" to the "objective" and to fit measurement of human capabilities into the same positivistic, natural science model as disciplines, such as physics, chemistry, meteorology, and so forth. It can be argued that measurement practices in psychophysics and behavior analysis do, indeed, adhere to objective measurement; but, in so doing, they stand alone among the social "sciences," and even these pursuits are inextricably related to subjective/social factors. Many of our measurement attempts in development, education, and psychology may provide the illusion of objective precision, but anyone who has tried to administer an "intelligence test" to a hyperactive 3-year-old with language impairments knows that precision is futile! In fact, standardized, norm-referenced instruments, when used with young children—especially those who have sensory, motor, language, affective, and cultural differences from the standardization group—yield results that not only are imprecise but that frequently are misleading and bogus.

Because our assessment purposes and practices have a social basis, it seems productive to adopt the emergent paradigm of *assessment as decision making* based on reliable, verifiable information. In this paradigm, validity refers not to scores but to the goodness of *decisions* made on the basis of data and information generated by one or several means. Our viewpoint is not that testing and scoring should be abandoned, but that performance on assessment instruments is subject to a host of factors that contribute to a "score." Countless hours of professional training, preoccupation with psychometric "validities," misguided policies that mandate standardized normative instruments, and commercial insistence on promoting traditional instruments have not and cannot rescue business-as-usual assessment.

We must always bear in mind that, rather than adhere to arbitrary cutoff scores for eligibility and diagnoses, the assessor uses instruments to gain *impressions* of child status. Test performance, interviews, observations, and clinical judgment merge to provide considered judgments. So often, as professionals, we are required to use instruments that we know may not faithfully portray a child's abilities. We do not believe the scores we obtain because we know *other things* about the child that contradict or delimit the scores. Indeed, "to assess" is derived from *assidere*, meaning to "sit beside" or "to get to know" someone. Our assessment standards and procedures should help us "get to know" the child in question.

Early childhood specialists are increasingly turning toward assessment that parents and professionals know is useful, worthwhile, and trustworthy. Several assessment materials and procedures have gained prominence rapidly; as noted, some of these (i.e., performance based, functional, authentic, curriculum based) are especially important to early intervention. These approaches to assessment are not independent of each other; in fact, they overlap considerably. In this text, we describe and encourage the use of **curriculum-based assessment of authentic, functional performance**. In this chapter and those that follow, we emphasize assessment materials and practices that capture the best properties of several recommended approaches—practices that LINK assessment and intervention.

2

Building a Model Curriculum
for the Early Childhood Years

∞∞∞

As discussed in Chapter 1, one of the most critical issues in early childhood education and early intervention is to identify and use authentic assessment and curricular materials (see Spodek & Saracho, 1994). In this chapter, we clarify the importance of choosing and using appropriate curricula, examine four curricular models, discuss primary uses and content items of curricula, discuss the need to use curricula to provide smooth transitions from early education programs to kindergarten, and present considerations to bear in mind when selecting a curriculum. This introduction to the uses and characteristics of curricula reinforces the importance of LINKing assessments and curricula through the six standards introduced in Chapter 1.

Several definitions of curriculum (Dunst, 1981; Lillie, 1975; Mori & Neisworth, 1983) provide a basis for the definition we offer here:

A curriculum is an organized set of anticipated outcomes fostered through planned experiences or circumstances.

All programs for young children that are beyond mere babysitting services have some sort of curriculum, planning, or schedule of activities and experiences believed to be wholesome and constructive. Conducting a program without a curriculum is something like taking an extended trip without a map or a destination. An aimless journey may bring surprises and, indeed, be enjoyable, but only by chance. To leave the education and development of young children to chance cannot be justified.

It is especially unprofessional and unethical to place children with developmental delays, atypical behavior, or special needs in programs that do not offer the structure and direction that are available through a well-planned curriculum. In keeping with recommended practices (Odom & McLean, 1996), we believe that good curricular materials provide the best method to chart and evaluate child progress. The process of selecting and using curricular materials for teaching and assessment can serve as a unifying and team-building experience for the participants. It is not easy, however, to decide *which* outcomes to encourage. Advocates of *developmentally appropriate practice* (DAP) (NAEYC, 1991) argue against any lock-step curriculum wherein preset objectives are imposed on all children enrolled in a program. Moreover, DAP advocates encourage a formative, or emergent, curriculum that unfolds as a child explores the physical circumstances and interacts with his or her peers and with adults. Note that even an emergent curriculum presumes a planned environment and experiences; children are not turned loose in a void with unknown objects, people, and possibilities.

Teachers are always faced with the question of what to teach; this is especially true at the preschool level. Later schooling usually becomes tilted toward academic achievement; reading, writing, arithmetic, social studies, vocational preparation, and so forth dominate the curriculum. At the preschool level, however, there is considerable and understandable controversy over what constitutes appropriate and teachable content. The curriculum becomes the center of this controversy because it provides the potential goals and objectives for children at various ages and stages of development. Most parents and professionals readily agree on program goals when they are stated in general and abstract terms. Few would object to such program goals as achieving self-respect, acquiring an appreciation of one's culture, caring about others, developing problem-solving skills, gaining independence, and so on. When general goals are broken down into smaller parts and specific behaviors are stated, the trouble begins.

It should not be surprising, in view of the controversy over desirable content, that a variety of preschool curricula have been developed and promoted by various factions in early childhood education (see Bagnato et al., 1986). Indeed, hundreds of published curricula are available. On the one hand, many of these curricula are essentially similar to, or mere variations of, one another. On the other hand, many curricula are quite distinct, reflecting differing philosophies concerning child development and the role of the early childhood experience.

Regardless of your view of child development or of how prescriptive a curriculum should be, you will probably agree that sequenced, organized experiences with constructive opportunities should be available to young children. The metaphor of planning and taking a trip can be extended to further the argument for a curriculum: All children cannot, will not, and should not reach the same destinations or travel by the same routes. A variety of destinations and main and alternate routes should be available and will prove useful as children wend their ways along their wonderful developmental paths. Teachers can use curricular "maps" in flexible ways to suggest outcomes, elaborate and enrich directions spontaneously taken by children, and chart and evaluate child progress. It is not possible to link assessment to program objectives when there are no objectives, nor is it possible to track and evaluate progress without some sequence of worthwhile objectives. A curriculum is the key to determining a program's impact and a child's progress, because it provides the array of goals to be fostered and allows for sensitive monitoring of attainment.

CURRICULAR MODELS

The content and methods presented in published curricula reflect the range of philosophies concerning appropriate practice. Moreover, the nature and extent of the special needs of the children for whom curricula are designed are crucial factors that dictate the kind of curriculum content and how it is best offered. Philosophies regarding child development and the special needs of children enrolled in various programs are perhaps the two major considerations in the design and content of available and emerging curricular materials. We identify and discuss four major curricular models (or approaches): developmental milestones, cognitive-constructivist, functional/adaptive, and interactive/transactional. (See Table 2.1 for a comparison of the four curricular models.)

A common concern that cuts across all curricular models is the issue of authenticity and performance as a basis for assessment. *Authentic assessment* and *performance-based assessment* (see Meyer, 1992; see Chapter 1) refer to the use of meaningful, real-life objectives for instruction with corresponding assessment approaches. Thus, children are not taught to perform tasks that in themselves have little or no relevance to natural play or functional activities. Authentic objectives and assessment do not use contrived tasks but, rather, emphasize useful, relevant activities. Putting on socks, going up steps, and using a telephone are examples of authentic activities that can be taught and used to assess cognitive, social, communication, motor, and other skills. Many curricula seem to be moving toward more real-life, functional content and away from splinter skills or psychometric tasks. A number of curricula are reviewed in Chapter 4, in which we ascertain the degree of authentic content included in each curriculum. We emphasize assessment/instructional materials that center on functional, interesting, useful, authentic activities.

Developmental Milestones Model

Empirical research in child development has accumulated much information about the landmark skills, or developmental milestones, evidenced by children at various ages (Bayley, 1969; Gesell, 1923;

Table 2.1. Comparison of four curriculum models

Model	Premise for objectives	Advantages/disadvantages
Developmental milestones	Skills evidenced by children without disabilities at various age levels Based on empirical research and observation of normal development Main objective to differentiate age groups, although subskills may be derived through task analysis or professional judgment	**Advantages:** Normative comparisons Ease of linkage with traditional developmental milestone assessment devices **Disadvantages:** Objectives based on assessment items that psychometrically differentiate among age groups Such objectives may not be developmentally important or systematically related to each other
Cognitive-constructivist (Piagetian)	Skills evidenced by typically developing children at various (theory-based) stage levels Stages and sequence of steps within stages somewhat invariant, although timing varies with disabilities	**Advantage:** Sequence of steps in teaching stage level specified, providing clear, instructional goals for what must be taught first **Disadvantage:** Piagetian theory somewhat restricted to cognitive and language development; other objectives must be provided
Functional/adaptive	Objectives are of immediate utility to child and for future success in predictable environments Readiness or precursive skills are identified through task analysis rather than developmental prerequisites	**Advantage:** Particularly suited for children with severe disabilities to provide immediate success, motivation, and mastery in current situation—especially because normal milestone may not be feasible or appropriate **Disadvantage:** Child may not be prepared to succeed in subsequent environments because broad developmental milestones and prerequisites are not emphasized
Interactive/transactional	Derived from child development research and theory Objectives are actually for caregivers, designed to promote constructive and progressive adult–child transactions; should produce optimal child attainment of developmental milestones	**Advantages:** Parent–child dynamic crucial for early learning Well suited to a family-systems approach and to improving parent as well as child capabilities **Disadvantage:** Promoting desirable interaction does not guarantee selection of child objectives; many parents may not be ready, willing, or able to transact

Havinghurst, 1956; Knobloch, Stevens, & Malone, 1980). This information base enables us to determine the usual direction, sequence, and onset of major typical capabilities. As discussed in Chapter 1, most norm-based early childhood assessment instruments rely on testing or observing to determine whether a child has reached such developmental milestones. Curricula that incorporate these developmental milestones usually also include objectives that are precursors to each milestone. Through task analysis, which breaks down milestones into simpler components, a given developmental milestone may be divided into dozens of subskills or "readiness" skills. The skill of eating with a spoon, for example, is preceded by mastery of many other skills, such as chewing and swallowing, eye–hand coordination, and grasping. If a child is unable to eat with a spoon, instruction can begin on tasks that appear earlier (i.e., lower) in the hierarchy of skills. If the child cannot perform the earlier skill, his or her teacher can keep moving down in the hierarchy until an objective that the child has mastered is found. Instruction can proceed forward from that point.

Hierarchies of objectives that progress from earliest (i.e., easiest) to latest (i.e., most difficult) are, therefore, provided in the developmental milestones approach. These hierarchies are developed through observation, empirical trials, task analysis, and sheer logic. Sometimes professional consensus (Bailey & Wolery, 1992) is used to provide a sequence of skills that are subordinate to a milestone.

The developmental milestones approach offers strong curriculum format and content. A child's development can be assessed; treatment, instruction, or other intervention can be delivered; progress can be tracked; and program impact can be evaluated—all with reference to developmental milestones. Developmental hierarchies, therefore, provide both instructional objectives and diagnostic profiles of a child's capabilities. Establishing where within a given hierarchy a child falls is a relatively rapid way to evaluate that child's developmental status compared with his or her peers and to provide points for instruction and assessment.

The developmental milestones included in most curricula and assessment instruments come from research conducted with typically developing children. Since the 1980s, however, information regarding developmental patterns that are typical of children with specific special needs has been published. Often the age at which a certain developmental milestone is evidenced is later for children with special needs than it is for their typically developing peers (see Table 2.2). In general, however, the sequence and pattern of development are the same for all children, although alternative paths to the same capability are sometimes developed. This variation has implications for when an educator should attempt to teach a skill and how he or she should task analyze it (see Lewis, 1987).

Developmental milestones curricula are used in many programs that include youngsters with special needs, because such cur-

Table 2.2.   Developmental norms for two groups of children with disabilities compared with typically developing children

Process	Typically developing children (months)	Children who are blind (months)	Children with cerebral palsy (months)
Reach and grasp	3–5	10	14
Tactile-auditory patterns	4–6	9–12	15–20
Repeats purposeful acts	4–8	14	18
Extends arms to parent	3–5	8–12	18
Spontaneous smile	1–2	12	4
Object constancy	6–8	15–20	18
Separation anxiety	8–12	24–36	24
Word/object/person match	12–14	20	18
Self-references (i.e., I, me)	30	36–54	42
Actual object representation	24–30	60	Incomplete
Reciprocal games (e.g., peekaboo)	6–8	14	12–14

Source: Langley (1980).

ricula are highly structured and sequenced and permit the use of informal developmental assessment measures. These curricula frequently are aimed at children with developmental ages (DAs) from birth to 5 years and are particularly useful for planning experiences and writing IEPs or IFSPs for children with mild to moderate delays. A developmental milestones approach, however, is often inappropriate for children with severe sensory or neurophysical difficulties, who must use alternative sensory or response modes to act on the environment (Bailey & Wolery, 1992; Haley, Hallenborg, & Gans, 1989). Because the standard milestones often are not relevant to these children, functional and adaptive curricular models (discussed below) that address these children's needs have been developed. Moreover, experts are increasingly questioning the appropriateness of imposing an average or normative template on any child (Pellegrini & Dresden, 1991; Zelazo & Barr, 1989).

Cognitive-Constructivist Model

Jean Piaget's speculations and research have produced major contributions to early childhood assessment and curricula, including cognitive-constructivist theory. In *The Origins of Intelligence in Children* (1952), as well as in later work (1987), Piaget provides the theoretical basis for practical applications in assessment and education. Note, however, that Piaget did not design practical materials; his theoretical propositions have been interpreted and used as rationales for various curricular designs and contents. Numerous early childhood professionals (Brazelton, 1973; Bricker, 1993; Dunst, 1981; Uzgiris & Hunt, 1975) have used Piaget's observations as a basis to devise developmental goals and objectives. Piaget (1952) identified six critical concepts that are assumed to be the foundations for later learning: 1) object permanence, 2) means–end relations,

3) operational causality, 4) imitation, 5) spatial awareness, and 6) object function. A cognitive-constructivist curriculum contains the virtually unvarying steps in the progression of each of these six concepts through the stages of the sensorimotor period. These hierarchies provide a blueprint for appraising conceptual skills and guiding instruction during the developmental period.

Curricula based on theories of development (such as Piaget's) contain objectives that are logically related and consistent. As a result, specific predictable sequences can be used to guide instruction. In contrast, the developmental milestones approach is not theory based; rather, it is an empirically based compilation of skills observed in typical children of various ages. These developmental skills may meet psychometric criteria (i.e., they may distinguish between age groups for norming purposes); this, however, does not necessarily mean that the skills are crucial teaching objectives or that they are sequenced in a teachable manner.

Another feature of a cognitive-constructivist approach to curriculum is the use of developmental stage rather than age attainment (although stages are related to ages). With such a curriculum, a teacher attempts to help each child progress through steps in the predicted stage. Once these steps have been accomplished, the next stage (dependent on the previous one) becomes the goal.

In addition to conceptual development, the cognitive-constructivist approach provides guidelines for the related areas of language and social development; however, other major curricular concerns (e.g., fine and gross motor development, adaptive skills, affective development) are not addressed adequately to permit the creation of comprehensive curricula.

Functional/Adaptive Model

A functional/adaptive curriculum has two major characteristics: First, it emphasizes the learning of skills that have immediate utility and motivation for the child. Authentic, or real-life, competencies are listed as suggested goals for education. Major life skills and adaptive behaviors are analyzed to identify components and sequences that can be taught and that have immediate relevance. Second, a functional/adaptive curriculum places an emphasis on the function of a behavior rather than on the form and shape of the behavior. For example, some emergent curricula for youngsters with neurological impairments (Haley et al., 1989) delineate desirable functions or effects (e.g., opens doors) rather than developmental skills (e.g., pincer grasp, eye–hand coordination). As a result, the functional/adaptive model offers great promise for children with more severe needs, who may have impaired, but also alternative, sensory or response capabilities.

Some functional/adaptive curricula have been designed to accommodate children with specific difficulties. Specialized curricula can be purchased for children with visual, auditory, or motor limitations; cognitive or language delays; and Down syndrome. These

dedicated curricula have clear advantages: Although they apply the developmental milestones approach, they are functional/adaptive in that they are sensitive to the alternative sensory or response modalities that are likely to be needed by children with specific limitations. In addition to such dedicated curricula, several more general functional/adaptive curricula provide suggestions for adapting or altering materials and activities for children with specific needs; by making the suggested adaptations, professionals can use these curricula in inclusive settings.

Interactive/Transactional Model

The interactive/transactional model responds to the ever-increasing interest in examining and facilitating caregiver–child interaction as a primary method for promoting child development. The quality of parent–child interaction during infancy may set the stage for subsequent cognitive and social development. Enhancing the stimulus–response opportunities offered by a child's social and physical contexts rather than addressing specific child behaviors is the focus of the interactive/transactional approach. Most important is the match between a caregiver's actions or environmental events and a child's capabilities, interests, and behavioral style (i.e., pace, mood, manner of reacting); teaching efforts that do not meet these three matching criteria are not considered productive under the interactive/ transactional approach. Both the content of an objective and how that objective relates to the child's interests and behavioral state are of major concern (Mahoney & Powell, 1986).

The interactive/transactional model is built on child developmental research (Bell, 1979; Bell & Harper, 1977; Sameroff & Chandler, 1975) that recognizes the impact of children's characteristics and behavior on the caregiver (and vice versa) and the need for parents to feel comfortable with their children (Bromwich, 1981). Given efforts to develop and implement IFSPs, various transactional curricula may be available to optimize family–child reciprocity and mutually satisfying adult–child exchanges. Unlike other curricular models, the interactive/transactional model emphasizes the dynamics of interaction (i.e., how to match and relate to the child) to promote child progress.

CURRICULUM CONTENT AND DELIVERY

In this section, we offer a brief description of the typical content and characteristics of available curricular packages and a discussion of two major approaches to delivering the content.

Curriculum Content and Characteristics

As stated at the outset of this chapter, a curriculum is a set or array of intended or possible outcomes. Many materials developed since the late 1980s go beyond supplying curricular goals and objectives and include 1) the philosophy or rationale for the materials, 2) instructions for optimal use, 3) descriptions of or suggestions for instructional activities, 4) materials for working with parents, and 5) an assessment system for evaluating a child's status and tracking progress within the curriculum.

The qualities of the assessment materials related to each curriculum are the focus of this book, but we hasten to note that assessment and intervention are reciprocal. The dynamic between assessment and teaching has allowed us to "teach to the test" and "test what we teach." We call special attention to three aspects of curricula: lesson planning, family participation, and the curriculum objectives (i.e., items) themselves. In addition, we discuss two approaches to *using* curriculum content for teaching or assessing. The *how* becomes as important as the *what* to teach or assess because authenticity depends on real-life activities (i.e., content) being taught or assessed in real-life contexts.

Lesson Planning

The instructional or intervention activities found in curricula are intended to be used as a resource to aid in lesson planning. Seldom do teachers use the activities as fixed recipes. Instead, they develop creative lessons inspired by the suggested activities provided in curricula. These suggested lessons or activities are often accompanied by explanations of procedures, such as matching to a sample, performing task analysis, using surprise, making deliberate teacher mistakes, interrupting an activity, and so forth. Several curricula offer in-service materials to help teachers make instruction more effective, adaptive, and fun. Chapter 4 highlights a number of useful curricula and offers examples of innovative features available for use in teaching and assessing.

Family Participation

A second aspect common to good materials is an emphasis on parent or family involvement. No longer are parents *apart* from professional efforts to promote child progress; instead, they are *a part* of the process—partners in our work. Family-centered practices are a central standard of recommended practice, which means that parents and other family members can be active in assessment and intervention. Curricular materials to foster family participation are especially helpful when they are written and presented in a family-friendly fashion (Bricker & Squires, 1989). Several prominent curricula go a long way to give parents a central role (see Chapter 4).

Assessment Materials

There are two basic methods of presenting curriculum-based assessment systems of curricular packages. On the one hand, in curriculum-embedded systems, separate booklets that contain instructions and the assessment items, which are the curriculum objectives themselves, accompany the curricula. Such systems are integral to a particular set of curricular materials. On the other hand, curriculum-compatible assessment systems are not part of a specific curriculum but are nevertheless useful for instructional planning and monitoring; these systems are designed to work with any of a number of curricula.

For both systems, the instructions typically describe how to estimate a child's current levels of performance in the several developmental domains. Sometimes, details, such as how to determine basal and ceiling scores, are provided. The instructions also specify whether observation, interview, or direct performance testing is preferred for given items. Because assessment procedures can be quite flexible, many instructions simply offer guidelines for use. Often teachers and other professionals adapt the assessment procedures to fit their needs—and their time constraints. In addition, parents are frequently able to use the assessment materials that come with a curriculum. Some packages contain separate instruments specifically for parents to use to rate a child's performance or to gather information. Finally, a curriculum-based assessment system should welcome collaborative assessment. Arena, play-based, and transdisciplinary assessment (discussed in Chapter 1) are all models based on the importance of using multiple perspectives. Most curriculum-based assessment materials make it easy for multiple people to gauge a child's performance, either simultaneously or independently.

It is important to remember that curriculum-based assessment entails using instructional objectives (curriculum objectives) as the assessment items. Because of their dual role, the actual content and organization of curriculum objectives are of paramount importance in curriculum-based systems. Objectives within the domains of a curriculum should be organized in hierarchies or clear sequences that are based on child development research. Curricula should provide opportunities for behavior expansion (Bagnato et al., 1986) for the child, the caregiver, or both. In particular, the addition of new skills to a child's repertoire can fill those gaps in development that often are experienced by children with special needs. Furthermore, the development of behavioral variability across materials, settings, and response modes can allow children to generalize skills to situations outside the teaching environment (Mori & Neisworth, 1983).

Curriculum Delivery

As stated previously, a curriculum is a collection of teachable objectives, the content of which varies according to the underlying approach. Depending on the nature of its content, a curriculum usually involves several areas (or domains). Most developmental curricula include the cognitive, social-emotional, communication, and motor domains or variants thereof. Typically, each domain comprises an array of related objectives; there may be dozens or hundreds of objectives grouped under each domain. Often domains are organized into subdomains, or strands, of related objectives to assist in instructional planning and assessment.

It is clear that our chopping up of development into domains creates artificial categories that are defied by many, if not most, genuine activities. Using a toy telephone, for example, allows children to develop and practice multiple abilities. Talking on a telephone is difficult to classify according to the conventional developmental domains: Is it a cognitive, motor, language, or social skill? Curriculum content and delivery should reflect the fact that real-life activities typically encompass interrelated abilities. Worthwhile childhood curricula 1) foster general development, 2) teach interrelated skills, and 3) teach specific competencies. Thus far, we have discussed the content of curricula. How curriculum objectives are taught and used for assessment is equally important.

There are two very different basic approaches to teaching and using curriculum content: Teaching may be either decontextualized (i.e., specific skills taught or practiced under contrived circumstances) or activity based (i.e., interrelated skills taught or practiced through ongoing child activities). Some explanation of these two extremes is needed because these issues of what and how to teach are so contentious.

Activity-based teaching occurs when children are learning on their own; they typically are at play, experiencing natural consequences, noticing changes, and so forth. Natural (i.e., authentic) circumstances are ideal for observing what children can do and want to do. Curriculum objectives can be woven into natural child-driven activities without resorting to special tricks, treats, or threats to create motivation. Child-centered routines permit the introduction and practice of related skills that cut across conventional domains. Having a tea party, for example, is an opportunity for children to learn and practice various related cognitive, language, motor, and social competencies in an authentic circumstance. Not all children will be at the same skill levels, and their IEPs should specify different goals for the same activity. When possible, we encourage teachers and parents to select curriculum goals and objectives in a formative manner that follows or anticipates each child's lead. Sense where a child is and seems to want to go, and use that child's interests and capabilities as avenues for teaching. Such "transactional teaching" allows the teacher to follow the child's lead while offering help and direction that is child centered. Repeated reference to selected curricular materials will guide the teacher in planning the next challenges for the child.

In contrast with such activity-based teaching is decontextualized teaching (i.e., using curriculum objectives to teach specific skills under specific, contrived circumstances). In one preschool, we overheard the following instruction, which captures the artificial nature of decontextualized teaching: "Now it is time to string

beads to practice eye–hand coordination." This command conveys the antithesis of authentic teaching. Indeed, unless these preschoolers were being trained or tested to work in a necklace or bead factory, stringing beads does not seem like a worthwhile or relevant activity!

Assessment activities are much the same as teaching; assessment can be performed in either natural or contrived ways. As discussed in detail in Chapter 1, distinct differences are inherent between the assumptions, approaches, and outcomes of psychometric assessment and those of authentic assessment. How a child strings beads, stacks blocks, or looks under a cloth for a tiny toy from a test kit are examples of inauthentic tasks and decontextualized circumstances that are scored during a psychometric assessment. The child who fails to look for a hidden bunny, for example, may do very well at finding a favorite toy at the bottom of his or her toybox. If the mission of the assessment is to determine whether a child has attained a level of object permanence, then is it not obvious which approach to assessment is more trustworthy? This issue becomes even more critical when inauthentic content and conditions are used to assess children who have special needs or cultural backgrounds that differ from those of the standardization sample. Often, sensory, motor, affective, or cultural differences invalidate completely the use of standardized procedures.

We hasten to note that, occasionally, it may be in the interest of a child's progress to teach specific skills in contrived, or decontextualized, circumstances. A child may, for example, have great difficulty with a particular behavior that cannot be addressed in his or her ongoing routine. Sometimes taking such a child aside for special instruction is the best solution. Sometimes, too, actual drills, rehearsals, and similar tactics performed out of the natural context may be indicated—but only as exceptions to the general real-life approach.

A good teacher can use most of the curricula described in this book and can embed the goals and objectives of a given curriculum into a program's ongoing child-centered activities. It seems clear that routine- or activity-based approaches promote more natural assessment and intervention. Several researchers have developed materials that promote the selection and teaching of important objectives within authentic child contexts and routines (e.g., Bricker, 1993; Bricker & Cripe, 1992; Bricker & Pretti-Frontczak, 1996; Bruder, 1993; Cripe et al., 1993).

Well-conducted criterion-referenced assessment allows both parents and professionals to observe and assess where a child is in the ongoing curriculum, anticipate or plan subsequent goals, and monitor progress. When a curriculum is used to endorse rather than thwart a child's interests, the concurrent assessment can be sensitive and helpful. An example of this best-case scenario as applied to making the transition from early childhood education to kindergarten is presented next.

CURRICULA AND TRANSITIONS

At some point, every child involved in an early childhood special education program must make a "transition" to a new program because of his or her age, issues particular to the service delivery model, or decisions made by his or her family. Inherent in the process of making the transition to kindergarten is the need to change from that which is known to the family and child (e.g., staff, curriculum, related services, schedules, location) to a new situation replete with unknowns. This period of transition causes significant stress for the family and child as they anticipate what the new program holds in store for them. Will (1984) likens the transition process to building a solidly anchored bridge that connects the known program to the new, unknown program. Responsibility for planning successful transitions for families and children clearly resides with the administration and staff of both the child's present program and the receiving program. Systematic planning for the transition to kindergarten will ensure continuity of services for the child with minimal disruption to the family and will ensure that each child is adequately prepared to adjust successfully to the new program.

Family Self-Assessment

The transition of a child from an early childhood special education program to a school-age kindergarten program must be carefully orchestrated by a designated conductor, and each player must perform his or her piece fluently. This process necessarily requires a positive collaborative relationship among the family and all preschool and school staff involved. It is of utmost importance that the family make all decisions relevant to the transition and that this decision be clearly specified in the child's IEP. The DEC (1993) recommends that all family members of young children with special needs be afforded the opportunity to choose their roles in the program-planning process. They may elect to coordinate the efforts of the IEP team in a leadership role, accept a position of parity in a situation in which all team members have an equal voice in decision making, or select another team member to lead the planning process. The first and most crucial assessment target during the transition planning stage is the family.

A child's parents must be surveyed to determine their preference for initiating the planning phase. They must first determine their preference for the composition of the team and decide who will assume the leadership or coordinator's role. Next, it is helpful to have the parents complete a written survey or an interview to determine their need for information regarding the transition process itself and/or the receiving kindergarten program. Hanline and Knowlton (1988) have developed a checklist to determine parents' need for information or assistance before initiating the transition process (Figure 2.1). Completion of this type of checklist will alert the designated transition team to the nature and degree of informa-

PARENT TRANSITION PREPARATION CHECKLIST

Do you need more information about or assistance in:

_____ _____ Preparing for your child's assessment?
Yes   No   If so, what do you need? _____
_____

_____ _____ Preparing for your child's IEP?
Yes   No   If so, what do you need? _____
_____

_____ _____ Obtaining appropriate related services?
Yes   No   If so, what do you need?
_____

_____ _____ Arranging for visits to preschool classrooms?
Yes   No   If so, what do you need? _____
_____

_____ _____ Preparing your child for the new classroom?
Yes   No   If so, what do you need? _____
_____

_____ _____ Communicating with your child's new teacher?
Yes   No   If so, what do you need to know? _____
_____

_____ _____ Your legal rights and responsibilities?
Yes   No   If so, what do you need to know? _____
_____

_____ _____ How and when you will be offered a preschool special
Yes   No   education placement for your child?
                     If so, what do you need to know? _____
_____

_____ _____ Preschool special education programs and services?
Yes   No   If so, what do you need to know? _____
_____

_____ _____ Education in the least restrictive environment?
Yes   No   If so, what do you need to know? _____
_____

_____ _____ Your involvement in preschool programs?
Yes   No   If so, what do you need to know? _____
_____

_____ _____ Community services?
Yes   No   If so, what do you need to know? _____
_____

Figure 2.1.   Parent transition preparation checklist. (From Hanline, M.F., & Knowlton, A. [1988]. A collabora-tive model for providing support to parents during their child's transition from infant intervention to preschool special education public school programs. *Journal of the Divison for Early Childhood, 12,* p. 120; reprinted by permission.)

tion and assistance desired by the family. As a matter of organiza-tion, it is also important to provide parents with a proposed time line that details the sequence of activities and target completion dates. We proposed one such time line (Bagnato & Neisworth,

1991a); this time line helps to allay parents' anxiety regarding the transition process and provides planning deadlines for the sending and receiving programs (Figure 2.2).

Assessing the Kindergarten Environment

To adequately prepare a child for a successful transition to the kindergarten program, a thorough assessment of the program's environment must be conducted by the sending and receiving program staff. This ecological assessment of the receiving environment will yield a list of social and academic skills that are requisite for the child to make a smooth transition into the new program as well as a

---

A TIMELINE FOR "ERRORLESS" TRANSITION

Time	Task initiated	Task completed
12 Months		
1. Transition calendar of events created		
2. Allocate team members responsible for events		
3. Arrange to meet with receiving kindergarten teacher(s)		
4. Ecological observation of receiving kindergarten setting		
5. Begin screening to determine readiness strengths and weaknesses		
10 Months		
1. Team members attend pre-planning meeting to review timeline, screening results and tentative child goals		
2. Schedule program planning with team members and parents		
3. Provide parents with a list of activities they can use at home with child		
9 Months		
1. Implement progress monitoring system with preschool teacher		
2. Initiate preschool curriculum objectives for approximating kindergarten setting		
3–4 Months		
1. Administer thorough follow-up assessment		
2. Meet with multidisciplinary members to determine appropriate services and program goals		
3. Meet with parent to discuss/receive input for child's program		
4. Conduct visitations of kindergarten with parents and child		
Posttransition		
1. Schedule staff meetings to monitor child's kindergarten progress		
2. Initiate progress reporting to parents		

Figure 2.2.   Time line for errorless transition and to facilitate the determination of IEP objectives and goals. (From Bagnato, S., & Neisworth, J. [1991a]. *Assessment for early intervention: Best practices for professionals,* p. 146. New York: Guilford Press; reprinted by permission.)

list of critical program elements that will support the child during and after the transition process.

One of us (Munson) has created Survival and Supports in the Next Environment (SSINE) to provide suggested target areas for conducting an ecological assessment of the receiving kindergarten program (Figure 2.3). SSINE is best completed through direct observation of the kindergarten program by family members and a representative of the preschool program. The receiving program may also provide information through interviews, written surveys, and printed material detailing the philosophy and goals of the kindergarten program. Completion of the SSINE assessment must occur as early as 9 months to 1 year before the targeted transition date.

SSINE includes three target areas to consider when conducting an ecological inventory of the proposed kindergarten class: program and staff, services, and curriculum and instruction. The *program and staff area* is concerned with the philosophy of the receiving program and training and experience of program personnel. An exemplary program espouses a child-centered philosophy of viewing each child as an individual and supports the belief that all children will learn when provided with appropriate curricular opportunities. In exemplary programs, parents are viewed as equal partners in the education process and are encouraged to actively participate in all aspects of their children's programs. Administrators, teachers, and staff maintain an open system of communication and are present in sufficient numbers to provide adequate support for each child. All program personnel are appropriately trained and certified and are willing to meet the diverse instructional needs of all children.

The *services area* focuses on the educational services available to children and families and on the range of related services (e.g., speech-language therapy, occupational therapy, counseling) in the receiving program that may be a part of the child's IEP and are deemed necessary to provide an appropriate program. Noneducational services that must be considered include accessible and efficient transportation; appropriate food service to meet dietary and feeding needs; and, most important, the accessibility of the target classroom and the entire building (e.g., ramps, doors, elevators, bathrooms, cafeteria, playground). In addition, before- and/or after-school care services are often needed to accommodate families' work schedules.

With regard to the *curriculum and instruction area*, exemplary programs for young children clearly address the standards and best practices of organizations such as the DEC (1993) and the NAEYC (1996). Curriculum, instructional strategies, and materials are developmentally appropriate and are adapted to meet the needs of individual children. Activities are based on authentic, functional tasks that are critical for experiencing success in the natural environment, and they encourage active exploration on the part of the child. The heterogeneous grouping of students facilitates cooperative learning of both social and academic outcomes. Adaptive equipment and aug-

SURVIVAL AND SUPPORT IN THE NEXT ENVIRONMENT (SSINE)

Target Area:	In the kindergarten program, this item is present to the degree of:				For this child's transition, the item is:		
	Exemplary	Adequate	Marginal	Not Present	Essential	Desirable	NA
Program and Staff							
Philosophy is child centered and based on an inclusive education model							
Appropriately certified and trained teachers							
Adequate number of professional and paraprofessional staff to provide needed support							
Willing to make reasonable accommodations according to the child's IEP							
Encourages parent participation in all aspects of the program							
Administrators are accessible for the family							
Services							
Range of related services available							
Transportation							
Building & rooms are accessible							
Food service							

Before-/after-school care programs

Curriculum & Instruction

Curriculum is developmentally appropriate with flexible outcomes

Instructional strategies are developmentally appropriate with accommodations for individual needs of students

Uses cooperative learning approaches to facilitate inclusion of child

Instructional materials & equipment are age appropriate

Use of adaptive/prosthetic devices, computer-assisted technology, and augmentative communication devices is possible if included in the child's IEP

Behavior management is child centered using positive practices

Evaluation is based on authentic assessment such as CBA and student portfolios

Figure 2.3.   SSINE form for assessing the receiving environment.

mentative communication devices are available as needed and are readily incorporated into the child's classroom activities. Carefully structured classroom routines with predictable schedules are in place, and clear expectations for children's behavior are explicit. Each child's mastery of specified outcomes is evaluated on an ongoing basis by using curriculum-embedded tasks and performance measures such as student portfolios.

The results of SSINE provide critical information about the presence or absence of program elements and supports that will facilitate a child's placement. First, parents and sending staff rate the elements of each SSINE target area of the receiving program as follows:

Exemplary: Target area is clearly observed as an integral part of the program and is consistently present.

Adequate: Target area is observed but either is not present on a consistent basis or is not seen as an integral part of the program.

Marginal: Target area is not present on a consistent basis and/or is not applied or implemented appropriately.

Not present: Target area is not observed in any form or to any degree.

Second, for each child, the level of priority for each target area is specified as essential, desirable, or not applicable. The resultant list of essential and desirable supports enables the IEP team to develop a transition plan and IEP to meet the needs of the child and family. An assessment of the child's academic and nonacademic survival skills for the kindergarten environment is another aspect of completing the SSINE process.

Assessing the Child

Rosenkoetter, Hains, and Fowler (1994) prepared a checklist of nonacademic survival skills that are thought to be necessary for children to function adequately in the kindergarten setting (Table 2.3). The child should be able to communicate with and respond to the teacher, adapt to the structure of classroom routine, and interact with other students in the class during both structured and unstructured activities. Although such a list never includes all of the critical skills and may not be relevant for every child in every kindergarten program, it does serve as a starting point for assessing a child's repertoire of survival skills before the actual transition occurs. It is also helpful for the sending program staff to visit the potential kindergarten program to observe both the setting and the behavior of successful students to determine the range of critical entry skills for that program.

The process of determining the goodness of fit between a child and a receiving program is referred to as "template matching" (Cone, Bourland, & Woods, 1986); that is, the child's competence in the critical survival skills is compared with the profiles of students who have performed successfully in the receiving kindergarten pro-

Table 2.3. Nonacademic skills useful for transition into kindergarten

NOTE: The following skills may be useful for goal writing, if they are developmentally appropriate for a given child. They should *never* be used as entrance criteria or to exclude any child from a classroom.

PLAYING AND WORKING INDEPENDENTLY AND COLLABORATIVELY

1. Plays and works appropriately with and without peers
2. Completes activities approximately on time
3. Stays with an activity for an appropriate amount of time
4. Plays and works with few individual prompts from the teacher

INTERACTING WITH PEERS

1. Imitates peers' actions when learning new routines
2. Initiates and maintains contact with peers
3. Responds to peers' initiations
4. Learns and uses names of peers
5. Shares objects and takes turns with peers
6. Plans activities with peers

FOLLOWING DIRECTIONS

1. Responds to adults' questions
2. Responds appropriately to multistep verbal directions
3. Responds appropriately to verbal directions that include common school-related prepositions, nouns, and verbs
4. Complies with group as well as individual instructions
5. Modifies behavior as needed when given verbal feedback
6. Recalls and follows directions for tasks previously discussed or demonstrated
7. Watches others or seeks help if he or she doesn't understand directions

RESPONDING TO ROUTINES

1. Learns new routines after limited practice
2. Moves quickly and quietly from one activity to another without individual reminders
3. Reacts appropriately to changes in routine
4. Cares for personal belongings

CONDUCTING ONESELF ACCORDING TO CLASSROOM RULES

1. Waits appropriately
2. Lines up if teacher requests that he or she do so
3. Sits appropriately
4. Focuses attention on the speaker, shifts attention appropriately, and participates in class activities in a manner that is relevant to the task or topic
5. Seeks attention or assistance in acceptable ways
6. Separates from parents and accepts the authority of school personnel
7. Expresses emotions and feelings appropriately

From Rosenkoetter, S.E., Hains, A.H., & Fowler, S.A. (1994). *Bridging early services for children with special needs and their families*, p. 143. Baltimore: Paul H. Brookes Publishing Co.; reprinted by permission.

gram. On the basis of this comparison, the family and preschool staff may either determine whether there is a need to teach the child specific survival skills before the transition or identify possible adaptations that could be made in the receiving environment to facilitate the transition process.

Curriculum-Based and Authentic Measures

Completing informal checklists of survival skills needed for transition is indeed helpful during the planning phase; however, it is also critical that a more comprehensive assessment be conducted to provide adequate information for developing the child's IEP and determining the goodness of fit with the receiving kindergarten program. The following commercially produced, curriculum-based measures, all of which are discussed in greater detail in Chapter 4, are appropriate for this purpose of assessment.

BRIGANCE Prescriptive Readiness: Strategies and Practice (Brigance, 1985) is a criterion-referenced measure of preacademic skills based on developmental milestones for children ranging from prekindergarteners to first graders. Results identify a child's pattern of strengths and areas of concern in a number of developmental domains and preacademic skills (e.g., language, writing, reading, social skills, adaptive skills, motor ability) (see Chapter 4).

WSS (Marsden et al., 1994; also see Chapter 1) is an excellent example of an authentic assessment system that is useful for determining a child's academic and nonacademic skills before the transition to kindergarten. WSS relies on portfolios of students' work samples and developmental checklists to assess children. Performance indicators in the kindergarten level of the personal and social domain demonstrate a child's grasp of nonacademic survival skills such as self-concept, self-management, approach to learning, and skill in peer interactions. Performance indicators in the remaining six domains focus on language and literacy, mathematics, arts, and physical development (see Chapter 4).

SPECS (Bagnato & Neisworth, 1990; also see Chapter 1) offers a team-based decision-making model for use in assessment for kindergarten transition. Section 10 of the D–Specs includes a readiness checklist for identifying potential learning and behavior problems that would prevent a smooth transition to kindergarten (Figure 2.4). After team members reach consensus on a child's areas of concern by completing the transition readiness items, they complete

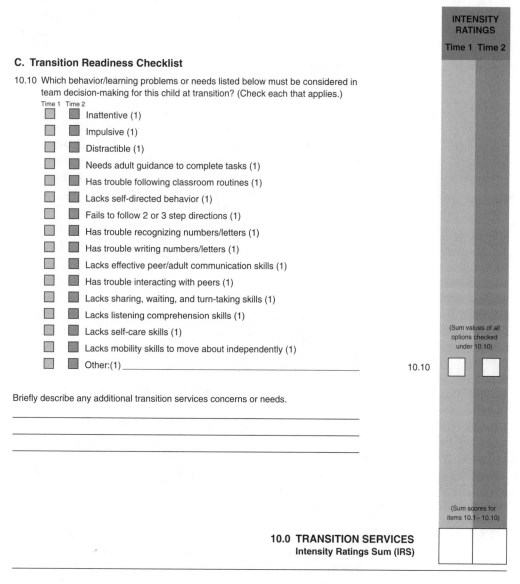

Figure 2.4.   Readiness checklist from section 10 of D–Specs. (From Bagnato, S.J., & Neisworth, J.T. [1990]. *System to Plan Early Childhood Services [SPECS]*, p. 13. Circle Pines, MN: American Guidance Service; reprinted by permission.)

the P–Specs to determine that child's need for specific transition services (Figure 2.5). Decisions reached on the P–Specs facilitate IEP team decisions regarding how to provide the most appropriate program and services for the child in the least restrictive environment (see Chapter 4).

Closure: Making the Transition

Deliberate planning for a child's transition to kindergarten is essential to minimize the family's stress and to maximize the child's success. Assessments of the family, the kindergarten environment, and the child generate the information necessary to plan a successful transition. It is imperative that both sending staff and receiving staff provide support to the child and family as they adjust to the new setting, staff, and program and that staff members maintain frequent contacts during the actual transition. Parents and the sending program staff should share information regarding how the actual transition is progressing.

After the transition process is complete, the posttransition activities suggested in Figure 2.2 should be implemented. These activities may include monitoring the child's progress through use of observations, curriculum-based measures, and a work portfolio. Meetings among parents, sending staff, and receiving staff may be required if unanticipated problems arise. A carefully orchestrated transition will result in a child who is able to successfully meet the demands of the new program and family members who experience minimal disruption as well as a sense of satisfaction regarding the next phase of schooling for the child.

CHOOSING A CURRICULUM

Curricula are usually designed for use with certain age ranges, special needs, and particular settings. The following considerations should prove helpful in selecting curricula that best meet particular child, family, and program needs:

- Target population: developmental ages and chronological ages (CAs), special needs
- Intended setting: for use with individuals or small groups, for use at home, early childhood education program, hospital
- Comprehensiveness and balance: all or most major domains addressed, adaptations included or suggested for use with children with disabilities
- Inclusion: opportunities for children at various stages to participate equally
- Family involvement: family-friendly materials, transactional curricula, forms and checklists designed for parents
- Required training and utility: level of training provided and needed, clarity and organization of lessons, ease of preparation, goodness of fit with children's needs and program's philosophy

10.0 TRANSITION SERVICES
(Complete only for children 4-1/2 to 6 years old.)

| INTENSITY RATINGS |
| Time 1 Time 2 |

From Team Specs: Service Average _____

Service Decision _____

A. Primary Placement

10.1 Will this child require related services to be successfully integrated and maintained in a regular kindergarten or first grade setting?

Time 1 Time 2

☐ ■ No (0)

☐ ■ Yes (1): (If yes, complete questions 10.2–10.10.)   10.1 ☐ ☐

10.2 Does this child require a special education placement?

Time 1 Time 2

☐ ■ No (0)

☐ ■ Yes (1): (If yes, which setting is most appropriate?)

Time 1 Time 2

☐ ■ Developmental or transitional kindergarten (1)

☐ ■ Resource room (2)

☐ ■ Part-time special education classroom (3)

☐ ■ Full-time special education classroom (4)   10.2 ☐ ☐

10.3 To what extent should this child participate in mainstream activities?

Time 1 Time 2

☐ ■ 50%–85% (1)

☐ ■ 15%–49% (2)

☐ ■ 0%–14% (3)   10.3

10.4 In which of the following activities should this child be excluded from participating with his nonhandicapped peers? (Check each that applies.)

Time 1 Time 2

☐ ■ Content areas (e.g., science) (1)

☐ ■ Physical education (2)

☐ ■ Playground/recess (2)

☐ ■ Math (1)

☐ ■ Reading (1)

☐ ■ Library (1)

☐ ■ Art (1)   (Sum values of all options checked under 10.4)

☐ ■ Music (1)

☐ ■ Lunch (2)   10.4 ☐ ☐

10.5 This child's daily special program should be:

Time 1 Time 2

☐ ■ Half-day (1)

☐ ■ Full-day (2)   10.5 ☐ ☐

Figure 2.5.   Transition services needs from P–Specs. (From Bagnato, S.J., & Neisworth, J.T. [1990]. *System to Plan Early Childhood Services [SPECS]*, p. 12. Circle Pines, MN: American Guidance Service; reprinted by permission.)

- Progress monitoring: simple way to perform formative and summative evaluations, clear criteria for mastery
- Database or information base: number and kinds of children with whom curriculum has been used, sites and lengths of use, progress information provided, teacher ratings provided
- Durability: kit format or manual with reproducible forms, well organized, adaptability and generalizability, supplemental materials needed, cost

In addition to addressing these considerations, the individual or individuals responsible for selecting the curriculum must have a clear understanding of and agreement with the child's family to ensure that the philosophy and goals of the family and program staff are clear and reflected in the materials. For example, program staff may elect to have a central, inclusive curriculum and to consult and use several supplemental materials to support children with special needs.

By learning about and helping to select curricular materials, family members will have a better understanding of what to expect of the program and what is expected of them. They will be better able to determine whether the program will meet the particular needs of their child and family. For some families, an intense home-based program may be the most helpful and valuable; for others, for a variety of reasons, a center-based program or a less intense home-based program may be better suited to their needs.

In addition, it is vital to consider the six standards introduced in Chapter 1 (detailed in Chapter 3) when selecting both assessment and curricular materials:

1. How *authentic* are the objectives and teaching practices?
2. Is *collaboration* with parents and other professionals made possible?
3. Are there two or more *convergent* ways to appraise progress (e.g., direct observation, permanent products)?
4. Are there clear suggestions on how to accommodate individual differences so that instruction is *equitable*?
5. Are there an adequate number of objectives in the several instructional domains to make possible *sensitive* increments of change?
6. Were the materials designed for and validated (i.e., *congruent*) with children who have the kinds of individual differences of concern?

Finally, remember that no materials will address all of your needs for assessing and teaching. Use curricular materials and curriculum-based assessment with discretion, flexibility, and always to the advantage of child and family.

3

Authentic Curriculum–Based
Evaluation Through LINK

Significant changes in assessment for early intervention have occurred since the early 1980s. These changes, nevertheless, pale and lag with the dramatic, parallel changes in early intervention, itself; the most notable of these are inclusion in natural settings and family-centered practices. In this respect, assessment for early intervention has been "retarded" in its own development. Although curriculum-based assessment has been the hallmark of important changes that have occurred in the objective of early childhood assessment (i.e., linking assessment to early intervention), few important changes have occurred in the methods or styles of assessment to complement inclusion and family-centered perspectives in the field. We believe that this stagnation in early childhood assessment is best described by Bronfenbrenner's (1979) reproach regarding developmental psychology, "Much of developmental psychology [early childhood assessment], as it now exists, is the science of the strange behavior of children in strange situations with strange adults for the briefest possible periods of time" (p. 19).

Assessment for infants and young children remains dominated by an approach that places a premium on inauthentic, contrived developmental tasks that are administered by various professionals in separate sessions using small toys from test kits, staged at a table or floor in a "clinic" setting, observed passively by parents, and interpreted through norms based solely on typical children. As this chapter's title implies, we believe that curriculum-based assessment transformed by an emphasis on authenticity will provide the necessary impetus to generate fundamental changes in the process of assessment for early intervention.

In Chapters 1 and 2, we examine the need for real-life relevant assessment and curricular materials; summarize the six standards of such linked materials; and discuss important models, recommended practices, and associated features of assessment and curriculum approaches—in particular, we consider how best to address the special needs of young children with developmental delays and/or disabilities.

In this chapter, we define and discuss in detail the LINK model of *authentic* curriculum-based assessment; demonstrate how LINK incorporates effectively the six standards gleaned from prominent assessment and curriculum models discussed in Chapters 1 and 2; provide examples of authentic and inauthentic tasks included in commercially available curriculum-based (i.e., curriculum-embedded and curriculum-compatible) instruments; illustrate our rating system (based on the six standards of LINKing) for the appropriateness of early childhood assessment instruments; introduce some of the best overall examples of linked materials; and apply our rating system to some of the traditional norm-referenced measures used by many interdisciplinary professionals.

We believe that a reformulation of curriculum-based developmental assessment into an authentic framework is the most feasible, desirable, and sensible solution to the assessment dilemma in early intervention. An authentic curriculum-based approach will move the field in a much-needed new direction—a direction that is authentic, collaborative, convergent, equitable, sensitive, congruent, and developmentally appropriate.

WHAT IS LINK?

LINK is both a philosophical perspective and an operationalizable set of guidelines for professionals that addresses the missions, content, methods, and applications for linking authentic curriculum-based assessment and early intervention. LINK includes the focused activities of assessment and the all-encompassing process of evaluation. We emphasize both the distinction and the close relationship between assessment and evaluation that was proposed by Peterson (1987), who defined *evaluation* as an overarching "process of making judgments about a child's behavior or development, an instructional procedure, a program, or anything else about which conclusions are to be drawn" (p. 282). The evaluation process (not a single event) synthesizes qualitative and quantitative information with a decision-making effort that requires the professional or professionals to make value judgments and interpretations on the basis of multidimensional information collected continuously over time. Peterson also defined *assessment* as the ongoing activity "of collecting data for purposes of evaluation" (1987, p. 282) through the use of diverse measurement instruments and procedures.

LINK blends the processes of assessment and evaluation to more effectively forge a link to instruction and therapy in early intervention; this link is both practical and authentic. LINK, as the procedures and process for authentic curriculum-based assessment, encompasses several primary characteristics: 1) an emphasis on natural and functional developmental competencies or goals that are displayed by children in everyday play and social activities, as well as by toys, materials, and settings; 2) a developmentally appropriate style with adaptive modifications to accommodate special needs and broad individual differences; 3) an individualized and longitudinal evaluation of children's developmental progress along a hierarchical curricular sequence; and 4) collaborative, intervention-focused decisions by parents and professionals about the service delivery needs of young children and their families.

LINK integrates the six standards found in the previously discussed alternative early childhood assessment models, blending the best elements of each model to form a more viable alternative strategy. LINK is an eclectic hybrid model that incorporates the developmental sequence of hierarchical competencies and intervention linkages from the criterion-referenced assessment model; the natural tasks and ecology of the authentic/performance assessment model; the distillation of multiple sources, settings, occasions, domains, measures, and collaborative parent–professional teamwork and decision making of the convergent assessment model; the adaptive accommodations of the functional/adaptive assessment model; the learning modes of the dynamic assessment model; and the developmentally appropriate materials, demands, and style of the play-based assessment model.

We propose the analogy of a prism to suggest the organic, or fluid, process by which the most desirable characteristics of the prominent alternative early childhood assessment models are transformed into the LINK approach via the six standards, which form the layers of the prism. These layers accept and isolate the most desirable features of the major assessment approaches, which are represented as separate streams of light entering the prism. The six layers of the LINK prism separate, realign, and magnify the light streams into a single beam, which represents LINK (see Figure 3.1).

THE STANDARDS OPERATIONALIZED AS DIMENSIONS OF LINK

Table 3.1 summarizes the dimensions of LINK that are culled from the alternative assessment approaches reviewed in Chapter 1. LINK, through these hybrid dimensions, operationalizes each of the six standards and transforms them into standards for rating the assessment measures and instructional procedures of curricula, in particular, authentic curriculum-based assessment materials.

Authentic Dimensions of LINK

LINK is based on a developmental hierarchy of the functional and natural competencies displayed in daily life by young children with and without developmental disabilities. LINK's central assessment instrument, into which all assessment data from multiple instruments, sources, settings, and occasions are integrated, is the func-

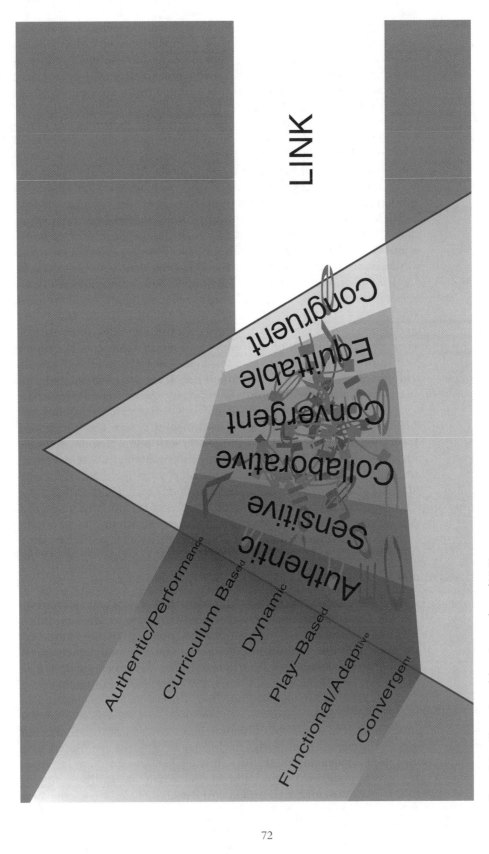

Figure 3.1.   Illustration of the prism analogy of LINK.

Table 3.1. The six operational LINK standards incorporating the most desirable early childhood assessment characteristics

Standard	LINK dimension
Authenticity	• Bases assessments on sequential authentic goals contained within a curriculum's developmental hierarchy or task analysis
	• Taps natural developmental competencies
	• Emphasizes areas of strength rather than areas of concern
	• Relies on child's actual performance, work samples, and videotaped records
	• Requires use of developmentally appropriate and familiar toys and materials or necessary adaptive toys
	• Promotes natural circumstances for assessments
	• Converts contrived test items into authentic tasks
	• Balances quantitative and qualitative performance information
Convergence	• Accepts/incorporates multiple data sources, including curriculum-compatible and authentic information
	• Focuses on assessment in natural contexts
	• Relies on play-style stagings of assessments to complement natural displays of behavior
	• Ensures broader coverage of the child and family's developmental ecology
	• Promotes inter- or transdisciplinary modes of teamwork
	• Is family centered in outlook process
Collaboration	• Relies on family as the primary source of authentic child performance data
	• Supports consensus decision making and use of collaborative problem solving and judgments as the most valid assessment process
	• Fosters in situ cross-talking and consensus decisions among parents and professionals about the child's capabilities, needs, and family priorities
Equity	• Adapts tasks to accommodate child's functional limitations
	• Emphasizes criterial task/competencies demonstrated by the child, irrespective of functional limitation
	• Uses test–teach–test approach to identify primary response mode and to generalize its use by the child with various materials, activities, and settings
	• Conducts assessments via a natural test–teach–test framework that blends testing and teaching
	• Seeks to uncover and foster the child's learning-to-learn skills and abilities
Sensitivity	• Uses sequential curricular goals and graduated metrics to monitor small increments of individual progress
	• Links authentic assessment tasks to authentic curriculum goals and authentic curriculum goals to authentic interventions
	• Underscores activity-based interventions in natural home and preschool settings and using natural activities
	• Links to real-life IEP/IFSP goals
Congruence	• Accomplishes major purposes and missions of early childhood and special education
	• Uses developmentally appropriate styles of assessment that emphasize play, natural observations, and parent reports
	• Contains tasks and procedures that allow flexible accommodations for young children with wide individual differences, in particular developmental delays and disabilities
	• Encompasses content and procedures that have field-derived social and treatment validities to support their suitability for use with young children, particularly those with special needs

tional curriculum used by early intervention programs and teams. The outcomes of linked assessment procedures for children and families emphasize strengths and individual competencies and resources rather than areas of concern and individual limitations, which are emphasized by traditional norm-referenced models. This emphasis enables parents and professionals to plan interventions that build on each child's unique functional capabilities while expanding the repertoire of behaviors necessary for more sophisticated skill development. Similarly, LINK procedures rely on everyday incidents of a child's functional skills (e.g., critical incidents of cause–effect or means–end behavior) or samples of the child's work (e.g., drawings, play constructions) to generate richer and more socially valid understandings of that child's personal competencies. Such authentic behavior occurs in those natural and typical settings of daily life that are unique to each child and family. Natural physical and social environments are important in LINKing and must use the child's own toys, common household items, common toys within the preschool setting, or toys with adaptive qualities or modifications (i.e., toys with microswitches, computers). LINK incorporates periodic videotaped records of a child's behavior to generate more vivid, truer, longitudinal portraits of a child's developmental progress.

Videotaping is perhaps the most authentic of all early childhood assessment strategies. The LINK model promotes the broader use of videotaping as a primary child and family appraisal technique. Increasingly, professionals in early intervention are using videotape analysis as the key method for linking assessment, intervention, and progress evaluation. Videotaping can be performed unobtrusively to capture natural child–environment interactions both at home and within the preschool setting. Professionals use videotape analysis to achieve consensus among professionals and parents about a child's areas of strength and areas of concern. Videotaped records from home and preschool can document situation-specific skills and authentic samples of everyday problem solving, social, language, and motor skills and can offer tangible examples of curricular goals and skills that must be developed during instruction and therapy. Such records also capture the nuances of child–child and child–adult interactions, on which that basis for intervention planning and parent education can be formed. These videotape records should be included in a child's portfolio so that behaviors and interactions that occur before, during, and after intervention can be preserved and compared. These permanent product records provide the richest, most representative, indisputable document of child progress. LINK procedures, such as videotaping, ensure a balance in the collection of quantitative and qualitative evidence of a child's capabilities and a family's resources.

Tables 3.2 and 3.3 show the types of authentic tasks that are contained in some of the commercially available, curriculum-based assessment materials reviewed in Chapter 4. These authentic tasks

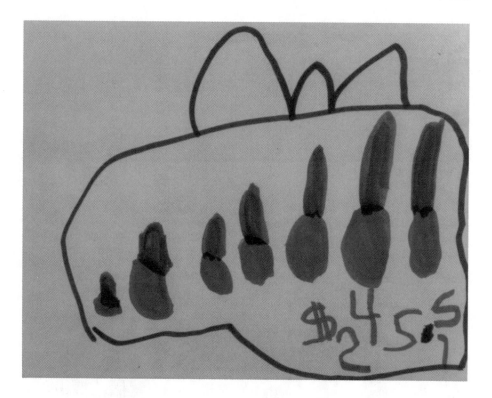

are contrasted with generic examples of the inauthentic and contrived tasks that are commonly found in traditional norm-referenced measures. One challenge met by LINK is to allow teams to convert some of these contrived assessment items/tasks into authentic competencies that are amenable to instruction and therapy.

Convergent Dimensions of LINK

In LINK, multiple sources of data converge and are incorporated into the curriculum-based assessment system; the information is translated into authentic tasks and observable, teachable competencies. Descriptive information is gathered from numerous sources to characterize the quality and impact of both the child's capabilities and the child's developmental ecology (i.e., the family's resources and environment, the preschool context). Preferably, a curriculum-based assessment is conducted during the child's natural play opportunities or play-based "stagings" within the home or preschool setting.

Collaborative Dimensions of LINK

LINK relies on collaboration: Parent–professional partnerships and transdisciplinary teams are emphasized. Parents become the primary source of information for determining a child's authentic, functional skills displayed in real-life home circumstances. Professionals use genuine behavior samples provided by parents to identify complementary examples of authentic behavior that apply to

Table 3.2. Authentic skills

Instrument	Motor	Cognitive	Social-emotional	Communicative	Adaptive
On Track	Rides a tricycle without crashing into stuff	Recites own telephone number	Speaks with "indoor" voice	Initiates conversation with other children	Hangs coat on hook
	Colors with pencils	Identifies time, after, before, during	Invites peers to play	Protests appropriately	Drinks from a water fountain
Assessment, Evaluation, and Programming System (AEPS) for Infants and Young Children	Rotates either wrist to turn part of an object (e.g., removes lid from jar, turns water faucet knob) Climbs up and down play equipment (e.g., jungle gym, slide)	Looks for object in usual location (e.g., child looks in toy box for favorite toy or goes to coat rack for coat) Navigates large object around barriers (e.g., doll carriage, grocery cart around furniture)	Responds to established social routine (e.g., mealtime, bath time; e.g., when adult turns on bath water child goes to tub and takes off clothes) Entertains self by playing with appropriate toys Initiates a social interaction Operates a simple or mechanical toy	Gains person's attention and refers to an object, person, or event (e.g., gain attention by looking at, reaching for a person); a child would look at a person and then point to a ball Uses proper names (e.g., child will look at parents and say "Mamma" or "Dadda")	Indicates awareness of soiled or wet pants/diapers Brings food to mouth using utensil
Carolina Curriculum for Preschoolers with Special Needs (CCPSN)	Plays with (pinching or rolling) messy materials like clay	Tells current age, how old he or she was last year, and how old he or she will be next year	Asks permission to use other's things	Talks on telephone and waits his or her turn to respond	Runs brush or comb through hair

(continued)

Table 3.2.   *(continued)*

Instrument	Motor	Cognitive	Social-emotional	Communicative	Adaptive
CCPSN (*continued*)	Rides bike with training wheels		Buys simple objects in a store without help (e.g., gets object, tells clerk what he or she wants, gives money, and gets change)	Requests assistance when needed	Fixes bowl of dry cereal with milk independently
Hawaii Early Learning Profile (HELP)	Spreads paste on one side of a paper and sticks it to another paper	Tells month and day of birth	Cleans up spills after eating	Carries on a conversation with another child	Serves self and carries tray in serving line
	Places key in lock of door and opens lock	Tells mom's and dad's first and last names when asked	Bargains with other children	Retells story with original sequence	Ask location of bathroom when in new location

the preschool setting: For example, parents may observe that the child can discriminate between Cheerios and Rice Krispies cereals at the grocery store, and the teacher may observe that the child can discriminate between a circle and a square in the preschool. LINK procedures stress that teamwork is the only valid format for early childhood assessment; in this context, teamwork does not apply to assessments completed by separate professionals in separate sessions. Transdisciplinary or interdisciplinary assessment is characterized by teaming professionals *and* parents (e.g., speech-language pathologist, teacher, parents). Because LINK entails a larger process than conducting the assessment "acts" themselves, the outcome of LINK is more than the sterile scoring of performances or child behaviors; LINK results in richer problem-solving partnerships among parents and professionals in which observations are compared, judgments are offered, discrepancies are resolved, and consensus is reached to form a real-life portrait of each child's capabilities and areas of concern, which, in turn, are linked to intervention plans.

Equitable Dimensions of LINK

LINK requires assessment procedures to be need specific (i.e., adaptive) or to contain or allow modifications to accommodate a child's functional limitations to ensure equity or parity in the assessment process for all children—both with and without disabilities. It is unacceptable to expect a child with a sensory, neuromotor, lan-

Table 3.3. Nonauthentic skills

Motor	Cognitive	Social-emotional	Communicative	Adaptive
Strings large beads	Sorts objects by shapes, colors, etc.	Eats items of meal in order	Locates common object	Laces and unlaces model shoe
Places small pegs in holes on board				
Gallops forward	Stacks 10 blocks	Eats with one hand on lap	Names object by function	Identifies pictures of comb, toothbrush, soap
Balances on one foot for 5 seconds with eyes open	Matches picture with objects	Responds to name	Uses predicate phrases with noun phrases	
Jumps with feet together	Selects one that doesn't belong or is different			Shows what to do with cup
Marches in time to repetitious beat				Places toy dishes, spoon, and fork correctly
Hangs from bar using overhand grip	Categorizes sounds			
Imitates a vertical stroke				

guage, or social behavior limitation(s) to perform tasks designed for and field-tested on typically developing children. Modification of the stimulus characteristics of objects (e.g., increase in size, tactile format) or the response modes available to the child (e.g., use of computers, communication boards, light wands, head pointers) are examples of functional accommodations. With LINK, however, we introduce the concept of *authentic criterial competencies*, which is arguably the most equitable modification in child assessment. Authentic criterial competencies are hierarchically sequenced functional skills that are defined by their function rather than by the topography of the behavior under examination. For example, "gets across the room by self," "initiates a social interaction," and "recognizes the McDonald's sign" are authentic criterial competencies that do not depend on any particular response mode: A child who uses a wheelchair does not have to walk independently to move across the room; a child without eye contact or language does not have to use words to begin playing with a friend; and a child without full sentence use does not have to talk to show his or her understanding of McDonald's. We believe that the future design of authentic assessment measures and procedures will stress standardization of the behavior being assessed and not standardization of situations (i.e., administration) or responses as the most equitable assessment strategy. Some of the curriculum-based assessment instruments included in Chapter 4 operationalize the concept of authentic criterial competencies and equity through the function rather than the form of expected behaviors.

Sensitive Dimensions of LINK

LINK is dedicated to forging connections among authentic assessment procedures, authentic curriculum goals, and authentic interventions; these connections depend on the range, density, and scope of the functional developmental hierarchical sequence and its tasks. LINK's sensitivity in detecting and gauging a child's progress hinges on the availability of a finely graded sequence of functional tasks ranging from the most primitive functional skills to the most sophisticated competencies. This functional hierarchy enables teams of parents and professionals to tailor interventions to a child's unique strengths and needs and to monitor the quality and quantity of a child's gains through such measures as the number of authentic curriculum goals achieved and the display of behavior under various conditions (e.g., prompts). LINK promotes the predominant use of intraindividual strategies rather than normative interindividual or group comparisons for monitoring each child's status and progress.

Congruent Dimensions of LINK

LINK corresponds directly to the philosophy and purposes of early intervention; therefore, the curriculum-based assessment systems chosen for use in LINKing are, by nature, congruent, or suitable for all young children in design, content, and procedures. The formats for evaluation, themselves, are developmentally appropriate; they rely on natural settings and natural observations of real-life behaviors made by multiple individuals working in collaboration. Most important, LINK procedures have been validated for use with young children who have special needs. LINK encompasses natural, but intentional, field-derived treatment and social validities; congruence is innate to the LINKing process.

LINK AND THE SIX STANDARDS AS A METHOD TO RATE EXISTING INSTRUMENTS

The six standards introduced in Chapters 1 and 2 are most important when selecting and using curriculum-based assessment systems to fulfill early intervention purposes. Linked curriculum-based systems for assessment and intervention must be authentic, convergent, collaborative, equitable, sensitive, and congruent. A discussion of the characteristics of each of these standards follows.

Authenticity

The processes and products of the assessment of child and family needs are considered authentic when 1) the assessment is conducted in natural, everyday settings that are typical for a given child and family; 2) methods of collecting functional information that are flexible, acceptable to the family, socially valid, and from multiple sources are used; 3) naturally occurring samples of real-life behavior elicited through toys and activities that are central to a family's daily life are emphasized; and 4) functional levels are readily translated into natural, activity-based goals that are amenable to instruction and therapy and represent worthwhile goals that have functional relevance to a child's increasing self-sufficiency in daily life. In addition, authentic assessments require low (if any) inferences about the capability being assessed; this characteristic is in contrast with the high inferences required by most traditional norm-referenced assessments, in particular, early intelligence tests. Finally, authentic assessments sample direct examples of real-life competencies in everyday situations.

Convergence

Assessment for early intervention must gather and synthesize diverse pieces of information about a child and family's needs and a program's requirements by using a multidimensional perspective. We refer to this multidimensional process of synthesizing, or funneling, functional data as convergent assessment because it involves collecting and interfacing data culled from multiple sources, measures, settings, domains, and occasions to fulfill multiple early intervention purposes.

Collaboration

Parent–professional partnerships are integral to comprehensive, family-centered early intervention services. In the early intervention field, the collaborative process becomes practical and real through models of teamwork. Teamwork is based on the shared purposes, aims, and methods of a relatively constant group of professionals who, in conjunction with a child's family, reach consensus about the needs of a child, his or her family, and the program in which he or she is enrolled. Collaborative decision making is a flexible process that results in richer, more accurate assessments that link to intervention.

Equity

Assessment for early intervention must accommodate the unique needs of each child and family. Assessment materials and practices are equitable when they are adjusted to the sensory, neuromotor, linguistic, affective, and behavior impairments of young children. This adjustment can be achieved by 1) modifying the stimulus characteristics of toys and objects used to perform the assessment; 2) accepting children's diverse functional responses; 3) using flexible avenues to stage assessments and gather information; 4) applying dynamic or responsive strategies to elicit child behaviors and to examine the impact of those behaviors on learning; and 5) empowering families to set priorities, pose questions, and suggest the activities that might best demonstrate both the child's optimal capabilities and most pressing areas of concern.

Sensitivity

The hallmark of the best linked curricular systems is a high degree of treatment validity. The most effective curriculum-based assessment systems are sensitive in their capacity to detect a child's current functional capabilities as well as his or her progress. Sensitivity refers to the clarity and density of prerequisite competencies contained in the functional hierarchy (i.e., developmental task analysis) of a curriculum-based assessment system to identify the current status of, and any change in, a child's functional capabilities as a result of intervention, even for a child with the most severe of disabilities and the smallest increment of progress.

Congruence

All too often, professionals are beguiled into using traditional assessment measures in early intervention on the basis of misleading and irrelevant information about a measure's supposed psychometric integrity. We believe that, rather than rely on such misleading psychometric data when selecting and using instruments, a professional should select an instrument on the basis of a number of practical considerations regarding the extent to which the instrument is *congruent* with the expectations and aims of early childhood intervention as well as the idiosyncrasies of both typical and atypical early childhood development. Congruence refers to a measure's suitability, developmental appropriateness, and field-tested validitiy for use in early intervention.

Table 3.4 illustrates how the six standards of LINK may be operationalized to varying degrees in linked assessment/curricular materials. Early intervention professionals can use these examples as a baseline from which to analyze and classify the extent to which various instruments are developmentally appropriate and valid for use with young children. The resultant rating scale, the LINK index (Figure 3.2), enables professionals to describe and compare different instruments according to those critical standards that compose the concept of developmentally appropriate assessment: authentic, convergent, collaborative, equitable, sensitive, and congruent. The LINK index consists of a simple but practical three-point Likert rating continuum for each of the six standards. A total LINK index score enables a professional to calculate an average rating to characterize a particular instrument according to its global adherence to the standards: ratings are 3.0, exemplary; 2.5, high; 2.0, acceptable; 1.5, low; and 1.0, negligible.

Chapter 4 of this volume presents LINK indexes, short summary "snapshots," and "close-ups" of unique features for a number of curriculum-based assessment systems that are available to early intervention professionals as well as for the most frequently used, traditional, norm-referenced tests, which are shown to be in stark contrast with the curriculum-based instruments, thereby demonstrating their grossly unacceptable nature for early intervention purposes.

These LINK rankings are culled from focus group reviews and qualitative "consumer satisfaction" surveys that we have conducted with more than 4,000 parents and professionals since 1989; in addition, we conducted a study of traditional scales, which re-

Table 3.4.   Developmentally appropriate assessment ratings to gauge the quality of authentic curriculum-based instruments

Standard	Major attributes
Assessment is	*When it is characterized by*
Authentic	Real-life activities, settings, and methods that provide goals for intervention
	3. Clear emphasis on skills or activities that are useful and worthwhile in natural settings.
	2. Many or most items have some relevance; items can be adapted or contextualized to be useful objectives.
	1. Emphasis on items with little real-life relevance; psychometric tasks that are neither required nor desired in typical activities and settings.
Collaborative	Consensual decision making through teamwork between parents and professionals
	3. Assessment items and methods are readily useful by parents and various professionals.
	2. Material can be used by professional teams after coaching, although parent use is minimal.
	1. Content and methods are discipline specific; use by parents and other professionals not feasible.
Convergent	A confluence of information from multiple sources, settings, occasions, domains, and measures for multiple purposes
	3. Emphasizes the use of multiple sources of information, including observation across settings and interview, as well as scoring of activity in context.
	2. Employs at least some information source other than testing (e.g., interview, observation in natural contexts).
	1. Focuses on direct testing, with little or no reliance on other avenues for information gathering.
Equitable	Flexible and adaptive modifications to accommodate the needs and priorities of young children and families
	3. Activity is phrased functionally (what gets done), rather than requiring specific sensory or motor capability.
	2. Administration permits normative skill or activity to be modified to accommodate special sensory, motor, or cultural needs.
	1. Normative tasks or activities not feasible for child with special sensory (seeing or hearing), motor, or cultural needs
Sensitive	Range and density of tasks in the functional hierarchy to detect even small increments of change
	3. Assessment procedures and wide range and high density of items designed to detect even small changes.
	2. Moderate array of items, but gaps between items that preclude tracking of modest changes.
	1. Psychometric high inference items; few items for gauging child attainment of major developmental stages and capabilities; spotty, low density.
Congruent	The extent to which an assessment instrument and its procedures correspond are compatible with the missions of early intervention, responsive to the developmental demands and special needs of young children, and suitable for and field validated with children similar to those to be assessed
	3. Assessment system shows specific design features, content and procedures to detect and accommodate individual early childhood needs; demonstrates its suitability through formative field validations and/or standardization and norming studies that establish its social and treatment validities.

(continued)

Table 3.4.   *(continued)*

Standard	Major attributes
	2. Assessment system shows general design features, content, and procedures that can accommodate individual early childhood needs; but evidence of field-derived social and treatment validities is weak or absent.
	1. Assessment system is developmentally inappropriate in design, content, and procedures; fails to demonstrate field-derived social and treatment validity with any special needs group(s) during its development; is normed and/or field-validated with typical children and misapplied to children with special needs.

flected both a focus group analysis and a consumer use survey of approximately 200 preschool psychologists in 41 states, who rated the invalidity and poor utility of early IQ tests for early intervention purposes with more than 7,000 young children (Bagnato & Neisworth, 1994). The LINK ratings were determined on the basis of shared characteristics of curriculum-based assessment materials that consensus consumer ratings identified as exemplars of the philosophy, purposes, and practices of early intervention. In turn, these rated measures are operationalized to form the foundation for the LINK model of authentic curriculum-based evaluation.

Tables 3.5, 3.6, and 3.7 present LINK index numbers derived from consumer ratings; these ratings identify and compare the acceptability of selected curriculum-embedded (Table 3.5) and curriculum-compatible (Table 3.6) versus traditional norm-referenced assessment

LINK Index			
Authentic	1	2	3
Convergent	1	2	3
Collaborative	1	2	3
Equitable	1	2	3
Sensitive	1	2	3
Congruent	1	2	3
	☐	☐	☐
Total LINK Index	☐		

Figure 3.2.   Sample LINK index. The materials being rated are assigned a score ranging from 3 (highest) to 1 (lowest) for each of the six standards. The scores in each rating category are added (i.e., all of the 1s are added, all of the 2s are added, all of the 3s are added) and entered into the boxes at the bottom of each column. Then, the column tallies are added to one another and divided by 6. The resultant number is the LINK index (3.0, exemplary; 2.5, high; 2.0, acceptable; 1.5, low; 1.0, negligible).

Table 3.5.   LINK index scores for exemplary curriculum-embedded assessment measures for use with young children

Standard	LINK index number					
	AEPS	CCIPSN	DPIYC	EMC	HELP	OPC
Authentic	3	3	2	3	3	3
Collaborative	3	2	3	2	3	3
Convergent	3	3	3	3	3	3
Equitable	3	3	3	3	3	3
Sensitive	3	3	2	3	3	2
Congruent	3	3	3	3	3	3
Total LINK index	3.0	2.8	2.7	2.8	3.0	2.8

Abbreviations: AEPS, Assessment, Evaluation, and Programming System; CCIPSN, Carolina Curriculum for Infants and Preschoolers with Special Needs; DPIYC, Developmental Programming for Infants and Young Children; EMC, Every Move Counts; HELP, Hawaii Early Learning Profile; OPC, Oregon Project Curriculum for Visually Impaired and Blind Preschool Children.

(Table 3.7) instruments in early childhood and early intervention. (These materials are reviewed in Chapter 4.)

Tables 3.5 and 3.6 reveal that consumers view the 12 curriculum-based assessment systems as exemplary or nearly exemplary (median LINK index, 2.7) in their operationalization of the six standards. On the basis of feedback received at our workshops and in response to our surveys, we conclude that HELP (VORT, 1995) and The Carolina Curriculum for Infants and Toddlers with Special Needs (2nd ed.; Johnson-Martin, Jens, Attermeier, & Hacker, 1991) are the most frequently employed curricular systems in the early intervention field. It is noteworthy that AEPS (Bricker, 1993) and Every Move Counts (Korsten et al., 1993) exemplify the new direction in curricular assessment and intervention toward more authentic, functional, treatment-linked, developmentally appropriate practices.

Table 3.6.   LINK index scores for exemplary curriculum-compatible assessment measures for use with young children

Standard	LINK index number					
	BDI	BDIED–R	DOCS	KIDS	PEDI	RZS
Authentic	2	2	3	3	3	2
Collaborative	3	2	3	3	3	3
Convergent	3	2	3	3	3	3
Equitable	3	2	2	2	3	3
Sensitive	2	2	3	2	3	3
Congruent	3	2	2	3	3	2
Total LINK index	2.7	2.0	2.7	2.7	3.0	2.7

Abbreviations: BDI, Battelle Developmental Inventory; BDIED–R, BRIGANCE® Diagnostic Inventory of Early Development–Revised; DOCS, Developmental Observation Checklist System; KIDS, Kent Infant Development Scale; PEDI, Pediatric Evaluation of Disability Inventory; RZS, Reynell-Zinkin Developmental Scales for Young Visually Handicapped Children.

Table 3.7. LINK index scores for widely used, traditional, norm-referenced assessment measures for use with young children

	LINK index number					
Standard	BSID II	DAS	MSCA	SBIS IV	WJPEB–R	WPPSI–R
Authentic	2	1	1	1	1	1
Collaborative	2	1	2	1	1	1
Convergent	2	1	1	1	1	1
Equitable	1	1	1	1	1	1
Sensitive	1	1	1	1	1	1
Congruent	1	1	1	1	1	1
Total LINK index	1.5	1.0	1.2	1.0	1.0	1.0

Abbreviations: BSID II, Bayley Scales of Infant Development (2nd ed.); DAS, Differential Ability Scales; MSCA, McCarthy Scales of Children's Abilities; SBIS IV, Stanford-Binet Intelligence Scale (4th ed.); WJPEB–R, Woodcock-Johnson Psycho-Educational Battery–Revised; WPPSI–R, Wechsler Preschool and Primary Scales of Intelligence–Revised.

In contrast, Table 3.7 reveals that the most widely used and respected traditional norm-referenced instruments, notably early tests of intelligence and mental development, are rated by consumers as being developmentally inappropriate for use in early childhood and early intervention. The LINK index range was from 1.0 to 1.5; this restricted, low range demonstrates that these instruments have unacceptably low to negligible inclusion of desirable qualities. Consider that norm-referenced tests, such as the Bayley Scales of Infant Development–Second Edition (Bayley, 1993), the Stanford-Binet Intelligence Scale (Terman & Merrill, 1960), and the Wechsler Preschool and Primary Scales of Intelligence–Revised (Wechsler, 1989), are touted as the most technically sound measures for young children and are advertised as being especially constructed to meet early intervention mandates and the requirements of young children with special needs. Paradoxically, these very measures are rated by consumers as being inauthentic, developmentally inappropriate, and incongruent with the purposes of early intervention! Each of these measures is an exemplar of how **not** to construct an assessment instrument for young children, in particular, those who have special needs.

These LINK index ratings assigned by consumers reveal the misrepresentations of test publishers about the applicability of traditional instruments to early intervention. On the basis of consumer reaction, we urge interdisciplinary professionals and their program administrators to advocate for the abandonment of the use of these traditional instruments for early childhood assessment in early intervention.

4

Snapshots and Close-ups
of Authentic Curriculum–Based
Assessment Systems

In this chapter, we examine an array of curriculum-based assessment instruments, systems, and procedures. The 52 instruments surveyed are divided into two kinds of curriculum-based measures: *curriculum embedded* (i.e., forming the foundation of an integrated curricular assessment system) and *curriculum compatible* (i.e., having content similar to the goals emphasized in curriculum-embedded systems). All of the assessment materials included have good or excellent features that are authentic, convergent, collaborative, equitable, sensitive, and congruent; in fact, a LINK index of 2.0 or greater in each of the six standards was the criterion for inclusion in this chapter.

Some of the systems included are geared toward use with infants and toddlers; others, toward use with preschool-age children; and still others, toward use with kindergarten-age children. Some address specific disabilities. Some are actually norm referenced but possess curriculum-compatible qualities and robust field-validation and norming data.

We present such diverse materials to highlight the strengths and weaknesses of each instrument and to acknowledge that each child (and each program) has individual needs, some of which may be best met by an assessment/curriculum system that does not necessarily have a high LINK index number. No single curriculum is a panacea; often, several curricula are useful with a group of children. Sometimes teachers and psychologists may even use two or more curricula for just one child. One curriculum may detail a particular domain (e.g., fine motor) in a way particularly appropriate for a given child, whereas another curriculum may include objectives

and activities that are excellent for other areas of that child's program.

For each set of assessment/curriculum materials, we provide both a "snapshot" and a "close-up." The snapshot can be consulted for ordering information and for a compressed review of the content and qualities of the materials. The instrument's ratings on each of the six standards, as well as an overall LINK index number, are provided for each set of materials. These snapshots and close-ups were analyzed and selected through surveys and a focus group process.

Each snapshot provides identifying information, including author(s); cost; and publisher's name, address, and phone number. In addition, the snapshot provides focused descriptions of the following specific content features: assessment type (curriculum embedded or curriculum compatible), age/focus group, domains/content, special needs options, curricular links (when applicable), authenticity, family involvement, scoring/sample, validation, and training needed. Finally, each snapshot concludes with several comments that highlight unique scale aspects, research citations (when applicable), and, most important, a LINK index number that identifies the developmentally appropriate quality of each instrument on the basis of its overall attainment of the six standards (authenticity, convergence, collaboration, equity, sensitivity, and congruence). Note the symbol system that is used in conjunction with the LINK index number. These symbols allow for at-a-glance appraisals of the materials by identifying the major characteristics of each instrument (e.g., if you are seeking a disability-specific instrument, simply look to see whether the symbol for disability specificity [a wheelchair] is featured by the instrument's LINK index number).

     Infants and toddlers

     Preschoolers

     Kindergarten-transition

   ♿   Disability specific
   ↔   Curriculum compatible
   ∞   Curriculum embedded

Each snapshot is followed by a close-up, which provides a more thorough description of the features of the instrument, and by at least one actual page reproduced from the instrument, which serves as a quick and trustworthy way to determine whether the format and content of a given instrument would work well with your child or program.

We believe that these snapshots and close-ups will enable parents, professionals, and administrators on early intervention teams to analyze and select the best combinations of curriculum-embedded and curriculum-compatible assessment materials to match the idiosyncratic needs of their children and their programs. Moreover, we hope that this organization enables professionals to fundamentally change their early childhood assessment practices by adopting observation and evaluation systems that are authentic, curriculum based, and developmentally appropriate.

Assessment, Evaluation, and Programming System (AEPS) for Infants and Children (Volumes 1 and 2)

Author(s): D. Bricker (Vol. 1); J. Cripe, K. Slentz, & D. Bricker (Vol. 2)
Year: 1993
Publisher: Paul H. Brookes Publishing Co.
Address: Post Office Box 10624, Baltimore, Maryland 21285-0624
Phone: 800-638-3775
Cost: $92.50 (Volumes 1 and 2 purchased as a set)
Volume 1 (*AEPS Measurement for Birth to Three Years*), $42.95; Volume 2 (*AEPS Curriculum for Birth to Three Years*), $59.95; *AEPS Data Recording Forms, Birth to Three Years* (package of 10), $23; *AEPS Family Report, Birth to Three Years,* (package of 10), $17; *AEPS Family Interest Survey* (Cripe & Bricker) (package of 30), $15; *AEPS Child Progress Record, Birth to Three Years* (package of 30), $18

Assessment type: Curriculum embedded.

Age/focus group: Designed for children who are at risk for or who have special needs in the developmental age range from birth to 3 years. Can be used in a home-based setting or a small-group, center-based program.

Scale(s): Data Recording Forms (one form for each domain) for professionals; parents can complete parallel assessments with the Family Report forms.

Data system: Child Progress Record forms and summary data forms.

Domain/content: Fine motor, gross motor, adaptive, cognitive, social-communication, and social.

Special needs options: Visual, motor, and hearing.

Authenticity: Natural child activity basis of the system ensures great authenticity.

Family involvement: Involvement encouraged by use of the Family Report for assessment of the child by the family, the IFSP

Planning Guide to promote involvement of family in program planning, the Child Progress Record to assist families in assessing the child's progress over time, and the Family Interest Survey to help families list and prioritize areas of interest in programming for children.

Training needed: Knowledge of early childhood development; useful to professionals for direct services. Developers of AEPS strongly encourage users to become familiar with the system before use by reading and understanding the measurement system and how it operates.

Validation: AEPS is the product of approximately 20 years of programmatic efforts and research on intervention relevant to assessment. Federal research funds and continual field validation provide a basis that is stronger than that for most other materials available.

Comments:
- *Strong family involvement*
- *Curriculum goals and objectives directly link with assessment items*
- *Periodic evaluations of child progress, sensitive tracking*
- *Activity-based, developmentally appropriate instruction*
- *Particularly useful and effective for close monitoring and individualized instruction*

LINK Index			
Authentic	1	2	③
Convergent	1	2	③
Collaborative	1	2	③
Equitable	1	2	③
Sensitive	1	2	③
Congruent	1	2	③
Total Index	☐ +	☐ +	18 ÷ 6 = 3.0
Overall quality: exemplary			

3.0, exemplary; 2.5, high; 2.0, acceptable; 1.5, low; 1.0, negligible.

Assessment, Evaluation, and Programming System (AEPS) for Infants and Children (Volumes 3 and 4)

Author(s): D. Bricker & K. Pretti-Frontczak (Vol. 3); D. Bricker & M. Waddell (Vol. 4)

Year: 1996

Publisher: Paul H. Brookes Publishing Co.

Address: Post Office Box 10624, Baltimore, Maryland 21285-0624

Phone: 800-638-3775

Cost: $96 (Volumes 3 and 4 purchased as a set)
Volume 3 (*AEPS Measurement for Three to Six Years*), $57.00; Volume 4 (*AEPS Curriculum for Three to Six Years*), $49; *AEPS Data Recording Forms, Three to Six Years* (package of 10), $24; *AEPS Family Report, Three to Six Years* (package of 10), $23; *AEPS Family Interest Survey* (Cripe & Bricker) (package of 30), $15; *AEPS Child Progress Record, Three to Six Years* (package of 30), $21
Note: Volumes 1–4 may be purchased as a set for $185.

Assessment type: Curriculum embedded.

Age/focus group: Designed for children who are at risk for or who have a disabilities in the developmental age range from 3 to 6 years. Can be used in a home-based setting or a small-group, center-based program.

Scale(s): Data Recording Forms (one form for each domain) for professionals; parents can complete parallel assessments with the Family Report forms.

Data system: Family Report, Family Interest Survey, and Child Progress Record forms.

Domain/content: Fine motor, gross motor, adaptive, cognitive, social-communication, and social.

Special needs options: Designed with and for preschoolers with a range of needs.

Authenticity: Natural child activity basis of the system ensures great authenticity.

Family involvement: Involvement encouraged by use of the Family Report for assessment of the child by the family, the Child Progress Record to assist families in assessing the child's progress over time, and the Family Interest Survey to help families list and prioritize areas of interest in programming for children.

Training needed: Developers of AEPS strongly encourage users to become familiar with the system before use by reading and understanding the measurement system and how it operates.

Validation: AEPS is the product of approximately 20 years of programmatic efforts and research on intervention relevant to assessment. Volumes 3 and 4 are undergoing examination of reliability and treatment validity.

Comments:
- *Strong family involvement*
- *Curriculum goals and objectives directly link with assessment items*
- *Activity-based intervention approach*
- *Information and suggestions for compatible planned intervention activities and other preschool curricula that target a particular goal or objective*

 ∞

LINK Index			
Authentic	1	2	③
Convergent	1	2	③
Collaborative	1	2	③
Equitable	1	2	③
Sensitive	1	2	③
Congruent	1	2	③
Total Index	☐ +	☐ +	18 ÷ 6 = 3.0

Overall quality: exemplary

3.0, exemplary; 2.5, high; 2.0, acceptable; 1.5, low; 1.0, negligible.

Assessment, Evaluation, and Programming System (AEPS) for Infants and Children (Volumes 1–4)

The Assessment, Evaluation, and Programming System (AEPS) is a curriculum-based assessment/evaluation system that encourages natural learning opportunities for children in the developmental age range of birth to 6 years. AEPS is perhaps the clearest and most outstanding example of assessment for intervention in which assessment and teaching are linked and reciprocal. Furthermore, the materials and strategies permit sensitive planning and tracking of a child's progress toward family-centered goals. By using the principles of activity-based intervention, AEPS provides a framework for developing worthwhile, individualized goals and objectives, which, in turn, guide selection of intervention content and strategies. AEPS is conveniently available in four spiral-bound volumes: Volume 1, *AEPS Measurement for Birth to Three Years*; Volume 2, *AEPS Curriculum for Birth to Three Years*; Volume 3, *AEPS Measurement for Three to Six Years*; and Volume 4, *AEPS Curriculum for Three to Six Years*.

Volume 1, *AEPS Measurement for Birth to Three Years*, provides a clear explanation of the AEPS process and parallel assessment/evaluation tools for families. Also included are the forms and plans needed to implement the AEPS program successfully. The AEPS assessment is curriculum based and allows the estimation of functional skills in infants and children in six key domains: fine motor, gross motor, adaptive, cognitive, social-communication, and social. Complete with teaching objectives and scoring criteria, this assessment tool is flexible enough to accommodate modifications for children with motor or sensory impairments. Assessment is not decontextualized and is performed in an ongoing manner while the child is engaged in naturally occurring activities. There is no question that this approach is a welcome one, especially from a developmentally appropriate perspective. The measurement system does not generate age-equivalent scores and so avoids all of the problems and issues surrounding such quantifications. Instead, measurement is based on the accomplishment of authentic skills and progress within the curriculum. A helpful appendix includes AEPS Data Recording Forms, AEPS Child Progress Record, AEPS Family Report, AEPS Family Interest Survey, and assessment activity plans.

Volume 2, *AEPS Curriculum for Birth to Three Years*, is linked directly to Volume 1, *AEPS Measurement for Birth to Three Years*, thereby creating a continuous relationship among assessment, IEP/IFSP development, and instruction and evaluation. The curriculum offers a complete set of learning activities to facilitate children's acquisition of functional skills. The curriculum's activity-based intervention approach promotes the integration of activities into children's daily routines, enabling them to generalize skills more easily. Each curricular activity is accompanied by helpful teaching strategies, instructional sequences, and recommendations for environmental arrangements.

AEPS Family Interest Survey is a 30-item checklist that helps to identify the interests and priorities that should be addressed in a child's IEP/IFSP. The AEPS Family Report, Birth to Three Years, is a 64-item questionnaire that asks parents to rank children's abilities on specific skills that correspond with the curricular areas in the AEPS Test.

Volume 3, *AEPS Measurement for Three to Six Years*, is divided into the same three sections as Volume 1. In Section I, Understanding the Assessment, Evaluation, and Programming System for Infants and Children, a description of AEPS is provided. In Section II, Assessment, Evaluation, and Programming System Test, AEPS test items in the six domains (fine motor, gross motor, adaptive, cognitive, social-communication, and social) are given; each domain contains a list of strands, goals, and associated objectives that allow the user easy identification of particular aspects. In Section III, Family Participation in AEPS, useful materials and suggestions for involving families in the assessment process are given. AEPS Family Report, Three to Six Years, and AEPS Family Interest Survey are two examples of forms that encourage family participation in the assessment process.

Volume 4, *AEPS Curriculum for Three to Six Years*, is linked directly to Volume 3, *AEPS Measurement for Three to Six Years*, thereby creating a continuous relationship among assessment, IEP/IFSP development, and instruction and evaluation. Volume 4 differs from Volume 2 in that Volume 4 provides information on recommended intervention practices but does not include programming. Instead, Volume 4 suggests activities and recommends the use of compatible curricula that focus on particular goals or objectives.

Space does not permit a sufficient discussion of the details and strengths of AEPS. In summary, there appears to be no instrument better than AEPS for providing precise yet family-friendly assessment for early intervention.

Sample from the Assessment, Evaluation, and Programming System (AEPS) for Infants and Children

AEPS

Cognitive Domain

S = Scoring Key	Q = Qualifying Notes
2 = Pass consistently	A = Assistance provided
1 = Inconsistent	B = Behavior interfered
performance	R = Reported assessment
0 = Does not pass	M = Modification/adaptation
	D = Direct test

Name: _____

Test Period: _____
Test Date: ___/___ ___/___ ___/___ ___/___
Examiner: _____

	IEP	S	Q	S	Q	S	Q	S	Q
A. Sensory stimuli									
1. Orients to auditory/visual/tactile events									
1.1 Orients to auditory events									
1.2 Orients to visual events									
1.3 Orients to tactile events									
1.4 Responds to auditory/visual/ tactile events									
B. Object permanence									
1. Visually follows object or person to point of disappearance									
1.1 Visually follows object moving in horizontal/vertical/circular direction									
1.2 Focuses on object or person									
2. Locates object in latter of two successive hiding places									
2.1 Locates object or person who hides while child is watching									
2.2 Locates object or person who is partially hidden									
2.3 Reacts when object or person hides from view									
3. Maintains search for object that is not in usual place									
3.1 Looks for object in usual location									
C. Causality									
1. Correctly activates mechanical toy									
1.1 Correctly activates simple toy									
1.2 Acts on mechanical or simple toy in some way									
1.3 Indicates interest in simple or mechanical toy									

(continued)

From Bricker, D. (Ed.). (1993). *Assessment, evaluation, and programming system: Vol. 1. AEPS measurement for birth to three*, p. 275. Baltimore: Paul H. Brookes Publishing Co.; reprinted by permission.

Strand B   Personal Hygiene

Definition   The ability to demonstrate bowel and bladder control in familiar and unfamiliar environments, to wash and dry hands, and to brush teeth with assistance.

GOAL 1   Initiates toileting

CRITERION   Child initiates toileting and demonstrates bowel and bladder control. Child may need help completing toileting routine. Occasional reminders are acceptable.

DIRECTIONS

Materials   Toilet or potty chair.

Position   Any position that is functional for the child.

Procedure   *Observation:* Observe child's ability to initiate toileting and to demonstrate bowel and bladder control. Child stays dry and unsoiled between self-initiated trips to the toilet. Child may need help completing routine. Occasional reminders are acceptable.
Direct Test: Direct test is not appropriate for this item.

Objective 1.1   Demonstrates bowel and bladder control

CRITERION   Child demonstrates bowel and bladder control when taken to the toilet on a regular basis. Occasional accidents are acceptable.

DIRECTIONS

Materials   Toilet or potty chair.

Position   Any position that is functional for the child.

Procedure   *Observation:* Observe child's ability to demonstrate bowel and bladder control when taken to the toilet on a regular basis. Child stays dry and unsoiled between trips to the toilet. Occasional accidents are acceptable.
Direct Test: Direct test is not appropriate for this item.

From Bricker, D. (Ed.). (1993). *Assessment, evaluation, and programming system: Vol. 1. AEPS measurement for birth to three,* p. 135. Baltimore: Paul H. Brookes Publishing Co.; reprinted by permission.

Autism Screening Instrument for Educational Planning, Second Edition (ASIEP–2)

Author(s): D.A. Krug, J.R. Arick, & P.J. Almond
Year: 1993
Publisher: PRO-ED
Address: 8700 Shoal Creek Boulevard, Austin, Texas 78757
Phone: 800-397-7633
Cost: $170+

Assessment type: Curriculum compatible; separately standardized subtests for diagnosis, placement, educational program planning, and analysis of progress of individuals with autism.

Age/focus group: The autism behavior checklist (ABC) is for use with individuals of any chronological age or functioning level; other instruments are appropriate for individuals functioning at language and social developmental ages between 3 and 49 months.

Domains/content: Consists of five instruments: ABC, Sample of Vocal Behavior, Interaction Assessment, Educational Assessment, and Prognosis for Learning Rate. ABC includes a list of 57 specific nonadaptive behaviors, each with a weighted score. Sample of Vocal Behavior includes analysis of four characteristics: repetitiveness, noncommunication, intelligibility, and babbling; Interaction Assessment measures spontaneous social responses and responses to requests; Educational Assessment gathers information to identify instructional need and curriculum placement and probes five areas: staying seated, receptive language, expressive language, body concept, and speech imitation.

Special needs options: Procedures and format are specific to the needs of individuals with autism.

Curricular links: Subscales of educational skills, language, and learning have general links to curricular goals.

Authenticity: Multisource approach; natural samples of vocal, language, and behavioral skills in multiple contexts (both structured and unstructured).

Family involvement:

Parent data about child behavior and some skills are gathered.

Scoring/sample:

Record forms for each subtest summarize performance; manual provides interpretation across subtest; and examples of scores among instruments include weighted scores converted to profiles, raw scores converted to age equivalents and percentiles, and behavior samples.

Validation:

Field validation studies with groups of individuals with various disability (i.e., autism, mental retardation requiring extensive supports, and deaf-blind).

Training needed:

The ASIEP–2 should be completed by a professional who is familiar with the syndrome of autism and who has at least 3 weeks of experience with the individual being assessed.

Comments:

- *Dedicated measure for people with autism*
- *Combines multiple measurement and information sources*
- *Emphasizes an interactive approach to development, behavior, and contexts*
- *The best noncurricular developmental scale for autism and related disorders*

LINK Index			
Authentic	1	②	3
Convergent	1	2	③
Collaborative	1	②	3
Equitable	1	2	③
Sensitive	1	②	3
Congruent	1	2	③
Total Index	☐ +	6 +	9 ÷ 6 = 2.5
Overall quality: high			

3.0, exemplary; 2.5, high; 2.0, acceptable; 1.5, low; 1.0, negligible.

Autism Screening Instrument for Educational Planning, Second Edition (ASIEP–2)

The structured and comprehensive appraisal of the functional capabilities of young children with autism or related self-regulatory disorders is one of the most difficult challenges faced by professionals. Few adequate tools were available to meet this challenge until the first edition of the Autism Screening Instrument for Educational Planning (ASIEP) was developed and published in 1980. The first edition of the system was very successful in combining a functional, curriculum-compatible approach and a structured norm-based methodology. The second edition, ASIEP–2 (1993), continues the advantages of this approach with great refinements in the subtests of the battery, increased normative data on each subscale resulting from field-tests with samples of children with severe disabilities (e.g., autism, mental retardation requiring extensive supports, deaf-blindness, emotional disturbances) and with typically developing children, and slight procedural changes. The major subscales remain Autism Behavior Checklist (ABC), Sample of Vocal Behavior, Educational Assessment, Interaction Assessment, and Prognosis of Learning Rate.

Although the ASIEP–2 is a hybrid, curriculum-compatible, norm-based instrument, it retains its effective and innovative functional and criterion-referenced qualities. The ASIEP–2 strives to provide an assessment of natural behaviors, both typical and atypical, in real-life settings (e.g., social interactions, vocal behavior samples) for the individual with autism so that appraisal is best linked to intervention.

The ASIEP–2 is the only comprehensive noncurricular assessment battery for children with autism (and individuals with autism who have developmental ages between 3 and 49 months). It fills a great need in the field for an integrated system that is flexible yet technically adequate to provide a multidimensional appraisal of the functional competencies of individuals with autism who function on a preschool level. The ASIEP provides a clear probing of curricular domains in its component for the educational assessment of functional skills; furthermore, it is compatible with the *Individualized Assessment and Treatment for Autistic and Developmentally Disabled Children* (Scholpler et al., 1979).

The ASIEP–2 is both technically and clinically solid. Most of the relevant studies have been conducted on the ABC component, which has been standardized on 1,049 individuals, including people with autism, mental retardation requiring extensive supports, emotional disturbances, and deaf-blindness. The standardization shows a clear clinical distinction between children with autism and the other diagnostic groups. The ASIEP–2 enables the clinician to assess children through various means, including structured performance assessments, naturalistic observations, clinical judgment ratings, and trial teaching that involves the use of prompts and demonstrations to evaluate learning rate. The flexible, but standardized, multi-source format provides an important adaptive feature, which enables the diagnostic specialist to obtain as accurate an assessment of the "untestable" atypical child as possible.

The authors are to be commended for developing a highly useful, technically sound system that integrates several critical assessment components. Some of the components (e.g., Interaction Assessment) are cumbersome to use and score. On balance, however, the ASIEP–2 provides invaluable diagnostic and programming features to programs that include young atypical children.

Adaptive procedures include the sources from which information about children and families is collected. Clinical judgment methods gather the impressions of various adults across several settings about the functional capabilities of young children with disabilities. This method provides social input regarding children's real-life capacities for interacting with people and objects in their world despite their disabilities. In this way, clinical impressions can supplement and even challenge the results of narrower and less flexible forms of assessment.

Sample Vocal Behavior Record Form from the Autism Screening Instrument for Educational Planning, Second Edition (ASIEP–2)

Sample of Vocal Behavior Record Form

Student's Name __JSD__   Date __11/12/92__

Evaluator __Maisie__   Minutes needed to obtain sample __17'__

SCORING

Autistic Speech Characteristics

- 2 Repetitive
- 34 Noncommunicative
- 34 Unintelligible
- + 24 Babbling

112 TOTAL RAW SCORE

Interpreted Language Age Raw Score

- 30 First Use
- 16 Communicative
- + 16 Intelligible

62 TOTAL

Average Length

STEP 1

2) 24   12 BAB SCORE / Babbling

STEP 2

12 BAB SCORE
+ 46 TOTAL WORDS
58 TOTAL LENGTH

STEP 3

1.16 = Average Length
50) 58 TOTAL LENGTH

STIMULI: (Circle one)
a. Books and Pictures
b. Toys *(circled)*
c. Physical Stimulation
d. Selected Environmental Setting

Description of setting and materials: Classroom; various toys

Verbatim Record of Spontaneous Utterances

#	Utterance
1	La
2	oo
3	La
4	throaty "sound
5	"
6	"
7	"
8	"
9	"
10	ah (points to shoe)
11	p
12	bo
13	oo
14	ah (gestures)
15	na
16	mum
17	Lugga
18	mum
19	oo
20	oo
21	ee yah
22	bunny
23	rabbit
24	La
25	wa wa (gestures)
26	ack
27	sanwick
28	yuk (makes face)
29	Lugga
30	this man
31	Lugga
32	Lugga
33	Lugga
34	I want to go
35	where live?
36	ee yah
37	ee yah
38	I like dis one
39	dis one
40	dis one
41	dis one
42	in the cup
43	ball in the cup
44	go to the beach
45	Kirby vacuum clean
46	its a Kirby
47	your name
48	ee yah
49	ah wa wa wa (sign)
50	m-m

TOTALS (bottom row): 30 20 16 34 16 34 24 46 | 15 4 11 1 3 3 18 6 3 7 6

COMMENTS: The statements: bunny, rabbit, sanwick, go to the beach, Kirby vacuum cleaner, and its a Kirby, were scored noncommunicative because there was no apparent stimulus and the comments were not directed to the examiner. (49) signed "I want water"

Battelle Developmental Inventory (BDI)

Author(s):   J. Newborg, J.R. Stock, & J. Wnek (initial development)
                J. Guidubaldi (pilot norming study)
                J.S. Svinicki (completion and standardization)
Year: 1988
Publisher: Riverside Publishing Co.
Address: 8420 Bryn Mawr Avenue, Chicago, Illinois 60631
Phone: 800-767-8420
Cost: $249

Assessment type: Norm based/curriculum compatible; used for diagnosis, linkage, and progress evaluation purposes.

Age/focus group: Birth to 95 months.

Domains/content: Personal-social, adaptive, motor, communication, and cognitive domains and 22 subdomains (e.g., coping, peer interaction, attention, memory, expression of feelings); 341 items.

Special needs options: General adaptations for various disabilities; standardized stimulus/response options for visual, hearing, neuromotor, and behavior/emotional disorders included with most items.

Curricular links: Compatibility of domains and items with commonly used preschool curricula; developmental task sequences by chronological age within each subdomain. Battelle curriculum development in progress.

Authenticity: Includes observations of typical behavior and competencies in everyday settings in the personal-social and adaptive domains; relies on convergent data from various sources.

Family involvement: Requires parent input on personal-social and other subscales.

Scoring/sample: Domain scores (developmental age, z-score, developmental rate, normal curve equivalent, percentile), structured assessment, observations, and interview data; norm group, $N = 800$, national sample continuum scoring (0, 1, or 2) of items. Recalibrated norms available as of 1988.

Validation: Reliability and validity based on prepublication version; field research supports concurrent validity, interrater reliability, and internal consistency; program efficacy research established.

Training needed: Although appropriate for nonpsychologists, supervised practice in administration for preschoolers with disabilities across the entire age span is critical.

Comments:
- *Consistent with the spirit of PL 94-142 and PL 99-457*
- *Merges norm-based, curriculum-based, and adaptive features*
- *Needs technical evaluation in field-test settings*
- *The best example of curriculum referencing and linking assessment, intervention, and evaluation beyond a curriculum*

LINK Index

Authentic	1	②	3
Convergent	1	2	③
Collaborative	1	2	③
Equitable	1	2	③
Sensitive	1	②	3
Congruent	1	2	③
Total Index	☐ +	4 +	12 ÷ 6 = 2.7

Overall quality: high

3.0, exemplary; 2.5, high; 2.0, acceptable; 1.5, low; 1.0, negligible.

Battelle Developmental Inventory (BDI)

The Battelle Developmental Inventory (BDI), a standardized development scale, is the only norm-referenced diagnostic measure that also integrates criterion-referenced features into its structure (it is not, however, a curriculum). The BDI analyzes the acquisition of 341 critical developmental skills within five functional domains and 22 subdomains in children from birth to 8 years of age. Functional capabilities are assessed in the following major domains: personal-social, adaptive, motor, communication, and cognitive. Unique clusters of subdomain skills are sampled in such areas as adult interaction, expression of feelings/affect, coping, attention, and reasoning (see the sample pages that follow). Recommendations from early intervention research are incorporated into the design and construction of the BDI.

The BDI assessment battery consists of components that are in keeping with the LINK model because they fulfill four interrelated purposes that link assessment and intervention: 1) screening and identification, 2) comprehensive assessment and goal planning, 3) programming and intervention, and 4) evaluation of child progress and program effectiveness. The BDI ensures norm-referenced identification of young children with special needs and highlights those developmental areas that require more comprehensive appraisal. The battery's multidimensional structure allows a comprehensive analysis of functional capabilities by incorporating diagnostic data from multiple people and sources (e.g., teachers, therapists, parents, observation, interviews, child performance). One unique adaptive feature of the BDI is its inclusion of assessment adaptations for specific sensorimotor impairments and general guidelines for presenting testing tasks for young children with various disabilities. In addition, the developmental and behavioral content of the BDI is congruent with the goals and tasks of frequently used infant and preschool curricula. Finally, the organization of the BDI enables interdisciplinary team members to assess children independently to complete formative and summative evaluations of progress and program efficacy.

Normative and technical data on the BDI support its use. Some questions have, however, been raised as to whether its developmental quotients might "overestimate" the number of preschoolers with developmental disabilities. In early 1988, the publisher issued a recalibrated normative manual for BDI that may resolve these problems. Additional research is needed to settle this question. The inventory was standardized on 800 children ranging in age from birth to 8 years using a national norming sample stratified according to age, race, and gender. Reliability (test–retest, interrater) and validity (content, construct, and criterion-rated) data reported in the manuals seem to support the stability of the battery, its factorial validity, and its relation with other developmental and intellectual measures. Child diagnostic data are reported in three forms for each major domain and subdomain: age equivalents (DA), percentiles, and standard scores (developmental quotients, z-scores and t-scores, and normal curve equivalents).

The BDI is an excellent multidimensional assessment battery that blends norm- and criterion-referenced features to link assessment and intervention. Its inclusion of adaptive evaluation strategies ensures the collection of more accurate and functional diagnostic and instructional data. Finally, the publisher plans to develop a curriculum based on the content of the BDI. A unique feature of this curriculum will be goals that are based on clusters of items rather than on each individual item in the test.

Sample from the Battelle Developmental Inventory (BDI)

ADAPTIVE DOMAIN

Subdomain: Attention

Basal = a score of 2 on all items at an age level
Ceiling = a score of 0 on two consecutive items

Item No.	Age (mos)	Behavior	Score	Cum Max	Comments
A 1	0–5	Turns eyes toward light source	___		
A 2		Visually attends to object for five or more seconds	___		
A 3		Attends to ongoing sound or activity for 15 or more seconds	___	6	
A 4	6–11	Visually attends to light source moving in 180-degree arc	___		
A 5		Visually attends to light source moving in vertical direction	___		
A 6		Occupies self for 10 or more minutes without demanding attention	___	12	
A 7	12–17	Looks at, points to, or touches pictures in book	___	14	
A 8	18–23	Attends to one activity for three or more minutes	___	16	
A 9	36–47	Attends to learning task or story in small group	___		
A 10		Focuses attention on one task while being aware of (but not distracted by) another activity	___	20	

Subdomain Score

DOMAIN	Cognitive	**AGE**	4 to 5 years	**CG 25**
SUBDOMAIN	Reasoning and Academic Skills		(48 through 59 months)	
BEHAVIOR	The child gives three objects on request.			
MATERIALS	Six cubes (other available objects)			

STANDARD PROCEDURES

PROCEDURE

Structured. Place the six cubes in a row on the table before the child. Say to the child, "**Give me three blocks.**" If the child does not respond, repeat one request. After the child has given you the three cubes, do not consider the response complete until the child has had time to give you another cube if he or she wishes. Consider the reponse complete when the child draws his or her hand back from the table and looks up at you as though waiting for your approval.

SCORING

Credit is given if the child gives or separates **three and only three** cubes from the six cubes on the table.

2 points = as above
1 point = 2 or 4 cubes
0 points = anything else

ADAPTATIONS FOR THE HANDICAPPED

Severe Motor Impairment—Arm or Hand. Credit is given if the child is able to push the three cubes to you. Place the cubes slightly further apart than they would be normally placed. If the child cannot physically move the cubes, pick up one cube at a time (while retaining all cubes previously picked up) and ask, "**Do I have three now?**" Do this for all six cubes.

Severe Visual Impairment. After the cubes are placed on the table, take the child's hand and place it on each of the six cubes individually. Do not count them. Say, "**Give me three blocks.**" Allow the child to feel the cubes, using both hands if he or she wishes, before giving them to you.

Severe Hearing Impairment or Emotional Disturbance. Hold up three fingers to indicate the number three but discontinue this sign before the child responds.

2 to 6: Instructional Activities for Children at Risk (links to BDI)

Author(s):	C. Bos, S. Vaughn, & L. Levine
Year:	1992
Publisher:	Science Research Associates (SRA)
Address:	Order Service, 220 East Danieldale Road, De Soto, Texas 75115-2490
Phone:	800-843-8855
Cost:	$199 (purchased as a set of seven books; $35 for each individual book [$245 if all seven are purchased separately])

Assessment type: Curriculum embedded; links to the Battelle Developmental Inventory for assessment.

Age/focus group: Designed for toddlers, preschoolers, and kindergarten-age children with special needs.

Scales: Developmental Inventory.

Data system: Participation Sheets and Progress Charts are provided. Battelle Developmental Inventory Sheets available with BDI.

Domains/content: Communication, motor, cognition, personal-social, and adaptive.

Special needs options: It is designed for children with special needs; therefore, it provides various adaptations and activities for a range of sensory and motor special needs.

Authenticity: Content shows predominance of natural skills and activities that are useful and relevant in real-life child settings.

Family involvement: Family involvement is emphasized. *Very Special Families*, an activity book for teachers, includes informational newsletters, calendars, ideas, and suggestions to share with families to help with their children's development.

Training needed: Knowledge of basic curriculum and assessment instrument is needed.

Validation: Validation is provided by the Battelle Developmental Inventory.

Comments:
- *Many useful activities and ideas provided*
- *Good resource and program for novice teachers*
- *Adaptations made for specific special needs*
- *See review of Battelle Developmental Inventory*

LINK Index			
Authentic	1	②	3
Convergent	1	②	3
Collaborative	1	②	3
Equitable	1	②	3
Sensitive	1	2	③
Congruent	1	2	③
Total Index	☐ +	8 +	6 ÷ 6 = 2.3
Overall quality: acceptable			

3.0, exemplary; 2.5, high; 2.0, acceptable; 1.5, low; 1.0, negligible.

2 to 6: Instructional Activities for Children at Risk

2 to 6 provides preschool and kindergarten teachers with five activity books that consist of instructional activities in five developmental domains: communication, motor, cognitive, personal-social, and adaptive. The activity books help teachers structure different activities to encourage learning that is fun, effective, and functional for the children.

The instructional activities include activities that correspond to the skills assessed in BDI in addition to other activities that are not related to the BDI. 2 to 6 also provides suggestions for adapting activities for children with vision, hearing, and/or physical impairments, although more severe needs are not accommodated. Each activity includes a learning objective, materials needed, procedures for teaching, additional experiences, and extensions that encourage adaptation of activities as needed.

In addition to the five books of instructional activities, two books for teachers and parents, *Special Times* and *Very Special Families*, are included in this program. These books include additional activities, ideas, newsletters, and suggestions to promote collaboration between teachers and parents. Several charts for monitoring the program and child progress are included: Participation Sheets (reports child's participation), Group Participation and Progress (facilitates report of progress of the group with other teachers), Individual Monitoring Chart (records the progress of each child), and Group Monitoring Chart (records progress of each child in the group).

2 to 6 is a practical "teacher-friendly" material, which, most will agree, is extremely helpful. The curriculum is geared toward children with typical development, but it has features that allow teachers to make the lessons less or more challenging to accommodate special needs. Used in tandem with BDI for assessment, this set of materials is valuable, especially for Head Start or similar inclusive programs.

Scope and Sequence Chart

DOMAIN:
COGNITIVE

SUBDOMAIN:
CONCEPTUAL
DEVELOPMENT

◉ = Developmentally Age Appropriate

Most activities can be extended downward or upward
to cover a wider developmental range.

Activity/Objective	Pages	Age Range In Years				
		1 to 2	2 to 3	3 to 4	4 to 5	5 to 6+
I Did It! Understand that people can cause things to happen	102–103	◉				
What Does It Do? Identify and demonstrate uses of familiar objects	104–105		◉			
I Have Lots of Parts Point to different body parts	106–107		◉	◉		
Small Fry and Big Bear Identify objects by size and describe as *big* or *little*	108–109			◉		
Gone Fishing Sort by colors and count up to ten objects in unison	110–111		◉	◉		
The Long of It Identify the longer of two objects	112–113			◉		
Shape Up by Sorting Sort forms by shape	114–115			◉		
It's Heavy! Identify the heavier of two objects	116–117			◉	◉	
What Color Is the Rainbow? Match colors and name colors of familiar objects	118–119			◉	◉	
Floaters and Sinkers Sort objects that float and objects that sink	120–121			◉	◉	
Bigger or Smaller Compare size of objects and animals from memory	122–123			◉	◉	◉

From Bos, C., Vaughn, S., & Levine, L. (1992). *2 to 6: Instructional Activities for Children at Risk*. New York:
SRA–McGraw-Hill Co.; reprinted by permission of the McGraw-Hill Company.

DOMAIN: COGNITIVE SUBDOMAIN: CONCEPTUAL DEVELOPMENT	ACTIVITY # What Does It Do?	

 Age: 2-0 to 3-0

Learning Objective

The children will identify and demonstrate the uses of familiar objects.

Materials

- familiar objects such as crayons, spoon, glass/cup, ball, wash cloth, various articles of clothing
- pictures of familiar objects

Teaching Procedures

1. Place several familiar objects in the center of the table or on the floor. Pick up and name each object. Have the children say the name of each object after you.

2. Select two familiar objects that have different uses; for example, a spoon and a ball. Say the name of each object and demonstrate and describe its use.

3. Let the children take turns selecting one of the objects, saying its name, and demonstrating its use.

4. Repeat the procedure with the other objects.

5. Combine names of objects and actions to form phrases and/or short sentences; for example, "Roll ball," "Roll the ball."

✛ Additional Experiences for Learning

1. Place the objects in front of the children when the demonstrations have been completed. Say to the children "Show me what you (function) with."

2. Help the children make a "Book of Functions." Paste a picture of an object on the first right-hand page. Paste a picture that illustrates its function on the next page; for example, a picture of a spoon might be on the first page. A picture of someone eating with a spoon would be on the second page. Show the picture of the object and have the children tell what they do with it. Then have the children turn the page to verify their answer.

3. Present books such as *Richard Scarry's Things That Go, Richard Scarry's Toy Book,* and *Richard Scarry's Cars & Trucks & Things That Go* to the children. Let the children pick out familiar objects, name them, and tell what they do. Encourage the children to look at these books independently.

▼ Downward Extensions

1. Introduce only two or three objects for the children to name and then pantomime.

2. Have the children actually use the object before they pantomime its use; for example, have them use a spoon to eat gelatin or applesauce before they pantomime eating with a spoon.

3. Let the children pantomime the different actions in a group instead of individually.

▲ Upward Extensions

1. Include more than two objects for the children to identify by function or use.

2. Repeat the procedures, using pictures of objects.

★ Special Adaptations

1. Provide assistance, such as using a hand-over-hand technique, if the children have difficulty demonstrating the use of an object.

2. Describe the actions for children with severe visual impairments.

From Bos, C., Vaughn, S., & Levine, L. (1992). *2 to 6: Instructional Activities for Children at Risk.* New York: SRA–McGraw-Hill Co.; reprinted by permission of the McGraw-Hill Company.

BRIGANCE® Diagnostic Inventory of Early Development, Revised Edition (BDIED–R)

Author(s):   A.H. Brigance
Year: 1991
Publisher: Curriculum Associates
Address: 5 Esquire Road, North Billerica, Massachusetts 01862-2589
Phone: 800-225-0248
Cost: $100

Assessment type: Curriculum-compatible developmental measure (with "developmental age notations derived from norms found in reference"). Offers assessment instrument, instructional guide, tracking system, tools for developing IEPs, and resources for parents and professionals.

Age/focus group: Infants and children younger than the developmental age of 7 years.

Domains/content: Eleven domains: preambulatory motor, gross motor, fine motor, self-help, speech and language, general knowledge and comprehension, social and emotional development, readiness, basic reading skills, manuscript writing, and basic math.

Special needs options: Contains no specific adaptations in either scoring or administration, offers some flexibility in data-gathering strategies, and falls on the more traditional end of the spectrum of measures used in early childhood assessment.

Curricular links: Assessments are based on developmental skills and behaviors and curriculum objectives. Results can be applied directly to planning and individualizing instruction primarily for children who are at risk for and those who have mild difficulties. BDIED–R is compatible with the *BRIGANCE Prescriptive Readiness: Strategies and Practice* (Brigance, 1985), and tasks on the BDIED–R and learning objectives and activities in the curriculum are cross-referenced and cross-coded.

Authenticity: Low authenticity; contains flexible information gathering for use in less natural settings for certain tasks.

Family involvement: Incorporates parent observations.

Scoring/sample: No validation sample reported; scoring performed by using traditional pass/fail metric.

Validation: Content validity is clear and strong; other field-validation data gathered with groups with special needs are not reported.

Training needed: Knowledge of child development and familiarity with procedures in the manual.

Comments:
- *One of the most frequently used criterion-referenced developmental measures because it is easy to use*
- *Motivating, flexible, and comprehensive*
- *Procedures blend assessment, selection of objectives, and evaluation of progress*
- *Coding to the* BRIGANCE Prescriptive Readiness: Strategies and Practice *for kindergarten-age children is a strength*
- *Appropriate only for children who are at risk for or who have mild disabilities*
- *Lack of field-validation studies with special needs samples is a weakness*

LINK Index

Authentic	1	②	3
Convergent	1	②	3
Collaborative	1	②	3
Equitable	1	②	3
Sensitive	1	②	3
Congruent	1	②	3
Total Index	☐ +	12 +	☐ ÷ 6 = 2.0

Overall quality: acceptable

3.0, exemplary; 2.5, high; 2.0, acceptable; 1.5, low; 1.0, negligible.

BRIGANCE® Diagnostic Inventory of Early Development, Revised Edition (BDIED–R)

The BRIGANCE Diagnostic Inventory of Early Development, Revised Edition (BDIED–R) refines and updates the information presented in the first edition (1978), thereby increasing its usefulness to the many preschool programs that rely on it as their primary assessment tool.

Two major changes in this revised edition are worth noting. First, the BDIED–R is more comprehensive and has been tailored to be responsive to the intent of PL 94-142 and PL 99-457 than is the BDIED, in large part through the addition of a social-emotional domain. The developmental competencies that are included focus on important social skills (e.g., understanding the need to share and take turns), play skills (e.g., playing cooperatively with two or more children), and self-regulatory or work-related behaviors (e.g., remaining at a task for 10–12 minutes). Second, the BDIED–R codes and cross-references developmental competencies with specific teaching activities in the *BRIGANCE Prescriptive Readiness: Strategies and Practice* (Brigance, 1985). This curriculum compatibility is especially evident for those kindergarten skills involving basic concepts and for beginning reading and arithmetic skills.

Aside from the two above-specified differences, the BDIED–R is quite similar to the first edition of the BDIED. It is based on a developmental task–analytic model, combines norm- and criterion-referenced features, and integrates assessment with curriculum goal planning. The BDIED–R surveys the age range of birth to 7 years and analyzes child performance across 98 skill sequences within 11 major developmental domains, including prespeech behaviors, general knowledge and comprehension, fine motor skills, preambulatory motor skills, and social-emotional development. Item placement and skill sequencing follow the organization of items in traditional developmental scales; the BDIED–R uniquely references the source of these age-level placements for each item. Multiple procedures for scoring child performance are provided (i.e., interview, observation, diagnostic teaching, pragmatic task modifications). The BDIED–R also accommodates different response styles; therefore, adaptations for various disabilities are possible, although not specifically indicated. Developmental ages are indicated for each sequence of developmental skills; the scale links assessment with intervention by arranging tasks in a hierarchical manner and by matching appropriate objectives to these tasks in each subdomain. Computer-based programs are available to translate child assessment data directly into BDIED–R plans.

The associated curriculum, *BRIGANCE Prescriptive Readiness: Strategies and Practice,* is a package of instructional activities that are appropriate for children at the preschool, kindergarten, and early first-grade levels and that correspond to assessment tasks on the BDIED–R. These activities detail objectives, rationales, instructional sequences, teaching recommendations, and indicators of learning diffi-culties for 400 developmental and behavior skills.

Although the BDIED–R is one of the best criterion-referenced measures of de-velopmental functioning available in a noncurricular format, many of its skill se-quences lack the detail needed to provide assessments sufficiently precise for preschoolers with severe disabilities (in auditory, visual, language, perceptual, and fine motor areas). BDIED–R is, therefore, most effective when used for children with mild to moderate disabilities.

Sample from the BRIGANCE® Diagnostic Inventory of Early Development, Revised Edition (BDIED–R)

G. Social and Emotional Development (continued)

Assessment: G–2   Page: 168

Play Skills and Behaviors:

0-3
1. Gets excited when a toy is presented.
2. Shakes rattle or other object when placed in hand.

0-7
3. Likes to reach for object and grab it.
4. Bites or chews toys in play.
5. Plays peek-a-boo.
6. Explores the environment with curiosity.
7. Plays pat-a-cake.

1-0
8. Plays with a variety of toys, doing different activities with each.
9. Engages in a simple game with others such as rolling a ball back and forth.
10. Engages in play that extends beyond self—brushes doll's hair, feeds doll, feeds mother.

1-6
11. Engages in play in which he/she pretends to sleep or eat.
12. Imitates environmental sounds during play.
13. Imitates in play an activity involving housework.
14. Imitates motions of an object.
15. Associates objects in play such as giving the doll a ride in a car or having the dog for a walk.

2-0
16. Watches other children play, and may attempt to join briefly.
17. Imitates self doing something such as crying or eating.
18. Plays alone in the presence of other children (parallel play).

19. Tends to like rough-and-tumble play.

2-6
20. Uses a doll or other toy to act out a scene.
21. Watches others play and plays near them (parallel play).
22. Engages in domestic make-believe play, imitating an adult activity for at least ten minutes.
23. Plays simple group games such as "Ring Around the Rosy."

3-0
24. Begins to play with other children with adult supervision.
25. Begins to take turns.
26. Can usually play cooperatively, but may need adult help.

3-6
27. Takes turns with assistance.

28. Has an imaginary companion/playmate.

4-0
29. Plays at least one table game with supervision.

4-6
30. Incorporates verbal directions into play activities.
31. Takes turns in play without adult supervision.

5-0
32. Plays cooperatively with one or two children for at least fifteen minutes.

5-6
33. Plays a pretend career/professional role in play.
34. Plays two or three table games.
35. Plays cooperatively with two or three children for at least twenty minutes. 6-0

Notes:

Assessment: G–3   Page: 173

Work-Related Skills and Behaviors:

0-6
1. Holds arms out to be picked up.
2. Searches for hidden (covered) object.
3. Works for toy out of reach.

2-6
4. Begins to link objects to functional relationships.

1-0
5. Imitates actions of others such as putting blocks into a box.

1-6
6. Imitates in play an activity involving housework.
7. Dramatizes adult activities.

2-0
8. Helps put things away.

9. Exhibits signs of developing independence by having the attitude that "I can do it myself."

2-6
10. Works with an adult by doing an activity for five minutes.
11. Engages in domestic make-believe play, imitating an adult activity for at least ten minutes.

3-0
12. Uses blocks or other objects to build simple enclosures such as pens or yards.

13. Engages in an activity, such as playing with his/her toys or watching TV, for at least twenty minutes.
14. Works in a small group for at least five minutes.

3-6
15. Works in a small group for at least twelve minutes.
16. Uses blocks or other objects to build more complex enclosures such as a house, barn, or garage.

4-0
17. Performs simple errands.

18. Usually remains at a ten- to twelve-minute task until it is time to quit or change.

5-0
19. Likes to finish what he/she starts with less dawdling than at an earlier age.
20. Pushes for autonomy (wants to be independent like an adult).

6-0
21. Works in a small group for at least twenty minutes.
22. Remains at a task when "school" distractions are present. 7-0

Notes:

Callier-Azusa Scale: Assessment of Deaf-Blind Children (CAS)

Author(s): R. Stillman
Year: 1974
Publisher: Callier Center for Communication Disorders
Address: 1966 Inwood Road, Dallas, Texas 75235
Phone: 214-905-3060
Cost: $12 per copy

Assessment type: Curriculum compatible; dedicated to a specific disability.

Age/focus group: Birth to 8 years.

Domains/content: Social, daily living, motor, language, and perceptual domains; observations in natural settings.

Special needs options: Dedicated to the multiple needs of children who are deaf-blind; emphasizes tactile modes of learning and experiencing.

Curricular links: Baseline developmental skills sequences are compatible with, and augment, those of existing developmental curricula.

Authenticity: Observations conducted in natural settings during everyday and play activities; data collected through multiple sources; focus on functional skills.

Family involvement: Relies on parent input as being integral to the results.

Scoring/sample: A 3-point scoring scale.

Validation: Handicapped Children's Early Education Programs–developed and field-validated scale for this population.

Training needed: Strong observation skills; transdisciplinary experience and/or training in language, positioning, and working with individuals with mental retardation requiring extensive supports.

Comments:

- *Dated scale retains great utility*
- *Strong treatment validity*
- *Authentic focus and methods*
- *Fulfills a challenging low-incidence need*
- *Matches levels in some low-incidence curricula*

LINK Index			
Authentic	1	2	③
Convergent	1	2	③
Collaborative	1	2	③
Equitable	1	2	③
Sensitive	1	②	3
Congruent	1	②	3
Total Index	☐ +	4 +	12 ÷ 6 = 2.7
Overall quality: high			

3.0, exemplary; 2.5, high; 2.0, acceptable; 1.5, low; 1.0, negligible.

Callier–Azusa Scale: Assessment of Deaf–Blind Children (CAS)

Few dedicated curriculum-compatible measures exist for use with young children with severe disabilities, particularly those with multiple impairments, such as deafness and blindness. The Callier-Azusa Scale (CAS) continues to offer distinct advantages over other traditional measures for the assessment and initial curriculum planning for infants and young children with sensory impairments. The CAS comprises five subscales: socialization, daily living skills, motor development, perceptual abilities, and language development. Although the CAS is not a curriculum, its density of task analysis shows enough fine gradations in the developmental sequence to enable professionals to make decisions about instructional goals for children from birth to 8 years of age who have multiple sensory impairments. The example on page 122 shows obvious adaptations for sensory impairments in its focus on tactile modes of learning and the use of "may" tags in items to denote those that a given child may have trouble exhibiting because of idiosyncrasies in functional capabilities. The CAS tasks target low-level capabilities: For example, "finds object that has been placed in textured material," "shows only reflexive responses to the environment," and "shows undifferentiated cry." We regard the CAS as a dated but important alternative assessment measure for young children with low-incidence disabilities. It is compatible with major developmental curricula and first included authentic assessment tasks and observational procedures in natural contexts before it was fashionable.

Sample Item Tasks and Sequences from the Callier-Azusa Scale (CAS)

PERCEPTUAL ABILITIES

ITEM	EXAMPLE
A. Visual Development	
0. Does not respond to visual stimulus	
1. Responds to visual stimulus	startle, blink, motor activity at presentation of light or bright object
2. (A) Attends to large object in the visual field within 30 seconds of its presentation	when an object (large ball, or similar object the child likes) is presented close to the child's eyes, he will direct his gaze to the object within 30 seconds
*(B) May look at caregivers face when held or in close contact with caregiver	
(C) Eyes follow object from center to side or side to center of body—but do not cross midline	
3. (A) Looks toward the source of light	
(B) Visually follows a moving person or large object	
4. Shows eye-blink response to a quickly approaching object	
5. (A) Attends to small objects	2" ball, cookie, or some object the child likes
(B) Anticipates a whole object by seeing only a part	when asked to find an object that is only partially in view (toy in a sandbox, half buried in sand and half visible), the child can find the object
B. Auditory Development	
0. No response to sounds	
1. Changes behavior in response to sound	when a loud noise is produced outside of the child's visual field, he startles, blinks, or exhibits general movement
2. Turns head or eyes in general direction of sound source	
3. (A) Attends to or responds to patterned sounds	stops other behaviors to listen to musical toy, touches vibrating object when hears sounds; tries to put record on after it stops
(B) Distinguishes intonation in voice	reacts differently to scolding, praising, soothing voices
4. Looks, moves, or reaches toward sound source *located in any direction*	
5. Anticipates a routine activity from sound cues	prepares to go outside when bell rings
C. Receptive Communication	
0. Unresponsive to the environment. Movements are not in response to stimulation and appear to have no goal or purpose.	–twisting and rolling movement of body; apparently random arm, leg and head movement
1. Changes behavior when stimulated.	–ceases activity, alerts, or attends to loud sounds, light, or bright objects –turns toward stimulus when touched near mouth –grasps object placed in palm –startles when body position abruptly changed
2. (A) Smiles or grimaces to tactile, visceral (internal), or kinesthetic stimulation	–smiles when tickled, stroked, rocked, or after eating
*(B) *May* distinguish between human voices or distinguish between human voices and other sounds.	–may attend rather than startle to human voices
3. (A) Systematically repeats movements. The focus of attention is on the child's own body movements and the stimulation of his own body.	–repeatedly scratches available object such as mat, table top, finger, toy –repeatedly makes guttural sounds –licks available objects –child makes a sound which the adult immediately repeats, the child continues to produce a sound –rocks –brings thumb to mouth to suck
(B) Anticipates a familiar event from whole body cues.	–opens mouth or turns head to search for bottle or spoon when held in a manner regularly associated with feeding –Teacher holds child, swings him from side to side and then quickly lowers him. After several repetitions of this sequence, teacher pauses before lowering child; child tenses or startles in anticipation of being lowered
*(C) *May* attend to a human voice.	–reduces or ceases activity

From Stillman, R. (Ed.). (1974). *Callier-Azusa Scale (CAS)*. Dallas: University of Texas at Dallas, Callier Center for Communication Disorders; reprinted by permission.

The Carolina Curricula:
The Carolina Curriculum for Infants and
Toddlers with Special Needs, Second Edition
(CCITSN)

Author(s):   N.M. Johnson-Martin, K.G. Jens, S.M. Attermeier, & B.J. Hacker
Year: 1991
Publisher: Paul H. Brookes Publishing Co.
Address: Post Office Box 10624, Baltimore, Maryland 21285-0624
Phone: 800-638-3775
Cost: $40
                 *Assessment Log and Developmental Progress Charts for The
                 Carolina Curriculum for Infants and Toddlers with Special
                 Needs* (package of 10), $20; also available, *Assessment Log and
                 Developmental Progress Charts for The Carolina Curriculum
                 (CCITSN and CCPSN, 12 Months to 3 Years)* (package of 10),
                 $23

Assessment type: Curriculum embedded.

Age/focus group: Designed for children who have mild to severe special
                            needs and who function in the birth to 24-month de-
                            velopmental range. It can be used individually in ei-
                            ther a home- or center-based program.

Scale(s):   Assessment Log and Developmental Progress Charts
                            for children from birth to 2 years and for children from
                            12 months to 3 years (the latter charts are designed for
                            children whose skills fall between those covered by
                            the infant curriculum and those covered by the
                            preschool curriculum).

Data system: Individual assessment logs and developmental progress
                            charts are provided.

Domains/content: Cognition, communication, social/adaptation, fine
                            motor skills, and gross motor skills.

Special needs options: Vision, motor, and hearing.

Authenticity: This curriculum is high in authenticity and includes many naturally occurring tasks.

Family involvement: It is emphasized that very young children receive most care from their families; therefore, the activities are structured so that families can be involved throughout.

Training needed: Knowledge of principles of learning in and assessment of children with special needs; can be used by professionals, assistants, and parents with some professional support.

Validation: Among the best technical data of any curriculum; reliability, validity, and program efficacy data are provided.

Comments:
- *Family involvement*
- *Specific adaptations are noted to accommodate sensory/motor needs*
- *Easy to implement with a good system for data collection*
- *Functional activities*
- *Great detail and suggestions for activities*

🛒 ∞

LINK Index			
Authentic	1	2	③
Convergent	1	2	③
Collaborative	1	②	3
Equitable	1	2	③
Sensitive	1	2	③
Congruent	1	2	③
Total Index	☐ +	2 +	15 ÷ 6 = 2.8
Overall quality: high to exemplary			

3.0, exemplary; 2.5, high; 2.0, acceptable; 1.5, low; 1.0, negligible.

The Carolina Curricula:
The Carolina Curriculum for Preschoolers with Special Needs (CCPSN)

Author(s): N.M. Johnson-Martin, S.M. Attermeier, & B.J. Hacker
Year: 1990
Publisher: Paul H. Brookes Publishing Co.
Address: Post Office Box 10624, Baltimore, Maryland 21285-0624
Phone: 800-638-3775
Cost: $34
Assessment Log and Developmental Progress Chart for the Carolina Curriculum for Preschoolers with Special Needs (package of 10), $22; also available, *Assessment Log and Developmental Progress Charts for The Carolina Curriculum (CCITSN and CCPSN, 12 Months to 3 Years)* (package of 10), $23.

Assessment type: Curriculum embedded.

Age/focus group: Designed for children who have mild-to-severe special needs and who function in the 2-year to 5-year developmental range. It can be used individually in either a home- or center-based program.

Scale(s):   Assessment Log and Developmental Progress Charts for children from 2 to 5 years and children from 12 months to 3 years (the latter charts are designed for children whose skills fall between those covered by the infant curriculum and those covered by the preschool curriculum).

Data system: Individual assessment logs and developmental progress charts are provided.

Domains/content: Cognition, communication, social adaptation, fine motor, and gross motor skills.

Special needs options: Vision, motor, and hearing.

Authenticity: This curriculum is high in authenticity and emphasizes many naturally occurring tasks.

Family involvement: The importance of family involvement is stressed, and activities are structured so that families can be involved throughout the entire assessment and instruction process.

Training needed: Knowledge of principles of learning in and assessment of children with special needs; can be used by professionals, assistants, and parents with some professional support.

Validation: Among the best technical data of any curriculum; reliability, validity, and program efficacy data are provided.

Comments:
- *Characteristics of specific disabilities, the effects of disability in the classroom, and classroom tips are noted*
- *Easy to implement with a good system for data collection*
- *Functional activities*
- *Family involvement*
- *Offers great detail (e.g., task analyses, alternative activities)*

LINK Index

Authentic	1	2	③
Convergent	1	2	③
Collaborative	1	②	3
Equitable	1	2	③
Sensitive	1	2	③
Congruent	1	2	③
Total Index	☐ +	☐2 +	☐15 ÷ 6 = ☐2.8

Overall quality: high to exemplary

3.0, exemplary; 2.5, high; 2.0, acceptable; 1.5, low; 1.0, negligible.

The Carolina Curricula:
The Carolina Curriculum for Infants and Toddlers with Special Needs, Second Edition (CCITSN) and The Carolina Curriculum for Preschoolers with Special Needs (CCPSN)

The Carolina Curriculum for Infants and Toddlers with Special Needs (CCITSN) organizes the five domains of child development into 26 subdomains. This jargon-free curriculum provides detailed teaching and needs assessment techniques to enhance the growth of children who have special needs or who are at risk for developmental delays. The CCITSN spans the birth to 24-month developmental age range and is replete with teaching procedures, sensorimotor adaptations, routine integration strategies, evaluation criteria, and a sample Assessment Log for recording a child's progress. These materials allow professionals to tailor programs to the special strengths and needs of each child.

The Assessment Log and Developmental Progress Charts for The Carolina Curriculum for Infants and Toddlers with Special Needs permits easy recording of each child's progress in a 24-page log that has four spaces for recording a child's performance in the 26 developmental subdomains over time. This log has an orderly format and keeps data organized and accessible.

The Carolina Curriculum for Preschoolers with Special Needs (CCPSN) begins where the first curriculum left off—with children between the developmental ages of 2 and 5 years who have special needs or who are considered at risk for developmental delays. The curriculum for preschoolers focuses on 25 specific subdomains of development, providing a detailed picture of a child's functioning. This "hands-on" curriculum tool enables the teacher to identify effective intervention techniques for use in the preschool classroom and to plan individual preschool programs for children with special needs. A sample Assessment Log for charting a child's progress is also included.

The Assessment Log and Developmental Progress Chart for The Carolina Curriculum for Preschoolers with Special Needs is a 28-page companion to the preschool curriculum; this form provides an efficient graphic system for charting individual preschool programs. Because the system is so easy to use, it encourages data collection of a child's performance on more that 400 discrete skills in the 25 developmental subdomains that are assessed. The log includes spaces for recording a child's performance on four occasions to demonstrate progress over time.

In 1995, the Assessment Log and Developmental Progress Charts for The Carolina Curriculum (CCITSN and CCPSN, 12 months to 3 years) was added. This log is a convenient, time-saving assessment log that permits charting the progress of children with skills in the 12-month to 36-month developmental range. The log straddles the age ranges of the two curricula and allows for evaluation of those skills that fall between the infant and preschool curricula, thereby assisting professionals in planning a toddler's transition to preschool placements.

These curricula and their accompanying materials are excellent choices and are especially helpful for children with more intense needs.

Sample from The Carolina Curriculum for Infants and Toddlers with Special Needs, Second Edition (CCITSN)

Using the Curriculum

Name: _____ Week: _____
Location: _____

Situation for activities	Opportunity to observe					Mastered (date)
	M	T	W	Th	F	
Child on back (e.g., diapering, playing) Visually tracks in circle						
Turns head to search for sound						
Feet in air for play						
Child on back or sitting supported Glance from toy to toy when one in each hand						
Plays with toys placed in hand(s)						
Places both hands on toy at midline						
Looks or reaches for ojbect that touches body out of sight						
Reacts to tactile stimulation with movement						
Repeats activities that get interesting results						
Social interactions, including meals Anticipates frequently occurring events in familiar games						
Responds differently to stranger and family members						
Laughs						
Repeats sounds when imitated						
Turns to name being called						
Repeats vocalizations that get reactions						
Smiles reciprocally						
Mealtime Munches food						
Vocalizes 5 or more consonant-vowel combinations						
Bathing and dressing Holds trunk steady when held at hips						

From Johnson-Martin, N.M., Jens, K.G., Attermeier, S.M., & Hacker, B.J. (1991). *The Carolina curriculum for infants and toddlers with special needs* (2nd ed.), p. 43. Baltimore: Paul H. Brookes Publishing Co.; reprinted by permission.

Sample from The Carolina Curriculum for Preschoolers with Special Needs (CCPSN)

Age (Years)	Curriculum Sequences	Date: ___	Date: ___	Date: ___	Date: ___
	19-I. Visual-Motor Skills: Pencil control and copying				
	a. Makes a crayon rubbing				
	b. Imitates vertical stroke				
(2.5)	c. Imitates horizontal stroke				
(3)	d. Copies a circle with a circular scribble				
	e. Copies a circle				
(3.5)	f. Copies a cross				
	g. Traces a 6″ × ¼″ line with no more than one deviation				
(4)	h. Holds marker with fingers in tripod position				
(4.5)	i. Copies a square				
	j. Traces outline of simple stencil				
(5)	k. Copies asterisk (*)				
	19-II. Visual-Motor Skills: Representational drawing				
(3.5)	a. Draws a person with a head and 1 feature				
(4)	b. Draws a person with a head and 4 features				
	c. Draws simple pictures of things seen or imagined				
(4.5)	d. Draws a person with a head and 6 features				
(5)	e. Draws a person with a head and 8 features				
	19-III. Visual-Motor Skills: Cutting				
	a. Snips with scissors				
(3)	b. Makes continuous cut across paper				
(3.5)	c. Cuts straight line, staying within ½″ of guideline				
(4)	d. Cuts a 5″ circle (at least three-fourths of the circle)				
(4.5)	e. Cuts a 5″ square				
(5)	f. Cuts out pictures following general shape				
	20-I. Locomotion: Walking				
	a. Walks backward 10 feet				
(2.5)	b. Walks on all types of surfaces, rarely falling				
(3)	c. Uses heel-toe walking pattern, arms swinging at side or free to carry objects				

From Johnson-Martin, N.M., Attermeier, S.M., & Hacker, B.J. (1990). *The Carolina curriculum for preschoolers with special needs,* p. 59. Baltimore: Paul H. Brookes Publishing Co.; reprinted by permission.

Visual-Motor Skills: Representational drawing

AREA: 19-II. Visual-Motor Skills: Representational drawing
BEHAVIOR: 19-IIc. Draws simple pictures of things seen or imagined

Materials: Paper, crayons, markers, pencils

Procedure	Group activities
Ask the child to draw a picture. If he or scribbles or makes little response, suggest something that he or she might draw, particularly something you know in which he or she is interested. Often it is helpful to suggest and demonstrate easy to draw pictures (e.g., rainbow, car, house, flower). Draw a very simple picture and ask the child to make one like yours. The goal is not that the child reproduce yours exactly, but rather to give him or her some ideas on how to draw simple objects; a foundation upon which he or she can expand. When the child does draw spontaneous pictures, ask him or her to tell you about the picture.	1. Ask the children to draw pictures related to a topic being explored that week or to a favorite story. 2. Have the children use a flannel board to construct a scene.

Criterion: The child draws simple pictures of things he or she has seen or imagined.

AREA: 19-II. Visual-Motor Skills: Representational drawing
BEHAVIOR: 19-IId. Draws a person with a head and 6 features

Materials: Paper, pencil (or markers or crayons)

Procedure	Group activities
Ask the child to draw a picture of him- or herself. This item expands on the skills demonstrated in item 19-IIb. Try having the child look in a mirror (preferably full length). Encourage the child to add a body to his or her picture, if he or she has not done this already. Show the child how arms and legs are attached to the body. Ask him or her what else is on the body that is not part of his or her picture. Draw a simple drawing of a person on a separate piece of paper as an example. On a different occasion, ask the child to draw a picture of him- or herself, without providing any cues initially. If he or she has limited success, repeat the teaching procedure.	1. Make body tracings of children by having them lie on a large piece of paper while you trace around them. Then, have the children fill in the details by looking in a mirror for clues. 2. Draw incomplete pictures of a person for the children to complete by adding the missing body parts.

Criterion: The child draws a head and 6 other features when asked to draw a picture of him- or herself.

From Johnson-Martin, N.M., Attermeier, S.M., & Hacker, B.J. (1990). *The Carolina curriculum for preschoolers with special needs*, p. 283. Baltimore: Paul H. Brookes Publishing Co.; reprinted by permission.

Carolina Record of Individual Behavior (CRIB)

Author(s):	R.J. Simeonsson (research group: Simeonsson, Huntington, Short, & Ware, 1982)
Year:	1985
Publisher:	Author
Address:	School of Education, CIREEH, Peabody Hall 037A, University of North Carolina, Chapel Hill, North Carolina 27514
Phone:	919-966-6634
Cost:	Research participation

Assessment type: Curriculum compatible, judgment based; clinical assessment of subtle response classes that characterize a child's response to the environment; particularly useful for young children with severe disabilities.

Age/focus group: Developmental range, birth to 48 months.

Domains/content: Twenty-two developmental (i.e., object orientation, receptive communication) and behavioral (i.e., reactivity, attention) domains and numerous rhythmic habit patterns (i.e., head bang, hand flap).

Special needs options: Structures observational assessment of children with severe disabilites; based on observation and impressions across people and situations.

Curricular links: Describes dimensions that influence the content, intensity, and organization of treatment; identifies general functional levels within important domains: goal-directed behavior, consolability; attention; and receptive and expressive language.

Authenticity: Relies on accumulated observations and ratings of important developmental and behavioral characteristics in home activities and program activities, both structured and unstructured.

Family involvement: Incorporates parent observations, but scales are difficult and professionally oriented.

Scoring/sample: Likert scale 1–9 (1 = primitive, 9 = advanced; or 5 = normal; 1 and 9 = extremes); 0, 1, and 2 assess severity of rhythmic habit patterns; uses multiple ratings across situations.

Validation: Based on Bayley Infant Behavior Record (Bayley, 1969) and Brazelton Neonatal Behavioral Assessment Scales (Brazelton, 1973); comparative data with norms, curricular instruments, and temperament scales; descriptive norms provided on $N = 600$ by disability group.

Training needed: Familiarity with operational definitions in scales.

Comments:
- *Provides valuable structure to clinical judgment data*
- *Assesses crucial child adaptive processes*
- *Operationalizes hard-to-observe, subtle response classes*
- *Item wording may be difficult for nonprofessionals to understand*

LINK Index			
Authentic	1	2	③
Convergent	1	2	③
Collaborative	1	②	3
Equitable	1	②	3
Sensitive	1	②	3
Congruent	1	2	③
Total Index	☐ +	6 +	9 ÷ 6 = 2.5
Overall quality: high			

3.0, exemplary; 2.5, high; 2.0, acceptable; 1.5, low; 1.0, negligible.

Carolina Record of Individual Behavior (CRIB)

In the search for precision in assessment, professionals are becoming increasingly sterile and test based in their approaches to evaluating children. Professionals often assess children without the benefit of an underlying conceptual framework to guide their observations and, as a result, tend to put their often valuable clinical judgments and expertise on hold. The Carolina Record of Individual Behavior (CRIB) offers a framework that enables observers to record their clinical impressions about a child's behavior in structured and naturalistic contexts. Its expanded content is based on the Bayley Infant Behavior Record (Bayley, 1969).

Focusing on the preschooler with severe disabilities who functions in the birth to 3-year age range, the CRIB provides an effective method of describing a child's developmental and behavioral competencies in noncategorical terms. It uses a 9-point rating scale to appraise such subtle response classes as motivation, reactivity, endurance, body tone/tension, attention, social orientation, and consolability. In addition, the CRIB enables the clinician to rate the severity of various stereotypies, such as head banging, hand flapping, body rocking, rumination, and tongue thrusting. The CRIB describes the child's characteristics in such a way that intervention programs that tailor the level of intensity of stimulation and the organization of the environment to the child's capacity to adjust to and benefit from the program can be developed. The CRIB can be a valuable addition to any prescriptive assessment battery. Descriptive norms on approximately 600 preschoolers with severe impairments generate a basis for individual comparisons. Because its wording is sometimes difficult, the CRIB is judged to be used more effectively by professionals than by parents or assistants. The CRIB represents an important and creative advance in alternative forms of assessment that are adaptive to each child's needs and, therefore, are disability sensitive.

Sample from the Carolina Record of Individual Behavior (CRIB)

Object Orientation

A7   Responsiveness to objects, toys or test materials: Score behavior which is spontaneous rather than in direct response to demonstration or elicitation. (Circle One)
1   Does not look at, show interest and/or seem aware of objects.
2   Looks at and/or turns toward only if object attracts attention (e.g., makes noise, flashes light, etc.) (high stimulus items only).
3   When presented with materials, turns to or looks at briefly but does not attempt to approach, reach for, or manipulate any object.
4   Sustained interest in objects as they are presented (e.g., turns to, looks at, smiles at, etc.).
5   Does attempt to approach or manipulate objects: uses in same manner regardless of form or function (e.g., bangs all objects, mouths all objects).
6   Reaches for and manipulates objects in a variety of exploratory ways—holding, feeling, visual examination, shaking, etc.
7   Manipulates object with some regard to form (e.g., puts block in cup, peers into box, sticks finger in hole, etc.).
8   Manipulates object with appropriate regard to form or function (e.g., rocks doll, pushes car, stacks blocks).
9   Plays imaginatively with materials, uses objects several ways.
X   Not applicable.

Reactivity

B2   The ease with which the child is stimulated to react in general; his sensitivity or excitability; reactivity may be positive or negative. (Circle One)
1   Only responds to physically intrusive and/or aversive stimuli (e.g., sudden change of position, pin prick, ice).
2   Reactive to strong and repeated nonintrusive stimulation (e.g., loud noises, bright lights; does not habituate).
3   Periodic reaction to strong stimulation; habituates rapidly.
4   Some tendency to be underreactive to usual testing stimuli and/or changes in the environment.
5   Shows appropriate awareness to usual testing stimuli and/or changes in environment.
6   Some tendency to be overreactive to changes in environment and/or testing stimuli.
7   Overreactive to changes in immediate environment; alerts, startles.
8   Overreactive to selected stimuli enough to cry and/or withdraw (e.g., noises, lights, people).
9   Very reactive—every little thing causes child to startle, cry, and/or withdraw; reacts quickly.
X   Not applicable.

From Simeonsson, R.J., Huntington, G.S., Short, R.J., & Ware, T. (1982). Carolina Record of Individual Behavior: Characteristics of handicapped infants and children. *Topics in Early Childhood Special Education, 2*(2); reprinted by permission.

Communication and Symbolic Behavior Scales, Normed Edition (CSBS)

Author(s): A.M. Wetherby & B.M. Prizant
Year: 1993
Publisher: Riverside Publishing Co.
Address: 8420 Bryn Mawr Avenue, Chicago, Illinois 60631
Phone: 800-767-8420
Cost: $661.25

Assessment type: Curriculum compatible; norm-referenced standardized assessment for identifying children who are at risk for communication impairment and for establishing a profile of and monitoring changes in a child's communicative, social-affective, and symbolic functioning.

Age/focus group: Children with chronological ages between 9 months and 6 years and functional communication ages between 9 months and 2 years.

Domains/content: Eighteen scales that measure aspects of communicative behavior (including joint attention, conventional gestures, syllables with consonants, inventory of words, rate, and gaze shifts) and four scales that measure symbolic development (including comprehension, inventory of action schemes, complexity of action schemes, and constructive play).

Special needs options: Superb focus on reciprocal communication regardless of mode.

Curricular links: Clear links to developmental curricula; provides the "missing" feature (i.e., pragmatic social communication) to the traditional receptive-expressive dichotomy.

Authenticity: This curriculum focuses on natural observations and videotaping of representative behavior in natural settings to profile true usable communication skills.

Family involvement: Integrates both parent and professional observations.

Scoring/sample: Behaviors rated according to twenty-two 5-point scales; scoring includes raw, scaled, cluster, percentile rank, and standard scores; determinations of language stages include prelinguistic, early one word, late one word, and multiword. Normative data on typical and atypical groups.

Training needed: Background in early communication skills and expertise in naturalistic observations of natural play behavior.

Validation: Supported by field-validation and psychometric studies.

Comments:
- *Arguably the best measure of early language*
- *Strong implications for treatment and intervention planning for reciprocal communication skills*
- *Extends the limited range of most developmental curricula in the language domain*
- *Strong authentic features*

LINK Index			
Authentic	1	2	③
Convergent	1	2	③
Collaborative	1	②	3
Equitable	1	2	③
Sensitive	1	2	③
Congruent	1	2	③
Total Index	☐ +	2 +	15 ÷ 6 = 2.8
Overall quality: high to exemplary			

3.0, exemplary; 2.5, high; 2.0, acceptable; 1.5, low; 1.0, negligible.

Communication and Symbolic Behavior Scales (CSBS)

One of the most difficult but pressing needs in early intervention is the authentic assessment of pragmatic communication competencies in infants, toddlers, and preschoolers with special needs. Most language assessment instruments rely on appraisals of the presence or absence of landmark speech and language skills that are age related (e.g., puts together two words, follows a simple direction). What is missing from such appraisals is an assessment of the extent to which a young child uses various forms of communication (e.g., gestures, facial expressions, signs) to communicate needs to adults and peers in everyday social situations. The link between social and language skills is intimate in observations of pragmatic communication skills. Communication and Symbolic Behavior Scales (CSBS) (Wetherby & Prizant, 1990) is one of the most useful, but little-known, scales in early intervention and is appropriate for young children between the developmental ages of 9 months and 2 years or between the chronological ages of 9 months and 6 years. We regard CSBS as an ecological assessment instrument for authentic communication skills. CSBS is a technologically sophisticated scale that relies on convergent information derived from parent interviews, direct observations of natural play routines, and videotaped excerpts. CSBS ratings are recorded on twenty-two 5-point rating scales that survey various domains: communicative functions, gestural and vocal communicative means, reciprocity, social/affective signaling, and verbal and nonverbal symbolic behaviors. The scales rely on the use of a child's own toys as well as certain strategic, standardized toys that invite response-contingent or action-oriented play behaviors from the child. In addition to its ecological basis, CSBS is compatible with most developmental curricula and enables interventionists to identify the degree of a child's impairment, plan IFSPs, and monitor progress and program impact. We regard CSBS as an exemplar of the type of authentic communication assessment devices that should be designed for use in early intervention programs.

COMMUNICATION AND SYMBOLIC BEHAVIOR SCALES

■ COMMUNICATION SCALES

COMMUNICATIVE FUNCTION

1. Range of Communicative Functions
Variety of behavioral regulation, social interaction, and joint attention

1	2	3	4	5
absence of differentiated functions		1 function in each major category		at least 6 functions in 3 major categories

2. Proportion of Functions
Behavioral regulation

1	2	3	4	5
no behavioral regulation acts		4-9 behavioral regulation acts		at least 15 behavioral regulation acts

3. Proportion of Functions
Joint attention

1	2	3	4	5
no joint attention acts		4-9 joint attention acts		at least 15 joint attention acts

COMMUNICATIVE MEANS

4. Gestural Means
Variety of conventional gestures

1	2	3	4	5
no conventional gestures		3 different conventional gestures		at least 5 different conventional gestures

5. Gestural Means
Distal hand gestures

1	2	3	4	5
no distal gestures		4-6 distal gestures		at least 10 distal gestures

6. Gestural and Vocal Means
Coordination of gestures and vocalizations

1	2	3	4	5
no coordinated gest. + voc. acts		4-9 coordinated gest. + voc. acts		at least 15 coordinated gest. + voc. acts

7. Vocal Means
Isolated vocal acts

1	2	3	4	5
no isolated acts		4-9 isolated acts		at least 15 isolated acts

8. Vocal Means
Inventory of consonants

1	2	3	4	5
no consonants		4-6 different consonants		at least 10 different consonants

9. Vocal Means
Syllable shape

1	2	3	4	5
no consonants		4-9 syllables with a consonant		at least 15 syllables with a consonant

10. Vocal Means
Multisyllables

1	2	3	4	5
no multisyllables		4-9 multisyllables		at least 15 multisyllables

From Wetherby, A.M., & Prizant, B.M. (1993). *Communication and Symbolic Behavior Scales* (Normed ed.), p. 3. Chicago: Riverside Publishing Co.; reprinted by permission.

Creative Curriculum for Early Childhood, Third Edition

Author(s):	D.T. Dodge & L. Colker
Year:	1992
Publisher:	Teaching Strategies
Address:	Post Office Box 42243, Washington, D.C. 20015
Phone:	202-362-7543
Cost:	$40

Assessment type: Curriculum embedded.

Age/focus group: Designed for preschool and kindergarten students; to be used in a center-based program.

Scale(s): Child Development and Learning Checklist.

Data system: Child Development and Learning Checklist is provided for ongoing assessment.

Domains/content: Social-emotional, cognitive, and physical development.

Special needs options: Numerous techniques are offered to accommodate special needs.

Authenticity: This curriculum focuses on carefully organized circumstances that provide a foundation for daily environmental interactions.

Family involvement: Suggestions for parent involvement and interactions, as well as activities for home use, are provided.

Training needed: Knowledge of child development and the early childhood education setting is helpful.

Validation: Curriculum has been implemented in a range of early childhood programs and public schools across the United States, Canada, and Australia.

Comments:

- *Promotes functional play*
- *Provides ongoing assessment*
- *Stresses individualized objectives and activities*
- *No specific suggestions for inclusion of children with special needs, although individualization can accommodate some needs*
- *Ten modules for learning centers*
- *Excellent basis for center-based program*

🐴 📖 ∞

LINK Index			
Authentic	1	2	③
Convergent	1	2	③
Collaborative	1	②	3
Equitable	1	②	3
Sensitive	1	②	3
Congruent	1	2	③
Total Index	☐ +	6 +	9 ÷ 6 = 2.5
Overall quality: high			

3.0, exemplary; 2.5, high; 2.0, acceptable; 1.5, low; 1.0, negligible.

Creative Curriculum for Early Childhood,
Third Edition

The Creative Curriculum for Early Childhood (3rd ed.) is an impressive package that celebrates and promotes the natural curiosity, playfulness, and energy of young children. The curriculum is built on activity or interest areas that promote learning across the major developmental domains. Interest areas include areas for blocks, house, table toys, art, sand and water, library, music and movement, cooking, computers, and outdoors. Teachers are encouraged to design plans to promote each child's social-emotional, cognitive, and physical development based on that child's individual strengths and interests. The manual explains how to use screening and assessment to determine a child's developmental status, in particular, with respect to the curriculum's goals and objectives.

Developmental status and curricular progress can be assessed by using the Development and Learning Checklist as well as by examining portfolios. The checklist reflects curricular goals and does not contain highly specific objectives. The goals are meaningful and high in authenticity and social validity. Parents can easily use the checklist and offer convergent, collaborative information.

A separate section of the curriculum manual includes a discussion on the inclusion of children with special needs. Guidelines that encourage teachers to provide a developmentally appropriate program for all children and to seek help from specialists or use special teaching techniques and materials when needed are included. Emphases on child-initiated activity and play are high priorities for professionals who advocate developmentally appropriate practices; these emphases, which may be problematic to "old guard" special educators, need not be obstacles to the use of the curriculum. The guidelines for inclusion of children with special needs stress techniques such as praise, task analysis, and environmental alterations. Furthermore, there is a strong focus on the design of the environment, observation of child activities, and changes in materials and settings to promote learning: All of these program features are hallmarks of good special education.

The third edition of the Creative Curriculum for Early Childhood would be a wise choice for use with most children and a good choice for programs that include children with mild delays. When children with more significant delays or special needs are included, the Creative Curriculum would be a good companion to other, more detailed, disability-specific curriculum systems.

Sample from the Creative Curriculum for Early Childhood, Third Edition

The *Creative Curriculum*® Child Development and Learning Checklist

Observation #1   Observation #2

Child's Name _____

Date of Birth _____

Date completed _____

Child's age when completed _____

Observer's signature _____

Socio-Emotional Development

SELF-ESTEEM

	Obs. #	Not yet	Some-times	Regu-larly	Comments
Identifies self as a boy or girl, and a member of a specific family and cultural group Examples: Refers to self by names and as a girl or boy Talks about family members Draws picture of self, family members	1	☐	☐	☐	
	2	☐	☐	☐	
Shows pride in heritage and background Examples: Talks about a family holiday Shares songs and traditions from cultural group Shares recipe, shows how to eat a special food	1	☐	☐	☐	
	2	☐	☐	☐	
Demonstrates confidence in growing abilities Examples: Shows pleasure (smiles, claps) in practicing new skills Brings attention to what he/she has done (drawing, building, printout, completed puzzle) Comments on accomplishments and skills ("I did it all by myself")	1	☐	☐	☐	
	2	☐	☐	☐	
Demonstrates increasing independence Examples: Chooses and returns table toys independently Washes hands without assistance Climbs a stepladder or slides down slide unassisted Selects a tape and operates tape recorder independently	1	☐	☐	☐	
	2	☐	☐	☐	
Stands up for rights Examples: States that "it's my turn" when appropriate Tells peer not to knock down his/her block structure Defends self when challenged	1	☐	☐	☐	
	2	☐	☐	☐	

From Dodge, D.T., & Colker, L. (1992). *Creative Curriculum for Early Childhood* (3rd ed.), p. 21. Washington, DC: Teaching Strategies; reprinted by permission.

SETTING THE STAGE

What Teachers Can Do to Promote Children's Self-Discipline

To develop self-discipline, children need to be offered choices and opportunities to make decisions, knowing what the logical consequences will be. Teachers must clearly state in advance the choices and the consequences. For example, you might say, "Sanchez, if you keep knocking down Tyler's blocks, you will have to leave the block area. You can make your own buildings and knock them down if you want. Or you can find something else to do." This type of guidance helps a child develop self-discipline because it sets limits and offers a choice. It results in less anger and fewer power struggles than does punishment.

You can use a variety of approaches to guide children's behavior. No one approach works for every child or every situation. The approach used should be based on your knowledge of the child and the particular problem. Positive guidance approaches include the following:

- *Anticipate and plan ahead* so that you can head off problems. "This new table toy is going to be very popular. I'd better set up a system for taking turns before I introduce it."

- *Look for reasons why a child is misbehaving.* Discuss the situation with a colleague. "Tyesha's mother is in the hospital. She is probably worried about her."

- *Focus on the child's behavior,* not the child's value as a person. "I like the way you wiped the table, Marguerite" (rather than "you're a good girl for wiping the table").

- *Help children understand the consequences of their actions.* "Shantaye and Annie, the doll broke when you were both pulling its arms. You will have to wait until it's fixed before you can play with it again."

- *Explain the choices available.* "If you want to drive your truck, Susan, you must drive on the rug, not under the easels."

- *Help children use problem-solving skills* to develop solutions. "I can see it is hard for you to share your bear, Carlos. Where can you put it until you go home?"

- *Help children refrain from dwelling on mistakes* so that they learn to move on. "Your paint cup spilled. Let's go find a sponge to clean up."

- *Watch for restlessness.* Give children room to release their energies and frustrations physically. "Kathy, you seem fidgety this afternoon. Why don't you and Leroy try out the climber for a little while? I'll watch you climb."

From Dodge, D.T., & Colker, L. (1992). *Creative Curriculum for Early Childhood* (3rd ed.), p. 22. Washington, DC: Teaching Strategies; reprinted by permission.

ACCOMMODATING CHILDREN WITH DISABILITIES

Language Delay	Expand on what child says; talk about what you are doing; model the correct usage and pronunciation instead of correcting. Provide frequent visual or concrete reinforcement. Keep directions simple; encourage child to repeat them for reinforcement. Explain new concepts or vocabulary.
Attention problems	Start with short group sessions and activities. Provide visual clues (e.g., define floor space with tape). Offer a limited number of choices. Provide positive reinforcement for sustained attention. Help child quiet down after vigorous play. Plan for transition times, including arrival and departure.
Developmental delays and learning disabilities	Allow for extra demonstrations and practice sessions. Keep all directions simple, sequenced, and organized. Offer extra help in developing fine and gross motor skills, if needed.
Emotional/social problems	Provide extra structure by limiting toys and defining physical space for activities. Allow shy child to observe group activities until ready to participate. Help aggressive child control behavior through consistent enforcement of rules. Observe dramatic play for important clues about feelings and concerns. Help child learn how to express feelings in appropriate ways.
Mental retardation	Establish realistic goals for each child. Provide frequent positive feedback. Sequence learning activities into small steps. Allow adequate time for performance and learning. Encourage cooperative play and help the child move from independent to parallel to group interaction.
Impaired hearing	Obtain child's attention when speaking; seat child close to voice or music. Repeat, rephrase as needed; alert other children to use same technique. Learn some sign language and teach signing to the entire class. Provide visual clues (e.g., pictures or . . — . . — to represent rhythm). Demonstrate new activities or tasks.
Impaired vision	Ensure child's safety at all times without being overprotective. Provide verbal clues for activities. Introduce child to equipment and space verbally and through touch. Use a "buddy" system.
Physical disability or poor coordination	*Accessibility* Organize physical space to accommodate child in wheelchair. Use tables that accommodate wheelchairs or provide trays on wheelchairs. Use bolsters or other supports for floor activities. Provide adaptive equipment for standing. Learn about the availability of assistive technology and devices. *Manual dexterity* Use magnetic toys to facilitate small muscle activities. Attach bells to wrist or ankles for musical activities. Use adaptive scissors or spoons as needed.

From Dodge, D.T., & Colker, L. (1992). *Creative Curriculum for Early Childhood* (3rd ed.), p. 23. Washington, DC: Teaching Strategies; reprinted by permission.

Developmental Communication Curriculum (DCC)

Author(s):	R.P. Hanna, E.A. Lippert, & A.B. Harris
Year:	1982
Publisher:	The Psychological Corporation
Address:	555 Academic Court, San Antonio, Texas 78204-2498
Phone:	800-228-0752, extension 5780
Cost:	$139 for kit (Curriculum Guide, Activity Handbook, 12 copies of the DCC Inventory, and 12 issues of the Parent Newsletter)

Assessment type: Curriculum embedded.

Age/focus group: Designed for children between the developmental ages of 12 months and 5 years. It can be used individually in home-based or center-based programs; designed specifically for children with communication delays and with hearing needs.

Scale(s) Developmental Communication Curriculum Placement Profile and Probe Data Record.

Data system: The Curriculum Guide contains probes that provide a means to monitor, organize, and record progress objectively.

Domains/content: Communication skills taught in the context of play, with related cognitive and social skills taught concurrently.

Special needs options: Flexibility and adaptation of activities are promoted to address children who are deaf or who have hearing impairments or clear language delays.

Authenticity: Clear emphasis on skills or activities that are useful and worthwhile in natural settings.

Family involvement: Parent News offers description of communication development that is designed to promote regular exchange of information between the parents and teachers.

Training needed: Can be used by special education teachers, speech-language pathologists, hearing therapists, preschool and primary teachers, and/or child developmental specialists who are familiar with speech-language development.

Validation: No formal field data provided concerning program efficacy; numerous professionals, however, report using these materials, especially with children with marked communication difficulties.

Comments:
- *Integrates language, cognitive, and social goals (no relay motor objectives)*
- *Organized by functional categories rather than by typical milestones*
- *Makes use of augmentative communication*
- *Uses pragmatic language approach*

LINK Index			
Authentic	1	②	3
Convergent	1	2	③
Collaborative	1	②	3
Equitable	1	2	③
Sensitive	1	②	3
Congruent	1	2	③
Total Index	☐ +	6 +	9 ÷ 6 = 2.5
Overall quality: high			

3.0, exemplary; 2.5, high; 2.0, acceptable; 1.5, low; 1.0, negligible.

Developmental Communication Curriculum (DCC)

The Developmental Communication Curriculum covers four chronologically ordered stages: birth to 12 months (prelinguistic relations); 9–21 months (symbolic relations); 18–36 months (symbolic relations); and older than 30 months (complex symbolic relations). Within each stage, the concept of communication is viewed from within three domains: function, form, and content; these serve to analyze communication in behavioral terms. The DCC seems especially well-suited for use with children with marked language delays and/or hearing impairments. Communication development is used as the cornerstone for, and is interrelated with, cognitive and social development; motor skills, however, are not really addressed.

The DCC includes a Placement Profile that allows behavioral objectives to be formulated and implemented. The DCC also has an activity handbook that contains more than 300 activities to encourage and stimulate language growth; flexibility and adaptation of activities are promoted. A range of activities are included for both individual and group participation. The authors also present 46 probes, with a general scheduling guideline that depends on student contact time. The probes are linked with objectives in the curriculum.

Additional features addressed in the DCC include 1) parent programs, 2) choosing an augmentative expressive system, 3) working with physical disabilities, 4) staff development and training, and 5) administration concerns.

ACTIVITY 187

Object Permanence Activity Set

MATERIALS   Series of small toys such as tiny babydoll, ball, miniature animal, etc., and set of 3 covers to obscure objects from view, e.g., pillows, blankets, small empty boxes, pieces of cardboard, etc.

PROCEDURE A

Engage child's interest in a series of toys, one at a time. Line up the little toys and partially cover some of them with a sheet or blanket. Say, "Where's the _____ ? Show me." This game can extend to people as well. Play a version of hide and seek using a sheet or blanket to cover one child in the group. Say, "Where's _____ ? Let's go find him/her." Help child uncover the child who is hidden.

PROCEDURE B

Show child a toy and then slip it completely under a pillow or other covering. Ask child, "Where's the _____ ." Encourage the child to search for the object.

PROCEDURE C

Place two coverings, such as empty small boxes, on a table between you and the child. Show child a toy and then place it under one of the two covers. Say, "Where's the _____ ?" and encourage the child to search.

*This activity is based on object permanence norms published by Cohen, A.M. and Gross, P.J., *The Developmental Resource: Behavioral Sequences for Assessment and Planning*, Vol 1 (New York: Grune & Stratton, 1979), pp. 81–91.

Administrator _____

Caretaker _____

PART TWO

Teacher/Caretaker Interview

Begin by explaining the following:
"We'd like to try to get a complete picture of (Name)'s communication. We can observe him/her here, but we need your help to fill us in on how he/she is doing at home and elsewhere. So I'll be asking you a lot of questions during this time together. Some may seem pretty simple and others may be harder for you to pinpoint. But you're in the best position to really know (Name) so whatever you can tell us will be of real value."

Stage I

		ans	comments
1.I	The first question deals with sensation. By this we mean hearing, feeling, seeing, smelling, and tasting. Does your child respond to or participate in some of these sensory experiences? e.g., attend to bright color or lights, play with texture such as play dough, allow touch.		
2.	Can you tell what mood your child is in? How?		
2.I	Expresses broad emotional ranges.		
2.II	Uses face and body together to show feelings, e.g., smiling and wriggling to show happy or excited; contorted features and tense body to show anger.		
2.III	Expresses mood variety. Labels moods.		
2.IV	Expresses subtle changes in attitude, e.g., word choice, rhythm, prosody, expression, etc.		
3.I	Does your child make any sounds?		
4.I	Does your child say consonant-vowel sounds like "ba-ba," "da-da," etc.?		
5.	Does your child look on command?		
5.I	Looks at you.		
5.II	Looks at what you designate by pointing or looking.		

13

Developmental Observation Checklist System (DOCS)

Author(s):   W.P. Hresko, S.A. Miguel, R.J. Sherbenou, & S.D. Burton
Year: 1994
Publisher: PRO-ED
Address: 8700 Shoal Creek Boulevard, Austin, Texas 78757
Phone: 512-451-3246
Cost: $80

Assessment type: Curriculum compatible; hybrid, standardized, norm-referenced screening device for identification of potential developmental delays and recommendation for early intervention.

Age/focus group: Children ages birth to 6 years, whose dominant language is English and who reside in the United States.

Domains/content: Three components: Developmental Checklist (DC), Adjustment Behavior Checklist (ABC), and Parental Stress and Support Checklist (PSSC); DC is divided into four domains: language, social, motor, and cognition. Areas measured include language, social ability, parental stress, parental support, fine and gross motor skills, child adaptability, cognitive, overall development, play skills, parent–child interaction, and environmental impact.

Special needs options: The inclusion of real-life tasks observed in everyday settings with flexible exemplars of acceptable performance is a strong adaptive feature.

Curricular links: Sequences and clusters of skills cross-referenced across domains fit with most of the major curricula.

Authenticity: Emphasizes many naturally occurring tasks (e.g., "recognizes the McDonald's sign") in natural settings.

Family involvement: Relies on parent response and observations about the child and family.

Scoring/sample: Provides raw scores, percentile ranks, standard scores, component quotients, normal curve equivalents, and age equivalents.

Validation: Standardized on 1,094 children residing in 30 states, from November 1989 to December 1992.

Training needed: "Basic understanding of tests and testing statistics; knowledge of general procedures governing test administration, scoring, and interpretation; and specific information about developmental evaluation" (p. 10).

Comments:
- *One of the first of the emergent, curriculum-compatible, authentic developmental assessment measures*
- *Excellent interdomain format operationalizes development as interactive*
- *Three-part battery on same norm base links developmental, behavioral, and family status*
- *Welcome focus on parent observations with professional collaboration*
- *Serves several interrelated early intervention assessment purposes*
- *The lack of a computer scoring disk to aid data analysis and reporting for individual children and classroom groups is a weakness*

LINK Index			
Authentic	1	2	③
Convergent	1	2	③
Collaborative	1	2	③
Equitable	1	②	3
Sensitive	1	2	③
Congruent	1	②	3
Total Index	☐ +	4 +	12 ÷ 6 = 2.7
Overall quality: high			

3.0, exemplary; 2.5, high; 2.0, acceptable; 1.5, low; 1.0, negligible.

Developmental Observation Checklist System (DOCS)

The Developmental Observation Checklist System (DOCS) is one of the most unique developmental assessment systems for the early childhood period produced by a commercial publisher. The DOCS is a three-part system that strives to examine and profile the transactional nature between a child's development and behavior and his or her family's coping ability and stress.

Within the early intervention field, the DOCS is one of the first breaks with the contrived developmental content common to most traditional norm-based developmental scales: DOCS represents one of the first attempts to infuse authentic or naturally occurring developmental skills as content in a developmental measure.

Although it is promoted primarily as a screening tool, we regard the DOCS as a sophisticated and relatively comprehensive instrument for observing and recording functional skills in natural settings. The format of the measure recognizes the interactive nature of early development and cross-references the recording and scoring of each of 475 developmental skills across four functional domains (i.e., motor, social, language, cognitive). Moreover, the DOCS is compatible with most developmental curricula and effectively combines norm-based, curriculum-compatible, and observational qualities.

Early interventionists will find that the three parts of the DOCS will aid in the design of full IFSP goals. We support the use of the DOCS for several purposes: eligibility determination, ensuring parent input into decision making, general goal setting, and progress monitoring. Our experience with the DOCS shows that it can have a unique role in enabling parents, with professional support, to document the loss of skills or regression overtime when used both retrospectively and prospectively for young children with various degenerative disorders (e.g., Rett syndrome). The DOCS is a strong addition to the category of early childhood measurement tools and an exemplar of the new directions in authentic assessment with a clear curricular focus.

Sample from the Developmental Observation Checklist System (DOCS)

Yes	No		Motor	Social	Language	Cognition
___	___	201. Drinks from a regular cup without help.	___			
___	___	202. Copies (says) unknown words (does not have to be accurate).			___	___
___	___	203. Bends over and looks through legs.	___			
___	___	204. Can identify his or her reflection in a mirror by saying his or her name.		___	___	
___	___	205. Points to one part of the body such as mouth, hands, tummy, or feet, when asked.			___	___
___	___	206. Puts a toy in a specific place when asked to.			___	___
___	___	207. Briefly stands on one foot while holding another person's hand.	___			
___	___	208. Steps over low objects without falling.	___			
___	___	209. Pretends play (examples: uses Kleenex as a blanket for doll, uses block as a truck).		___		
___	___	210. Walks up stairs while holding another person's hand.	___			
___	___	211. Paints or colors using such big arm movements that the drawing sometimes goes off the page.	___			
___	___	212. Practices new words so that gradually he or she becomes easier to understand.			___	
___	___	213. Indicates (points, cries) when diapers are wet or dirty.			___	___
___	___	214. Puts two words together ("want more").			___	
___	___	215. Uses one object to get another object that is out of reach.	___			___
___	___	216. Throws a ball overhand with some degree of accuracy.	___			
___	___	217. Refers to him- or herself by name.		___	___	
___	___	218. Opens containers to get something inside.	___			___
___	___	219. Works at getting objects into narrow-necked containers.	___			___
___	___	220. Points or says name when looking at him- or herself in photographs.			___	___
___	___	221. Fits smaller objects into larger objects (smaller pots into larger pots).	___			___
___	___	222. Participates in and enjoys nursery rhymes and finger plays.		___		
___	___	223. Tries to start a mechanical toy with some success.	___			___
___	___	224. Begins to sort objects.			___	___
___	___	225. Explores cabinets and drawers.			___	___
___	___	226. Matches sounds to animals.			___	___
___	___	227. Plays next to other children but not with them.		___		
___	___	228. Names a few pictures.			___	
___	___	229. Squats down without falling.	___			
___	___	230. Writes on paper or a chalkboard with pencil, crayon, or chalk.	___			
___	___	231. Always uses the names of at least 20 familiar objects.			___	
___	___	232. Enjoys rough-and-tumble play.		___		
___	___	233. Points to at least three to five major body parts (leg, arm, hair, hand, head, or foot).			___	___
___	___	234. Runs, but falls sometimes.	___			
___	___	235. Puts both feet on each step while walking up stairs.	___			

Total for page 8

From Hresko, W., Miguel, S., Sherbenou, R., & Burton, S. (1994). *Developmental Observation Checklist System (DOCS)*, p. 6. Austin, TX: PRO-ED; reprinted by permission.

Developmental Profile II (DP II)

Author(s):	G. Alpern, T. Boll, & M. Shearer
Year:	1980; 1986
Publisher:	Western Psychological Services
Address:	12031 Wilshire Boulevard, Los Angeles, California 90025
Phone:	800-648-8857
Cost:	$90+

Assessment type: Curriculum compatible; judgment-based, norm-based appraisal of a child's developmental capabilities, based on interview of parent/caregiver.

Age/focus group: Children from birth to 9 years.

Domains/content: Five domains: physical, adaptive skills, social, academic, and communication (217 tasks).

Special needs options: Caregiver judgments provide observational data; combined report and observational data can facilitate assessment of children with autism.

Curricular links: Domains and landmark skills are comparable with those typically included in preschool curricula.

Authenticity: Targets behaviors for parent observations referring to "does" or "can do" stems for readily observable skills.

Family involvement: Parent observations are primary.

Scoring/sample: Pass–fail, yes/no scaling; developmental age, developmental quotient, and significant difference cutoffs for impairments; observation, interview/report samples.

Validation: Norms are based on 3,008 children; validity and reliability are adequate for general screening purposes; concurrent validity with Stanford-Binet Intelligence Scale (Terman & Merrill, 1960), Learning Accomplishment Profile (Glover, Preminger, Sanford, & Zelman, 1995), and Infant Psychological Developmental Scale.

Training needed: Thorough reading of the manual, knowledge of child development, and practice and experience interviewing parents.

Comments:
- *Structures caregiver perceptions about developmental skills*
- *Remains the best available early childhood interview scale*
- *"Does" and "can do" question stems for parents are easily understood*
- *Tasks are instructionally relevant and developmentally sequenced*
- *Exceeds the Vineland Adaptive Behavior Scale in clinical usefulness for young exceptional children in terms of family friendliness*

LINK Index

Authentic	1	②	3
Convergent	1	②	3
Collaborative	1	2	③
Equitable	1	②	3
Sensitive	1	②	3
Congruent	1	②	3

Total Index ☐ + ☐10☐ + ☐3☐ ÷ 6 = ☐2.2☐

Overall quality: acceptable

3.0, exemplary; 2.5, high; 2.0, acceptable; 1.5, low; 1.0, negligible.

Developmental Profile II (DP II)

Parent reports of child capabilities are often considered unreliable. Their accuracy depends on many factors, including the clarity of the child skills in question and how the question is asked. Many parents systematically overestimate child capabilities. Parents of children with severe impairments, however, tend to portray their children's status more accurately. For these reasons, tests such as the Developmental Profile II (DP II) are considered indispensable in comprehensive diagnosis.

The DP II is a norm-referenced developmental screening measure that relies on a structured interview with the parents to estimate a child's current level of functioning. The DP II is unique among screening measures in that it is multidimensional, reliable, valid, and well standardized.

The DP II surveys the age range from birth to 12 years and contains 217 developmental tasks ordered within five functional domains: physical, adaptive, social, academic, and communication. The tasks are presented as questions that tap the developing child's level of competence in each area. The DP II is probably the most well-standardized interview screening measure available because it is standardized on 3,008 children.

Scoring is done by circling a zero for a failure or the "month number" opposite an item to indicate a pass. Basal and double-ceiling levels are established, as on other measures, to represent the upper and lower limits of functioning. The total number of items passed determines the developmental age score for each functional domain. Questions are asked in terms of whether the child "does" and "can" perform a particular activity to obtain notions of actual functioning and capability. Scores, which represent functioning, are interpreted in terms of the degree of "developmental lag" between chronological age and current levels of functioning and the discrepancies between developmental levels across the multiple domains. The significance of lags is determined from the norm tables.

The DP II presents certain unique characteristics and is invaluable as part of a larger diagnostic battery. It facilitates the use of parent judgments in formulating interventions and aids in standardizing the diverse perceptions of involved adults who know and serve the child. As an interview measure, it accurately portrays the perceived needs of children with developmental delays and provides a potential basis for counseling and parent training. Finally, it provides a valid and reliable basis for multisource assessment and establishes initial targets for curriculum prescriptions by highlighting perceived capabilities and impairments.

Sample Communication Subscale Questions from the Developmental Profile II (DP II)

Newborn: 0–6 months

1. Does the child use vocal noises for play? The child must PLAY with sounds (not just cry, gurgle, or laugh when something happens).

Infant I: 7–12 months

4. Does the child sometimes imitate spoken "words" such as "da-da" or "ma-ma"? The child may not know what these words mean.

Infant II: 13–18 months

8. Does the child say the names of at least five things (not in imitation and not including names of people)? The words must be said well enough to be understood by a stranger.

Toddler I: 19–24 months

12. Does the child put two or more words together to form sentences? "Me, go," "You give," "Tom want," are all examples of passes. But, if the child ALWAYS uses the same two words together (so that they are really one word to the child), that does not rate a pass.

Toddler II: 25–30 months

13. Does the child either repeat parts of nursery rhymes or join in when others say them?

Developmental Programming for Infants and Young Children (DPIYC): Developmental Programming for Infants and Young Children (0–36 months; Revised Edition)

Author(s): S.J. Rogers, & D.B. D'Eugenio
Year: 1981
Publisher: University of Michigan Press
Address: Post Office Box 1104, Ann Arbor, Michigan 48106
Phone: 313-764-4392
Cost: Volume 1 (*Assessment and Application*), $15; Volume 2 (*EIDP*), $3 (minimum of 5 copies); Volume 3 (*Stimulation Activities*), $16
Note: Volumes 1–3 may be purchased as a set for $30.

Assessment type: Curriculum embedded.

Age/focus group: Designed for children within the developmental age range from birth to 36 months. It can be used individually in a home-based program or in a center-based program.

Scale(s): Early Intervention Developmental Profile (EIDP).

Data system: Forms for recording entries of pass, no pass, and emergent skills and dates to permit progress checks. Format is easy to use.

Domains/content: Perceptual/fine motor, cognition, language, social-emotional, adaptive, and gross motor.

Special needs options: Visual, motor, and hearing.

Authenticity: Although this curriculum includes many authentic objectives, it also includes many tabletop-type test items.

Family involvement: The material contains some jargon (especially in the motor section), but, in general, assessment can include parent input. The stimulation activities are designed for parent use.

Training needed: Professionals train parents; consultation with other professionals is recommended.

Validation: Published reliability and validity data are provided.

Comments

*   *Parents are focus of simulation program*
*   *Adaptations are noted*
*   *Short-term goals, suggested activities, and adaptations are provided in Volume 3*
*   *Designed especially for interdisciplinary teams*

	LINK Index		
Authentic	1	②	3
Convergent	1	2	③
Collaborative	1	2	③
Equitable	1	2	③
Sensitive	1	②	3
Congruent	1	2	③
Total Index	☐ +	4 +	12 ÷ 6 = 2.7
Overall quality: high			

3.0, exemplary; 2.5, high; 2.0, acceptable; 1.5, low; 1.0, negligible.

Developmental Programming for Infants and Young Children (DPIYC): Developmental Programming for Infants and Young Children (3–6 Years)

Author(s):   S. Brown, D. D'Eugenio, J. Drews, S. Haskin, E. Whiteside Lynch, M. Moersch, & S. Rogers

Year: 1981

Publisher: University of Michigan Press

Address: Post Office Box 1104, Ann Arbor, Michigan 48116

Phone: 313-764-4392

Cost: *(Preschool Assessment and Application)*, $20; Volume 5 *(Preschool Development Profile)*, $2 (5 copies)

Assessment type: Curriculum embedded.

Age/focus group: Designed for children within the developmental age range from 3 to 6 years with mild to severe special needs. It can be used individually in a home-based program and in a center-based program.

Scale(s):   Preschool Developmental Profile (PDP).

Data system: Easy-to-read recording forms allow entry of dates for assessment, pass, no pass, and emergent skills.

Domains/content: Perceptual/fine motor, cognition, language, social-emotional, adaptive, and gross motor.

Special needs options: Visual, motor, and hearing.

Authenticity: This curriculum clearly emphasizes skills/activities that are useful and worthwhile in natural settings, although numerous tasks are of the conventional test type.

Family involvement: Professionals offer training and support when needed and monitor progress.

Training needed: Professionals train parents; consultation with other professionals is recommended.

Validation: Published reliability and validity data are provided.

Comments:

- *Parents are the focus of the intervention program*
- *Adaptations are noted*
- *Designed especially for use by interdisciplinary teams*
- *Provides information on linking the assessment to objectives and developing activities beyond those described in the manual*
- *The preschool content is adequate for most assessment purposes but is not as dense as that of the companion volumes for children ages birth to 36 months*

LINK Index			
Authentic	1	②	3
Convergent	1	2	③
Collaborative	1	2	③
Equitable	1	2	③
Sensitive	1	②	3
Congruent	1	2	③
Total Index	☐ +	4 +	12 ÷ 6 = 2.7
Overall quality: high			

3.0, exemplary; 2.5, high; 2.0, acceptable; 1.5, low; 1.0, negligible.

Developmental Programming for Infants and Young Children (DPIYC): DPIYC (0–36 Months; Revised Edition) and DPIYC (3–6 Years)

Developmental Programming for Infants and Young Children (DPIYC) is organized in five volumes. Volumes 1, 2, and 3 contain an assessment, a profile, and intervention activities for infants from birth to 3 years. Volumes 4 and 5 contain an assessment, a profile, and application activities for preschoolers ages 3–6 years. The curriculum content is arranged in a parallel mode with a crossover of specific objectives. The activities are designed for professionals who are training parents and are meant to supplement specific therapies conducted by specialists. Ongoing consultation with other members of a multidisciplinary or transdisciplinary team is essential to the formalization and implementation of an appropriate program for each child. The volumes for children from birth to 3 years were first published in 1977 and were revised when the preschool portion became available in 1981.

Volumes 1 and 4 provide assessment instruments: Early Intervention Developmental Profile (EIDP) and Preschool Developmental Profile (PDP). These instruments are used in conjunction with information from other evaluations to determine a child's strengths and limitations. The program's profiles are used to record the results of the assessment, assist in program planning, and provide a means for summative evaluation. Recording sheets are useful for periodic evaluations of child progress. The recording forms are easy to use and often are used in arena-type situations.

The home is the focus of this program. The activities for infants are designed to increase parents' confidence and to improve parent–child interactions. For preschoolers, the opportunity for socialization with their peers is best served in a center-based program. To ensure that the activities are consistent at home and at the center, a simple chart can be developed, and parents can assist in collecting information and graphing the progress.

This program offers a complete package that links assessment to curriculum. All of the basic elements are provided, which makes the program a useful tool. The curriculum can be used for children with and without special needs, thereby permitting use in inclusive settings. The DPIYC is often the choice of teams when a simpler, easy-to-use assessment is needed to act as a common tool in conjunction with discipline-specific measures. It should be noted that the separate domains (e.g., gross motor, fine motor) were developed by specialists in the various areas and, as such, are acceptable to specialists. Because of some domain specificity, some jargon is used; this jargon may reduce the program's "friendliness" to parents or professionals who are not specialists in a given domain. The infant curricular objectives/assessment items are more dense (i.e., provide greater sensitivity for assessment) than are the preschool materials. In general, the DPIYC materials are thought to be stronger in volumes for children from birth to 36 months, and the program is recommended for use at this level.

Sample from Developmental Programming for Infants and Young Children (DPIYC)

9–11 Months

***Child will cry, fuss, or search when
separated from his parent in a strange environment.***   ***Attachment***

Activities

Take the child with you when you shop, visit friends, eat out. The more social opportunities he has, the better able he will be to get through the attachment-separation period.

Let other people hold the child for short periods or until he fusses.

CAUTION: When the child begins meeting this objective, comfort him by talking to him, holding him, and rocking him. Leaving him with a sitter for short periods may upset him, but he will adjust nicely over time.

Hearing Impaired: *NC*

Motorically Involved: *NC*

Visually Impaired: *NC*

***Child will play pat-a-cake and peek-a-boo
games, giving some appropriate gesture.***   ***Social Play***

Activities

1. Ask the child how big she is. Raise her arms above her head and say, *So big!* Do this several times throughout the day and note whether she begins to help you raise her arms.

2. Play pat-a-cake and peek-a-boo with the child, manipulating her through the actions. Concentrate on a particular gesture such as *clapping* and encourage her to imitate you.

3. Encourage the child to imitate you through the complete pat-a-cake game.

Hearing Impaired: *The child will learn to imitate the gestures even though she may not be able to hear the words.*

Motorically Involved: *NC*

Visually Impaired: *Manipulate the child through all the games many times while saying the words. After several weeks, ask the child if she can play pat-a-cake. If she does not respond, manipulate her through the actions. If she claps, reward her with a hug and praise.*

***Child will repeat actions or
vocalizations when laughed at.***   ***Social Play***

Activities

1. When the child does something funny or cute, laugh at him and ask him to do it again.

2. Repeat the child's vocalizations. When he imitates you, reward him.

Hearing Impaired: *MA*

Motorically Involved: *NC*

Visually Impaired: *NC*

From Rogers, S.J., & D'Eugenio, D.B. (1981). *Developmental Programming for Infants and Young Children (DPIYC): Vol. 2. Early Intervention Developmental Profile (EIDP)*, p. 84, Ann Arbor: University of Michigan Press.

Sample from the Developmental Programming for Infants and Young Children (DPIYC)

NAME _____   **Social/Emotional**

ITEM NUMBER	*DEVELOPMENTAL LEVELS AND ITEMS*	DATE	DATE	DATE	DATE
	0–2 months				
136	Quiets when picked up				
137	Quiets to face or voice				
138	Maintains brief periods of eye contact during feeding				
139	Smiles or vocalizes to talk and touch				
	3–5 months				
140	Watches adult walk across room				
141	Reflects silent adult's smile				
142	Smiles or reaches to familiar people				
143	Smiles or laughs during physical play				
144	Smiles spontaneously				
145	Smiles at image in mirror				
	6–8 months				
146	Prefers to be with people				
147	Laughs and smiles at pat-a-cake and peek-a-boo games				
148	Reaches for image of self in mirror				
149	Explores features of a familiar person				
	9–11 months				
150	Leaves physical contact with familiar person momentarily				
151	Participates in pat-a-cake and peek-a-boo games				
152	Performs for social attention				
153	Offers toy				
	12–15 months				
154	Responds differentially to young children				
155	Gives toy to adult				

Developmental Programming for Infants and Young Children
Volume 2: Early Intervention Developmental Profile

From Rogers, S.J., & D'Eugenio, D.B. (1981). *Developmental Programming for Infants and Young Children (DPIYC): Vol. 2. Early Intervention Developmental Profile (EIDP)*, p. 12. Ann Arbor: University of Michigan Press.

Sample Profile Graph from the Developmental Programming for Infants and Young Children (DPIYC)

TABLE 4. Profile Graph

Name ___ *K.S.* ___ Birth Date *12/26/73*

Evaluation Dates *12/4/78 ; 6/26/79*

Developmental Level in Years	Perceptual/ Fine Motor	Cognition†					Speech and Language	Social Emotional	Self-care	Gross Motor
		C	N	Sp	S	T				
5½–6	35* ↑ 32	44 43		62 61		79 78	110 ↑ 106	140 ↑ 139	157	213 ↑ 204
5–5½	31 ↑ 27	42 41	53		68	77 76	105 ↑ 103	138 ↑ 135	154	203 ↑ 193
4½–5	26 ↑ 22		52 51 50	60	67 (66)	75 (74)	102 ↑ 98	134 ↑ 129	153 (151)	192 ↑ 187
4–4½	21 ↑ 11		(49) 48	59 (58)			(97) ↑ 92	(128) ↑ 120	148	186 ↑ 172
3½–4	10 ↑ 8	(40) (39)	47 38	57 (46)	65 (64)	(73) 72 71 70	91 (89)↑ 87	(119) ↑ 116	147 (145)	171 ↑ (167) 166
3–3½	(7) ↑ (1)	37 36	45	(55) 54	63	69	86 ↑ 80	115 ↑ 111	142F 141F	(164) 165 ↑ 158

*Profile item numbers
†C=Classification
N=Number
Sp=Space
S=Seriation
T=Time
– – – 6/26/79
——— 12/4/78

From Rogers, S.J., & D'Eugenio, D.B. (1981). *Developmental Programming for Infants and Young Children (DPIYC): Vol. 2. Early Intervention Developmental Profile (EIDP),* p. 9. Ann Arbor: University of Michigan Press.

Sample from the Developmental Programming for Infants and Young Children (DPIYC)

Gross Motor

ITEM NUMBER	*DEVELOPMENTAL LEVELS AND ITEMS*	DATE	DATE	DATE	DATE
181	Throws: tennis ball overhand with trunk rotation				
182	Bounces: large playground ball				
183	Kicks: large playground ball with accuracy				
184	Rides: tricycle expertly				
185	Turns: forward somersaults				
186	Imitates: body movements with integration of both sides of body				

$4\frac{1}{2}$–5 years

187	Stands: heel-to-toe				
188	Jumps: backward				
189	Jumps: a stationary rope 4 inches high				
190	Slides: down slide				
191	Swings: self on swing				
192	Body Image: places body in spatial relationships to objects				

5–$5\frac{1}{2}$ years

193	Stands: one foot, without visual feedback				
194	Walks: balance beam forward, backward, and sideward				
195	Runs: 35 yards in 10 seconds				
196	Hops: 15 yards in 10 seconds				
197	Throws: tennis ball with trunk rotation and forward weight shift				
198	Catches: bounced tennis ball with hands				
199	Hits: suspended ball with bat				
200	Skips or Gallops				
201	Marches: keeping time to music				
202	Uses: skates, sled, wagon, or scooter well				
203	Imitates: body movements requiring finer coordination of body parts				

Developmental Programming for Infants and Young Children
Volume 5: Preschool Developmental Profile

From Rogers, S.J., & D'Eugenio, D.B. (1981). *Developmental Programming for Infants and Young Children (DPIYC): Vol. 2. Early Intervention Developmental Profile (EIDP),* p. 12. Ann Arbor: University of Michigan Press.

Early Childhood Environment Rating Scale (ECERS)

Author(s): T. Harms & R.M. Clifford
Year: 1980
Publisher: Teachers College Press
Address: 1234 Amsterdam Avenue, New York, New York 10027
Phone: 212-678-3929
Cost: $30+

Assessment type: Curriculum compatible for programming purposes; ecological; judgment-based observation, rating, and analysis of the features of the preschool classroom that influence a child's adjustment and learning.

Age/focus group: Preschool to kindergarten.

Domains/content: A total of 37 features in seven domains: personal care routines, furnishings and displays, language-reasoning experiences, fine and gross motor activities, creative activities, social development, and adult needs.

Special needs options: Recent revisions include items that are sensitive to the needs, in both integrated and specialized settings, of young children with disabilities.

Curricular links: Scale serves as a criterion-referenced tool to detect factors that require modification to optimize the early childhood classroom setting.

Authenticity: Highly ecological in its focus on program elements and environmental features that are critical to a child's adaptation and success; adaptations for special needs occur in the same format.

Family involvement: Primarily for professional use, although family dimensions are included.

Scoring/sample: A 7-point rating scale (ranging from 1 = inadequate to 7 = excellent) with operational definitions.

Validation: Field use in general, inclusive, and specialized early childhood settings.

Training needed: Knowledge of child development and educational implications; thorough reading and practice with the scale.

Comments:
- *Simple, economical, yet effective*
- *Valuable for evaluating the match between setting and an individual child's needs*
- *Excellent administrative tool to enable programs to "self-evaluate"*
- *Disability revision must be better field-tested and standardized*

LINK Index			
Authentic	1	2	③
Convergent	1	②	3
Collaborative	1	②	3
Equitable	①	2	3
Sensitive	1	②	3
Congruent	1	②	3
Total Index	$\boxed{1}$ +	$\boxed{8}$ +	$\boxed{3}$ ÷ 6 = $\boxed{2.0}$
Overall quality: acceptable			

3.0, exemplary; 2.5, high; 2.0, acceptable; 1.5, low; 1.0, negligible.

Early Childhood Environment Rating Scale (ECERS)

The influence of the preschool environment on child behavior and developmental progress is an area of strong interest and concern. Early Childhood Environment Rating Scale (ECERS) is one of the few instruments that both operationalize features to distinguish adequate and inadequate settings and offer suggestions for rearrangement and improvement of those settings. ECERS is a "curriculum" that addresses effective preschool program design for administrators. ECERS comprises 37 items organized into seven sections: 1) personal care routines, 2) furnishings and display for children, 3) language-reasoning experiences, 4) fine and gross motor activities, 5) creative activities, 6) social development, and 7) adult needs. Through direct observation, administrators can rate these program dimensions to develop a profile of preschool program characteristics. Ratings are based on a 7-point scale. ECERS focuses on both the physical aspects of the preschool environment and teacher–child and child–child interactions.

Although it is typically used in general early childhood settings, ECERS has increasingly been used in preschool special education environments. Research with the scale to evaluate preschool children with disabilities indicates that, on 32% of the items, preschoolers in special education settings were rated much lower than were those in general settings (Bailey, Clifford, & Harms, 1982). A revision of ECERS includes additional items for inclusive preschool programs, and a complementary measure—Family Day Care Rating Scale (Harms & Clifford, 1989)—addresses the best characteristics for home child care programs.

ECERS fulfills a pressing need in a relatively uncharted early intervention area. Whereas most environmental observation systems are cumbersome and time consuming for data collection, ECERS uses a simple procedure to focus on important factors that influence the child's adjustment and learning. With the trend toward integration into more general settings, early interventionists must address these program design issues that influence the success of treatment of young children with disabilities.

GREETING / DEPARTURE

ITEM		PERSONAL CARE ROUTINES
Inadequate	1	No plans made. Greeting children is often neglected; departure not prepared for.
	2	●
Minimal	3	Informally understood that someone will greet and acknowledge departure.
	4	●
Good	5	Plans made to insure warm greeting and organized departure. Staff member(s) assigned responsibility for greeting and departure of children. (Ex. Conversation on arrival; art work and clothes ready for departure).
	6	●
Excellent	7	Everything in 5 (*Good*) plus parents greeted as well as children. Staff use greeting and departure as information sharing time to relate warmly to parents.

Early Coping Inventory (ECI)

Author(s):	S. Zeitlin, G. Williamson, & M. Szczepanski
Year:	1988
Publisher:	Scholastic Testing Service
Address:	480 Meyer Road, Bensenville, Illinois 60106
Phone:	800-642-6787
Cost:	$40+

Assessment type: Curriculum compatible; judgment based; observation and rating of the young child's capability to respond to, adapt, and control the environment.

Age/focus group: 4–36 months.

Domains/content: Three coping clusters: sensorimotor organization, reactive behaviors, and self-initiated behaviors; multiple ratings across situations.

Special needs options: Functional ratings focus on competence in coping with the environment and compensating for sensorimotor impairments.

Curricular links: Ratings highlight specific coping strategies used by a given child; these ratings are arranged hierarchically by maturity level and, thus, guide the planning of goals and environmental arrangements.

Authenticity: Observation of natural adaptive coping behaviors of children with special needs in everyday settings and activities and ways to improve coping, self-efficacy, and resilience are stressed.

Scoring/sample: Adaptive behavior index, coping effectiveness scores, and coping profile are based on conversion tables that rely on a 1- to 5-point Likert rating scale, with 1 as low (not effective) and 5 as high (consistently effective across situations).

Validation: Based on coping theory research studies with infants and the transactional model; field-test data on 1,040 infants and toddlers with disabilities and 227 infants/toddlers without disabilities in early intervention and child care settings.

Training needed: Thorough knowledge of infant development and practice in reading manual and using scale; appropriate for use by assistants.

Comments:
- *Unique clinical judgment scale*
- *Specialized focus on coping competencies*
- *"Task analysis" of coping patterns*
- *Clear functional interpretation*
- *Derived scores lack normative meaning*
- *Should be interpreted and used only by multiple assessors*

LINK Index			
Authentic	①	2	③
Convergent	1	②	3
Collaborative	1	②	3
Equitable	1	2	③
Sensitive	1	2	3
Congruent	1	2	③
Total Index	1 +	4 +	9 ÷ 6 = 2.3
Overall quality: acceptable			

3.0, exemplary; 2.5, high; 2.0, acceptable; 1.5, low; 1.0, negligible.

Early Coping Inventory (ECI)

The Early Coping Inventory (ECI) is an exemplar of adaptive behavior measures for infants. The ECI is a judgment-based observational scale that samples infant adaptive or coping patterns across three dimensions: 1) sensorimotor organization, 2) reactive behaviors, and 3) self-initiated behaviors. The 5-point Likert rating scale offers a multidimensional scoring system to quantify and qualify the "effectiveness" of interaction with the child's environment. Effectiveness has three criteria: The behavior must be 1) appropriate for the situation, 2) appropriate for the child's developmental level, and 3) successfully used by the child (i.e., the behavior results in a consequence).

The coping behaviors in each cluster are not truly task analyzed, but they do represent a loose functional hierarchy in which less mature competencies (e.g., child tolerates different intensities of touch) are precursors to more mature competencies (e.g., child demonstrates ability to comfort self). Although the scale is not a curriculum, the ratings do alert a program's team members to the "what" and "how" of an infant's interaction with the environment. This knowledge is important for arranging the home or classroom/therapy environment to promote more adaptive patterns.

When this volume went to press in late 1996, field-test and technical adequacy research had been conducted only by the authors. Nevertheless, the authors must be commended on their commitment to studying the scale with its intended population. The ECI has been field-tested on 1,040 infants and toddlers with disabilities—one of the largest samples of children with disabilities for any available measure—and 227 infants and toddlers without disabilities. Means and standard deviations allow individual comparisons between samples with and without disabilities.

Users must be aware that, despite the ECI's strengths, the measure should not be used by itself but should be grouped as part of a larger diagnostic battery. Because it is a clinical judgment measure, the inconsistent item definitions can be interpreted differently by parents and professionals. Care should be exercised to use multiple assessors and to determine congruence among them—a point that is not stressed sufficiently in the manual itself.

The ECI has numerous strengths that support its wide use in pediatric rehabilitation and early intervention programs, particularly those for children with severe impairments. As curricula are developed to emphasize the infant's transactions with the environment and the generalization of behavior across situations, the ECI will stand as a complementary clinical and diagnostic instrument for prescriptive purposes.

Sample Coping Competencies from the Early Coping Inventory (ECI)

Sensorimotor organization

Child responds to a variety of sounds (e.g., voices, toys soft-to-loud noises).   1 2 3 4 5

Child adjusts to irrelevant sounds in the environment.   1 2 3 4 5

Reactive behavior

Child accepts warmth and support from familiar persons.   1 2 3 4 5

Child reacts to feelings and moods of other people.   1 2 3 4 5

Self-initiated behavior

Child expresses likes and dislikes.   1 2 3 4 5

Child initiates action to communicate a need.   1 2 3 4 5

From Zeitlin, S., Williamson, G.G., & Szczepanski, M. (1988). *Early Coping Inventory (ECI)*. Bensenville, IL: Scholastic Testing Service; reprinted by permission.

Every Move Counts (EMC)

Author(s):	J.E. Korsten, D.D. Dunn, T.V. Foss, & M.K. Francke
Year:	1989 (accompanying manual, 1993)
Publisher:	Therapy Skill Builders/The Psychological Corporation
Address:	555 Academic Court, San Antonio, Texas 78204-2498
Phone:	800-228-0752, extension 5780
Cost:	$129 (manual and accompanying video)

Assessment type: Curriculum embedded.

Age/focus group: Designed for children with severe to profound disabilities, developmental delays, or autism. It is designed for program planning and monitoring when small but significant skill progress is likely.

Scale(s): Criterion-based sensory response and communication assessment.

Data system: Environmental Observation Forms, Response Significance Forms, Activity Logs, Response Inventory Forms, Individual Trials Record Forms, Daily Routines Record, and Symbol Choice-Location Logs.

Domains/content: Sensory-based communication development.

Special needs options: Numerous techniques are offered to accommodate the range of cognitive and physical abilities presented by this special population.

Authenticity: Clear emphasis on real-life activities, settings, and methods that provide goals for intervention.

Family involvement: Parent participation is encouraged. Parent's Guide helps promote communication with children and provides helpful ideas and activities to use at home.

Training needed: Although 1-, 2-, and 3-day Every Move Counts workshops are provided for interested individuals, they are not required. Manual is self-explanatory and easy to implement.

Validation: No supporting data for program efficacy are provided.

Comments:
- *A major contribution to curriculum-based assessment and intervention for special needs populations*
- *Ten-minute video shows Every Move Counts at work*
- *Four levels of instruction offer clearly defined goals and objectives*
- *Encourages a transdisciplinary approach*
- *Materials are confusing initially*

LINK Index			
Authentic	1	2	③
Convergent	1	2	③
Collaborative	1	②	3
Equitable	1	2	③
Sensitive	1	2	③
Congruent	1	2	③
Total Index	☐ +	☐2 +	☐15 ÷ 6 = ☐2.8

Overall quality: high to exemplary

3.0, exemplary; 2.5, high; 2.0, acceptable; 1.5, low; 1.0, negligible.

Every Move Counts (EMC)

Every Move Counts (EMC) offers strategies for recognizing and improving communication for any individual (from infancy through adulthood) who either is unable or is perceived as being unable to communicate. It is appropriate for use with people with autism, developmental delays, and severe multiple disabilities. A variety of techniques are offered to accommodate the range of cognitive and physical abilities presented by the targeted populations.

The EMC program presents sensory-based activities in a structure that encourages communication. The Sensory Response Assessment identifies sensory activities that an individual may enjoy and identifies how that enjoyment is or may be communicated. The person's natural response then becomes a means to request these preferred activities. As the individual moves through the four levels of the program, this basic response is defined, refined, and expanded into a more functional communication system.

The goal of the EMC approach is to provide a link to the development of an individual's communication system. The activities and techniques in the Program Manual, Implementation Guide, and Parent's Guide are intended to provide the types of stimulation most likely to elicit a response, thereby encouraging the individual to exert some type of control.

EMC presents materials and suggestions in an orderly and logical progression, but it is not a "cookbook" of ideas. It is important to utilize creativity and flexibility as an integral part of implementing this program.

Stimulation Protocol from Every Move Counts (EMC)

Activity	Presentation/ Withdrawal Intervals	Symbolic Representations				
		Object	Picture	Symbol	Gesture	Sign
Sock massage— rub client's hands and forearms firmly using a hand inside a tennis sock	5 sec./5 sec.	Tennis sock	Photo of object	Drawing of object, rebus symbol or Blissymbol, or a two-dimensional representation of same color and shape as equipment	Reaching for stimulus; holding out arm to be rubbed	Sign for "rub"
Massage with rubber vegetable scrubber	5 sec./5 sec.	A slender cylinder of color as handle of scrubber	↓		↓	Sign for "rub"
Hand/ball massage— rub client's palms firmly with a tennis ball	5 sec./5 sec.	Tennis ball or smaller ball				Sign for "rub"
Swinging in swing or sheet	10 sec./ 5 sec.	Something that represents swing or sheet			Any movement pattern that represents the motion	Sign for "swing"
Wagon ride	20 yards or to a pre-determined destination/ 5 sec./resume ride	Toy wagon or block with wheels added	Photo of object	Drawing of object, rebus symbol, or Blissymbol	Pointing to object	Sign for "ride" or "go"
Toy play	3 min./5 sec.	Similar toy	↓	↓		Sign for "play"
Switch activation	Naturally occurring interval/ 5 sec.	Object representing whatever is being activated			Point to item to be activated	Sign for the item to be activated
Participation in group snack	Naturally occurring turn/5 sec.	Cup and/or spoon			Point to item or bring hand to mouth	Signs for "eat," "drink," "cookie" . . .
Participation in group play	Naturally occurring turn/5 sec.	Object associated with play; carpet swatch for floor activity	↓	↓	Joining group	Sign for "play"

From Korsten, J.E., Dunn, D.D., Foss, T.V., & Francke, M.K. (1993). *Every Move Counts*. San Antonio, TX: Therapy Skill Builders/Psychological Corporation; reprinted by permission.

Family Day Care Rating Scale (FDRS)

Author(s):	T. Harms & R.M. Clifford
Year:	1989
Publisher:	Teachers College Press
Address:	1234 Amsterdam Avenue, New York, New York 10027
Phone:	212-678-3929
Cost:	$30+

Assessment type: Curriculum compatible for programming purposes; ecological rating scale; direct observations of family child care settings for program self-evaluations and changes.

Age/focus group: Early childhood.

Domains/content: Adaptation of ECERS; seven environmental domains: space and furnishings for care and learning, basic care, language and reasoning, learning activities, social development, adult needs, and provisions for exceptional children; developed to address the criteria for Child Development Associate Family Day Care credentials.

Special needs options: Includes a separate supplementary rating scale that surveys all seven major environmental domains and adaptive options in each area for accommodating children with special needs.

Curricular links: Provides a superb addition to the methods sections of IEPs and IFSPs that address quality and changes needed in the family child care environment.

Authenticity: Strong environmental focus.

Family involvement: Addresses some family aspects but is primarily for staff.

Scoring/sample: A 7-point rating scale that ranges from inadequate to excellent.

Validation: Field validations and basic psychometric studies.

Training needed: Designed to be used collaboratively by program supervisors and staff for self-evaluations.

Comments:
- *Simple to use but invaluable as an environmental rating scale for family child care settings*
- *Superb authentic characteristics*
- *One of the few commercially available ecological scales with special needs adaptations and specific field validations*

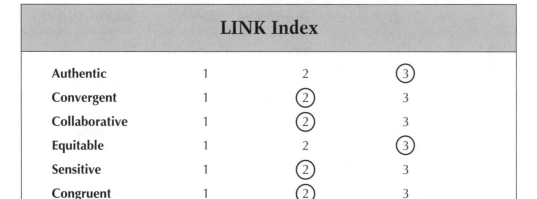

LINK Index			
Authentic	1	2	③
Convergent	1	②	3
Collaborative	1	②	3
Equitable	1	2	③
Sensitive	1	②	3
Congruent	1	②	3
Total Index	☐ +	8 +	6 ÷ 6 = 2.3
Overall quality: acceptable			

3.0, exemplary; 2.5, high; 2.0, acceptable; 1.5, low; 1.0, negligible.

Family Day Care Rating Scale (FDRS)

Like the ECERS, the Family Day Care Rating Scale (FDRS) provides a naturalistic evaluation of the dimensions in the home setting of a family day care arrangement and of the extent to which such a setting accommodates the unique needs of young children with developmental delays or disabilities when they are cared for in the same settings as their typically developing peers. The FDRS covers the same basic areas as does the ECERS and uses the same 7-point rating scale.

Unique to the FDRS are supplemental items that document field-validated provisions for children with special needs. For example, the adequacy of adaptations to meet basic care and physical activity needs, changes in scheduled routines, and modifications for communication/language problems and the adequacy of preparation of caregivers to provide care for young children with physical impairments are included in the FDRS. These provisions are an excellent step toward an authentic appraisal of the young child's day care environment, the modifications that are needed to promote inclusion and adjustment, and the training of family day care providers to meet the challenges of individual differences.

Sample from the Family Day Care Rating Scale (FDRS)

Supplementary Items: Provisions for Exceptional Children

Items 33–40 are to be rated in addition to the preceding 32 items only when a child with special needs is included in the child care home. The terms *exceptional*, *special needs*, and *handicapped* are used interchangeably.

Since some handicapping conditions are not readily observable, it is neces-sary to know the nature of the child's handicap in order to correctly assign scores. While these items have been extensively field-tested and used in assessing programs that integrated children with special needs, they have not undergone the formal reliability testing given to the main body of the scale.

Item	Inadequate 1	2	Minimal 3	4	Good 5	6	Excellent 7
33. Adaptations for basic care (physically handi-capped)	› Adaptive equipment needed for basic care routines is lacking (eating, sleeping, toileting, grooming), or not clean and in good repair. › Child's special basic care needs not met consistently. Caregiver does not perform special basic care procedures competently (Ex. child positioned inappropriately for feeding).		› Special adaptive equipment for basic care routines is clean and in good repair. › Caregiver consistently and competently follows special basic care routines (Ex. catheterization, turning bed-ridden child).		› Careprovider does not allow child's need for adaptive equip-ment and special procedures to isolate him from the group during routines (Ex. child eats at table with or very near other children). › Careprovider is gentle and respectful in the performance of the special basic care and health routines (Ex. respects child's need for privacy, handles special equipment with care).		› Caregiver plans and provides learning activities to develop higher levels of child's self-help skills (Ex. gradually intro-duces more advanced forms of solid food to child with chew-ing problems, encourages child to do as much as he can by himself). › Caregiver responds sensitively to child's special basic care needs (Ex. anticipates when nonambulatory child feels tired of sitting and changes his position).
34. Adaptations for activities (physically handicapped)	› Barriers limit child's use of space and materials and caregiver doesn't compensate. (Ex. toys out of reach, steps prevent easy movement). › Needed adaptive equipment not present or used, thus preventing child from joining learning and social activities.		› Barriers may be present but caregiver helps child gain access to activities when needed (Ex. moves non-walker to area where other children are playing). › Some adaptive equipment present, clean, safe, and in good repair. › Adequate space for adaptive equipment.		› Needed adaptive equipment available for self-help, learning, and play activities, both indoors and out. › Environment permits child free use of space and materials (Ex. toys put within child's reach, barriers to movement indoors managed effectively).		› Caregiver encourages independent use of adaptive equipment. › Careprovider plans activities for child to learn to use adap-tive equipment, where needed. › Caregiver helps other children accept adaptive equipment (Ex. by telling what it is for, answering questions, quieting fears, letting children try out equipment and help handi-capped child).

Family Needs Survey (FNS)

Author(s):	D.B. Bailey & R.J. Simeonsson
Year:	1990
Publisher:	Author
Address:	Frank Porter Graham Child Development Center, University of North Carolina, Chapel Hill, North Carolina 27514
Phone:	919-966-6634
Cost:	Research participation

Assessment type: Curriculum compatible for IFSP goals; judgment based; parent self-report of personal, social, child, economic, health, and family needs.

Age/focus group: Infants, toddlers, and preschoolers.

Domains/content: Six clusters: information needs, support needs, explaining to others, community services, financial needs, and family functioning; includes an open-ended essay question.

Special needs options: Parent reports of family and child needs.

Curricular links: Clearly identifies parent perceptions of the greatest areas of need and highlights goals for counseling, support, problem solving, and social services and medical interventions.

Authenticity: Strongly authentic; emphasizes parent interviews, ratings, and essay-type questions regarding family strengths, resources, and needs for incorporation into IFSP.

Family involvement: The focal purpose of this instrument.

Scoring/sample: Three-point Likert rating scale (1, definitely do not need help; 2, not sure; 3, definitely need help).

Validation: Preliminary field-testing and technical studies on 34 two-parent families; moderate mother–father agreement and stability over a 6-month period.

Training needed: Thorough knowledge of manual and parent interview skills is needed, despite self-report format.

Comments:
- *One of the best of the parent/family measures*
- *Addresses areas of chronic need that affect family coping*
- *Simple and readable*
- *Answers suggest immediate intervention goals/ options*
- *Field-testing with various family types (e.g., single parent, grandparent), developmental disabilities, and cultural groups is needed*

LINK Index			
Authentic	1	2	③
Convergent	1	2	③
Collaborative	1	2	③
Equitable	1	2	③
Sensitive	1	②	3
Congruent	1	2	③
Total Index	☐ +	2 +	15 ÷ 6 = 2.8
Overall quality: high to exemplary			

3.0, exemplary; 2.5, high; 2.0, acceptable; 1.5, low; 1.0, negligible.

Family Needs Survey (FNS)

The Family Needs Survey (FNS) is an important example of this type of instrument. As the sample on page 187 illustrates, its self-statements are organized into six clusters that tap the feelings and concerns of parents about themselves, their infants, and their families (e.g., "I need help locating a doctor who understands me and my child's needs," "I need to have more friends that I can talk to"). In a sense, these clusters focus on the concerns of the parent and identify specific areas of pressing need. They are criterion referenced—or, more accurately, intervention focused—so that they immediately suggest program goals and strategies (e.g., "I need more information about my child's condition or disability"). The developers have completed initial field-testing of the FNS with parents of infants with various disabilities. Preliminary technical adequacy data in terms of stability and mother–father agreement are encouraging (Bailey & Simeonsson, 1988a).

The FNS represents a very important advance in the field. It is an instrument that blends authenticity, technical soundness, and intervention utility.

Selected Self-Report Statements from the Family Needs Survey (FNS)

	No Help	Not Sure	Need Help
Needs for information			
1. I need more information about my child's condition or disability.	1	2	3
2. I need more information about how to handle my child's behavior.	1	2	3
Needs for support			
1. I need to have someone in my family that I can talk to about problems.	1	2	3
2. I need to have more friends that I can talk to.	1	2	3
Explaining to others			
1. I need more help in explaining my child's condition to either my parents or my spouse's parents.	1	2	3
2. My spouse needs help in understanding and accepting our child's condition.	1	2	3
Community services			
1. I need help in locating a doctor who understands me and my child's needs.	1	2	3
2. I need help locating a dentist who will see my child.	1	2	3
Financial needs			
1. I need more help in paying for expenses such as food, housing, medical care, clothing, or transportation.	1	2	3
2. I need more help in getting special equipment for my child's needs.	1	2	3
Family functioning			
1. Our family needs help in discussing problems and reaching solutions.	1	2	3
2. Our family needs help in learning how to support each other during difficult times.	1	2	3

From Bailey, D.B., & Simeonsson, R.J. (1990). *Family Needs Survey (FNS)*. Chapel Hill, NC: Frank Porter Graham Child Development Center; reprinted by permission.

Hawaii Early Learning Profile (HELP): HELP (Birth to 3)

Author(s): S. Parks, S. Furono, K. O'Reilly, T. Inatsuka, C.M. Hoska, & B. Zeisloft-Falbey

Year: 1984, 1985, 1987, 1988, 1992, 1994

Publisher: VORT Corporation

Address: Post Office Box 60880, Palo Alto, California 94306

Phone: 415-322-8282

Cost: *HELP at Home*, $69.95 (Spanish translation of handouts, $49.95); *HELP Checklist* (Furuno et al.), $2.95 each for 1–9 copies, $2.45 each for10–99 copies, and $1.95 each for 100 or more copies (Spanish version available at the same prices); *HELP Family-Centered Interview* (Parks), $1.50 each (package of 25, $17.95); *HELP Charts* (Furuno et al.), $2.95 each (set of three) for 1–9 sets, 2.45 each for 10–99 sets, and $1.95 each for 100 or more sets; *HELP Activity Guide* (Furuno et al.), $24.95; *HELP: When the Parent is Handicapped* (Parks), $27.95; *HELP Together* (software with 0–3 database), $595 (single-user version) and $1,295 (network version).
Note: HELP Together (software with 0–6 database) is available for $795 (single-user version) and $1,595 (network version).

Assessment type: Curriculum embedded.

Age/focus group: Designed for infants with special needs from birth to 3 years. It can be used individually in a home- or center-based program.

Scale(s): HELP charts, HELP Checklist (ages birth to 3 years).

Data system: HELP charts are used to identify current mastery of skills, needs, and objectives. They are also used for recording and visually tracking progress of child. HELP Together software/database is available for maintaining and reporting IFSP/IEP records for children.

Domains/content: Six developmental domains: gross motor, fine motor, cognition, expressive language, social and emotional development, and adaptive.

Special needs options: General and specific recommendations to accommodate several special needs.

Authenticity: Stresses observation of natural adaptive behaviors of children with special needs in everyday settings and activities; promotes activity-based learning.

Family involvement: Two guides for parents are provided: *When a Parent Is Handicapped* (techniques for involving parents who are blind or deaf or who have physical disabilities or mental retardation) and *HELP for Parents of Children with Special Needs* (additional parent information and a means of record keeping).

Training needed: Knowledge of and experience with infants and toddlers with disabilities; consultation with other professionals encouraged.

Validation: One of the most widely used instruments. It does not provide supporting data for program efficacy. It is based on the six developmental domains/areas.

Comments:
- *Clearly written plans and a variety of activities*
- *Precautions and suggestions for intervention in children with particular special needs conditions*
- *Some material is available in Spanish and on computer software*
- *Computer software available for planning and reporting*

<table>
<tr><td colspan="4">LINK Index</td></tr>
<tr><td>Authentic</td><td>1</td><td>2</td><td>③</td></tr>
<tr><td>Convergent</td><td>1</td><td>2</td><td>③</td></tr>
<tr><td>Collaborative</td><td>1</td><td>2</td><td>③</td></tr>
<tr><td>Equitable</td><td>1</td><td>2</td><td>③</td></tr>
<tr><td>Sensitive</td><td>1</td><td>2</td><td>③</td></tr>
<tr><td>Congruent</td><td>1</td><td>2</td><td>③</td></tr>
<tr><td>Total Index</td><td>☐ +</td><td>☐ +</td><td>18 ÷ 6 = 3.0</td></tr>
<tr><td colspan="4">Overall quality: exemplary</td></tr>
</table>

3.0, exemplary; 2.5, high; 2.0, acceptable; 1.5, low; 1.0, negligible.

Hawaii Early Learning Profile (HELP): HELP for Preschoolers (3–6)

Author(s): VORT Corporation
Year: 1995
Publisher: VORT Corporation
Address: Post Office Box 60880, Palo Alto, California 94306
Phone: 415-322-8282
Cost: *HELP for Preschoolers Assessment and Curriculum Guide,* $49.95; *HELP for Preschoolers Assessment Strands,* $3.25 each for 1–9 copies, $2.75 each for 10–99 copies, and $2.10 each for 100 or more copies; *HELP for Preschoolers Charts,* $2.95 each (set of three) for 1–9 sets, $2.45 each for 10–99 sets, and $1.95 each for 100 or more sets; *HELP for Preschoolers Checklist,* $2.95 each for 1–9 copies, $2.45 each for 10–99 copies, and $1.95 each for 100 or more copies; *HELP for Preschoolers Activities at Home,* $55.95; *HELP Together* (software with 3–6 database), $595 (single-user version) and $1,295 (network version).
Note: HELP Together (software with 0–6 database) is available for $795 (single-user version) and $1,595 (network version).

Assessment type: Curriculum embedded.

Age/focus group: Designed for children with special needs ages 3–6. It can be used individually in a home- or center-based program.

Scale(s): HELP for Preschoolers Assessment Strands; Preschoolers Charts and Preschoolers Checklist.

Data system: HELP charts are used to identify current mastery of skills, needs, and objectives. They are also used for recording and visually tracking child progress. HELP Together software/data base is available for maintaining and reporting IFSP/IEP records for children.

Domains/content: Six developmental domains: gross motor, fine motor, cognition, expressive language, social and emotional development, and adaptive.

Special needs options: General and specific recommendations to accommodate several special needs.

Authenticity: Stresses observation of natural adaptive behaviors of children with special needs in everyday settings and activities; promotes activity-based learning.

Family involvement: Guide for parents is provided: *HELP for Parents of Children with Special Needs* (additional parent information and a means of record keeping).

Training needed: Knowledge of and experience with preschoolers with disabilities; consultation with other professionals encouraged.

Validation: One of the most widely used instruments. It does not provide supporting data for program efficacy. It is based on the six developmental domains/areas.

Comments:
- *Clearly written plans and a variety of activities*
- *Precautions and suggestions for intervention in children with particular special needs conditions*
- *Some material is available in Spanish and on computer software*
- *Computer software available for planning and reporting*

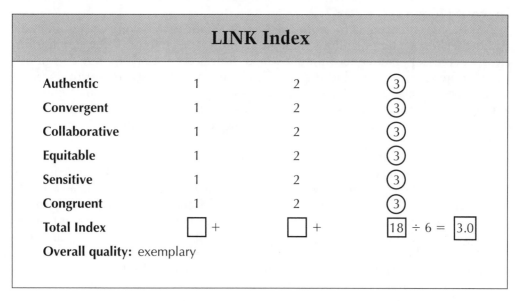

LINK Index			
Authentic	1	2	③
Convergent	1	2	③
Collaborative	1	2	③
Equitable	1	2	③
Sensitive	1	2	③
Congruent	1	2	③
Total Index	☐ +	☐ +	18 ÷ 6 = 3.0
Overall quality: exemplary			

3.0, exemplary; 2.5, high; 2.0, acceptable; 1.5, low; 1.0, negligible.

Hawaii Early Learning Profile (HELP):
HELP (Birth–3) and HELP for Preschoolers (3–6)

The Hawaii Early Learning Profile (HELP) is a remarkable set of resources for professionals, parents, and children. The materials span the age range from birth to 6 years, provide a comprehensive continuum of worthwhile skills, and promote activity-based, developmentally appropriate program practices. Indeed, the HELP package is complete and comprehensive—almost to a fault (13 separate materials)—but administration manuals (e.g., *Inside HELP*) provide clear explanations and instructions for using the array of materials. The 1995 complete revision welds together the materials to produce a package that is highly desirable for assessment, program planning, teaching, and parent participation. In fact, a software program, *HELP Together*, is now available that can save much time and effort in putting together assessment results and recommended activities for IFSP/IEP reports.

The HELP system is organized into strands that identify a range of skills within important dimensions of competence. For example, the 3- to 6-year-old strands within the cognitive area include valuable sequences on problem solving; matching; classifying; paying attention; and readiness for reading, writing, and math. The 58 birth to 3-year-old strands are extended and elaborated to 75 strands at the 3- to 6-year-old level. The more than 1,300 skills within and across the strands allow for sensitive curriculum-based assessment as well as a rich content for writing IEPs/IFSPs.

Assessment materials for both the birth-to-3 and 3-to-6 components include HELP checklists, charts, and assessment strands. The content of these materials clearly addresses practice recommendations. Especially noteworthy are the guidelines for preparing and conducting assessment and accommodating various special needs. Specific suggestions are offered for assessment and instruction of children with visual, hearing, motor, speech, or attention impairments. Assessment rests on observations of child activity under ongoing or arranged circumstances as well as parent interviews.

The *HELP Family-Centered Interview* is a strong illustration of meaningful, uncontrived honoring of parent information and preferences. The HELP curriculum is an excellent choice for inclusive programs and encompasses both typically developing children and those with mild to moderate special needs. (Children with severe developmental difficulties require focused materials and even greater intervention details [available through specialized curricula].) The continuous "seamless" congruence of the infant/toddler and toddler/preschooler materials permits smooth transitions between programs and preempts jolts and parent disappointment.

The HELP materials could very well be used as a short course in quality assessment and instruction for infants, toddlers, and preschoolers; they really do help.

Sample from a Hawaii Early Learning Profile Activity Guide

1.01 QUIETS WHEN PICKED UP (0–1 mo.)

The child stops crying, momentarily, when picked up.

1. Try to anticipate the child's needs. In this way you are prepared to meet the immediate needs. For example:
   a. Prepare a bottle or make sure the backrest you need for breast feeding is ready. Your child will be hungry after a three hour nap.
   b. Prepare clean diapers and whatever else you need to change the child's diapers quickly.
2. Call the child's name when approaching her to let her know you are coming. Pick the child up gently and slowly, not quickly with a jerk. Keep your voice calm.
3. Hold the child firmly so she feels secure being picked up and in your arms. Place the child snugly against your body. Do not hold the child too tightly, restrict her movements or hold her partially suspended.
4. Mold your body to the child's so she fits securely against your body. Lean slightly back to compensate for the child's weight and the angle at which she is held.
5. Pick up the child and gently rub or pat her back as you soothingly talk to her.
6. Rock gently and sing softly as you pat the child's back.

1.02 SHOWS PLEASURE WHEN TOUCHED AND HANDLED (0–6 mo.)

1. Talk to the child as if he understands everything you are saying to him. As you share and talk, activities are made more pleasant for you and for the child.
2. Gently stroke the child's head, hold his hand or rub his arm while you cuddle and feed the child from the bottle or breast.
3. Tap and rub the child's back very gently, and at times, playfully, when burping him.
4. Carry and rock the child to the beat of rhythmic music.
5. Pat and rub the child's legs and arms when checking to see if he is cold or hot.
6. Talk to the child, sing simple songs or nursery rhymes while bathing him.
7. Use terry cloth towels or smooth materials to rub different parts of the child's body, naming parts as you go along.
8. Blow on the child's stomach, hair, face, toes, or fingers.
9. Play a game like "This Little Piggy Went to Market" with the child's toes.
10. Sing nursery rhymes, such as "Hickory Dickory Dock." Use your two hands as the "mouse," and run up the child's body from toes to chin.
11. Sit in back of the child supporting him in sitting and do motions to songs, such as hands up, to the side, waving, rolling, tapping stomach or legs.

1.03 RESPONDS TO SOUNDS (0–1 mo.)

The child may show she has heard the sound in a number of different ways. She quiets after having been active, she changes her breathing pattern, she becomes more active after having been quiet by kicking her feet, moving her arms, widening her eyes or making a verbal sound.

1. Shake a bell eight to ten inches from the child's chest first to the left and then to the right of her head while the child is in supine.
   a. Use bright colored rattles with *low* tones, such as a wooden rattle.
   b. Use bright colored rattles (yellow) with *high* tones.
   c. Use rattles with faces on them.
   d. Use a squeak toy.
   e. Clap your hands suddenly (be careful not to scare her).
2. Shake the bell or rattle loudly and softly.
3. Repeat activity #1 with the child in different positions:
   a. In prone.
   b. In a carrying seat or held in sitting against an adult.
   c. In an upright position over the shoulder of an adult.
4. Place the rattle in the child's hands so she can feel its texture and shape. Assist the child in shaking the rattle to produce a sound.
5. Rock or move to a song on the radio. Stand very still when the music stops.
6. For the older delayed child:
   a. Place him in different positions when ringing a bell or rattle. Touch the cheek or arms of the child so she feels the vibration of the sound. Use a triangle or tuning fork.
   b. Hold the child very still and listen for a sound another person makes or for environmental sounds, such as a ringing telephone or flying airplanes. Turn the child toward the source of the sound.
   c. Make different sounds by knocking on wood or cans, or by using toys, such as xylophones, jack-in-the-boxes. Immediately acknowledge the sound by smiling and showing pleasure. Show excitement by asking, "Did you hear that?" or "That was a clown!"

1.04 RESPONDS TO VOICE (0–2½ mo.)

Initially, the child shows his awareness of a sound by a response, such as an eyeblink or a startle response depending on the intensity of the sound. He quickly adjusts to the sound and his response diminishes. The child adjusts to almost any kind of environmental noise and sleeps in quiet or noise, whichever is typical of his environment. A change either way to more noise or more quiet is apt to result in a response of increased activity or alertness demonstrating his awareness of the change.

1. Comfort the child by soothing him and by talking to him during the first two weeks. Speak to him in a soft, friendly voice. This will help quiet him when he is upset, provided he is not hungry or in pain.

From VORT Corporation. (1995). *HELP for Preschoolers,* p. 1. Palo Alto, CA: VORT Corporation; reprinted by permission.

Sample from the Hawaii Early Learning Profile (HELP)

0.0 Regulatory/Sensory Organization   (see *Inside* HELP - page 1)

+ - o	Skill	Age *	Skill/Behavior	Responses Observed **
	1.01	0-1	**Quiets when picked up** — *(under 3 months) calms with some external support*	
	1.03	0-1	**Responds to sound** — *enjoys and attends to a wide range of sounds*	
	5.01	0-3	**Enjoys and needs a great deal of physical contact and tactile stimulation** — *relaxes, smiles, vocalizes or looks at caregiver; also in 5-1*	
	5.05	0-3	**Molds and relaxes body when held; cuddles** — *shapes body to "fit" adult; also in 5-5*	
	1.02	0-6	**Shows pleasure when touched and handled** — *tolerates routine handling, rocking*	
	1.05	1-2	**Inspects surroundings** — *easy to engage , can remain calm & focused*	
	1.07	1-3	**Listens to voice for 30 seconds** — *easy to engage; able to focus*	
	6.04	1-3	**Stays awake for longer periods without crying - usually in p.m.** — *begins to establish sleep and feeding patterns*	
	1.06	1-6	**Shows active interest in person / object ≥ 1 min.** — *able to focus on a variety of sights, sounds & people; also in 2-4A*	
	1.15	3-6	**Uses hands and mouth for sensory exploration of objects** — *freely touches & mouths (if less than 1 year)a variety of textures; also in 1-1*	
	5.08	3-6	**Stops unexplained crying** — *can usually self-calm, e.g., suck fingers, rock self*	
	5.15	3-6	**Enjoys social play** — *that involves movement & touch, e.g., nuzzling tummy, "Pat-a-cake"; also in 5-5*	
	1.22	4-6	**Localizes tactile stimulation by touching the same spot or searching for object that touched body** — *e.g., piece of tape on leg*	
	5.18	4-8	**Enjoys frolic play** — *e.g., being held up in air; tolerates movement in all planes*	
	1.34	6-12	**Smells different things** — *no adverse responses to routine odors*	
	1.35	6-9	**Plays 2-3 minutes with a single toy** — *explores with sustained attention; also in 1-1*	
	1.54	9-11	**Listens to speech without being distracted by other sources** — *typical background sights and sounds*	
	6.23	7-12	**Drools less except when teething** — *also in 6-1*	
	6.25	9-12	**Finger feeds self** — *touches/eats variety of textured foods; also in 6-3*	
	6.27	9-12	**Sleeps nights twelve to fourteen hours** — *usually sleeps through night; falls asleep within 20 mins. if tired; also in 6-2*	
	6.29	10.5-12	**Cooperates with dressing by extending arm ,leg** — *does not mind clothing touching skin, also in 6-2*	
	1.68	12-18	**Enjoys messy activities** — *e.g., water and food play*	
	1.69	12-18	**Reacts to various sensations such as extremes in temperature and taste** — *e.g., warm, cold; sweet, sour*	
	1.99	18-24	**Uses playdough and paints** — *freely explores*	
	5.60	18-24	**Enjoys solitary play for a few minutes** — *sustained attention; symbolic and purposeful play*	
	5.61	18-24	**Enjoys rough and tumble play** — *e.g., "piggy-back" rides; rocking horse*	
	6.61	24-26	**Handles fragile items carefully** — *e.g., a drink, flowers; also in 6-7*	
	1.127	24-29	**Enjoys tactile books** — *freely explores*	
	1.120	24-36	**Plays with water and sand** — *freely explores*	
	1.151	30-36	**Identifies familiar objects by touch** — *e.g., spoon, ball, block hidden in a bag*	
	1.152	30-36	**Enjoys being read to and looks at books independently**	
	5.93	30+	**Participates in circle games; plays interactive games** — *interacts; follows "rules"; also in 5-5*	

Special Credit Notes (see *Inside* HELP for criteria): A+ Hyper- or overreactive response   * Age emerges
A- Hypo- or underreactive response   ** Preferences, dislikes, reactions

From VORT Corporation. (1995). *HELP for Preschoolers,* p. 3. Palo Alto, CA: VORT Corporation; reprinted by permission.

2. Begin by saying the words in the group. If the children are having difficulty, provide a cue of a visual representation. As the children become skilled in responding, increase the difficulty of the word groupings. To modify this activity, divide the children into two teams, giving points for the team that gives the correct answer. To prevent focusing on a single child's right or wrong answer, make sure that the team, and not individual members of the team, is asked to name the words.

1.184 Identifies missing parts of a picture storybook that has been read several times

Strand: 1-9 **Age:** 42-48m 3.6-4y

Definition

The child is read a story that he is very familiar with, and part of the story is left out on purpose. The child is able to identify the part that has been omitted and is able to retell the part correctly. This can also include the modification of the story content. The child is able to tell what has been changed, and what the original story-line was.

Assessment Materials

Select a short story with a clear story line and an easily identified sequence of events.

Assessment Procedures

1. Seat the child beside you so he can see the pictures in the book.
2. Read the story several times to the child.
3. Point to the pictures that correspond with the events or actions in the story.
4. Discuss the plot of the story with the child and include the sequence of each episode, the characters, the ending, etc.
5. Read the story again, and if the child wants to assist in the storytelling, allow him to do so.
6. Read the story again, but this time leave out a segment, making sure that the part left out is pictured.
7. Make a note if the child recognized the error and if the child filled in the correct section.
8. If the child did not recognize the error, read the story again and eliminate another part. Make a note if the child recognized the error and if he filled in the correct section.

Adaptations

The child must be able to recall what he has heard when needed. Recall involves understanding what is said and making critical judgments. Many children can provide answers to questions, follow directions, and even draw conclusions, but when critical listening is involved, a child may have a tendency to not trust his recall. The "inner voice" says, "What you just heard is probably right, you just forgot that part." If you are

working with a child that does not trust his "recall," ask him such questions as, "Do you think I read that right?" "Does that sound right to you?" "I think I just made a mistake in the story."

Instructional Materials

Select a large picture book that has language patterning such as word repetition and rhyming semantics. The book should be a story the child enjoys and wants to hear again and again. The large book should also have a duplicate in a child size. Good Listener Awards.

Instructional Activities

1. Invite the child to story time. It is important that the environment be comfortable; perhaps the child would enjoy sitting on a rug or a pillow.
2. Explain to the child that you are going to read a story from a large book. Show the child the cover of the book and discuss the picture and title.
3. Ask the child to listen while you read the story.
4. Read the story again.
5. Read the story once more, and encourage the child to recite the parts of the story he knows.
6. Give the child the duplicate, smaller book and tell him to follow along while you read the story. Encourage him to look at the pictures and turn the pages correctly.
7. Read the story one more time and omit an obvious part of the story.
8. If the child identified the missing part, give him a Good Listener Award or a chance to pick out the next story for story time.

1.185 Starts a task only when reminded, some prompting

Strand: 1-8 **Age:** 42-48m 3.6-4y

Definition

One of the most important elements of not beginning an activity until prompted is determining the cause. Some causes are: lack of motivation, sense of inability to achieve, disinhibition, low self-image, inappropriate role model, etc..

Assessment Materials

Select a topic that the child is interested in. Examples: cars, dogs, turtles, dolls, etc. Prepare or secure a variety of different activities (not more than four) within the scope of the child's interest levels and based on the selected topic. These activities could include picture books, puzzles, models, tracing activities, simple drawing tasks, etc.

Assessment Procedures

1. Engage the child in a discussion about the topic, including questions about factual information. Then move to questions that require interpretation and allow the child the chance to respond to judgmental

HICOMP

Author(s):	S.J. Willoughby-Herb & J.T. Neisworth
Year:	1983
Publisher:	Author
Address:	The Pennsylvania State University, 207 CEDAR Building, University Park, Pennsylvania 16802-3109
Phone:	814-863-2280
Cost:	$75

Assessment type:　　Curriculum embedded.

Age/focus group:　　Designed for children with and without special needs, ages birth to 5 years. It can be used in small group or individual center-based programs; behavioral emphasis is especially useful for children with behavioral special needs.

Scale(s):　　Assessment for Placement and Instruction (API) and HICOMP Track Record.

Data system:　　Easily scored formative system.

Domains/content:　　Communication, adaptive, motor, and problem solving (COMP).

Special needs options:　　Can be used with children with developmental delays, in particular, those with conduct disorders.

Authenticity:　　Content shows predominance of natural skills or activities that are useful and worthwhile in natural settings.

Family involvement:　　Activities can be used in a home-based program in which parents participate.

Training needed:　　Thorough study of curriculum guide; workshop suggested (half day for professionals, full day for assistants). Behavior modification strategies are stressed.

Validation: HICOMP objectives are linked to parallel items found in several other widely used assessment instruments, thereby permitting informal estimates of concurrence and age norms.

Comments:
- *A total of 800 objectives and lesson plans*
- *Includes goal/objectives in creativity, humor, and ethics*
- *Source for inclusive programs*
- *Good data collection system, parent friendly*
- *Especially useful with children who may be developing social/conduct disorders*

LINK Index		
Authentic 1	②	3
Convergent 1	2	③
Collaborative 1	2	③
Equitable 1	②	3
Sensitive 1	2	③
Congruent 1	2	③
Total Index ☐ +	4 +	12 ÷ 6 = 2.7
Overall quality: high		

3.0, exemplary; 2.5, high; 2.0, acceptable; 1.5, low; 1.0, negligible.

HICOMP

The HICOMP package allows professionals to estimate a child's placement into the curriculum's array of objectives rapidly (Assessment for Placement and Instruction [API]). After API has been performed, teachers can more precisely plan and track child progress throughout the 800 items. Progress is graphically displayed on the Track Record, a literal set of concentric tracks that show progress to the "finish lines" in each of the four domains. The formative monitoring and display of progress is especially appreciated by parents. Although HICOMP is based on developmental milestones, it includes task analyses and professional elaborations of objectives that result in an array of authentic objectives and activities. Goals include refreshing suggestions for guiding ethical development, humor, and creativity.

Materials include a booklet that suggests 10 ways to collect information about child progress (e.g., frequency, duration, anecdotal) and 10 ways to help (e.g., shaping, modeling, reinforcement). The program is not a "cookbook," but it presents alternatives for teachers who want to use this resource but be creative in their planning and intervention.

Sample from HICOMP

COMMUNICATION

Year	Language Related Play	Self-Expression	Language Responding	Imitation Related to Language	Language Related to Attention	Materials
1	T — Vocalizes when presented with a toy	O — Uses a word to make wants and needs known (observed or reported to use 10 different words)	T — Indicates yes/no when asked a question	T — Imitates familiar gestures accompanied by vocalizations (e.g., child waves and says, "bye-bye")	T — Looks attentively at objects (child sustains gaze at five different objects or toys)	5 toys (e.g., doll, ball)
2	T — Imitates the functional use of a toy and vocalizes appropriately (e.g., child pushes car and says "zoom!")	O — Uses two-word combinations to describe actions, objects (e.g., child says, "big dog," or "dog barking")	T — Follows a simple two-step direction (e.g., tester says, "Put a block in front of your chair and give one to me.")	T — Imitates simple sentences (e.g., "I am happy," or "Toys are fun.")	T — Looks at named pictures (e.g., "Show me the ball.")	A toy car or a toy telephone; a block; picture cards
3	O — Uses 4-5 words to communicate in a familiar role-playing game (e.g., child pretends to be the "mommy")	O — Asks a 3-4 word question using "WH" words such as *what, where, when* (one or more words observed or reported).	T — Identifies specific information about self: first and last name, age, sisters and brothers, pets	T — Imitates six-word sentences (e.g., I like chocolate milk and cake. Sun and rain make flowers grow.)	O — Looks at pictures while an adult reads a story	
4	T — Claps hands to the beat of a song (e.g., "Old MacDonald")	T — Retells a story from personal experience	T — Names major body parts: head, arm, hand, knee, foot, heel, elbow, little finger, ankle	T — Imitates (i.e. sings) a short, simple melody line	O — Looks attentively at peers and teacher during show and tell	
5	O — Plays group games involving if-then rules (e.g., duck-duck-goose)	T — Tells a story from three pictures arranged in sequential order	T — Answers simple questions about family, home, school	T — Says a nursery rhyme by imitating an adult model	O — Attends to various signs in the environment: restroom signs, walk-don't walk signs, exit signs, teacher's signal to be quiet.	3 sequential picture cards

2

Sample from HICOMP

YEAR 1

High/Scope Child Observation Record (COR)

Author(s):   High/Scope Staff
Year: 1992
Publisher: High/Scope Press
Address: 600 North River Street, Ypsilanti, Michigan 48198-2898
Phone: 800-407-7377
Cost $91

Assessment type: Curriculum embedded.

Age/focus group: Designed for children, from preschoolers to third graders, with diverse background, strengths, and interests. It can be used in an early childhood setting, preschool, child care, home-based, or Head Start program.

Scale(s):   The High/Scope Child Observation Record Assessment Booklet.

Data system: Recording forms, summarizing forms, and parent report forms.

Domains/content: Based on observation of the child's behavior and activities in six developmental categories: initiative, social relations, creative representation, music and movement, language and literacy, and logic and mathematics.

Special needs options: No special needs options are specified.

Authenticity: Real activities that are typical of children within typical settings; emphasis is on social activities.

Family involvement: Parent Report Forms are provided as a basis for discussion at parent conferences.

Training needed: The COR should be completed by staff members or people most familiar with the child. COR training is recommended.

Validation:

On-going field studies with children who are at risk; there is, however, little support for use with children who have more serious special needs.

Comments:

- *Based on natural behaviors and activities of the child*
- *Helps identify skills and strengths of each child*
- *Provides a vehicle for charting child's development and progress*

LINK Index			
Authentic	1	2	③
Convergent	1	2	③
Collaborative	1	2	③
Equitable	1	②	3
Sensitive	1	②	3
Congruent	1	②	3
Total Index	☐ +	6 +	9 ÷ 6 = 2.5
Overall quality: high			

3.0, exemplary; 2.5, high; 2.0, acceptable; 1.5, low; 1.0, negligible.

High/Scope Child Observation Record (COR)

The Child Observation Record (COR) is the core curriculum-embedded instrument for High/Scope. To survey skills in the 2½- to 6-year age range, COR relies first on the collection of anecdotal records and portfolio information by parents, teachers, and staff in early childhood settings over several weeks or months. COR is then completed by using a 5-point scale to denote a child's highest levels of accomplishment for each of six major developmental competencies: initiative, social relations, creative representation, music and movement, language and literacy, and logic and mathematics. COR's anecdotal record strategy relies on authentic information gathered across time, people, and situations—the hallmark of a strong, authentic, curriculum-based approach.

Sample High/Scope Child Observation Record (COR) Anecdotal Notecard

---

Observer's name: SHARON SMITH

Child's name: LA TANYA PHILLIPS

High/Scope
Child Observation
Record (COR) for
Ages 2½ – 6

Initiative

(9/16) COLLECTS ALL THE BALLS WHEN ASKED TO PUT GYM EQUIPMENT AWAY

(10/2) HELPS SARA PUT THE BLOCKS UP WITHOUT BEING ASKED

(10/17) PUTS ON COAT AND HAT WITHOUT HELP; ZIPS ZIPPER

(11/4) MAKES CHOICES EASILY EACH DAY AT PLANNING TIME

(11/4) HAS TROUBLE TURNING TRAIN AROUND; TRIES MOVING IT FORWARD AND BACKWARD; THEN REARRANGES TRACK, AND THAT WORKS!

Social Relations

(9/16) WORKS WITH JIM WITH BLOCKS; J–SAYS, "LET'S PUT A ROOF ON THIS"; L–SAYS, "I'LL GET YOU MORE LONG BLOCKS"

(10/2) HELPS SARA PUT BLOCKS AWAY

(10/17) HOLDS TEACHER'S HAND, SAYS, "I LOVE YOU"

(11/4) LETS OTHER KIDS PLAY WITH TRAINS: "YOU CAN PLAY, TOO"

(11/4) DANIELLE BEGINS TEARING UP TRAIN TRACK; LATANYA CRIES AND GETS ME TO SOLVE THE PROBLEM; L–SAYS TO D–, "IT MAKES ME SAD," AFTER I ASK HER TO TELL D–HOW SHE FELT ABOUT THE TRAIN TRACK

Creative Representation

(9/16) WORKS WITH JIM TO BUILD A GAS STATION; USES WOODEN BLOCKS, SMALL CARS AND PEOPLE

(10/2) DRAWS PICTURE OF SELF–HAIR, FACE, NOSE, MOUTH, EYES, BODY, ARMS, LEGS, SHOES, AND DRESS

(10/17) MAKES COLLAGE—USED GLUE, PAINT, RIBBON, BUTTONS, STYROFOAM, PAPER

(11/4) SHOWS ME TRAIN TRACKS, TRAINS, CARS, AND A BUILDING MADE FROM BLOCKS; L–SAYS TO ME, "THIS IS MY TRAIN CITY"

(12/6) SELLS "TICKETS" (REALLY JUST BITS OF PAPER) FOR HER "SHOW"

©1992 HIGH/SCOPE EDUCATIONAL RESEARCH FOUNDATION

Observer's name: SHARON SMITH

Child's name: LA TANYA PHILLIPS

High/Scope
Child Observation
Record (COR) for
Ages 2½ – 6

Music and Movement

(9/16) HOPS ON ONE FOOT, SKIPS, JUMPS FROM SMALL PLATFORM, BOUNCES BALL DURING GYM

(10/2) CUTS PAPER W/SCISSORS W/OUT HELP

(11/4) MANIPULATES SMALL PUZZLE PIECES WITH THUMB AND FOREFINGER

(11/17) WRITES WITH PENCIL, ROLLS PLAYDOH INTO TINY BALLS

(12/6) DANCES TO A STEADY BEAT AT GROUP TIME

Language and Literacy

(9/16) TELLS ABOUT LAST NIGHT'S OUTING: "LAST NIGHT I WENT TO MC DONALD'S AND I GOT A HAPPY MEAL AND I GOT A TOY"

(10/2) CHOOSES BOOK AND TURNS PAGES; LOOKS AT EACH PAGE

(10/17) LOOKS AT BOOKS WITH ME, POINTS TO SOME PICTURES, NAMES THEM

(11/4) SAYS, "I WANT TO PLAY IN THE BLOCK AREA AND MAKE A TRAIN STATION"

(11/13) WRITES THE "L" IN LA TANYA

(12/6) READS "K MART" FROM NEWSPAPER; RECOGNIZES "THE END" IN A STORY

Logic and Mathematics

(9/16) HELPS SORT BOTTLE CAPS, CORKS, AND BUTTONS INTO CANISTERS AT CLEAN-UP TIME

(10/2) TELLS MEGAN AT SNACK TIME THAT THE APPLES ARE RIGHT IN FRONT OF HER

(10/17) SAYS, "FROGS ARE GREEN"

(11/4) WHEN I ASK IF THERE ARE ENOUGH MARKERS FOR SIX KIDS, LA TANYA COUNTS THEM CORRECTLY, TOUCHING EACH AS SHE DOES SO

(12/6) L–TELLS A SHORT STORY AND SAYS, "NEXT TIME I'LL TELL A LONGER STORY"

©1992 HIGH/SCOPE EDUCATIONAL RESEARCH FOUNDATION

Front and back sides of sample COR Anecdotal Notecard.

From High/Scope Staff. (1992). *High/Scope Child Observation Record (COR).* Ypsilanti, MI: High/Scope Press; reprinted by permission.

Sample High/Scope Child Observation Record (COR)

I. Understanding and expressing feelings		Time 1	Time 2	Time 3
Child does not yet express or verbalize feelings.	(1)	_____	_____	_____
Child expresses or verbalizes feelings, but sometimes in unacceptable ways.	(2)	_____	_____	_____
Child shows awareness of the feelings of others.	(3)	_____	_____	_____
Child usually expresses feelings in acceptable ways.	(4)	_____	_____	_____
Child responds appropriately to the feelings of others.	(5)	_____	_____	_____

Notes:

_____

_____

_____

III. Creative Representation

J. Making and building		Time 1	Time 2	Time 3
Child does not yet explore or use making-and-building materials such as clay, sand, or blocks.	(1)	_____	_____	_____
Child explores making-and-building materials.	(2)	_____	_____	_____
Child uses materials to make something (a stack of blocks, a sand pile) but does not say whether it is meant to represent something else (a tower, a beach).	(3)	_____	_____	_____
Child uses materials to make simple representation and says or demonstrates what it is (says a stack of blocks is a tower; says a stack of balls is a snowman).	(4)	_____	_____	_____
Child uses materials to make or build things withat least three details represented (a house with a door, windows, and a chimney).	(5)	_____	_____	_____

Notes:

_____

_____

_____

From High/Scope Staff. (1992). *High/Scope Child Observation Record (COR)*. Ypsilanti, MI: High/Scope Press; reprinted by permission.

Home Observation for Measurement of the Environment (HOME)

Author(s):	B. Caldwell & R.A. Bradley
Year:	1978
Publisher:	University of Arkansas
Address:	Child Development Research Unit, University of Arkansas, Thirty-third University Avenue, Little Rock, Arkansas 72204
Phone:	501-569-3362
Cost:	Research participation

Assessment type: Curriculum-compatible for IFSP goals; ecological; judgment-based analysis of the social and physical home environment.

Age/focus group: Birth to 72 months (two sections: birth to 36 months, 36–72 months).

Domains/content: For the birth to 36-month section, 45 items in six categories: emotional responsibility of mother, avoidance of restriction, environmental organization, play materials, maternal involvement, and stimulation opportunities; for the 36- to 72-month section, 80 items in seven categories: stimulation, mature behavior, language environment, avoidance of restriction, pride/affection/thoughtfulness, masculine stimulation, and independence.

Special needs options: Revision needed to be sensitive to the interactive needs and issues of children with disabilities and parents.

Curricular links: Serves as a criterion-referenced tool to detect factors that require modification to optimize the home environment.

Authenticity: Stresses natural observations in the home setting but has limitations in use with children who have serious delays/disabilities.

Family involvement: Includes family input but does not clearly match current family-centered practices.

Scoring/sample: Yes/no scoring; multiple assessors are helpful.

Validation: One of the most widely researched early childhood de-vices; norm-based data for comparative purposes; adequate reliability and validity for screening purposes.

Training needed: Good observational skills and sensitivity to family needs, integrity, and dignity, especially under difficult circumstances; for use by professionals and assistants.

Comments:
- *Premier ecological assessment scale*
- *Essential in family services operations*
- *Revision required to address cultural differences, disability appropriateness, and family-centered practices*

LINK Index

Authentic	1	2	③
Convergent	1	②	3
Collaborative	1	②	3
Equitable	①	2	3
Sensitive	1	②	3
Congruent	1	②	3
Total Index	$\boxed{1}$ +	$\boxed{8}$ +	$\boxed{3}$ ÷ 6 = $\boxed{2.0}$

Overall quality: acceptable

3.0, exemplary; 2.5, high; 2.0, acceptable; 1.5, low; 1.0, negligible.

Home Observation for Measurement of the Environment (HOME)

Perhaps the most widely used measure of the content, quality, and responsiveness of young children's home environments is the Home Observation for Measurement of the Environment (HOME). The reliability and validity of the HOME inventory for normal infants and preschoolers has been well established, but research on its application in populations of children with developmental disabilities is only emerging. The HOME inventory is appropriate for children ranging in age from birth to 72 months. The first section (birth to 36-month age range) appraises such clusters of home ecological attributes as emotional and verbal responsibility of the mother, avoidance of restriction and punishment, organization of the physical and temporal environment, provision of adequate play materials, and opportunities for variety in daily stimulation. Similar dimensions are tapped in the second section for the 37- to 72-month-old child: provision of stimulation through equipment; ride, affection, and thoughtfulness; masculine stimulation; and independence from parental control.

HOME is an effective tool for analyzing the stimulating quality of the home environment and for providing tangible guidelines about ways to intervene when necessary. Its adaptation for infants and preschoolers with disabilities and their families is overdue.

Much interest is apparent in the design and development of instruments to assess the social and physical aspects of the child's environment. These are termed ecological assessment procedures; they include appraisals of family dynamics, parent–child interaction and stress, characteristics of the preschool classroom setting, and aspects of the home environment. Given federal mandates to devise IFSPs, such family or ecological measures are increasingly needed.

Sample Items from the Home Observation for Measurement of the Environment (HOME)

Ages 0–36 Months

I. Emotional and verbal responsivity of mother

	Yes	No
1. Mother spontaneously vocalizes to child at least twice during visit (excluding scolding).		
2. Mother responds to child's vocalizations with a verbal response.		
3. Mother tells child the name of some object during visit or says name of person or object in a "teaching" style.		
4. Mother's speech is distinct, clear, and audible.		
5. Mother initiates verbal interchanges with observer—asks questions and makes spontaneous comments.		
6. Mother expresses ideas freely and easily and uses statements of appropriate length for conversation (e.g., gives more than brief answers).		
7. Mother permits child occasionally to engage in "messy" type of play.		
8. Mother spontaneously praises child's qualities of behavior twice during visit.		
9. When speaking of or to child, mother's voice conveys positive feeling.		
10. Mother caresses or kisses child at least once during visit.		
11. Mother shows some positive emotional responses to praise of child offered by visitor.		

Ages 36–72 Months

II. Stimulation of mature behavior

22–29 Child is encouraged to learn the following:

	Yes	No
22. Colors.		
23. Shapes.		
24. Patterned speech (nursery rhymes, prayers, songs, TV commercials, etc.).		
25. The alphabet.		
26. To tell time.		
27. Spatial relationships (up, down, under, big, little, etc.).		
28. Numbers.		
29. To read a few words.		
30. Tries to get child to pick up and put away toys after play session—without help.		
31. Child is taught rules of social behavior which involve recognition or rights of others.		
32. Parent teaches child some simple manners—to say, "Please," "Thank you," "I'm sorry."		
33. Some delay of food gratification is demanded of the child, e.g., not to whine or demand food unless within ½ hour of mealtime.		

From Caldwell, B., & Bradley, R.A. (1978). *Home Observation for Measurement of the Environment (HOME)*, p. 121. Little Rock: University of Arkansas; reprinted by permission.

Individualized Assessment and Treatment for Autistic and Developmentally Disabled Children (IATA)

Author(s):	E. Schopler, R. Reichler, A. Bashford, M. Lansing, & L. Marcus
Year:	1979
Publisher:	PRO-ED
Address:	8700 Shoal Creek Boulevard, Austin, Texas 78757-6897
Phone:	512-451-3246
Cost:	Volume I, *Psychoeducational Profile–Revised (PEP–R) Complete Program* (manual and summary sheet), $59; Volume II, *Teaching Strategies for Parents and Professionals*, $29; Volume III, *Teaching Activities for the Autistic Child*, $69; Volume IV, *Adolescents and Adults*, $49

Assessment type: Curriculum embedded.

Age/focus group: Designed for children functioning at the preschool level within the chronological age range from 1 to 12 years and for preschoolers with autism. It can be used in an individual, center-, or home-based program.

Scale(s):   Individualized Assessment and Treatment for Autistic and Developmentally Disabled Children Tracking Progress Chart and Weekly Home Log.

Date system: PEP sheets.

Domains/content: Imitation, perception, fine and gross motor, eye–hand coordination, cognitive performance, and cognitive verbal skills.

Special needs options: Designed specifically for use with children with atypical development and special behavioral needs.

Authenticity: Clear emphasis on real-life activities, settings, and methods that provide goals for intervention.

Family involvement: The importance of cooperation between teachers and parents is emphasized through the curriculum. Strategies for involving parents are provided.

Training needed: Knowledge of and experience with working with children and families of the target population is recommended. Careful review of materials and manual is also helpful.

Validation: Data concerning the effectiveness of the program can be found in Mittler (1981).

Comments:
- *Linkage suggestions for IEP/IFSP and program development*
- *In all, 250 teaching activities and goals*
- *Individual tracking of progress*
- *Family involvement is stressed*

LINK Index			
Authentic	1	②	3
Convergent	1	②	3
Collaborative	1	2	③
Equitable	1	②	3
Sensitive	1	②	3
Congruent	1	2	③
Total Index	☐ +	8 +	6 ÷ 6 = 2.3
Overall quality: acceptable			

3.0, exemplary; 2.5, high; 2.0, acceptable; 1.5, low; 1.0, negligible.

Individualized Assessment and Treatment for Autistic and Developmentally Disabled Children (IATA)

Individualized Assessment and Treatment for Autistic and Developmentally Disabled Children (IATA) is organized into three volumes. Volume I, the *Psychoeducational Profile* (PEP), is used to assess the abilities of the child. Seven learning functions are examined: imitation, perception, gross motor, fine motor, eye–hand integration, cognitive performance, and cognitive verbal.

Volume II contains teaching strategies for parents and teachers. Volume III provides teaching activities. There is no attempt to provide a general curriculum for the target population; because of the truly individual characteristics of this population, such a curriculum is not conceivable. Progress toward individual goals can be tracked through forms such as the Tracking Progress form.

Knowledge of the target population and experience working with children and their families are essential. A careful study of the materials and ongoing communication with other professionals will aid in planning and implementation. The importance of cooperation between teachers and parents is emphasized throughout the curriculum. Regular personal contact between teacher and parent is essential to implementation. Parents are encourage to observe in the classroom and to share ideas they may have used successfully with their children. Home visits by the teacher are also considered important.

Communication and recording procedures are guided by both the parents' and the professional's need for information. Weekly home logs and parent–teacher notebooks are used to facilitate communication.

The curriculum and assessment offer a well-planned and reasonable program for children with those disabilities that continue to puzzle educators. A variety of activities are provided, and strategies are explained carefully. Cooperation between home and school greatly enhances the potential for progress.

B-2   SELF-ABUSE

Problem: Head banging.

Background: Sherry is a well-coordinated, active 4-year-old girl. She functions generally at a 2-½ year level, but has an expressive vocabulary of less than five words. Sherry is aware of others and able to predict their responses to her behavior. Her moods fluctuate unpredictably. For a year she has been banging her head frequently whenever she is upset either by mood or by interruptions in her self-chosen play. This behavior is distressing to her parents but does not cause obvious physical damage. Neither punishment nor special affection seemed to help decrease the behavior.

Analysis: Sherry's head banging brings immediate attention from others. She does not seem to care whether this attention is angry and punitive or concerned and affectionate. She does seem to know that banging her head will make you change your demands and let her have her way.

Objective: To decrease head banging by changing your response to this behavior, that is, not giving her attention or changing your demands.

Intervention: During the table activities (puzzles, peg board, and crayons) place the table and her chair so she cannot bang the wall behind her. Whenever Sherry starts to bang her head on the table, pull the materials toward you and turn your body away from her. Count to 10 (approximately 10 seconds) and then turn back, giving her the materials again. Give her a little help with the first step only. Praise her when she begins to work. Repeat this response each time she bangs, but do not discontinue the tasks until they are finished (you can shorten the tasks if she is feeling particularly upset that day, but be sure she puts in the last piece so she knows she is not getting out of the task). Continue this for 2 weeks, marking on your chart each time she bangs (see Figure 10.1). It is important to pay lots of attention and give praise when she is not banging.

Date	Activity	Head banging episodes (one mark for each time you turned away)
1–20	Ring stack	III

From Schopler, E., Reichler, R., Bashford, A., Lansing, M., Marcus, L., & Waters, L. (1979). *Individualized Assessment and Treatment for Autistic and Developmentally Disabled Children (IATA)*, p. 226. Austin,TX: PRO-ED; reprinted by permission.

Index III
BEHAVIORAL INTERVENTIONS

Type	No.	Specific Problem	Estimated Language Age	Page No.
Self-Abuse	B¹-1	Biting hand	2 years	225
	B-2	Head banging	1 year	226
	b-14	Head banging	0–1 year	238
	b-15	Face slapping	0–1 year	238
Aggression	B-3	Spitting at people	2½ years	227
	B-4	Slapping adult's face	0–1 year	238
	b-16	Biting others	0–1 year	238
	b-17	Pulling hair	1½ years	239
Disruption	B-5	Throwing objects	2 years	229
	B-6	Screaming, crying, yelling	3 years	230
	B-7	Jumping up from table	2½ years	231
	b-21	Jumps up from table	2½ years	240
	b-18	Silliness	1½ years	239
	b-19	Provocative teasing	3 years	239
	b-20	Whining	1½ years	240
	b-22	Makes loud noises	2½ years	240
Repetition	B-8	Mouthing objects	2½ years	232
	B-9	Perseverative questions	3 years	233
	b-23	Perseverative noises	2 years	241
	b-24	Object attachment	1½ years	241
	b-25	Object attachment	2 years	242
	b-26	Infantile clinging	0–1 year	242
Deficit	B-10	Short attention span	1 year	234
	B-11	Lacks initiative	5 years	235
	B-12	Disinterest in physical contact	0–1 year	236
	B-13	Impulsivity	3 years	237
	b-27	Poor eye contact	3 years	243
	b-28	Impulsive grabbing	2 years	243
	b-29	Lacks initiative	1½ years	244

From Schopler, E., Reichler, R., Bashford, A., Lansing, M., Marcus, L., & Waters, L. (1979). *Individualized Assessment and Treatment for Autistic and Developmentally Disabled Children (IATA)*, p. 17. Austin,TX: PRO-ED; reprinted by permission.

Infant–Toddler Developmental Assessment (IDA)

Author(s):	S. Provence, J. Erikson, S. Vater, & S. Palmeri
Year:	1995
Publisher:	Riverside Publishing Co.
Address:	8420 Bryn Mawr Avenue, Chicago, Illinois 60631
Phone:	800-323-9540
Cost:	$350

Age/focus group: Birth to 42 months.

Assessment type: Curriculum-compatible structured format to integrate the "clinical process" of developmental assessment and parent–professional team decision making about early needs.

Scoring/sample: Three-level graduated scoring system: present, absent, and emerging; percentage delay computations based on norm-based (age), but not norm group, statistics. Field-validation sample: 100 infants and toddlers, ages birth to 3 years.

Domains/content: IDA consists of three instruments/forms—IDA/Provence Birth-to-Three Developmental Profile, IDA Parent Report, and IDA Health Recording Guide—which focus on motor, language, cognitive-adaptive, feelings, social adaptation, and personality trait domains, as well as various subdomains, and integrated developmental concerns, health concerns, and family strengths and priorities to create the IFSP.

Special needs options: Flexible clinical process of collaborative problem solving allows professionals to focus on adaptations and special needs in IFSP; IDA scale contains no adaptations.

Curricular links: IDA scale items are compatible with general goals or entry points in prominent developmental curricula.

Authenticity: Flexible process emphasizes each child's developmental context; items and assessment strategies stress observation of real-life competencies in natural settings, at home, and during play.

Family involvement: Promotes parent partnership and collaboration.

Validation: Field validations and psychometric analyses on reliability (interrater and internal consistency); validity (i.e., content, construct, concurrent, criterion); and efficacy and efficiency-of-use data.

Training needed: Familiarity with team processes and parent–professional collaborations.

Comments:
- *Superb operational format to facilitate an integrated process of early developmental assessment and decision making*
- *Provides a general link between assessment and intervention*
- *Ensures parent participation in the process*
- *Integrates health concerns into decision making*
- *Exemplar of a more authentic and collaborative form for future assessments procedures in early intervention*

LINK Index			
Authentic	1	2	③
Convergent	1	2	③
Collaborative	1	2	③
Equitable	1	②	3
Sensitive	1	②	3
Congruent	1	②	3
Total Index	☐ +	6 +	9 ÷ 6 = 2.5
Overall quality: high			

3.0, exemplary; 2.5, high; 2.0, acceptable; 1.5, low; 1.0, negligible.

Infant–Toddler Developmental Assessment (IDA)

One of the enduring challenges of early intervention has been to identify the most effective ways to synchronize and coordinate the process of team assessment and parent partnerships, shared decision making, and service delivery, especially for infants and toddlers. Widely used practices, however, still involve largely unintegrated multidisciplinary procedures.

Infant-Toddler Developmental Assessment (IDA) is described as "an integrated clinical process" to be facilitated by an interdisciplinary or transdisciplinary team of parents and professionals for the youngest children with developmental delays. The IDA phases and methods exemplify many characteristics of authentic, convergent, and curriculum-compatible assessment procedures that are recommended practices in early intervention.

IDA consists of six coordinated phases that must be implemented in a unified fashion because each phase is a prerequisite to the next, so that the sequence of assessment/decision-making/intervention/monitoring activities is integrated. These six phases include 1) referral and prereferral data gathering, 2) initial parent interview, 3) health review, 4) developmental observation and assessment, 5) integration and synthesis, and 6) results sharing.

Three instruments facilitate the linkage among phases. These instruments are IDA/Provence Birth–Three Developmental Profile, IDA Health Recording Guide, and IDA Parent Report. The IDA/Provence Profile contains landmark developmental and self-regulatory competencies that provide clear, albeit general, linkages to various early intervention curricula. The scale samples both traditional and unique domains: gross motor, fine motor, relationship to inanimate objects, language/communication, self-help, relationship to people, emotions and feeling states, and coping behavior. While most tasks are traditional, many items tap competencies in real-life circumstances (e.g., uses toy to relieve tension or distress, recovers from small hurts by self). The IDA manual describes in detail each of the six phases and how to implement each through a team process that is guided by the forms. Case vignettes show the integrated IDA process in action.

The authors are to be commended for conducting sensible field-validation studies on the system; they study approximately 100 infants and toddlers with delays and their parents. Reliability and validity studies included content, construct, concurrent, interrater, and criterion-related research as well as important efficiency studies. Although it is not technically adequate, we support the confident use of the IDA percentage delay criteria for eligibility determination reported in the manual, because such flexibility and comprehensiveness, rather than mere psychometric considerations, should be the deciding factors in systems developed for use in early intervention.

Sample of the Infant-Toddler Developmental Assessment (IDA)

Feelings, Social Adaptation, and Personality Traits

SH — 5. Self-Help	P — 6. Relationship to Persons	E — 7. Emotions & Feeling States	C — 8. Coping Behavior	Age (mos.)
☐ 5. Pushes adult hand away. (P 8, C 7) ☐ 6. Works to obtain toy out of reach. (RI 8, C 6)	☐ 8. Pushes/moves to avoid. (SH 5, C 7) ☐ 8.1 Reacts to strangers. (E 10) ☐ 8.2 * Clings to familiar adult in distress. (C 7.1) ☐ 9. Plays peek-a-boo. ☐ 9.1 Responds to pickup gesture. (L 7.3) ☐ 10. * Plays pat-a-cake; bye; so-big. (L 8.1) ☐ 11. Expresses affection, anger. (E 11) ☐ 11.1 Understands "no." (L 8.3) ☐ 11.2 Responds to names of parents. (L 8.2) ☐ 11.3 Begins to object to separation. (E 12)	☐ 10. Shows distinct stranger reaction. (P 8.1) ☐ 11. * Expresses many recognizable emotions (large repertoire and wide range). (P 11) ☐ 12. * Begins to show anxiety at separation from parent. (P 11.3)	☐ 6. Seeks or avoids objects by rolling. (RI 8, SH 6) ☐ 6.1 Uses vocal signals to gain assistance. (L 6.1) ☐ 7. * Pushes away an unwanted person or object. (SH 5, P 8) ☐ 7.1 Actively seeks familiar persons when distressed. (P 8.2)	7 to 10
☐ 7. Feeds self cookie or cracker. ☐ 8. Extends toy back and forth. (L 9, P 12, RI 12.1) ☐ 9. Actively "helps" in dressing.	☐ 12. Hands toy or other object back and forth. (RI 12.1, L 9, SH 8) ☐ 13. * Rolls ball to another. (FM 11.2) ☐ 13.1 Imitates actions. (FM 12, RI 13.1) ☐ 14. * Hugs parent.	☐ 13. * Expresses affection toward familiar persons actively. ☐ 14. Shows anger toward persons or objects.	☐ 8. Uses locomotion to seek or avoid. ☐ 8.1 Uses toys to relieve tension or distress. ☐ 9. Uses transitional object for self comfort.	10 to 13
☐ 10. Wakes alone with signs of pleasure. (E 16, C 12) ☐ 10.1 Partially feeds self with spoon or fingers. (C 13)	☐ 15. Indicates wants by pointing. (L 11, C 12.1) ☐ 16. * Plays "Where is your eye?" etc. (L 13.1) ☐ 16.1 Shows oppositional behavior. (E 15, C 12.2) ☐ 16.2 Seeks affection or reassurance. ☐ 16.3 Kisses with a pucker.	☐ 15. Expresses oppositional feelings. (P 16.1, C 12.2) ☐ 16. Shows pride in new accomplishments. (SH 10, C 12)	☐ 10. * Looks for hidden object. (RI 13, RI 14.1) ☐ 11. Begins to detour around obstacles. ☐ 12. Shows pleasure in new skills. (SH 10, E 16) ☐ 12.1 Points or asks for desired object. (L 11, L 14.1, P 15, P 17) ☐ 12.2 * Rejects unwanted object or attention. (P 16.1, E 15)	13 to 18

Infant/Toddler Environment Rating Scale
(ITERS)

Author(s): T. Harms, D. Crier, & R.M. Clifford
Year: 1990
Publisher: Teachers College Press
Address: 1234 Amsterdam Avenue, New York, New York 10027
Phone: 212-678-3929
Cost: $30+

Assessment type: Curriculum compatible for programming purposes; ecological rating scale; observation-based decisions regarding program elements and needed changes.

Age/focus group: Infants and toddlers.

Domains/content: Seven domains: furnishings and display for children, personal care routines, listening and talking, learning activities, interaction, program structure, and adult needs.

Special needs options: Scale targets typically developing children; authors are developing modifications for children who are at risk for and those who have disabilities.

Curricular links: Links to instructional, behavioral, and environmental aspects of the IFSP that address the impact of the environment on individual child adaptation and adjustment.

Authenticity: Clear, authentic features focus on program elements and environmental modifications that are amenable to change.

Family involvement: Primarily for professionals but surveys some family aspects.

Scoring/sample: A 7-point rating scale that ranges from inadequate to excellent; graph of acceptability of various program elements.

Validation: Field validations and reliability and validity studies in early childhood programs in North Carolina; content developed according to NAEYC criteria.

Training needed: Can be completed collaboratively by program supervisors and staff for self-appraisals.

Comments:

- *One of the few readily available program rating systems*
- *Shows valuable use for program self-evaluations*
- *Validated adaptations are required to address the special needs groups that are identified in the manual*
- *Can be modified by experienced staff for other applications*
- *Contributes to more complete IFSP development and individual programming changes for specific children*

LINK Index			
Authentic	1	2	③
Convergent	1	②	3
Collaborative	1	②	3
Equitable	①	2	3
Sensitive	1	②	3
Congruent	1	②	3
Total Index	1 +	8 +	3 ÷ 6 = 2.0

Overall quality: acceptable

3.0, exemplary; 2.5, high; 2.0, acceptable; 1.5, low; 1.0, negligible.

Infant/Toddler Environment Rating Scale (ITERS)

Also based on the ECERS format is the Infant/Toddler Rating Scale (ITERS), which surveys the common environmental domains by using the 7-point rating scale format of ECERS. The items focus on the needs of infants and toddlers and the adequacy of caregiver training. The adaptive provisions for infants and toddlers with special needs are not as broad as are those contained in the FDRS; for example, item 31 of the ITERS includes a generic category, Provisions for Exceptional Children, which surveys the adequacy of all modifications that are instituted, including basic physical needs, changes in daily schedules and routines, and staff communication with parents.

Sample from the Infant/Toddler Environment Rating Scale (ITERS)

	Inadequate 1	2	Minimal 3	4	Good 5	6	Excellent 7
31. Provisions for exceptional children*	−No attention to the special needs of the exceptional child. −Only the child's basic physical needs are met (Ex. fed and toileted). −Child not included in play activities.		−Minor changes made in the schedule, environment, and routines to get through the day. −Child involved in some play activities provided for the other children.		−Caregiver provides activities, adapts schedule to meet the child's needs. (Ex. finds toys child can use, provides daily activity on child's level). −Caregiver adapts physical environment if necessary (Ex. adds ramps or hand rail). −Caregiver interacts with exceptional child as much as with other children.		−Caregiver follows programs developed by or with trained professional. −Caregiver uses information from assessment in care of child. −Close communication among staff, parents, and other professionals working with the child and family.
ADULT NEEDS							
32. Adult personal needs*	−No special areas for staff (Ex. no separate restroom, lounge, storage for personal belongings). −No time provided away from children to meet personal needs (Ex. no time for breaks).		−Separate adult restroom. −Some adult furniture available outside of children's area. −Some storage for personal belongings. −At least one scheduled time for caregiver to be away from job responsibilities. −Some staff available to cover unscheduled, necessary breaks (Ex. phone calls, restroom).		−Adult lounge area available; lounge may have dual use (Ex. office, storeroom). −Adult furniture in lounge. −Convenient storage for personal belongings with security provisions if necessary. −Morning, afternoon, and lunch breaks provided. −Facilities provided for staff meals/snacks (Ex. refrigerator space, cooking facilities).		−Separate adult lounge area. −Comfortable adult furniture in lounge. −Flexible break times.

Reprinted by permission of the publisher from Harms, T., Cryer, D., & Clifford, R.M., INFANT/TODDLER ENVIRONMENT RATING SCALE (ITERS) (New York: Teachers College Press, © 1990 by Thelma Harms, Debbie Cryer, & Richard Clifford. All rights reserved.), p. 37.

Instrument for Measuring Progress (IMP)

Author(s): J. McAllister
Year: 1994
Publisher: Author
Address: Children's Hospital, Child Development Unit, 3705 Fifth Avenue,
Pittsburgh, Pennsylvania 15213
Phone: 412-692-5560
Cost: Research participation

Assessment type: Curriculum-compatible, comprehensive developmental assessment system.

Age/focus group: Birth to 8 years.

Domains/content: Academic, language, motor, self-help, and social domains; serves clinical and administrative purposes; system encourages the evaluation of individual and group progress and reflects on program impact.

Special needs options: Graduated scoring links performance and small increments of change determined by extent of instructional/ behavioral help needed.

Curricular links: Specific links between IMP tasks and comparable tasks in most commercially available developmental curricula.

Authenticity: Emphasizes the use of direct observation of skills in both structured and unstructured settings; includes parents as partners in assessment process.

Scoring/sample: Graduated scoring options; developmental ages; graphing intra-individual progress.

Family involvement: Incorporates parent reports and observations.

Validation: Field-validation in clinics and school district preschool programs for young children with special needs.

Training needed: Used by parents, professionals, and assistants in collaboration.

Comments:
- *Not available commercially*
- *Unique curriculum-based assessment measure that blends norm-referenced, curricular, and authentic features*
- *Graduated scoring system is one of the most useful systems available*
- *Excellent treatment validity*

LINK Index			
Authentic	1	②	3
Convergent	1	2	③
Collaborative	1	②	3
Equitable	1	2	③
Sensitive	1	2	③
Congruent	1	②	3
Total Index	☐ +	6 +	9 ÷ 6 = 2.5
Overall quality: high			

3.0, exemplary; 2.5, high; 2.0, acceptable; 1.5, low; 1.0, negligible.

Instrument for Measuring Progress (IMP)

The Instrument for Measuring Progress (IMP) is an integrated computer-based system for curriculum-based developmental assessment, program evaluation, ongoing parent–preschool communication (i.e., behavioral report cards), and computer output of IEPs and data for progress monitoring. A computer bank of 800 developmentally sequenced objectives provides the foundation of IMP, which spans the birth-to-8-years age range. Child performance is quantified according to pass, fail, or emergent criteria; once transitional skills as objectives have been chosen for the child, the computer program automatically calculates developmental age levels for each child; developmental scores are stored automatically and graphed across the major domains (i.e., adaptive, academic/cognitive, receptive language, expressive language, fine motor, gross motor, and social). The cumulative data are stored and graphed longitudinally to monitor child progress and program impact for individual children and for groups of children within classrooms. A unique feature of the IMP is that each developmental objective includes graduated scoring criteria of progress toward mastery, which often involves a number of successful learning trials or performance under various instructional conditions (e.g., visual cues, verbal cues). This evidence of progress toward mastery provides a powerful tool for helping parents and professionals recognize and value small increments of change. We regard the IMP as a prototype for the future of curriculum-based developmental measurement that combines authenticity with clear utility for teaching and program planning.

Sample for theInstrument for Measuring Progress (IMP)
Developmental Continuum Display

+ 1.0 Annual Goal: Increase expressive language skills

+ **Short Term Instructional Objective:**
+ • Tony will use noun phrases with adjectives (e.g., "big ball")
+ Step 1: Perform target behavior 2×/day when modeled
+ Step 2: Perform target behavior 2×/day when modeled
+ Mastery: Perform target behavior spontaneously, 3×/day

+

+ 2.0 Annual Goal: Increase expressive language skills

+ **Short Term Instructional Objective:**
+ • Tony will convey simple message
+ Step 1: Perform target behavior with multiple repetitions, 2/4×
+ Step 2: Perform target behavior with multiple repetitions, 2/4×
+ Mastery: Perform target behavior on request, 3/4×

+

− 3.0 Annual Goal: Increase expressive language skills

− **Short Term Instructional Objective:**
− • Tony will respond to "what" questions involving noun response, no visual cues
− Step 1: Perform target behavior 2/5× with concrete referent present
± Step 2: Perform target behavior 4/5× with concrete referent present
− Mastery: Perform target behavior 4/5 presentations, within vocabulary constraints

—

− 4.0 Annual Goal: Increase expressive language skills

− **Short Term Instructional Objective:**
− • Tony will relate immediate experiences to others
± Step 1: Perform target behavior with visual or verbal cues, 3×/session
− Step 2: Perform target behavior spontaneously or when asked, 3×/session
− Mastery: Perform target behavior spontaneously or when asked, 5×/session

—

− = Absent Skill
+ = Mastered Skill
± = Emerging Skill

From McAllister, J. (1994). *Instrument for Measuring Progress (IMP)*, p. 12. Pittsburgh, PA: Children's Hospital of Pittsburgh; reprinted by permission.

Kendall Demonstration Elementary School (KDES) Preschool Curriculum Guide

Author(s):	Pre-College Programs, Gallaudet University
Year:	1989
Publisher:	Pre-College Outreach Services, Kendall Demonstration Elementary School
Address:	800 Florida Avenue, NE, Washington, D.C. 20002
Phone:	202-651-5380 (Gallaudet University Bookstore)
Cost:	$16

Assessment type: Curriculum embedded.

Age/focus group: Designed for preschool-age children who are deaf or have a hearing impairment. It can be used individually or in a center-based program.

Scales: Scope and Sequence Charts, used to plan and monitor curricular progress.

Data system: Scope and Sequence Charts are provided as the main record-keeping tool for individual student progress.

Domains/content: Personal, social, physical, and affective domains.

Special needs options: Program modifications for students with special needs are provided; these include modifications for class size, physical space, and yearly objectives and expectations.

Authenticity: The curriculum is based on a detailed scope and sequence of objectives that describe the content of material to be learned and the order in which it should be learned.

Family involvement: Family involvement is encouraged. Parent–Infant Program is an integral part of the curriculum development.

Training needed: Knowledge of target population and experience working with families of target population are useful. Care-
ful review of manual is helpful.

Validation: Curriculum guide represents the culmination of several years of work by teachers and other staff at the
Kendall School, but no formal data are provided for reliability and validity. It is noted, however, that all activities and objectives were tested extensively in classrooms with children of the same approximate ages and
levels of hearing loss.

Comments:
- *Tailored to preschoolers with hearing impairments*
- *Covers language development and cognitive, mo-
  tor, and social areas*
- *Introduces basic subject matter in arithmetic,
  writing, and so forth*
- *Provides extensive lesson plans in all domains*
- *Scope and sequence charts provide tracking sys-
  tem*
- *Inexpensive!*

LINK Index			
Authentic	1	2	③
Convergent	1	②	3
Collaborative	1	②	3
Equitable	1	2	③
Sensitive	1	2	③
Congruent	1	2	③
Total Index	☐ +	4 +	12 ÷ 6 = 2.7
Overall quality: high			

3.0, exemplary; 2.5, high; 2.0, acceptable; 1.5, low; 1.0, negligible.

Kendall Demonstration Elementary School (KDES) Preschool Curriculum Guide

The Kendall Demonstration Elementary School (KDES) Preschool Curriculum Guide was developed over a number of years at the Kendall Preschool at Gallaudet University. It is designed to provide a comprehensive program for children between 2 and 5 years of age who are deaf or who have hearing impairments. The curriculum consists of six domains: intellectual, communicative, personal, social, physical, and affective development. A total communication approach is used to work toward mastery of more than 750 objectives.

The curriculum is built around routines and themes that incorporate objectives across developmental domains. The six themes are 1) beginning of school, 2) self and others, 3) families, 4) homes and neighborhoods, 5) concept of change, and 6) close of school.

Objectives related to major themes are displayed in the scope and sequence charts. These charts can also be used to plan and monitor progress. Resource units provide greater detail and topics appropriate within the major themes. All resource units include main ideas, learning objectives, suggested activities, evaluation procedures, and resources. Student Achievement Records are provided to monitor individual and group progress for each resource unit.

Although the KDES is dedicated to children with hearing impairments, sensible suggestions are also offered to accommodate additional special needs. To be certain, youngsters with hearing impairments often display behavior and learning delays and difficulties. The authors offer five major tenets that underlie the KDES. These are 1) importance of the family, 2) use of total communication, 3) communication with both the hearing and the deaf communities, 4) foundations for academic competence, and 5) activity- or experience-based simultaneous development across domains. The Kendall Preschool Curriculum is part of a series of programs available from Gallaudet University.

KDES PRESCHOOL CURRICULUM

SCOPE AND SEQUENCE--LANGUAGE

Proficiency (P) Scale*

Attention Skills

	0+	1	2	3	4
1. Demonstrate awareness of surroundings by actively inspecting the area visually or physically.	X				
2. Visually track moving objects or people.	X				
3. Show interest in an adult or object by maintaining eye contact	X				
4. Show anticipatory response to the approach of a familiar person or object.	X				
5. Follow adult's gaze after adult breaks eye contact, looks elsewhere, alone or in a group.	X				
6. Attend to an adult long enough to establish a shared reference.	X				
7. Attend to short games, stories, songs when student is actively involved.		X			
8. Attend to short games, stories, songs when student is passively involved.			X		
9. Attend to face and hands of adult using language to describe situation or time.	X	X	X	X	
10. Attend to movies, live performances independently.			X		
11. Attend to ongoing dialogues between adults.			X		
12. Imitate simple actions and facial expressions when asked to do so.		X			
13. Imitate words and phrases when asked to do so: one word		X			
two words			X		
two--three words				X	
three words					X

From Pre-College Programs, Gallaudet University. (1989). *Kendall Demonstration Elementary School (KDES) preschool curriculum guide,* p. 17. Washington, DC: Pre-College Outreach Services, Kendall Demonstration Elementary School; reprinted by permission.

Sample from Kendall Demonstration Elementary School (KDES)
Preschool Curriculum Guide

PRESCHOOL CURRICULUM GUIDE

Student Achievement Record

NAME: _____   Date: _____

Taught From _____ through _____

EVALUATION KEY

1. <u>Not Competent</u>: Student cannot demonstrate performance of this skill or behavior.

2. <u>Emerging Competence</u>: Student is able to demonstrate some performance of this skill or behavior.

3. <u>Competent</u>: Student consistently shows this skill. Behavior is now generalized.

OBJECTIVES	CRITERIA	COMMENTS
1. Predict the next activity in the daily routine.	1 2 3	_____
2. Identify classmates and teachers in photos.	1 2 3	_____
3. Differentiate between the concepts of school and home.	1 2 3	_____
a. Identify children who came to school and those who stayed home.	1 2 3	_____
b. Imitate the teacher by counting the number of students and the quantity of materials needed to supply them.	1 2 3	_____
c. Identify a school bus.	1 2 3	_____
d. List activities done in school.	1 2 3	_____
e. State whether they are at home, at school, or on a school bus.	1 2 3	_____
f. Categorize things as associated with either school or home.	1 2 3	_____

From Pre-College Programs, Gallaudet University. (1989). *Kendall Demonstration Elementary School (KDES) preschool curriculum guide,* p. 95. Washington, DC: Pre-College Outreach Services, Kendall Demonstration Elementary School; reprinted by permission.

Kent Infant Development Scale,
Second Edition (KIDS)

Author(s): J. Reuter & L. Bickett
Year: 1985
Publisher: Kent Developmental Metrics
Address: 126 West College Avenue, Post Office Box 3178, Kent, Ohio 44240
Phone: 216-678-3589
Cost: $30

Age/focus group:	Infants with either chronological or developmental ages between birth and 12 months.
Assessment type:	Curriculum compatible; norm based; observational determination of developmental age status by parents and professionals.
Scoring/sample:	A (yes), B (did but outgrew), C (no longer able), or D (cannot do yet); parent report; developmental ages, percentiles, and delays.
Domains/content:	Five domains—cognitive, motor, language, self-help, and social—that encompass 252 behavioral descriptions.
Special needs options:	Relies on parent report; focuses on clear behavioral characteristics by age level; some items emphasize emotions and visual recognition rather than motor responses.
Curricular links:	Multidomain profile of developmental capabilities; emergent behaviors offer gross prescriptive objectives.
Authenticity:	Task content shows predominance of natural behaviors in natural settings; uses observational data from parents and professionals flexibly.
Family involvement:	Relies on parent reports and observations.

Validation: Normed on 480 infants in Northeastern Ohio in well-baby clinics and pediatricians' offices; test–retest validity, 88+; concurrent validity with Bayley Scales of Infant Development (Bayley, 1969), 70+; and reliability with infants with severe disabilities, 96+.

Training needed: Comprehensive knowledge of the scale and strong parent interview skills.

Comments:
- *Specialized and comprehensive measure for the first year of life*
- *Couples technical adequacy with economy and practicality*
- *Few adaptive qualities*
- *Should not be considered an infant curriculum but can be prescriptive*

 ↔

LINK Index			
Authentic	1	2	③
Convergent	1	2	③
Collaborative	1	2	③
Equitable	1	②	3
Sensitive	1	②	3
Congruent	1	2	③
Total Index	☐ +	4 +	12 ÷ 6 = 2.7
Overall quality: high			

3.0, exemplary; 2.5, high; 2.0, acceptable; 1.5, low; 1.0, negligible.

Kent Infant Development Scale, Second Edition (KIDS)

The Kent Infant Development Scale (KIDS) contains the most complete sample of competencies of infant behavior in the first year of life of any available norm-based measure (252 skills). Despite the fact that it is primarily a parent/caregiver reporting instrument, the KIDS's structure and content make it highly curriculum compatible and, therefore, prescriptive.

The KIDS surveys the infant's behavioral repertoire in five domains: cognitive, language, motor, self-help, and social. Within these domains, the scale taps many nontraditional characteristics and competencies, such as "gets startled by sudden voices or noises," "remembers where things are kept in the house," "imitates an action of an adult long after it occurred," and "shows jealousy." Care was taken to phrase items simply and to select colloquial terms so that parents and nonprofessionals could reliably judge the behavior. The KIDS offers several categories of scoring but unfortunately does not allow the recording of emergent skills.

Although no truly adaptive features are included in the scale, the KIDS has been field tested with children who have severe brain damage and who function within the infant developmental range. The authors advocate direct observation as an important supplement to caregiver information that covers such areas as rumination, temperamental style, attention, and motivational level for program planning. An important and valuable feature of the KIDS is computer scoring of the scale, which includes the response given for each item, the developmental age level for each domain, and the total raw score of behaviors within each of the five areas. In addition, a computer-generated report is offered.

The manual for the KIDS shows care in design and development. The norms, although they are not national, are clearly representative of infant expectancies. Spanish versions of the scale are available, and normative efforts are under way in Germany, The Netherlands, Spain, and Chile. The KIDS has been studied concurrently with the Bayley Scales of Infant Development (Bayley, 1993). At this time, no studies are available to compare its use with early developmental curricula. Nevertheless, the KIDS has compatibility in structure, content, and sampling, which makes it valuable for infant programming. Field-testing with children who have severe impairments adds a possible special needs–sensitive dimension.

The KIDS is a judgment-based normative assessment measure and, given the limitations of reported behaviors versus observed behaviors, should not be used as a sole program instrument. However, we believe that the KIDS can be a valuable component in a prescriptive assessment battery for infants who are at risk for and those who have disabilities. Its careful developmental base; active, clear item descriptions; and broad analysis of developmental competencies support its use as an initial prescriptive instrument. For example, the KIDS could be paired with The Carolina Curriculum for Infants and Toddlers with Special Needs or the Early Learning Accomplishment Profile to offer an exemplary assessment/curriculum linkage.

Selected Sample Tasks from the Kent Infant Development Scales, Second Edition (KIDS)

181. gets startled by sudden voices or noises
182. makes sounds when smiled at or tickled by an adult
183. walks holding onto furniture
184. crawls up stairs
185. smiles if an adult makes a funny face
186. plays with hands
187. smiles at the sight of a favorite toy
188. plays with two toys at the same time
189. shakes head "no"
190. picks up small objects the size of a pea
191. throws or flings a ball
192. sits up alone for a long time
193. walks, if both hands are held for balance
194. holds and drinks from a cup
195. pulls off socks
196. drinks from a cup held by an adult
197. holds spoon for a second when it's placed on his/her hand
198. laughs if an adult makes a funny face
199. reaches and pats image in mirror
200. plays with feet

From Reuter, J., & Bickett, L. (1985). *The Kent Infant Development Scale (KIDS)*, p. 13. Kent, OH: Kent Developmental Metrics; reprinted by permission.

Learning Accomplishment Profiles: Early Learning Accomplishment Profile (E–LAP)

Author(s): E. Glover, J. Preminger, & A. Sanford
Year: 1995
Publisher: Chapel Hill Training–Outreach Project
Address: 800 Eastowne Drive, Chapel Hill, North Carolina 27514
Phone: 919-490-5577
Cost: *E–LAP Development Kit*, $275; *E–LAP* (Spanish edition available at the same price), $8; *E–LAP Scoring Booklets*, $21; *Early Learning Activity Cards*, $50

Assessment type: Curriculum embedded.

Age/focus group: Designed for children from birth to 3 years old. It can be used in home- or center-based programs for individuals or some small groups.

Scale(s): E–LAP Profile Summative Recording Form.

Data system: Profile for summative recording is provided and is easily used by teams.

Domains/content: Fine and gross motor, language, self-help, social-emotional, and cognitive skills.

Special needs options: Cautions are stated regarding the need to adapt materials and procedures when assessing; in addition, specifics are not offered.

Authenticity: Items are based on the usual milestones and often are less authentic and more psychometric.

Family involvement: Activities can be used with parents in home-based programs, although special family-centered materials are not featured.

Training needed: Knowledge of target population; 2-day workshop is suggested.

Validation: No documentation of field use, reliabilities, and so forth.; norm referencing based on developmental literature is provided.

Comments:
- *Low density of items (less sensitivity) but easy to use, not time consuming*
- *Format invites multidisciplinary use*
- *Developmental milestone basis; questionable teachability/worth of some of the content*
- *Some family-friendly materials; child profile easily understood by parents*
- *Supplemental materials, audiovisual aids available*

LINK Index			
Authentic	1	②	3
Convergent	1	2	③
Collaborative	1	2	③
Equitable	1	②	3
Sensitive	1	②	3
Congruent	1	②	3
Total Index	☐ +	8 +	6 ÷ 6 = 2.3
Overall quality: acceptable			

3.0, exemplary; 2.5, high; 2.0, acceptable; 1.5, low; 1.0, negligible.

Learning Accomplishment Profiles:
Learning Accomplishment Profile–Revised (LAP–R)

Author(s): E. Glover, J. Preminger, A. Sanford, & J. Zelman
Year: 1995
Publisher: Chapel Hill Training–Outreach Project
Address: 800 Eastowne Drive, Chapel Hill, North Carolina 27514
Phone: 919-490-5577
Cost: *LAP–R Development Kit*, $207; *LAP–R Manuals* (set of 10), $65; *LAP–R* (Spanish edition available at the same price), $8; *LAP–R Scoring Booklets* (set of 20), $21; *Classroom Profile*, $5; *Learning Activities for Young Children*, $50

Assessment type: Curriculum embedded.

Age/focus group: Designed for children from 3 to 6 years old. It can be used in a small group or individually in either a center- or home-based program.

Scale(s): LAP Summative Recording Form.

Data system: LAP provides for summative recording of child's behavior.

Domains/content: Fine and gross motor, language, prewriting, self-help, personal-social, and cognitive skills.

Special needs options: No adaptations for special needs are provided.

Authenticity: Mixture of milestone/psychometric and authentic content.

Family involvement: Supplemental materials helpful in working with parents.

Training needed: Knowledge of the target population; 2-day workshop is suggested.

Validation: No field data or reliabilities data are provided. Literature-based norms for items are suggested.

Comments:

- *Caution against teaching to the assessment because many items are deemed not useful or worthwhile*
- *Kit is expensive*
- *Item coverage is not dense (i.e., not sensitive) but is relatively easy to use*
- *No adaptations for special needs*
- *Supplemental materials, audiovisual aids for staff and parent training*

LINK Index			
Authentic	1	②	3
Convergent	1	②	3
Collaborative	1	②	3
Equitable	1	②	3
Sensitive	1	②	3
Congruent	1	②	3
Total Index	☐ +	12 +	☐ ÷ 6 = 2.0
Overall quality: acceptable			

3.0, exemplary; 2.5, high; 2.0, acceptable; 1.5, low; 1.0, negligible.

Learning Accomplishment Profiles: Learning Accomplishment Profile–Diagnostic Standardized Assessment (LAP–D) (1992 Revision and Standardization)

Author(s):	A.D. Nehring, E.F. Nehring, J.R. Bruni, & P.L. Randolph
Year:	1992
Publisher:	Chapel Hill Training–Outreach Project & Kaplan School Supply
Address:	800 Eastowne Drive, Chapel Hill, North Carolina 27514
Phone:	919-490-5577
Cost:	$525

Assessment type: Curriculum-compatible with E–LAP and LAP and generically with others; formal standardized, norm-referenced assessment used to make educational decisions for young children and developing appropriate instructional objectives and strategies.

Age/focus group: 30–72 months.

Domains/content: Four domains (fine motor, gross motor, language, and cognition) and eight subscales (fine motor manipulation, fine motor writing, cognitive matching, cognitive counting, language naming, language comprehension, gross motor body movement, and gross motor object movement) are included.

Special needs options: Practitioners can use the LAP–D with special groups (e.g., children with low-incidence disabilities) as a criterion-referenced assessment but are advised against using normative data for comparison to special groups.

Curricular links: Content of the LAP–D shows approximately 80% compatibility with the LAP curriculum and its sequence of goals; LAP–D functions as the norm-referenced instrument for the LAP curriculum to link eligibility determination and individualized curriculum planning and IEP development.

Authenticity: General authenticity is low for the LAP materials because they contain traditional, contrived developmental tasks as inferential exemplars of underlying capabilities.

Family involvement: Incorporates parent observations for selected items.

Scoring/sample: Raw scores convert to percentile ranks, age equivalents, and standard scores.

Validation: Normative data on 800+ children ages 30–72 months; basic reliability and validity studies show acceptable technical adequacy.

Training needed: Can be administered by teachers, psychometrists, psychologists, or others with adequate preparation and training in administration of assessments.

Comments:
- *Provides an external norming structure for the LAP developmental sequence*
- *Facilitates the linking of assessment, curriculum planning, and intervention*
- *Continues the outmoded tradition of inauthentic developmental appraisal*
- *Appropriate only for children who are at risk for or who have mild disabilities*

LINK Index			
Authentic	1	②	3
Convergent	1	②	3
Collaborative	1	②	3
Equitable	1	②	3
Sensitive	1	②	3
Congruent	1	②	3
Total Index	☐ +	12 +	☐ ÷ 6 = 2.0
Overall quality: acceptable			

3.0, exemplary; 2.5, high; 2.0, acceptable; 1.5, low; 1.0, negligible.

Learning Accomplishment Profiles: Early Learning Accomplishment Profile (E–LAP), Learning Accomplishment Profile–Revised (LAP–R), and Learning Accomplishment Profile–Diagnostic Standardized Assessment (LAP–D)

The Learning Accomplishment Profile (LAP) curriculum content is centered around developmental milestones, as are most materials. Both the manual and the profile contain careful documentation of the original sources for individual items.

The LAP system includes three sets of materials: 1) Early Learning Accomplishment Profile (E–LAP) provides a wide selection of skills within each age range for ongoing assessment for children ages birth to 3 years and offers an easy way to appraise child status on milestone attainment; 2) Learning Accomplishment Profile–Revised (LAP–R) serves as a means of ongoing assessment of progress by the teacher/parent who is most familiar with the child (3–6 years); and 3) Learning Accomplishment Profile–Diagnostic Standardized Assessment (LAP–D), designed for use with children from birth to 6 years of age, is used to achieve three primary purposes—evaluation of the child's entry skills prior to the start of intervention, evaluation of the child's exit skills after participation in a given program, and validation of the intervention program itself. LAP–D is norm referenced and not a curriculum-based instructional program, per se.

Additional products extend the use of the program and provide a variety of activities. These include *Planning Guide: The Preschool Curriculum*, learning activity cards for both LAP and E–LAP, *Planning Guide for Gifted Preschoolers*, and supplemental books and audiovisual aids for staff and parents. These products assist in the development of inclusive programs. The LAP curriculum can be used in both center- and home-based programs with individuals or small groups. There are no special adaptations noted for specific special needs. When developing alternative activities, it is advisable to consult with specialists.

In 1992, Kaplan School Supply, in collaboration with the Chapel Hill Training Outreach Project, conducted a standardization and norming of the widely used LAP–R. The LAP–D retains the original characteristics of LAP–R, such as a criterion-referenced measure of developmental status in young children ages 30–72 months that also links to the LAP curriculum. This new revision and norming is timely and will strengthen the use of the LAP–D for eligibility determination and progress evaluation. Users of the entire LAP system will find that this hybrid, norm-/curriculum-based scale allows a closer fit between formal and more flexible assessment procedures.

Nevertheless, the LAP–D has several attributes that should signal caution to interdisciplinary teams. The norms should be applied very cautiously to young children with developmental delays because the field-validation and norming on special samples is unclear; the task analysis lacks sufficient density for detailed curricular linkages; the self-help scale has been eliminated from the revision; and the landmark nature of the tasks that are included limit the LAP–D, as well as the companion LAP curriculum, to use only with young children who are at risk for or who have mild delays.

LAP–D and its associated curriculum materials, which are products of the Chapel Hill Outreach Project, represent one of the most frequently used criterion-referenced curriculum scales covering the birth to 5½-year range. The LAP–D is an expanded compilation of various developmental tasks culled from traditional instruments (e.g., Bayley Scales of Infant Development [Bayley, 1993]) and placed at similar age levels, as determined by norm-referenced measures. The LAP–D scale combines the advantages of normed sequencing of developmental skills with precise targets for initiating individualized program planning.

The LAP–D is a developmental task–analytic diagnostic instrument that details functioning in five distinct areas: fine motor, gross motor, language, cognition, and self-help. Unlike narrower-scope, norm-based scales, it divides its major domains into subareas, including manipulation, writing, matching, object movement, counting, comprehension, and grooming. The detailed scale covers the age range of birth to 6 years across these functional areas and helps generate a diagnostic profile of a child's range of fully acquired (+), absent (−), and emergent (±) developmental capabilities. The profile forms the diagnostic basis for individualized goal planning by establishing developmental targets and age reference points rather than comparative statistical quotients.

Several features of the LAP–D make it unique among curriculum-based measures. First, it is one of the most colorful and interesting of the curriculum scales. The large red carrying case contains a rich variety of tasks that involve using a formboard, placing pegs, drawing, playing with a beanbag, color matching, puzzle working, block building, bead stringing, dressing an "octopus toy," and lacing. Although these activities are contrived and decontextualized, they are appealing to many young children and provide a motivational support for obtaining the child's maximum level of performance. Furthermore, the variety of tasks allow some adaptive accommodations to be made. Second, because of the colorful, high-interest tasks and flip-card administration format, a teacher can administer the scale in approximately 1.5 hours to obtain relevant educational goals and qualitative descriptions of a child's developmental and instructional needs. Finally, the LAP–D is based on continuing research efforts to establish a normative and technical basis in terms of reliability and validity, although the technical manual cites current data on only 35 children. Total scale test–retest reliability is reportedly 0.98, and subscale correlations are 0.91–0.97.

As part of a total assessment-intervention process, the LAP–D helps a professional formulate an adaptive and individualized program for prescriptive teaching. In brief, the LAP–D accomplishes the following six major objectives in early special education: 1) providing a record of functional skills, 2) establishing an initial developmental task analysis to guide teaching in multiple areas, 3) allowing for creative additions to the goal sequence, 4) providing a means for measuring progress, 5) highlighting individual strengths and weaknesses, and 6) enabling the teacher to initiate curriculum-based assessment within the classroom environment.

Sample from the Early Learning Accomplishment Profile (E–LAP)

From Glover, E., Preminger, J., & Sanford, A. (1995). *Early Learning Accomplishment Profile (E–LAP)*. Chapel Hill, NC: Chapel Hill Training–Outreach Project; reprinted by permission.

244

Sample from the Early Learning Accomplishment Profile (E–LAP)

Cognitive

BEHAVIOR	MATERIALS AND PROCEDURES	CRITERIA	SCORE + –	DATE ASSESS	DATE ACHIEV	COMMENTS
12 MO 1. Removes lid of box to find hidden toy (BAY)	**Materials:** 3 small objects Shoe box with lid **Procedure:** Say, **"Watch me."** Place an object in shoe box and cover with lid. Open box and replace cover. Hand closed box to child and say, **"Find the _____."** Demonstration may be repeated 2–3 times. Repeat procedure 2 additional times with remaining objects.	Credit if child removes cover to find toy at least 2 of the 3 times requested.				
16 MO 2. Obtains object from bottle (CAT)	**Materials:** Small object (i.e., peg, bead, raisin) Bottle (approximately 3" tall with 1½" diameter at opening) **Procedure:** Say, **"Watch me."** Place object in bottle. Give bottle to child and say, **"Now get it out."** Do not demonstrate.	Credit if child obtains object from bottle.				
17 MO 3. Attains toy with stick (BAY)	**Materials:** Small (rubber) toy Stick (approximately 8" long and ½" in diameter) **Procedure:** Place toy on table in front of child, just out of reach. Place stick so that it touches toy and points towards child. Say, **"See how I make the (toy) come."** Pull toy toward child using stick. Replace toy and stick and say, **"(child's name) make the (toy) come."** Demonstrate again if child seems unsure.	Credit if child makes purposeful attempt to attain toy by using stick, even if poor coordination prevents success.				
24 MO 4. Pulls mat to get object (BANGS)	**Materials:** Mat Toy or other desirable object **Procedure:** Place mat with object on top, out of child's reach except for one corner of mat. Say, **"Get the _____."** Do not demonstrate, but pick object up, show to child and replace on mat.	Credit if child pulls mat to retrieve object.				
5. Gives object similar to a familiar object (DOLL)	**Materials:** 2 balls 2 1" cubes 2 toy cars (Each object should be a different color)	Credit if child gives correct object at least 2 of the 3 times requested. Allow 1 trial for each request.				

From Glover, E., Preminger, J., & Sanford, A. (1995). *Early Learning Accomplishment Profile (E–LAP)*, p. 44. Chapel Hill, NC: Chapel Hill Training–Outreach Project; reprinted by permission.

Sample from the Learning Accomplishment Profile–Revised (LAP–R)

LANGUAGE/COGNITIVE: COMPREHENSION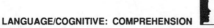

DEV AGE	ITEM#	DESCRIPTION	Pre +/-	Post +/-	COMMENT
15	LC1	Looks toward indicated area when told to "Look!"			
15	LC2	Gives 3 (out of 5) common objects upon request			ball/spoon/block/car/book
15	LC3	Points to 3 (out of 5) pictures of common objects			car/dog/house/ball/girl
24	LC4	Points to 6 (out of 7) body parts upon request			mouth/nose/eyes/hand/foot/head/ear
24	LC5	Follows 8 (out of 10) simple commands			stand/jump/sit/look/put/close/open/clap pick/throw
30	LC6	Responds appropriately to 2 (out of 3) prepositions			on/behind/in front of
30	LC7	Follows two 2-step commands in exact order			block in - open book/book on - block out
30	LC8	Points to 5 (out of 6) pictured objects by use			eat/ride/cool/wear/sleep/cut
36	LC9	Points to 5 (out of 10) pictures of common actions			eating/drawing/sleeping/playing reading/running/riding/jumping climbing/swimming
36	LC10	Points to 10 (out of 18) pictures of common objects			snake/dog/ball/car/wagon/flowers house/fish/tree/shoe/candy/fire/bed turtle/lamp/airplane/banana/rabbit
48	LC11	Points to 9 (out of 10) pictures of common actions			SCORE BASED ON LC 9 ABOVE
48	LC12	Points to 15 (out of 18) pictures of common objects			SCORE BASED ON LC10 ABOVE
48	LC13	Points to 8 colors			red/yellow/green/blue/black/orange purple/brown
48	LC14	Responds appropriately to 3 (out of 4) prepositions			in/under/over/beside
48	LC15	Selects 4 (out of 5) pictures related to a sentence read			eggs/play/swimming/sandwich/flowers
54	LC16	Points to 5 Printed numerals between 1 and 10			10/7/9/4/5
54	LC17	Selects 7 (out of 9) pictures that match verbal description			catching/summertime/nighttime/in box heavy/not/open/many/under
60	LC18	Selects pictures that belong to 4 (out of 5) named categories			2 items each (none incorrect) for: people/clothes/food/animals/furniture
60	LC19	Selects pictures that show who, what, where of a story			squirrel/tree/ax/acorn
72	LC20	Follows two 3-step commands in exact order			ring - hit - open/hit - close - ring
72	LC21	Shows left and right			right/left/left/right
72	LC22	Points to 5 printed letters between A and Z			F/H/Z/C/W
72	LC23	Points to 4 (out of 5) printed words			daddy/pie/milk/home/sat
		Number of last item of the ceiling			
		Subtract (minuses between basal/ceiling)			
		Raw Score			

From Glover, E., Preminger, J., Sanford, A., & Zelman, J. (1995). *Learning Accomplishment Profile–Revised (LAP–R)*, p. 7. Chapel Hill, NC: Chapel Hill Training–Outreach Project; reprinted by permission.

Sample from Learning Accomplishment Profile–Revised (LAP–R)

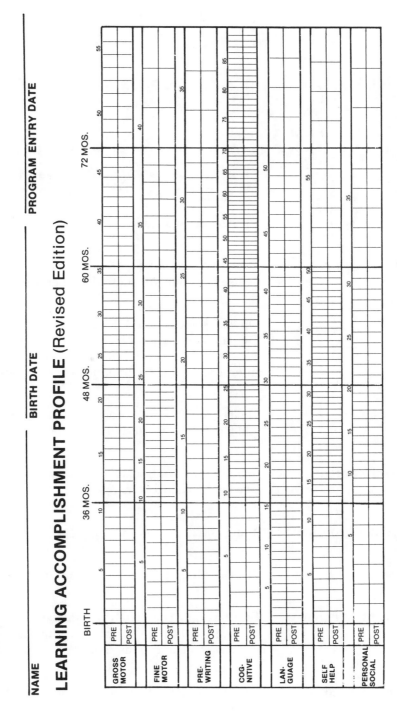

From Glover, E., Preminger, J., Sanford, A., & Zelman, J. (1995). *Learning Accomplishment Profile–Revised (LAP–R)*, p. 110. Chapel Hill, NC: Chapel Hill Training–Outreach Project; reprinted by permission.

On Track (A Comprehensive System for Early Childhood Intervention)

Author(s): S. Neilsen, R.A. van den Pol, J. Guidry, E. Keeley, & R.A. Honzel
Year: 1994
Publisher: Sopris West
Address: 1140 Boston Avenue, Longmont, Colorado 80501
Phone: 303-651-2829
Cost: $48

Assessment type: Curriculum embedded.

Age/focus group: Designed for young children with special needs. Can be used in home- or center-based programs.

Scale(s): On Track Individual Education Plan Assessment and On Track Family Interview Form. Scales can be administered by direct assessment, observation, family interview, or any combination of these methods.

Data system: On Track Teaching Record, On Track Planning Sheet, and On Track Quarterly Progress Report.

Domains/content: Social-emotional, adaptive, communication, cognitive, and physical domains.

Special needs options: None noted.

Authenticity: Stresses observational assessment of child.

Family involvement: Families may complete the optional Family Interview Form. In addition, they can participate in assessment by answering questions about their children.

Training needed: Easy to implement; knowledge of child development is helpful.

Validation:	Ongoing field-validation; no formal published reports on efficacy.

Comments:

- *Designed to expedite work of teachers*
- *Home, preschool, and kindergarten skill expectations compose content*
- *Assessment forms included*
- *Lesson-planning procedures and forms included*
- *Valuable for annual reporting and accountability*

LINK Index

Authentic	1	2	③
Convergent	1	2	③
Collaborative	1	②	3
Equitable	1	2	③
Sensitive	1	2	③
Congruent	1	2	③
Total Index	☐ +	2 +	15 ÷ 6 = 2.8

Overall quality: high to exemplary

3.0, exemplary; 2.5, high; 2.0, acceptable; 1.5, low; 1.0, negligible.

On Track (A Comprehensive System for Early Childhood Intervention)

On Track is designed for busy teachers of children in inclusive early childhood programs. The prospect of "churning out" and then monitoring a dozen or more IEPs is often enough to thwart the good intentions and work of even excellent teachers. The pace and demands of work often result in professionals complying with the letter but not the spirit of well-intentioned regulations; On Track was developed to make "compliance" both easier and more useful and meaningful. The materials serve as tools to ease the work involved with estimating a child's strengths and needs and a family's preferences, planning programs, and monitoring progress.

The assessment section comprises the Family Interview Form (families participate during the assessment process by reporting observations of the child's development and by prioritizing skill areas that are important to them) and the IEP Assessment, which is criterion referenced and assesses the five developmental domains identified by PL 101-476 (i.e., social-emotional, adaptive, communication, physical, cognitive).

The curriculum section consists of Planning Sheets, Teaching Records, and Progress Reports. A Tell-Show-Help-Praise model is the instructional strategy employed in the more than 100 Teaching Records. It is a gentle, nonintrusive model of instruction that allows the child the opportunity to learn skills first in the least restrictive way and then with gradually increasing directiveness. Three features of On Track are especially noteworthy. First, the content is clearly authentic and relevant to home and program expectations (i.e., no bead stringing, no decontextualized testing). Second, the materials respond to the demands that are routinely placed on teachers; they expedite useful assessment and lesson planning. Third, the skills are appreciated and easily monitored by parents. All assessment, planning, and reporting materials are formatted to make them easy to use, see, and share. The On Track materials are a real gift to teachers.

Sample from On Track (A Comprehensive System for Early Childhood Intervention)

Individual Education Plan Assessment

Cognitive Domain (continued)		Pretest Date:			Posttest Date:		
CODE: R/N = Rarely/Never S/H = Sometimes or With Help U/A = Usually/Always		R/N	S/H	U/A	R/N	S/H	U/A
14.6	Completes task						
14.7							
	Notes:						
15.0	**Classification**						
15.1	Sorts objects						
	15.1.1 Sorts objects by shape (square/circle/ triangle/rectangle/diamond)						
	15.1.2 Sorts objects by color (red/blue/green/ yellow/purple/orange)						
	15.1.3 Sorts objects by size small/medium/ large)						
15.2	Tells whether objects/pictures are same or different (Which one doesn't belong?)						
15.3	Describes similarities and differences in objects						
15.4	Demonstrates concepts						
	15.4.1 Identifies prepositions (in/on/under)						
	15.4.2 Identifies measurement (heavy/light, big/little)						
	15.4.3 Identifies temperature (hot/warm/cool)						
	15.4.4 Identifies time (before/after, early/later)						
15.5							
	Notes:						
16.0	**Memory**						
16.1	Recalls familiar objects						
16.2	Recalls facts from a story presented orally						
16.3	Identifies missing parts of objects						
16.4							
	Notes:						

On Track Teaching Record

Student:	Annual Goal (domain): Cognitive
Academic Year:	Objective (skill): Recalls Familiar Objects

Lesson Plan

Recalling familiar objects requires well-developed memory and cognitive skills. Obtain a small set of objects familiar to the child (e.g., pencil, shoe, hat, glove, eraser, toy). Hide the set and remove one object. Present remaining set and instruct. Repeat procedure, removing a different object. As the child succeeds, present larger numbers of objects and remove more than one at a time.

1. TELL the child, "(Name), tell me the one that is missing."

2. SHOW the child by repeating entire lesson plan procedure and instruction.

3. HELP the child by repeating instruction and presenting object in view but apart from other objects.

4. PRAISE the child by enthusiastically telling what was correct.

SCORING KEY: + = Correct S = Shown H = Helped I = Incorrect / = Not Applicable	INDICATE TYPE OF SESSION: O = Observation DI = Direct										%
10.											100
9.											90
8. Recalls four objects											80
7. Recalls four objects											70
6. Recalls three objects											60
5. Recalls three objects											50
4. Recalls two objects											40
3. Recalls two objects											30
2. Recalls one object											20
1. Recalls one object											10
Date											0
% Correct											
Initials											
Cumulative Correct Average											
Comments (on back)											

16.1

On Track Individual Plan Assessment

Child: Susan L.	Date of Birth: 3/15/91
Teacher: Mary Smith	Preschool: CO-TEACH
Enrollment Date: 9/15/94	Anticipated Transition Date: 5/96

Write an asterisk (*) next to skills which are parent priorities.

Adaptive Domain		Pretest Date:			Posttest Date:		
CODE: R/N = Rarely/Never S/H = Sometimes or With Help U/A = Usually/Always		R/N	S/H	U/A	R/N	S/H	U/A
7.0	**Classroom Entry and Exit**						
7.1	Responds to greeting			✓			
7.2	Removes coat independently		✓				
7.3	Hangs up coat on own hook		✓				
7.4	Removes outer wear independently (hat/boots/mittens)			✓			
7.5	Goes to next activity		✓				
7.6	Puts on coat independently		✓				
7.7	Puts on outer wear independently (hats/boots/mittens)		✓				
7.8							
	Notes:						
8.0	**Snack Skills**						
8.1	Washes and dries hands		✓				
8.2	Waits turn		✓				
8.3	Indicates "Yes" and "No" to teacher's offers			✓			
8.4	Makes requests appropriately			✓			
8.5	Uses "Please" and "Thank you"		✓				
8.6	Consumes food and beverage at moderate rate			✓			
8.7	Maintains lip closure		✓				
8.8	Does not spill food or choke on it		✓				
8.9	Eats only own food			✓			
8.10	Uses utensils correctly		✓				
8.11	Uses napkin correctly		✓				
8.12	Leaves only when excused			✓			

Oregon Project Curriculum for Visually Impaired and Blind Preschool Children (OPC)

Author(s):	S. Anderson, S. Boigon, & K. Davis
Year:	1991
Publisher:	Jackson County Education Service District
Address:	101 North Grape Street, Medford, Oregon 97501
Phone:	503-776-8580
Cost:	$119; additional packet of 20 inventory booklets is available for $40

Assessment type:　　Curriculum embedded.

Age/focus group:　　Designed for use with children who are blind or who have visual impairments and who range in age from birth to 6 years. It can be used in either a home- or center-based program with individuals or small groups.

Scale(s):　　Skills Inventory Booklet.

Data system:　　Weekly recording is suggested, and recording sheets are provided; permission to duplicate is given. A Skills Inventory is provided for summative evaluation.

Domains/content:　　Cognitive, language, self-help, socialization, fine motor, and gross motor.

Special needs options:　　Items and administration are tailored to children with visual limitations, thereby permitting equitable assessment. Curriculum is also available in Spanish.

Authenticity:　　This curriculum stresses observation, in everyday settings and activities, of natural adaptive behaviors of children who are blind or visually impaired.

Family involvement:　　Need for cooperation between teacher and parents is emphasized. The activities are designed for home use and incorporate the family into the process.

Training needed: Knowledge of development of preschool children with visual impairments is recommended. Skills in the use of prescriptive teaching methods are useful.

Validation: The Skills Inventory is based on records of preschoolers in the Southern Oregon's program for students with visual impairments. Input from preschool teachers of children who are blind is included.

Comments:
- *Family involvement*
- *Clear summative data system*
- *Precursors to independent skills at 6 years of age*
- *Spanish version available*
- *Clever items circumvent visual limitations*

LINK Index			
Authentic	1	2	③
Convergent	1	2	③
Collaborative	1	2	③
Equitable	1	2	③
Sensitive	1	②	3
Congruent	1	2	③
Total Index	☐ +	2 +	15 ÷ 6 = 2.8
Overall quality: high to exemplary			

3.0, exemplary; 2.5, high; 2.0, acceptable; 1.5, low; 1.0, negligible.

Oregon Project Curriculum for Visually Impaired and Blind Preschool Children (OPC)

The format of Oregon Project Curriculum for Visually Impaired and Blind Preschool Children (OPC) is a sequence that matches that of typically developing children. Six areas of development are emphasized: cognitive, language, self-help, socialization, fine motor, and gross motor. A coding system is used to note skills that are appropriate for a child with a particular visual problem or whose development is slower than other children. Compensatory skills are included in the curriculum. Goals and objectives are included both for children with low vision and those with no vision. There are a sufficient number of curricular assessment items to make this sensitive enough to track progress.

Assessment of the child in the home is viewed as the best approach for this program because early intervention will likely take place in that setting. A skills inventory that links assessment with curriculum objectives is provided. Long-range goals and short-range objectives for IEP or IFSP development can be formulated from the results of the inventory. Progress can be monitored through the use of the weekly recording sheets and the profile. The OPC curriculum is designed to be used with prescriptive teaching procedures.

OPC ranks as one of the best curriculum systems and is the clear choice for use with children who have visual impairments and those who are blind. If asked to recommend a curriculum-based assessment system for children with visual difficulties, we would recommend the OCP.

Sample from the Oregon Project Curriculum for Visually Impaired and Blind Preschool Children (OPC) Sample

COMPENSATORY 2–3 YEARS		ASSESSMENTS			HAS SKILL
16	Identifies familiar objects, toys, foods.				
17	Identifies an object by its sound.				
18	Interested in books with textures or moveable parts.				
19	Matches textures (finds the same kind when given a choice of 2–3).				
20	Independently explores familiar rooms in own home.				
21	Knows the arrangement of furniture, doors, stairs within own home.				
22	Maintains sustained search for dropped toy.				
		/7	/7	/7	

COMPENSATORY 3–4 YEARS		ASSESSMENTS			HAS SKILL
23	Tactually discriminates among items with similar characteristics (child's own hairbrush from Mom's).				
24	Identifies activities by sound (closing door, washing dishes) and smell (bakery, gas station) in the home/neighborhood.				

From Brown, L.B., Simmons, J.C., & Methvin, E. (1994). *Oregon Project Curriculum for Visually Impaired and Blind Preschool Children (OPC)*, p. 48. Medford, OR: Jackson County Education Service District; reprinted by permission.

Sample from the Oregon Project Curriculum for Visually Impaired and Blind Preschool Children (OPC)

FUNCTIONAL COMMUNICATION EVALUATION

OR Project

Name: _Randy_

Date: _10/5/90_

	Reactive	Non-Conventional	Conventional Intentional
Protest	Cries, fusses	Pushes object away.	
Requests Attention		Uses voice. Puts hand in adult's face.	"Shares" objects.
Requests Object		Reaches & fusses	
Requests Action		Pulls adult about, but not always to object.	
Greetings/ Social Exchange		Extends hand.	Waves, on request from parent.
Denial			Shakes head NO.
Imitation		Vocal play with self; occasional turn-taking.	
Social Games			

The Oregon Project for Visually Impaired and Blind Preschool Children - Fifth Edition
Anderson, S., Boigon, S., Davis, K. (1991)
Medford, OR: Jackson Education Service District

From Brown, L.B., Simmons, J.C., & Methwin, E. (1994). *Oregon Project Curriculum for Visually Impaired and Blind Preschool Children (OPC)*, p. 103. Medford, OR: Jackson County Education Service District; reprinted by permission.

Parenting Stress Index (PSI)

Author(s):	R.R. Abidin
Year:	1990
Publisher:	Psychological Assessment Resources, Inc.
Address:	Post Office Box 998, Odessa, Florida 33556
Phone:	1-800-331-TEST
Cost:	$30+

Assessment type: Interactive/norm based; diagnostic profile of perceived child and parent stress.

Age/focus group: 1–60+ months.

Domains/content: 13 subdomains within four major domains: total stress, child domain, parent domain, life stress.

Special needs options: Based on parent perceptions and report, thereby providing social validity to the assessment and broadening the information base for treatment; 5-point rating scale of degree of agreement/disagreement with item content.

Curricular links: Individual items bear directly on degree of life stress and disruption in the parent–child interaction. Items regarding mood, anxiety, and child misbehavior offer goals for the IFSP and therapy or counseling.

Authenticity: Shows obvious and strong authenticity by relying on parent's perceptions and rankings of true examples of stress in daily life; focuses on how stress affects parent–child and parent–parent interactions.

Family involvement: Based on parent interview and collaboration in a counseling relationship between a counselor and a parent or family .

Scoring/sample: Raw scores convert to percentile ranks for each domain and subdomain, yielding descriptive and diagnostic data and cutoffs of "pathology"; broad interview, self-report data.

Validation: Normed on 534 families; adequate reliability and validity for diagnosis and prescription; separate norms for four diagnostic groups.

Training needed: Thorough familiarity with manual and procedure; good interviewing skills; should be administered to and monitored with parent by social worker or psychologist.

Comments:
- *Effectively phrases items in "self-statements" to capitalize on parent emotions*
- *Sensitively samples broad moods and behaviors*
- *Should add parent–infant items to extend its use*
- *Shows excellent disability-specific field-validations*

LINK Index			
Authentic	1	2	③
Convergent	1	2	③
Collaborative	1	2	③
Equitable	①	2	3
Sensitive	1	2	③
Congruent	1	2	③
Total Index	1 +	☐ +	15 ÷ 6 = 2.7
Overall quality: high			

3.0, exemplary; 2.5, high; 2.0, acceptable; 1.5, low; 1.0, negligible.

Parenting Stress Index (PSI)

One of the most important and elusive ecological dimensions is the analysis of a family's interactive stress. Parenting Stress Index (PSI) is the best available example of an economical, sensitive, practical strategy for assessing this stress factor. PSI allows parents to rate their level of agreement with a series of "self-statements" reflecting the feelings, emotional turmoil, and images they experience in dealing with their children within the family context. The self-statements are worded personally to tap the specific moods, anxieties, and expectations that most parents typically report (e.g., "My child is so active that it exhausts me," "I feel trapped by my responsibilities as a parent"). PSI samples stressful feelings related to the child, such as hyperactivity, demandingness, and the tendency to reinforce the parent. Similarly, PSI taps various parent perspectives, such as sense of competence, health, and relationship with spouse. PSI characterizes the child's contribution to the problem, as well as various parent factors that interact to result in a stressful life experience.

PSI is a technically adequate instrument that can be used with confidence. Its use of parent perceptions allows for immediate and practical programming implications to plan family goals and reduce stress in various relationships. The system can be used to diagnose degree of interaction pathology or stress, plan goals focused on reducing anxiety and promoting behavioral control (and, perhaps, economical and social support), and evaluate the impact of treatment. PSI serves to link diagnosis and programming and progress evaluation, with the parent–child and family dynamics being selected as the targets of treatment.

Caution should be observed, however, in the use of the scale with children with disabilities. The wording of PSI suggests that the scale is most effectively used with parents of children with learning disabilities and behavior and affective disorders. Use of the scale with children who have more severe disabilities (e.g., autism, cerebral palsy, mental retardation requiring extensive supports) is judged to be least effective because the items do not sample many of the unique attachment problems that add stress to the parents' relationships with their children. We find this caution to be warranted despite the fact that PSI was normed partially on 40 children with cerebral palsy and their parents.

The author is to be commended for developing a practical tool that is both norm referenced and loosely criterion referenced in its content. The separate profiles on children and families with various problems, including hyperactivity; cerebral palsy; child abuse; and developmental delay, as well as normal patterns, offer a precious comparative resource. The item content poignantly samples real-life parent perceptions and distress and, as a result, holds tangible implications for therapy and counseling.

In response to the mandates of PL 102-119, researchers have begun to design and field-test instruments that integrate parents and families into the early intervention process. An important point to remember, however, is that such instruments must enable parents to self-report their various social, economic, health, personal, and child-related needs, while helping program personnel and the parents identify the program that is best tailored to both the infant's and the parents' needs. Such instruments are experimental, few in number, and generally of undetermined technical adequacy; nonetheless, they represent an important development for the future in the early intervention field.

Examples of Domains, Subdomains, and Items from the Parenting Stress Index (PSI)

Domains	Sample Items

Child Domain Score
  Adaptability
  Acceptability
  Demandingness
  Mood
  Distract/Hyper
  Reinforces Parent
 	
Parent Domain Score
  Depression
  Attachment
  Restriction of Role
  Sense of Competence
  Social Isolation
  Relation to Spouse
  Parent Health
 	
Life Stress
  (Optional Scale)
	1. When my child wants something, my child usually keeps trying to get it.
	2. My child is so active that it exhausts me.
	3. My child appears disorganized and is easily distracted.
	4. Compared to most, my child has more difficulty concentrating and paying attention.
	5. My child will often stay occupied with a toy for more than 10 minutes.
	6. My child wanders away much more than I expected.
	7. My child is much more active than I expected.
	69. I find myself giving up more of my life to meet my children's needs than I ever expected.
	70. I feel trapped by my responsibilities as a parent.
	71. I often feel that my children's needs control my life.
	62. It takes a long time for parents to develop close, warm feelings for their children.
	63. I expected to have closer and warmer feelings for my child than I do and this bothers me.

Adapted and reproduced by special permission of the Publisher, Psychological Assessment Resources, Inc., Odessa, FL, from the Parenting Stress Index by Richard Abidin, Ed.D., Copyright 1990 by PAR, INC. Further reproduction is prohibited without permission from PAR.

Pediatric Evaluation of Disability Inventory (PEDI)

Author(s):   S.M. Haley, W.J. Coster, L.H. Ludlow, J.T. Haltiwanger, & P.J. Andrellos

Year: 1992

Publisher: PEDI Research Group

Address: Department of Rehabilitative Medicine, New England Medical Center Hospital, 750 Washington Street, Boston, Massachusetts 02111-1901

Phone: 617-956-5031

Cost: $85 ($185 with scoring software)

Assessment type: Curriculum-compatible, hybrid, clinical instrument, standardized on normative sample, for pediatric functional capabilities and performance; detects functional difficulties/delays; evaluates individual and group progress in rehabilitation.

Age/focus group: 6 months to 7 years.

Domains/content: Three measurement scales: functional skills, caregiver assistance, and modifications; three content domains: adaptive, mobility, and social function; subdomains include brushing teeth, fastening fasteners, eating, floor locomotion, getting in and out of a car, climbing stairs, word comprehension, social interactive play, self-protection, and joint problem solving.

Special needs options: Entire scale is dedicated to functional impairments, capabilities, and extent of caregiver or technological assistance required for self-reliance.

Curricular links: Sequenced functional skills and levels of assistance required match the features of many developmental curricula; adaptive elements have many advantages not evident in most curricula.

Authenticity: Functional, real-life tasks; performances judged on the basis of multiple information sources.

Family involvement: Incorporates parent observations.

Scoring/sample: Graduated scoring system; Rasch Scale and frequency counts to produce normative standard scores and scaled scores; frequency counts can also be calculated to provide descriptive information on the frequency and degree of modifications.

Validation: Excellent field validation on disability groups with normative data.

Training needed: "Clinicians and educators who regularly evaluate functional performance in children with disabilities."

Comments:
- *Arguably the best adaptive assessment instrument available to professionals*
- *Clear links between assessed capabilities, goals, and therapeutic help needed*
- *Sensitive to small increments of change outside of a dense curriculum*
- *Prototype for the development of scales combining norm, curricular, convergent, and authentic features*

LINK Index			
Authentic	1	2	③
Convergent	1	2	③
Collaborative	1	2	③
Equitable	1	2	③
Sensitive	1	2	③
Congruent	1	2	③
Total Index	☐ +	☐ +	18 ÷ 6 = 3.0
Overall quality: exemplary			

3.0, exemplary; 2.5, high; 2.0, acceptable; 1.5, low; 1.0, negligible.

Pediatric Evaluation of Disability Inventory (PEDI)

Much research since the mid-1980s has focused on developing more sensitive, adaptive, and functional assessment instruments for young children with various sensory, motor, and neurological impairments. Progress in this area has been diligent but slow, and only a few scales have been developed (primarily as research editions). In fact, the biggest strides in this area have been in the development of adaptive curricular systems (e.g., The Carolina Curricula).

Pediatric Evaluation of Disability Inventory (PEDI) is arguably the only standardized, norm-referenced (n = 412), curriculum-compatible instrument designed to provide a functional assessment of the capabilities of young children with physical, sensory, and neuromotor impairments. PEDI is an authentic assessment instrument that addresses real-life survival skills in the adaptive, motor, and social domains. The authors observe that "The PEDI combines elements of adaptive developmental measures utilized in special education and characteristics of functional assessments used in rehabilitation medicine" (Haley et al., 1992, p. 3). Although it is extremely useful in community-based early intervention programs, PEDI was designed to be used to describe functional status, plan individualized programs, monitor progress, and evaluate the efficacy of inpatient and outpatient services in pediatric rehabilitation settings.

Several key features distinguish the scale: First, through the Functional Skills Scales, PEDI samples crucial functional capabilities (able/unable) that link directly to intervention rather than to measures of categorical disability. Second, the Caregiver Assistance Scale enables professionals and parents to examine the extent to which a caregiver must provide support or physical help in typical everyday situations. Third, the Modifications Scale allows professionals to cite the types and frequencies of environmental modifications or equipment used by the child daily. (PEDI is based in theory on the definitions of functional impairments apparent in the *International Classification of Impairments, Disabilities, and Handicaps* [World Health Organization, 1980].)

We regard the PEDI as one of the most sorely needed and technically adequate advances in functional assessment procedures for young children. It creatively combines the best of authentic, curriculum-based, adaptive, and norm-based assessment procedures in an easily used, accessible, practical format.

Sample from the Pediatric Evaluation of Disability Inventory (PEDI)

UNABLE · CAPABLE

C. Functional Use of Communication — 0 1

11. Names things
12. Uses specific words or gestures to direct or request action by another person
13. Seeks information by asking questions
14. Describes an object or action
15. Tells about own feelings or thoughts

D. Complexity of Expressive Communication — 0 1

16. Uses gestures with clear meaning
17. Uses single word with meaning
18. Uses two words together with meaning
19. Uses 4–5 word sentences
20. Connects two or more thoughts to tell a simple story

E. Problem-resolution — 0 1

21. Tries to show you the problem or communicate what is needed to help the problem
22. If upset because of a problem, child must be helped immediately or behavior deteriorates
23. If upset because of a problem, child can seek help and wait if it is delayed a short time
24. In ordinary situations, child can describe the problem and his/her feelings with some detail (usually does not act out)
25. Faced with an ordinary problem, child can join adult in working out a solution

F. Social Interactive Play (Adults) — 0 1

26. Shows awareness and interest in others
27. Initiates a familiar play routine
28. Takes turn in simple play when cued for turn
29. Attempts to imitate adult's previous action during a play activity
30. During play child may suggest new or different steps, or respond to adult suggestion with another idea

G. Peer Interactions: (Child of similar age) — 0 1

31. Notices presence of other children, may vocalize and gesture toward peers
32. Interacts with other children in simple and brief episodes
33. Tries to work out simple plans for a play activity with another child
34. Plans and carries out cooperative activity with other children; play is sustained and complex
35. Plays activities or games that have rules

H. Play with Objects — 0 1

36. Manipulates toys, objects or body with intent
37. Uses real or substituted objects in simple pretend sequences
38. Puts together materials to make something
39. Makes up extended pretend play routines involving things the child knows about
40. Makes up elaborate pretend sequences from imagination.

I. Self-Information — 0 1

41. Can state first name
42. Can state first and last name
43. Provides names and descriptive information about family members
44. Can state full home address; if in hospital, name of hospital and room number
45. Can direct an adult to help child return home or back to the hospital room

J. Time Orientation — 0 1

46. Has a general awareness of time of mealtimes and routines during the day
47. Has some awareness of sequence of familiar events in a week
48. Has very simple time concepts
49. Associates a specific time with actions/events
50. Regularly checks clock or asks for the time in order to keep track of schedule

K. Household Chores — 0 1

51. Beginning to help care for own belongings if given constant direction and guidance
52. Beginning to help with simple household chores if given constant direction and guidance
53. Occasionally initiates simple routines to care for own belongings; may require physical help or reminders to complete
54. Occasionally initiates simple household chores; may require physical help or reminders to complete
55. Consistently initiates and carries out at least one household task involving several steps and decisions; may require physical help

L. Self-Protection — 0 1

56. Shows appropriate caution around stairs
57. Shows appropriate cautions around hot or sharp objects
58. When crossing the street with an adult present, child does not need prompting about safety rules
59. Knows not to accept rides, food or money from strangers
60. Crosses busy street safely without an adult

M. Community Function — 0 1

61. Child may play safely at home without being watched constantly
62. Goes about familiar environment outside of home with only periodic monitoring for safety
63. Follows guidelines/expectations of school and community setting
64. Explores and functions in familiar community settings without supervision
65. Makes transaction in neighborhood store without assistance

SOCIAL FUNCTION DOMAIN SUM

PLEASE BE SURE YOU HAVE ANSWERED ALL ITEMS.

Comments

From Haley, S.M., Coster, W.J., Ludlow, L.H., Haltiwanger, J.T., & Andrellos, P.J. (1992). *Pediatric Evaluation of Disability Inventory (PEDI): Development, standardization, and administration manual*, p. 4. Boston: PEDI Research Group and New England Medical Center Hospital; reprinted by permission.

Sample Form from the Pediatric Evaluation of Disability Inventory (PEDI)

Parts II and III: Caregiver Assistance and Modification

Circle the appropriate score for Caregiver Assistance and Modification for each item.

	Caregiver Assistance Scale						Modification Scale			
	Independent	Supervision	Minimal	Moderate	Maximal	Total	None	Child	Rehab	Extensive

SELF-CARE DOMAIN

	5	4	3	2	1	0	N	C	R	E
A. **Eating**: eating and drinking regular meal; do not include cutting steak, opening containers or serving food from serving dishes	5	4	3	2	1	0	N	C	R	E
B. **Grooming**: brushing teeth, brushing or combing hair and caring for nose	5	4	3	2	1	0	N	C	R	E
C. **Bathing**: washing and drying face and hands, taking a bath or shower; do not include getting in and out of a tub or shower, water preparation, or washing back or hair	5	4	3	2	1	0	N	C	R	E
D. **Dressing Upper Body**: all indoor clothes, not including back fasteners; include help putting on or taking off splint or artificial limb; do not include getting clothes from closet or drawers	5	4	3	2	1	0	N	C	R	E
E. **Dressing Lower Body**: all indoor clothes; include putting on or taking off brace or artificial limb; do not include getting clothes from closet or drawers	5	4	3	2	1	0	N	C	R	E
F. **Toileting**: clothes, toilet management or external device use, and hygiene; do not include toilet transfers, monitoring schedule, or cleaning up after accidents	5	4	3	2	1	0	N	C	R	E
G. **Bladder Management**: control of bladder day and night, clean-up after accidents, monitoring schedule	5	4	3	2	1	0	N	C	R	E
H. **Bowel Management**: control of bowel day and night, clean-up after accidents, monitoring schedule	5	4	3	2	1	0	N	C	R	E

Self-Care Totals — **SELF-CARE SUM** [ ]

Self-Care Modification Frequencies

MOBILITY DOMAIN

	5	4	3	2	1	0	N	C	R	E
A. **Chair/Toilet Transfers**: child's wheelchair, adult-sized chair, adult-sized toilet	5	4	3	2	1	0	N	C	R	E
B. **Car Transfers**: mobility within car/van, seat belt use, transfers, and opening and closing doors	5	4	3	2	1	0	N	C	R	E
C. **Bed Mobility/Transfers**: getting in and out and changing positions in child's own bed	5	4	3	2	1	0	N	C	R	E
D. **Tub Transfers**: getting in and out of adult-sized tub	5	4	3	2	1	0	N	C	R	E
E. **Indoor Locomotion**: 50 feet (3-4 rooms); do not include opening doors or carrying objects	5	4	3	2	1	0	N	C	R	E
F. **Outdoor Locomotion**: 150 feet (15 car lengths) on level surfaces; focus on physical ability to move outdoors (do not consider compliance or safety issues such as crossing streets)	5	4	3	2	1	0	N	C	R	E
G. **Stairs**: climb and descend a full flight of stairs (12-15 steps)	5	4	3	2	1	0	N	C	R	E

Mobility Totals — **MOBILITY SUM** [ ]

Mobility Modification Frequencies

SOCIAL FUNCTION DOMAIN

	5	4	3	2	1	0	N	C	R	E
A. **Functional Comprehension**: understanding of requests and instructions	5	4	3	2	1	0	N	C	R	E
B. **Functional Expression**: ability to provide information about own activities and make own needs known; include clarity of articulation	5	4	3	2	1	0	N	C	R	E
C. **Joint Problem Solving**: include communication of problem and working with caregiver or other adult to find a solution; include only ordinary problems occurring during daily activities; (for example, lost toy; conflict over clothing choices.)	5	4	3	2	1	0	N	C	R	E
D. **Peer Play**: ability to plan and carry out joint activities with a familiar peer	5	4	3	2	1	0	N	C	R	E
E. **Safety**: caution in routine daily safety situations, including stairs, sharp or hot objects and traffic	5	4	3	2	1	0	N	C	R	E

Social Function Totals — **SOCIAL FUNCTION SUM** [ ]

Social Function Modification Frequencies

From Haley, S.M., Coster, W.J., Ludlow, L.H., Haltiwanger, J.T., & Andrellos, P.J. (1992). *Pediatric Evaluation of Disability Inventory (PEDI): Development, standardization, and administration manual*, p. 5. Boston: PEDI Research Group and New England Medical Center Hospital; reprinted by permission.

Preschool and Kindergarten Behavior Scales (PKBS)

Author(s):	K.W. Merrell
Year:	1994
Publisher:	PRO-ED
Address:	8700 Shoal Creek Boulevard, Austin, Texas 78757-6897
Phone:	512-451-3246
Cost:	$30+

Assessment type: Curriculum compatible for behavior and social skills domains; norm-referenced, standardized, hybrid instrument for use in assessing young children in a variety of settings, by a variety of behavioral informants.

Age/focus group: Ages 3–6 years.

Domains/content: Two domains: social skills and problem behavior; subscales of social skills include cooperation, interaction, and independence; subscales of problem behaviors include self-centered/explosive, attention problems/overactive, antisocial/aggressive, social withdrawal, and anxiety/somatic problems.

Special needs options: None.

Curricular links: Clear links with general goals in most developmental curricula (for social skills domain).

Authenticity: Strong authentic features with multiple observations of typical/atypical behavior in home and preschool contexts without contrivances.

Family involvement: Parent observations compose at least 50% of the interpretation of results.

Scoring/sample: Raw scores converted to standard scores, percentile ranks, and functional levels; functional levels for social skills include high functioning, average functioning, moderate deficit, and significant deficit; functional levels for problem behaviors include no prob-lem, average level, moderate problem, and significant problem. Normed on 2,855 preschool- and kinder-garten-age children.

Validation: Field-validations on typical and special needs groups.

Training needed: A basic understanding of the principles of educational and psychological testing; specific training in under-standing and assessing child behavior and emotional problems.

Comments:

- *Excellent dual measure of social skills and prob-lem behaviors that impede prosocial develop-ment*
- *Advantage of social skills and behavior problems on same normative structure*
- *Strong authentic features*
- *Excellent treatment validity*
- *Clear, active wording of items supports parent par-ticipation*
- *Definite links to goals in most developmental cur-ricula*
- *Excellent for determining eligibility, planning goals, and monitoring progress*

LINK Index			
Authentic	1	2	③
Convergent	1	2	③
Collaborative	1	2	③
Equitable	①	2	3
Sensitive	1	2	③
Congruent	1	②	3
Total Index	1 +	2 +	12 ÷ 6 = 2.5
Overall quality: high			

3.0, exemplary; 2.5, high; 2.0, acceptable; 1.5, low; 1.0, negligible.

Preschool and Kindergarten Behavior Scales (PKBS)

Social skills, language impairments, and behavior problems have a clear and understandable interrelationship. Preschool and Kindergarten Behavior Scales (PKBS) helps parents and professionals collaborate in the assessment and treatment of social behavior problems. PKBS was standardized on both typically developing preschoolers and those with developmental delays. It is a curriculum-compatible scale that relies on authentic and convergent data. PKBS is very useful for eligibility determination, IEP/IFSP development, and progress/program evaluation. It is one of the most family-friendly measures in terms of the wording of items, which are rated on a 4-point continuum (0, never; 1, rarely; 2, sometimes; and 3, often). Sample items with high treatment validity include "adapts well to new situations," "follows rules," "seeks comfort from adult when upset," and "takes turns with toys and other objects." Another advantage of PKBS over similar measures is that the same form and normative structure are used by parents and professionals. PKBS enables parents and professionals to rate 34 landmark social skills and 42 major problem behaviors. PKBS is an invaluable addition to a convergent assessment battery for preschoolers with mild to moderate developmental impairments.

Sample from the Preschool and Kindergarten Behavior Scales (PKBS)

SOCIAL SKILLS SCALE

Subscale A1, Social Cooperation
Is cooperative
Uses free time in an acceptable way
Shares toys and other belongings
Takes turns with toys and other objects

Subscale A2, Social Interaction
Tries to understand another child's behavior ("Why are you crying?")
Participates in classroom or family discussions
Stands up for other children's rights ("That's his!")
Invites other children to play

Subscale A3, Social Independence
Works or plays independently
Plays with several different children
Attempts new tasks before asking for help
Is able to separate from parent without extreme distress

BEHAVIOR PROBLEM SCALE

Subscale B1, Self-Centered/Explosive
Has temper outbursts or tantrums
Will not share
Defies parent/teacher/or caregiver
Is easily provoked; has a "short fuse"

Subscale B2, Attention Problems/Overactive
Acts impulsively without thinking
Has difficulty concentrating or staying on-task
Is restless and "fidgety"
Disrupts ongoing activities

Subscale B3, Antisocial/Aggressive
Is physically aggressive (hits, kicks, pushes)
Calls people names
Bullies or intimidates other children
Destroys things that belong to others

From Merrell, K.W.. (1994). *Preschool and Kindergarten Behavior Scales (PKBS)*, p. 91. Austin, TX: PRO-ED; reprinted by permission.

Reynell–Zinkin Developmental Scales for Young Visually Handicapped Children (RZS)

Author(s): J. Reynell & K. Zinkin
Year: 1979
Publisher: Stoelting Company
Address: Oakwood Centre, 620 Wheat Lane, Wood Dale, Illinois 60191
Phone: 708-860-9700
Cost: $100

Assessment type: Curriculum compatible, in particular with the Oregon Project Curriculum; norm based; provides a detailed flexible assessment procedure for infants and young children with visual impairments and a basis for program planning; shuns prediction; advocates profiles of current abilities.

Age/focus group: Birth to 60+ months.

Domains/content: Seven domains: social adaptation, sensorimotor understanding, exploration of environment, response to sound and verbal comprehension, vocalization and expressive language (structure), expressive language (vocabulary and content), and communication.

Special needs options: Focuses on functional assessments for children who are blind and who may have additional disabilities; norms for both children who are blind and those who have visual impairments include children who also have cerebral palsy and hearing impairments; premium on tactile/auditory tasks.

Curricular links: Tasks within domains hierarchically arranged but not task analyzed; developmental tasks and processes congruent with most curricula; items have adaptive and instructional features; scale assesses serial progress.

Authenticity: Strong authentic features in sampling competencies in the domains of social adaptation and social communication through both observation and structured probes.

Family involvement: Uses joint parent and professional data.

Scoring/sample: 1 (+), 0 (−); raw scores, subtest totals generate developmental age equivalents for children who are blind, those who have visual impairments, and those with full vision; based on performance assessment, report, and naturalistic observation.

Validation: *N* = 203 "recordings" for 109 children in three diagnostic groups: blind (97), partial (86), borderline (20); few data available on technical adequacy data.

Training needed: Direct experience with typical stages and behaviors for children who are blind; supervised administration of the scale; primary use by psychologists.

Comments:
- *Promotes assessment rather than testing*
- *One of the few measures to include "norms" for children who are typically developing and those who have disabilities*
- *Includes tasks that are sensitive to multiple impairments*
- *Enables profiling of functional status*
- *Developmental progressions typical of blind children (e.g., later sensory coordination)*

LINK Index			
Authentic	1	②	3
Convergent	1	2	③
Collaborative	1	2	③
Equitable	1	2	③
Sensitive	1	2	③
Congruent	1	②	3
Total Index	☐ +	4 +	12 ÷ 6 = 2.7
Overall quality: high			

3.0, exemplary; 2.5, high; 2.0, acceptable; 1.5, low; 1.0, negligible.

Reynell–Zinkin Developmental Scales for Young Visually Handicapped Children (RZS)

There is a need for assessment instruments that are both functionally appropriate for and normed on children with a specific disability. Reynell-Zinkin Developmental Scales for Young Visually Handicapped Children (RZS) is one of the few such disability-specific tools; it is also one of the most unique. A child's performance on the scales does not yield an IQ or DQ estimate; rather, the scales characterize functioning in terms of a developmental age "range." Similarly, the child's observed completion of tasks reveals current competencies that, within the developmental progression, provide goals for developmental intervention and support. The administration procedures are flexible so that different child response modes can be accommodated and stimulus features of objects and activities can be altered, as long as the intent and process requirements of the task remain intact.

The norms on RZS are also unique and valuable, because they enable you to distinguish a child's capabilities compared with those of children who are blind, those with visual impairments, and those with normal vision. The norm sample is also realistic and natural because some children with multiple disabilities are included (e.g., children with mild cerebral palsy, children with hearing impairments). Although it is limited in technical terms, this sample offers a valuable comparative framework in which to characterize the status and needs of individual children using three different points of reference. The authors admonish clinicians, especially psychologists and pediatricians, to conduct an assessment rather than a testing of a child's capabilities.

RZS is compatible with a curriculum-based approach that strives to discover a child's current competencies and programming needs. The items themselves place a weighted emphasis on auditory and tactile modes of experiencing and learning rather than on vision. Performance assessments should be supplemented by naturalistic observations of the child's interaction with the environment and should use different people, objects, and settings to obtain the most representative results. However, assessors should already be familiar with the behaviors of young children with visual impairments before attempting to use and interpret the scales. It is obvious that RZS needs greater refinement in design and technical adequacy. For example, no reliability studies are reported in the manual; these can and should be conducted, despite the authors' contention that profile analysis does not lend itself to statistical evaluation.

RZS is unique and much needed as a hybrid norm-referenced and curriculum-compatible developmental measure for young children who are blind. All early interventionists should be familiar with the content, design, and appropriate use of RZS when matched to the child's functional limitations and needs.

Sample from the Reynell-Zinkin Developmental Scales for Young Visually Handicapped Children (RZS)

Item No.	Item Description	Score
1	Active grasp of object put into hand	
2	Orientation of hand for grasping, e.g. turning over	
3	Bimanual exploration of objects	
4	Hand-mouth exploration of objects	
5	Explorative manipulation of shape	
6	Explorative manipulation of texture	
7	Searching momentarily for something lost from grasp	
8	Extensive search for lost object	
9	Relating 2 objects. Stage (i) Taking objects out of container	
10	Relating 2 objects. Stage (ii) Putting things into container or any other creative relationship (e. g. building)	
11	Exploration of moveable parts of objects, e.g. box with lid	
12	Getting small object out of simple round box with lid	
13	Replacing toy and lid	
14	Getting sweet out of screw-capped bottle	
15	Replacing screw-cap	
16	Large and small round boxes. Putting correct lids on	
17	Same for 3 boxes	
18	Sorting beads into big and small	
19	Sorting beads into round and square	
20	Sorting 'different' one out of four:— a) size / b) shape	
	SCORE (Max. 20)	

From Reynell, J., & Zinkin, K. (1979). *Reynell-Zinkin Developmental Scales for Young Visually Handicapped Children (RZS)*, p. 37. Wood Dale, IL: Stoelting Company; reprinted by permission.

Scales of Early Communication Skills for Hearing-Impaired Children (SECS)

Author(s):   J.S. Moog & A.V. Geers
Year: 1975
Publisher: Central Institute for the Deaf
Address: 818 South Euclid Avenue, St. Louis, Missouri 63110
Phone: 314-652-3200
Cost: $20+

Assessment type: Curriculum compatible for global curriculum entry purposes; norm based; hierarchical sequences of critical language/communication skills.

Age/focus group: 24–96 months.

Domains/content: Four subscales: receptive language skills, expressive language skills, nonverbal receptive skills, and nonverbal expressive skills.

Special needs options: Includes nonverbal skill samples and criteria for use of prompts and demonstrations to observe learning.

Curricular links: Developmental sequencing guides identification of functional communication levels and, thus, instructional/therapeutic goals.

Authenticity: Relies on natural communication skills observed in everyday interactions and contexts.

Family involvement: Incorporates parent observations.

Scoring/sample: Observation of elicited behavior in naturalistic and structured settings (+, −, and ± ratings).

Validation: Field-testing in 14 oral programs in the United States for individuals with hearing impairments. $N = 372$ children; percentile ranks and standard scores, x; standard deviation = 10 for each age, scale, and total.

Training needed: Thorough knowledge of the manual, critical skills, and typical behavior of young children with hearing impairments.

Comments:

- *One of the few developmental measures for children with hearing impairments*
- *Adequate field-testing and norms for deaf children*
- *Important nonverbal subscales*
- *Better as a screening tool than as a criterion/prescriptive measure*

🐎 📖 ♿ ↔

LINK Index			
Authentic	1	②	3
Convergent	1	②	3
Collaborative	1	②	3
Equitable	1	2	③
Sensitive	①	2	3
Congruent	1	②	3
Total Index	1 +	8 +	3 ÷ 6 = 2.0
Overall quality: acceptable			

3.0, exemplary; 2.5, high; 2.0, acceptable; 1.5, low; 1.0, negligible.

Scales of Early Communication Skills for Hearing-Impaired Children (SECS)

Few adequate measures are available for young children with hearing impairments. Scales of Early Communication Skills for Hearing Impaired Children (SECS) (Moog & Geers, 1975) are often used to assess the range of verbal and nonverbal abilities of young children with disabilities to pinpoint goals for programming. SECS is a norm-based instrument that appraises prerequisite communication skills in four major areas. The skills are arranged in hierarchical sequences to enable the clinician to screen functional capabilities and highlight starting points for instruction and therapy.

SECS is solidly based on data from 14 programs in the United States that emphasize the use of oral methods with preschoolers who have hearing impairments. The scales cover a wide range (24–96 months), however, and survey only 34 (albeit critical) communication skills. SECS must, therefore, be considered an interim screening measure. It is, nevertheless, very useful for initial program goal planning. For novices working with children who have hearing impairments, the scales provide important structure to the assessment. Moreover, SECS can easily be linked with other scales in a battery. In addition, SECS is compatible with the few available criteria for young children with hearing impairments.

Sample Items from the Scales of Early Communication Skills
for Hearing-Impaired Children (SECS)

I. Receptive language skills
   A. Demonstrates awareness that the mouth and/or voice convey information.
      1. Responds to a verbal stimulus.
      2. Watches and/or listens to the speaker spontaneously.
   B. Demonstrates comprehension of a few words or expressions.
      1. Identifies at least one word or expression from a choice of 2 or 3.
      2. Demonstrates comprehension of at least one word or expression in a natural situation.

II. Expressive language skills
   A. Demonstrates awareness that vocalizations are used to communicate.
      1. Vocalizes when expected to imitate speech.
      2. Vocalizes spontaneously while looking at another person or to get someone's attention.
   B. Demonstrates the ability to use a few syllables, words, or expressions.
      1. Imitates at least one phoneme, syllable, or word.
      2. Uses at least one syllable, word, or expression consistently and meaningfully.

III. Nonverbal receptive skills
   A. Demonstrates the ability to respond appropriately to a simple gesture.
   B. Demonstrates the ability to respond to subtle or elaborate gestures when the situation does not make the meaning obvious.

IV. Nonverbal expressive skills
   A. Communicates by using simple gestures.
   B. Communicates by using elaborate gestures.

From Moog, J., & Geers, A. (1975). *Scales of Early Communication Skills for Hearing Impaired Children (SECS)*, p. 1. St. Louis, MO: Central Institute for the Deaf; reprinted by permission.

Social Skills Rating System (SSRS)

Author(s): F.M. Gresham & S.N. Elliott
Year: 1990
Publisher: American Guidance Service
Address: Publisher's Building, Circle Pines, Minnesota 55014-1796
Phone: 800-328-2560
Cost: $105+

Assessment type: Curriculum compatible for behavior and social skills domains; standardized, norm-referenced scales for a broad, multiple-rater assessment of student social behaviors and development of interventions to improve the student's interactions with others. Information yielded includes identification of students who are at risk for behavior problems and poor academic performance; differentiation between students with and without disabilities; categorization of behavior difficulties and identifying social strengths; selection of behaviors for intervention; and enhancement of communications among parents, teachers, and students.

Age/focus group: Parent and teacher rating scales at three developmental levels: preschool, kindergarten through sixth grade, and seventh grade through twelfth grade; student self-rating at two levels: third grade through sixth grade and seventh grade through twelfth grade.

Domains/content: Three domains: social skills, problem behaviors, and academic competence; subdomains of social skills include cooperation, assertion, responsibility, empathy, and self-control; subdomains of problem behaviors include externalizing, internalizing, and hyperactivity.

Special needs options: Best used with children who are at risk for or who have moderate functional limitations; few adaptive provisions for social skills impairments; "importance" rankings aid decision making about priorities for goal planning.

Curricular links: Developing intervention or instructional plans is major purpose. Social tasks align directly with general levels in most curricula; Assessment-Intervention Record translates data for intervention; "importance" rankings guide collaborative decision making.

Authenticity: Strong authentic features with multiple observations of typical/atypical social and problem behaviors in home and preschool settings without contrivances.

Family involvement: Interpretation of results relies on strong parent observation and preparation.

Scoring/sample: Subscale and scale frequency raw scores for norm-referenced score interpretations; scores convert to descriptive behavior levels, standard scores, and percentile ranks. Normative sample = 4,000+ children.

Validation: Strong psychometric data on reliability and validity; some field trials on samples of individuals with disabilities.

Training needed: Users should have training in psychological test interpretation and an understanding of the basic principles and limitations of educational and psychological testing.

Comments:
- *Preeminent among the few social skills measures for preschoolers*
- *Strong authentic features*
- *Strong treatment validity*
- *Excellent for eligibility determination and intervention planning*
- *Matches the general goals of most curricula in the social-emotional domain*

LINK Index			
Authentic	1	2	③
Convergent	1	2	③
Collaborative	1	2	③
Equitable	①	2	3
Sensitive	1	2	③
Congruent	1	②	3
Total Index	1 +	2 +	12 ÷ 6 = 2.5
Overall quality: high			

3.0, exemplary; 2.5, high; 2.0, acceptable; 1.5, low; 1.0, negligible.

Social Skills Rating System (SSRS)

Preschool programs have increasingly begun to stress building social skills and social communication skills in young children with developmental delays and disabilities. In most curricula, the social domain is the weakest area. Given the emphasis on measuring and building social skills in natural environments, professionals have sought dedicated measures in this area. Social Skills Rating System (SSRS) is a curriculum-compatible scale that addresses a critical need in the early intervention field.

SSRS relies on convergent data (from parents and professionals) from across home, preschool, and community settings to collect a representative sample of a child's prosocial behaviors. We regard the SSRS as an ecological instrument with norms. The preschool version of the SSRS (for children ages 3–5 years) consists of three forms: Teacher Form, Parent Form, and Assessment-Intervention Record (AIR). AIR enables parents and professionals to produce a collaborative plan that prioritizes social skills for development on the basis of rankings of the "importance" of a particular skill to parents or teachers (e.g., not important, important, critical). A 3-point rating scale (0, 1, and 2) enables a rater to quantify, on the basis of direct observation, the degree to which a child has acquired landmark social skills (e.g., cooperates with peers without prompting, waits turn in games or other activities, controls temper in conflict situations with peers, attends to the instructions of parents, makes friends easily). In addition, SSRS contains brief screeners of major problem behaviors (e.g., appears lonely, disobeys rules or requests, has temper tantrums, argues with parents). The use of t-scores allows a team to determine the extent of social skill limitations and to isolate particular clusters of skills that require curriculum planning and intervention across situations. SSRS is a good fit with the early intervention emphasis on activity-based teaching in natural settings. In addition, SSRS gives parents a strong voice in the collaborative process of planning ways to develop important social communication and self-regulatory skills in both home and preschool settings. SSRS simultaneously serves the interrelated purposes of eligibility determination, IEP/IFSP development, and progress/program evaluation.

Sample from the Social Skills Rating System (SSRS)

FOR OFFICE USE ONLY How Often? C	A	S	Social Skills (cont.)	How Often? Never	Sometimes	Very Often	How Important? Not Important	Important	Critical
			17. Says nice things about himself or herself when appropriate.	0	1	2	0	1	2
			18. Uses free time in an acceptable way.	0	1	2	0	1	2
			19. Acknowledges compliments or praise from peers.	0	1	2	0	1	2
			20. Controls temper in conflict situations with peers.	0	1	2	0	1	2
			21. Follows rules when playing games with others.	0	1	2	0	1	2
			22. Finishes class assignments within time limits.	0	1	2	0	1	2
			23. Compromises in conflict situations by changing own ideas to reach agreement.	0	1	2	0	1	2
			24. Initiates conversations with peers.	0	1	2	0	1	2
			25. Invites others to join in activities.	0	1	2	0	1	2
			26. Receives criticism well.	0	1	2	0	1	2
			27. Puts work materials or school property away.	0	1	2	0	1	2
			28. Responds appropriately to peer pressure.	0	1	2	0	1	2
			29. Joins ongoing activity or group without being told to do so.	0	1	2	0	1	2
			30. Volunteers to help peers with classroom tasks.	0	1	2	0	1	2
C	A	S	SUMS OF HOW OFTEN COLUMNS						

FOR OFFICE USE ONLY How Often? E	I	Problem Behaviors	How Often? Never	Sometimes	Very Often	
		31. Has temper tanturms.	0	1	2	Do not make importance ratings for items 31–40
		32. Fidgets or moves excessively.	0	1	2	
		33. Argues with others.	0	1	2	
		34. Disturbs ongoing activities.	0	1	2	
		35. Says nobody likes him or her.	0	1	2	
		36. Appears lonely.	0	1	2	
		37. Is aggressive toward people or objects	0	1	2	
		38. Disobeys rules or requests.	0	1	2	
		39. Shows anxiety about being with a group of children.	0	1	2	
		40. Acts sad or depressed.	0	1	2	
E	I	SUMS OF HOW OFTEN COLUMNS **Stop. Please check to be sure all items have been marked.**				

Social Skills Rating System by Frank M. Gresham & Stephen N. Elliott © 1990 American Guidance Service, Inc., 4201 Woodland Road, Circle Pines, MN 55014-1796. Adapted and reproduced with permission of the Publisher. All rights reserved.

Syracuse Scales of Infant and Toddler Development (SSITD) (Syracuse Assessments for Birth to Three)*

Author(s): G. Ensher, E. Gardner, T. Bobish, C. Michaels, K. Butler, & P. Meller

Date: 1997

Publisher: Authors

Address: Applied Symbolix, 16 West Erie, Suite 300, Chicago, Illinois 60610

Phone: 312-787-3772

Cost: Research participation

Assessment type: Curriculum-compatible, norm-based hybrid with age-reference points.

Age/focus group: Appropriate for children from birth to 36 months representing a range of populations. Designed for individual eligibility determination based on norms.

Scale(s): Developmental milestones.

Data system: Three Record Forms, Observation Forms, Play in the Early Months, and Toddler Play Based Scenarios are provided.

Special needs options: Administration is flexible and encourages accommodating individual differences; but no special needs populations are included in norming/standardization.

Authenticity: Remarkably high for this type of instrument; play based.

Family involvement: Caregiver interview guides designed to assist service providers in collecting information concerning child and family. Caregiver Report of Home and School Environment invites parents to contribute to a child's as-

---

*At the time this book was going to press in early 1997, the Syracuse Scales of Infant and Toddler Development (SSITD) was in press at Applied Symbolix and had been retitled the Syracuse Assessments for Birth to Three (by Gail Ensher, Tasia Bobish, Eric Gardner, Cynthia Michaels, Katherine Butler, Daniel Foertsch and Christine Cooper). The scales will include two measures: 1) the Syracuse Dynamic Assessment for Birth to Three (SDA) and 2) the Syracuse Play-Based Assessment (SPBA).

sessment and participate with intervention planning and implementation.

Training needed: Professional skills, knowledge of development and content of assessment manual. Training tape and workshop available.

Validation: Research and trials spanning 10 years support the item content, standardized procedures, reliabilities, and approximate norms; norming and validation are ongoing across the United States.

Comments:
- *Play focused*
- *Activity-based skills assessed together instead of separate domain testing*
- *Supports parent–professional collaboration*
- *Designed for transdisciplinary teams*

LINK Index			
Authentic	1	2	③
Convergent	1	2	③
Collaborative	1	2	③
Equitable	1	②	3
Sensitive	1	2	③
Congruent	1	②	3
Total Index	☐ +	4 +	12 ÷ 6 = 2.7
Overall quality: high			

3.0, exemplary; 2.5, high; 2.0, acceptable; 1.5, low; 1.0, negligible.

Syracuse Scales of Infant and Toddler Development (SSITD)
(Syracuse Assessments for Birth to Three)

Many current assessment instruments are organized by developmental area or domain, with each area being administered to a child separately. SSITD, however, is structured so that multiple developmental areas are evaluated from a common set of play activities that require integrated abilities. These activities are meaningful and natural to children and caregivers because responses are elicited in the context of play activities that use novel and engaging toys or objects. SSITD play activities, therefore, can be regarded as a series of structured interactions among examiner, child, and caregiver that may be used to evaluate developmental abilities and behaviors, thereby obviating the need for repetitious evaluations across separate disciplines.

The SSITD approach to assessment features a balance between standardized procedures and examiner flexibility that is responsive to each child's readiness, temperament, and diverse abilities. For example, examiners may depart from the standard administration sequence of items or activities when an infant or toddler has become distracted, disinterested, or upset because state or temperament may affect performance under such circumstances. In addition, the scales contain both unstructured and structured play activities that allow examiners and team members to observe how a child behaves in various different situations. Also conducive to the needs of the child are flexible "time-out" activities that may be used at any time during the assessment; for instance, if a toddler becomes hungry during the evaluation, examiners may set up a snack time and administer play activities that involve eating and drinking. Finally, another important feature of SSITD is the incorporation of numerous skills, abilities, and behaviors that may be displayed spontaneously by the child and noted in the absence of specific administration. It is clear that this quality of SSITD offers a more natural, authentic context than do conventional methods for evaluating infants or toddlers.

A final point regarding the SSITD approach to assessment concerns the role of caregivers. Teams are encouraged to include caregivers or parents as active participants in evaluation. Such involvement may take the form of actual administration of certain activities, but other types of participation may largely consist of support for the child (e.g., holding, sitting nearby). In addition, for some items, a child's responses to familiar and unfamiliar people are evaluated separately. Such differences are especially important in terms of a child's display of speech, language, and communicative abilities.

The developmental portion of SSITD includes three major sections: 1) observations, 2) play development in the first year, and 3) later play development. Items in the observations portion differ from activities in the remainder of the test. Unlike activities in play development in the first year and later play development, observation items span the entire age range of SSITD (i.e., birth to 36 months) and are intended to afford a collection of samples of behavior occurring at any time during the evaluation. The first part of observations (occurrence of spontaneous behaviors) requires observers to record whether a specific behavior occurs during the assessment, and the second part (frequency of spontaneous behaviors) requires team members to rate the relative frequency or consistency of specific behaviors that have been noted during the evaluation.

The second major section of SSITD, play development in the first year, is organized around the child's position (i.e., play on back, play on stomach, play in sitting position, play in upright and standing position) with the exception of the time-out activities. Items within and across these positions are ordered developmentally between birth and 12 months. Paralleling the integrated activities of the later play section, items represent five primary areas, including neuromotor, sensory-perceptual, cognitive, language, and social-emotional development, as well as adaptive behavior.

The third major section of the test, later play development, spans the period from 13 to 36 months. These items, unlike those of the early play section, are clustered across toys, materials, and activities rather than position. As with the earlier sections of SSITD, however, special adaptations are offered for children who have physical or other disabilities.

Caregiver Guide I is designed to help team members collect important information concerning the child, his or her family, and key circumstances affecting him or her. Guide I focuses on identifying information and a brief history obtained from the primary caregivers during the first visit, whereas *Caregiver Guide II* offers a flexible interview schedule for looking at the current status of the child/family and resources. Guide II is especially helpful to teams gathering essential information about particular patterns of feeding and eating, moving, preferences, temperament, and other special strengths and limitations of the child before the actual administration of the SSITD. Finally, the Self-Reporting Guide on *Caregiver Priorities for Home and Program* is a short questionnaire that asks parents and caregivers to identify their priorities and needs for support and intervention. The questionnaire contains three sections: 1) home and family, 2) transition to services, and 3) progress in the program. The home and family section is appropriate for all infants and toddlers with whom SSITD is used. The remaining two sections of the questionnaire are designed for families of children receiving early intervention services.

Sample from the Syracuse Scales of Infant and Toddler Development (SSITD)

Observations

Occurrence of Spontaneous Behaviors

1-6 1. Differential Vocalization   L

○ Not Applicable/Appropriate _____

○ No Response/Not Observed

Check ANY/ALL

Grunts	☐
Squeals	☐
Sighs	☐
Changes in pitch	☐
Single vowel sounds	☐
Early consonant-vowel combinations	☐

3-8 2. Vocal Play   L

○ Not Applicable/Appropriate _____

○ No Response/Not Observed

Check ANY/ALL

"Raspberry"	☐
Early consonant-vowel (CV) combinations	☐
Later consonant-vowel (CV) combinations	☐
Duplicated syllables	☐

1-12 3. Surveying Environment   SE

○ Not Applicable/Appropriate _____

○ Does Not Survey

Surveying of Persons

_____ Number of persons present to child

_____ Number of persons surveyed

Range of Surveying   *Check ANY/ALL*

Less than 3 feet	☐
Between 3 feet and 4 feet	☐
Greater than 4 feet	☐

1-12 4. Crying   L

○ Not Applicable/Appropriate _____

○ No Response/No Crying Observed

Amplitude/Quality   *Check ANY/ALL*

Weak	☐
Strained	☐
Piercing	☐
Strong	☐

Pitch Level   *Check ANY/ALL*

Low	☐
Moderate	☐
High	☐

Variation of Pitch   *Check ONE*

No changes in pitch	○
Changes in pitch	○

3-18 5. Joint Referencing   L

○ Not Applicable/Appropriate _____

○ No Response/Not Observed

Check ANY/ALL

	Not Observed	Nonverbal	Verbal
Attends	☐	☐	☐
Gains attention	☐	☐	☐
Directs attention	☐	☐	☐
Continues familiar routine	☐	☐	☐

9-18 6. Babbling   L

○ Not Applicable/Appropriate _____

○ No Response/Not Observed

Check ANY/ALL

Single consonant-vowel (CV) combinations	☐
Reduplicated babbling	☐
Variegated babbling	☐
Jargon-like vocalizations	☐

Page 4   ☐ *Check ANY/ALL*   ○ *Check ONE*   **Occurrence of Spontaneous Behaviors**

From Ensher, G.L., Bobish, T.P., Gardner, E.F., Michaels, C.A., Butler, K.G., Foertsch, D., & Cooper, C. (1996). *Syracuse Scales of Infant and Toddler Development (SSITD)*, p. 4. Chicago, IL: Applied Symbolix; reprinted by permission.

Sample from the Syracuse Scales of Infant and Toddler Development (SSITD)

Listing of Later Play Development Items

Exploring Through Blowing and Touch

13-36 122. Blowing Bubbles
13-36 123. Play with Masking Tape

Shapes and Containers

13-18 124. Play with Blocks and Container
13-36 125. Block Recognition with Shape Sorter
13-36 126. Nesting Cups
13-36 127. Stacking Cups

Mazes, Designs, and Puzzles

13-36 128. Playing with a Bead Maze
15-36 129. Matching Shapes
19-36 130. Doing a Puzzle

Book, Picture, and Crayon Activities

13-36 131. Looking at a Child Book
13-36 132. Picture Recognition
13-36 133. Play with Crayon and Paper

Doll Play

13-36 134. Initiating Play in Unstructured Activity
13-36 135. Variety and Complexity of Pretend Play in Unstructured Activity
13-36 136. Poking and Inspecting Baby Doll
13-36 137. Identifying Body Parts on Doll/Self
13-36 138. One- and Two-Step Directions and Wh- Questions
13-36 139. Comprehending Objects Named
13-36 140. Holding and Dressing Baby Doll

Caring for Self

13-36 141. Combing/Brushing Hair
13-36 142. Putting on Hat
13-36 143. Undressing and Dressing Self
13-36 144. Taking Off and Putting On Socks
13-36 145. Unfastening and Fastening

Problem-Solving

13-24 146. Play with Pop-up Toy
13-24 147. Problem-Solving with Screens
13-24 148. Putting Finger Food in Container
13-24 149. Picking Up Finger Food
13-24 150. Eating Finger Food
23-36 151. Play with Toy Garage
31-36 152. Social Solutions/Real Decisions
31-36 153. Social Solutions/Torn Book Story
31-36 154. Identifying Objects by Touch
23-36 155. Building with Interlocking Blocks

Early Social/Verbal Games

13-18 156. Patty-Cake
13-18 157. Response to Bye-Bye
13-36 158. Phonological Awareness by Imitation
19-36 159. Identifying Different Sounds

Ball Play

13-16 160. Ball Play in Sitting
17-36 161. Throwing
17-36 162. Catching
17-36 163. Kicking a Rolling Ball
17-36 164. Sitting on a Ball

From Ensher, G.L., Bobish, T.P., Gardner, E.F., Michaels, C.A., Butler, K.G., Foertsch, D., & Cooper, C. (1996). *Syracuse Scales of Infant and Toddler Development (SSITD)*, p. 2. Chicago, IL: Applied Symbolix; reprinted by permission.

System to Plan Early Childhood Services (SPECS)

Author(s):	S.J. Bagnato & J.T. Neisworth
Year:	1990
Publisher:	American Guidance Service
Address:	Publisher's Building, Circle Pines, Minnesota 55014-1796
Phone:	800-328-2560
Cost:	$100+

Assessment type: Curriculum compatible for general curriculum entry points and programming purposes; service delivery emphasis. Convergent and authentic assessment measure with strong treatment utility and validity; focus on systematizing the process of team assessment and team decision making through consensus building among parents and professionals.

Age/focus group: Children 2–6 years of age; infant version in progress; Infant SPECS rating scale is in the field-validation phase (contact authors to participate).

Domains/content: Six clusters (communication, sensorimotor, physical, self-regulation, cognition, and self-social); 19 developmental dimensions (receptive language, expressive language, hearing, vision, gross motor, fine motor, health, growth, normalcy, temperament, play, attention, self-control, basic concepts, problem solving, self-esteem, motivation, social competence, and adaptive skills); three major instruments: Developmental Specs, Team Specs, and Program Specs.

Special needs options: Clear focus on individual levels of ability/disability; field-validation and diagnostic data on 10 special needs groups; focus on adaptive modifications to intervention options and service delivery arrangements.

Curricular links: The 19 developmental dimensions align with general curricular entry points and match domains in major developmental curricula; specific IEP/IFSP items link with decisions on specific instructional, service, and programmatic options weighted to derive a graph of "program intensity" for each child in the Program Specs component.

Authenticity:
Focuses on natural behavior in everyday settings; relies on structured observations from many individuals; translates assessment data into clear decisions about program needs and options for service delivery; links assessment, intervention, and progress evaluation in specific ways.

Family involvement:
Especially designed and dedicated to parent–professional collaboration and consensus decision making.

Scoring/sample:
Uses 5-point ratings of functional capabilities: typical, at risk, mild, moderate, severe; weighted scores for program options and intensities.

Validation:
Based on 10 years of reliability and field validation on 10 disability groups; content, concurrent, diagnostic, criterion, discriminant function, and generalizability theory studies in team decision making; Sample of 1,300 children (typical and atypical), 300 professionals, and 100 parents.

Training needed:
Natural data from formal and informal sources are converged by using input from parents, assistants, and professionals to reach consensus decisions; requires facilitation by a team leader.

Comments:
- *Most sophisticated and technically adequate team assessment measure*
- *Facilitates team decision-making process*
- *Arguably the only instrument with field validations on children with every major disability*
- *Links assessment, intervention, and progress evaluation in specific ways*
- *Requires parent–professional partnerships in team co-leadership and decision making*
- *Fulfills major early intervention purposes*
- *Exemplary assessment system combining convergent, authentic, and collaborative methods*

LINK Index

Authentic	1	2	③
Convergent	1	2	③
Collaborative	1	2	③
Equitable	1	②	3
Sensitive	1	②	3
Congruent	1	2	③
Total Index	☐ +	4 +	12 ÷ 6 = 2.7
Overall quality: high			

3.0, exemplary; 2.5, high; 2.0, acceptable; 1.5, low; 1.0, negligible.

System to Plan Early Childhood Services (SPECS)

Effective early intervention requires teamwork, and teamwork requires collaborative decisions by teams of parents and professionals. Assessment for early intervention, therefore, relies on the convergence of data from multiple sources, settings, and occasions to plan and evaluate programs for young children with developmental disabilities.

System to Plan Early Childhood Services (SPECS) is an authentic and convergent team assessment and decision-making battery composed of three primary instruments with synchronized uses. Developmental Specs (D–Specs) allows individual team members to rate and profile a child's level of functional capability in six domains (i.e., communication, sensorimotor, physical, self-regulation, cognition, self-social) and 19 developmental and behavioral dimensions on a 5-point rating continuum. Team Specs (T–Specs) summarizes D–Specs ratings and offers a mechanism by which the team can reach consensus about the extent of a child's needs and can translate those needs into general estimates of consultative or direct services. Program Specs (P–Specs) is a collaborative 45-item questionnaire that enables a team to detail a child's specific needs in 10 early intervention service areas and to graph the comparative intensity of those needs.

SPECS accomplishes several critical early intervention purposes: 1) it provides a common language for interdisciplinary parent–professional team assessments about developmental, mental health, and medical concerns; 2) it offers a sensible means for enabling parents to be partners in decision making; 3) it documents the severity of functional developmental deficits; 4) it translates assessment data into estimates of the need for direct or consultative services; 5) it gauges the specific intensities and arrangements for early intervention services that will likely promote developmental progress; and 6) it monitors a child's progress and a program's impact via the inverse relationship between increasing developmental competence and decreasing program intensity.

The diagnostic and treatment validity of SPECS is well-established through extensive field-validation studies performed over a 10-year period on 1,300 children (typical and atypical) with various developmental diagnoses, 300 professionals, and 100 parents; these studies included content, construct, concurrent, convergent, diagnostic, discriminant function, and criterion studies.

SPECS Components

1. **Developmental Specs** (D–Specs)
   - rates 20 competencies
   - profiles functional levels

2. **Team Specs** (T–Specs)
   - generates team consensus
   - classifies 10 service needs

3. **Program Specs** (P–Specs)
   - scores 45 specific program needs
   - profiles "program intensity"

Sample Team Consensus Profile from the System to Plan Early Childhood Services (SPECS)

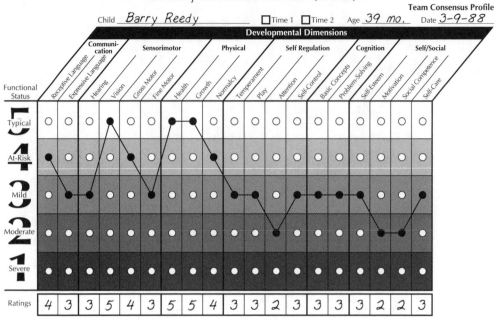

Team Consensus Profile

Child **Barry Reedy** ☐ Time 1 ☐ Time 2 Age **39 mo.** Date **3-9-88**

Ratings: 4 3 3 5 4 3 5 5 4 3 3 2 3 3 3 3 2 2 3

Service Matrix

Service Option	Receptive Language	Expressive Language	Hearing	Vision	Gross Motor	Fine Motor	Health	Growth	Normalcy	Temperament	Play	Attention	Self-Control	Basic Concepts	Problem-Solving	Self-Esteem	Motivation	Social Competence	Self-Care	Total	÷	Service Average	Service Decision
1.0 Early Education	4	3			4	3			4		3	2	3	3	3	3	2	2	3	42	÷14	3.0	DSN
2.0 Adaptive Services	4	3	3	5	4	3			3										3	28	÷8	3.5	CR
2.0 Adaptive Services									4	3	3	2	3			3	2	2		22	÷8	2.8	DSN
4.0 Speech/Language Therapy	4	3										3								10	÷3	3.3	DSN
5.0 Physical Therapy					4														3	7	÷2	3.5	CR
6.0 Occupational Therapy						3													3	6	÷2	3.0	DSR
7.0 Vision Services				5																5	÷1	5.0	NS
8.0 Hearing Services			3																	3	÷1	3.0	CR
9.0 Medical Services			3	5	4	3	5	3												25	÷6	4.1	CR
10.0 Transition Services (ages 4-1/2 to 6)																					÷19		

Enter Team Consensus ratings in the gold boxes, sum across the rows, and divide to obtain an average.

Service Decision Criteria

(Compare each Service Average to the criteria below. Round down to the next lowest whole number.)

5 – No Service Needed (NS)
4 – Consult Recommended (CR)
3 – Direct Services Recommended (DSR)
2/1 > Direct Services Needed (DSN)

Temperament Assessment Battery for Children (TABC)

Author(s): R.P. Martin
Year: 1988
Publisher: PRO-ED (no longer in print)
Phone: Please check your local library system for copies of this publication.
Cost: N/A

Assessment type: Curriculum compatible for behavior and personal-social domains. Battery of multiple-source, multiple-setting rating scales that measure individual differences in social-emotional functioning; scales produce descriptions of temperamental and regulatory characteristics of child and comparison of other children in same age range (consultative-ecological assessment as opposed to clinician-based assessment).

Age/focus group: Children 3–7 years of age.

Domains/content: Three instruments (parent form, teacher form, and clinician form) that measure six variables: activity, adaptability, approach/withdrawal, emotional intensity, distractibility, and persistence.

Special needs options: None are included; focus is on predictable extremes in self-regulatory behavior.

Curricular links: Items are worded in simple and active terms so that behavioral/temperamental needs are clear priorities for IEP/IFSP goal planning.

Authenticity: Strong authentic features with multiple observations of typical/atypical behavior in clinic, home, and preschool settings without contrivances.

Family involvement: Interpretation of results relies on integral participation of parents.

Scoring/sample:

Uses a 7-point frequency scale to determine raw scores, *t*-scores, percentiles, and verbal categories. Normed on 1,300+ children; some field trials with special needs populations.

Validation:

Internal consistency; test–retest, and interrater reliability.

Training needed:

"At minimum, careful study of technical data provided in manual" needed to administer; a higher level of interpretive skill required to interpret whether battery is used for psychological examination.

Comments:

- *Perhaps the most efficient and practical measure of temperamental attributes*
- *Facilitates eligibility determination for the social-emotional domain*
- *Breaks from the psychopathological model of premature and inappropriate psychiatric diagnoses for early problems in behavior and temperament; presents a regulatory model*
- *Operationalizes a multiple-source assessment model*
- *Excellent treatment validity; sensitive to behavior changes*
- *Exemplar of more authentic observational measures of temperamental style*

LINK Index			
Authentic	1	2	③
Convergent	1	2	③
Collaborative	1	2	③
Equitable	①	2	3
Sensitive	1	2	③
Congruent	1	②	3
Total Index	1 +	2 +	12 ÷ 6 = 2.5
Overall quality: high			

3.0, exemplary; 2.5, high; 2.0, acceptable; 1.5, low; 1.0, negligible.

Temperament Assessment Battery for Children (TABC)

Appraisals of the behavioral characteristics and "styles" of young children have begun to emphasize aspects of temperament and self-regulation rather than traditional classifications of developmental psychopathology or behavior/emotional disorders (e.g., attention-deficit/hyperactivity disorder). The majority of the newer assessment methods rely on observations and ratings completed by parents and professionals in natural settings. The objective of these assessments is to describe individual patterns of social behavior and self-regulation so that extremes can be defined and intervention can be targeted on reducing inappropriate behaviors and increasing specific prosocial and self-control skills that are germane to IFSP development and amenable to intervention.

One of the most useful of these curriculum-compatible behavior rating scales is Temperament Assessment Battery for Children (TABC). TABC consists of separate but complementary rating scales for parents, teachers, and individual clinicians that allow a description of extremes in aspects of temperamental styles (t-scores) in natural settings and across multiple domains (e.g., activity level, persistence, distractibility, adaptability, emotional intensity, approach/withdrawal). The items are clearly worded, are personalized, and invite individual judgments along a 7-point continuum from "hardly ever" to "almost always" (e.g., when first meeting new children, my child is bashful; the child shows little reaction when his or her toy is taken away by another child). A major strength of the TABC is that it is an observational rating scale with norms. Its intended use is as an authentic assessment instrument of behaviors that constitute temperament and self-regulation in real-life situations. TABC is both very useful for describing patterns and extremes in self-regulation and invaluable as a way to identify behavioral goals and family priorities for IFSP development. In this respect, TABC is an authentic curriculum-based scale with high treatment validity.

Sample Teacher Form from the Temperament Assessment Battery for Children (TABC)

TEMPERAMENT ASSESSMENT BATTERY FOR CHILDREN

Teacher Form

Child's
Name _____

Age (in
Months) _____ Date _____

Sex **M F**   Ethnicity   Caucasian, Black, Hispanic, Oriental,
  (Circle)   Other _____
          (circle one)

Respondent's
Name _____

Relation: Teacher, Aide
    Other _____
       (circle one)

This questionnaire is designed to gather information on the way a child behaves in different situations. Each statement asks you to judge whether that behavior occurs *"hardly ever, infrequently, once in a while, sometimes, often, very often,* or *almost always."* Please circle the number "1" if the behavior *hardly ever* occurs, the number "2" if it occurs *infrequently*, etc. Please try to make this judgment to the best of your ability, based on how you think the child *compares to other children about the same age*. Also, please make these judgments based on the child's behavior during the *last 3 months*.

1 hardly ever	2 infrequently	3 once in a while	4 sometimes	5 often	6 very often	7 almost always

1.	Child seems to have difficulty sitting still, may wiggle a lot or get out of seat.	1 2 3 4 5 6 7
2.	Child is shy with adults he/she doesn't know.	1 2 3 4 5 6 7
3.	If child's activity is interrupted, he/she tries to go back to the activity.	1 2 3 4 5 6 7
4.	Child seems to take things matter-of-factly (such as a visitor to class, trips, or other special events), without getting very excited.	1 2 3 4 5 6 7
5.	When teacher establishes safety rules (such as behavior during fire drill), child quickly learns to obey.	1 2 3 4 5 6 7
6.	When telling a story, such as what happened on the weekend or during a vacation, the child talks about it loudly, with enthusiasm and excitement.	1 2 3 4 5 6 7
7.	Child is easily drawn away from his/her work by noises, something outside the window, another child's whispering, etc.	1 2 3 4 5 6 7
8.	Child will initially avoid new games and activities, preferring to sit on the side and watch.	1 2 3 4 5 6 7
9.	Child quickly becomes impatient with a task he/she cannot grasp and goes on to something else.	1 2 3 4 5 6 7
10.	Child is among the first to notice if a messenger, parent, or another teacher comes into the room.	1 2 3 4 5 6 7
11.	If initially hesitant about entering into new games and activities, child quickly gets over this.	1 2 3 4 5 6 7
12.	Child's responses are loud.	1 2 3 4 5 6 7
13.	Child is distracted by other children's movement or talk when teacher is reading a story.	1 2 3 4 5 6 7
14.	Child runs rather than walks.	1 2 3 4 5 6 7
15.	After an absence of many days or after a long holiday, it takes time for this child to readjust to school routine.	1 2 3 4 5 6 7
16.	Child immediately gets involved in new learning situations.	1 2 3 4 5 6 7
17.	Child's attention to teacher reading stories is shorter than other children's.	1 2 3 4 5 6 7
18.	In outdoor play, child is active and energetic, rough and tumble, compared to other children.	1 2 3 4 5 6 7
19.	Child takes a long time to become comfortable in a new physical location (e.g., different classroom, new seat, etc.).	1 2 3 4 5 6 7
20.	If another child tries to interrupt when this child is engaged in activity, he/she will ignore them.	1 2 3 4 5 6 7
21.	Child will show little or no reaction when another child takes his/her toy or possession away.	1 2 3 4 5 6 7

From Martin, R.P. (1988). *Temperament Assessment Battery for Children* (TABC), p. 2. Austin, TX: PRO-ED; reprinted by permission.

Therapeutic Education for the Child with Traumatic Brain Injury: From Coma to Kindergarten

Author(s): D. McKerns & L. McKerns Motchkavitz
Year: 1993
Publisher: Psychological Corporation
Address: 555 Academic Court, San Antonio, Texas 78204-2498
Phone: 800-228-0752, extension 5780
Cost: $79

Assessment type: Curriculum embedded.

Age/focus group: Young children with traumatic brain injury. It can be used individually in a home- or center-based program.

Scale(s): Coma levels, developmental scales, criterion-based and ecological assessments, and task analysis.

Data system: Data Bank Questionnaire and Daily and Monthly Planner.

Domains/content: Learning behavior/cognitive and communication and motor.

Special needs options: Designed for children in need of sensitive assessment and therapy.

Authenticity: Sensory/motor measurement and therapy are essential; as authentic as circumstances permit.

Family involvement: Manual devotes a section to parent questions about the child with brain injury. It promotes the role of "parent as child advocate."

Training needed: Professionals, including cognitive teacher, occupational therapist, physical therapist, and speech-language pathologist, as well as parents, can use this tool.

Validation: Developed through a series of programmatic research efforts and case study validations.

Comments:

- *Family involvement*
- *Multiple means for assessment of current levels*
- *Provides baseline data useful for planning goals*

LINK Index			
Authentic	1	2	③
Convergent	1	2	③
Collaborative	1	2	③
Equitable	1	2	③
Sensitive	1	2	③
Congruent	1	2	③
Total Index	☐ +	☐ +	18 ÷ 6 = 3.0
Overall quality: exemplary			

3.0, exemplary; 2.5, high; 2.0, acceptable; 1.5, low; 1.0, negligible.

Therapeutic Education for the Child with Traumatic Brain Injury: From Coma to Kindergarten

Therapeutic Education for the Child with Traumatic Brain Injury is a curriculum that is intended for use with young children who have traumatic, or acquired, brain injury. Its purpose is to provide parents, health care providers, teachers, and therapists with information for restructuring the life of children with traumatic brain injuries. It promotes the role of "parent as child advocate" and provides teachers and therapists with many means of assessing a child's current performance levels to lead to goal setting within the curriculum. These materials should be considered for use when assessment must be sensitive to very small increments of change.

The skills that are taught in the program are organized into six activity kits: adapted art; manipulative toys; communication; gross motor; adaptive positioning, sensory integration, and coma stimulation; and therapeutic feeding. The kits contain 180 activities in total, and each activity is organized into a lesson plan found in the manual. Each lesson plan includes a description of the activity, the materials needed, a rationale for using the activity, variations in positioning, some cautions for certain activities, and skill objectives addressed by the activity. The skill objectives are broken into the three domains, and specific skills to be learned are delineated.

The program provides its own record-keeping system with two forms: The Monthly Planner and The Daily Planner. The Monthly Planner has two parts. The first part is completed at the beginning of each month to identify monthly goals and the specific activities that will lead to the attainment of these goals. The second part is completed at the end of each month and summarizes the child's progress. The Daily Planner is used to record intended lesson plans as well as which specific skill objectives to target. It is also used to record any adaptations used and the observations of the instructor.

The curriculum provides a direct way of determining entry performance levels for children with traumatic brain injury. It defines what a child can actually do instead of establishing a developmental level or IQ score. It provides baseline information that can be used to plan reasonable goals for the child. Parents and professionals will find these materials very helpful.

Itemized Components (Skill Objectives) of the Three Traumatic Brain Injury (TBI) Domains

Domain: *Learning Behavior/Cognitive*

Subdomains: Perceptual, Social Interactive, Sensory

- Arousal
- Attending
- Attention to task
- Attention span
- Understanding the nature of tasks
- Task completion
- Following directions
- Task accuracy
- Participation
- Cooperation
- Voluntary responding
- Developing flexibility; knowing when the task has been changed and being able to "shift gears"
- Reasoning and problem solving
- Generalizing
- Remembering and carryover
- Comprehension
- Developing initiative
- Awareness of the environment
- Sensory awareness (tactile, visual, auditory, olfactory, taste)
- Sensory discrimination (tactile, visual, auditory, olfactory, taste)
- Sensory integration (tactile, visual, auditory, olfactory, taste)
- Sequencing
- Classification (what belongs, what doesn't belong)
- Comparison
- Contrast
- Cause-effect
- Association/relationships
- Sorting
- Matching
- Directionality
- Spatial relations
- Observation
- Manipulation
- Colors
- Numbers
- Shapes
- Alphabet
- Basic counting
- Figure/ground discrimination

Domain: *Communication*

Subdomains*: Oral Motor, Oculo Motor, Hand-Eye Coordination, Social Interactive, Language

- Understanding the concept of communication
- Interest in communicating
- Response to communication
- Communicating basic needs
- Turn taking
- Describing (basic)
- Interchange of communication
- Understanding vocabulary
- Using vocabulary
- Understanding requests
- Requesting
- Initiating communication
- Understanding questions
- Using questions
- Oral motor skills for pre-speech
- Eye-hand coordination for manipulation of communication devices
- Augmentative/alternative communication
- Rapport
- Listening
- Making choices

---

*Many of these motor skills are necessary for augmentative/alternative communication modes for those who are nonverbal.

Domain: *Motor*

Subdomains: Gross Motor, Fine Motor, Oculo Motor, Visual Motor (Eye-Hand Coordination), Oral Motor, Sensory Motor

- Body awareness
- Position in space
- Range of motion
- Mobility
- Motor planning
- Posture
- Postural control (includes head control)
- Balance
- Balance reactions
- Task sequence
- Reach
- Stamina
- Speed of response
- Graded movement
- Hip flexion
- Knee flexion
- Ankle flexion
- Active leg extension
- Reach
- Grasp (active)
- Grasp/release
- Development of grasp patterns
- Targeting

- Eye-hand coordination
- Manipulation
- Arm pronation
- Arm supination
- Active wrist extension
- Active finger extension
- Flexion
- Extension
- Abduction
- Adduction
- Manipulation
- Visual motor (eye-hand coordination)
- Oculo motor (visual targeting, focusing, tracking)
- Oral motor: facial muscle movement, tongue movement, lip movement (opening, closing, closure around object, rounding), jaw depression (mouth opening), sucking, chewing, swallowing, sequential movement, swallowing, breathing, protective cough

Manipulative Toys Kit

Activity #27
Lesson Plan

Activity	Child places and releases rings on ring stacker
Materials	Ring stacker Velcro® (optional)

Rationale Rings are large, colorful, firm shapes in graduated grip sizes.

Activity provides opportunities for child to follow directions and exercise eye/hand coordination.

Task provides graded degrees of difficulty.

Adaptations For increased figure/ground discrimination, use a black cloth underneath base.

Hold unit horizontally to eliminate lift against gravity.

For added stability, base may be fixed to a stable surface with Velcro®.

Variations Positional changes: Upright, prone, sidelying

Skill Objectives

Domain Learning Behavior/Cognitive

Attending	Following directions
Attention span	Color recognition
Understanding nature of task	Sequencing by size
Task completion	Spatial concepts

Velcro® is a registered trademark of Velcro U.S.A., Inc.

Transdisciplinary Play–Based Assessment (TPBA) and Transdisciplinary Play–Based Intervention (TPBI)

Author(s):	T.W. Linder
Year:	1993
Publisher:	Paul H. Brookes Publishing Co.
Address:	Post Office Box 10624, Baltimore, Maryland 21285-0624
Phone:	800-638-3775
Cost:	$115 (TPBA, TPBI, and summary forms purchased separately) *Transdisciplinary Play-Based Assessment: A Functional Approach to Working with Young Children, Revised Edition* (TPBA) (Linder), $39; *Transdisciplinary Play-Based Intervention: Guidelines for Developing a Meaningful Curriculum for Young Children* (TPBI) (Linder with invited contributors), $49; *Transdisciplinary Play-Based Assessment and Transdisciplinary Play-Based Intervention Child and Program Summary Forms* (Linder) (package of 5 tablets containing all key forms from both manuals), $27; TPBA and TPBI purchased together, $79; TPBA, TPBI, and summary forms purchased together, $106
	Note: Two videotapes are also available (*And You Thought They Were Just Playing: Transdisciplinary Play-Based Assessment*, $175; *Observing Kassandra: A Transdisciplinary Play-Based Assessment for a Child with Severe Disabilities* and accompanying booklet and Summary Forms tablet, $165).

Assessment type: Curriculum embedded.

Age/focus group: Designed for young children from infancy to age 6 years. It is especially useful in arena settings.

Scale(s): Worksheets, Summary Sheets, Cumulative Summary Sheets, and Final Written Report.

Data system: Team ideas of play, team assessment of play, and play-based curriculum planning sheets are provided.

Domains/content: Cognitive, social-emotional, communication and language, and sensorimotor.

Special needs options: This curriculum is flexible and accommodates several different special needs.

Authenticity: Content shows predominance of natural skills and activities that are useful and worthwhile in real-life settings.

Family involvement: A chapter devoted to family participation, as well as materials concerning the importance of family involvement, are included.

Training needed: Can be used by professionals with expertise in the content areas in conjunction with parents.

Validation: Few supporting data provided for program efficacy; however, TBPA is widely used and is endorsed in a number of states.

Comments:
- *Provides a good foundation for program planning*
- *Highly individualized*
- *Natural and functional*
- *Group assessment allows for discussion of observations and real transdisciplinary assessment*
- *Some child development professionals voice concern about "staging" play circumstances*

LINK Index			
Authentic	1	2	③
Convergent	1	2	③
Collaborative	1	2	③
Equitable	1	②	3
Sensitive	1	2	③
Congruent	1	②	3
Total Index	☐ +	4 +	12 ÷ 6 = 2.7
Overall quality: high			

3.0, exemplary; 2.5, high; 2.0, acceptable; 1.5, low; 1.0, negligible.

Transdisciplinary Play–Based Assessment (TPBA) and Transdisciplinary Play–Based Intervention (TPBI)

Transdisciplinary Play-Based Assessment: A Functional Approach to Working with Young Children, Revised Edition (TPBA) is based on what children like to do: play. The TPBA approach is useful for children with special needs, children who are at risk for developmental delays, and children with typical development. TPBA is a valuable assessment tool that helps collect data and develop individualized, play-based intervention activities for young children in home- or center-based environments. It assesses the four domain areas of cognitive, social-emotional, communication and language, and sensorimotor development through child-directed play interactions. TPBA describes each of these four domains thoroughly by identifying the child's developmental level, learning style, temperament, motivation, and interaction patterns in each area of development.

TPBA contains observation and summary worksheets that include more detailed subcategories of abilities in each developmental domain. By using the observation and age charts for each developmental area along with observation and summary worksheets, team members are able to identify child strengths, areas of concern, and areas of readiness.

Transdisciplinary Play-Based Intervention: Guidelines for Developing a Meaningful Curriculum for Young Children (TPBI) is a more recent addition to the materials and is a curriculum that is linked to the assessment. TPBI helps families and other transdisciplinary team members determine the child's goals and behavioral objectives on the basis of TPBA assessment summary sheets. TPBI can guide the team through creative strategies for tackling the child's objectives by focusing on pleasurable interactions and functional activities that are a natural part of the child's day. The Team Ideas for Play (TIP) sheet provides a summary of activity suggestions across all areas of the child's life to ensure the development of an integrated and ecological intervention program.

TPBA is a jargon-free curriculum guide that provides instruction on how to adapt the curriculum to home-based interventions. Parents and facilitators together learn how to plan the play environment, play materials, and the overall structure of the day to facilitate enjoyable, child–parent interactions. Some experts suggest problems with the staging of play in arena circumstances and note that such assessment is not actually an observation of the child's play in real-life contexts. Although these criticisms merit consideration, the role of family information and involvement probably minimizes misinformation. TPBA and TPBI are a clear alternative to psychometric measurement and represent a major step toward authentic and collaborative assessment of young children.

The author plans to introduce a TPBI storybook curriculum, which will provide lesson plans based on popular children's stories.

Sample Cognitive Observation Worksheet from Transdisciplinary Play-Based Assessment (TPBA)

Name of child: _____ Date of birth: _____ Age: _____

Name of observer: _____ Discipline or job title: _____ Date of assessment: _____

IV. Symbolic and Representational Play

A. Symbolic object use

    1. Abstracting a concept *(circle one)*:

        a. Necessary real objects   c. Substituted unrealistic objects

        b. Substituted realistic objects   d. Pretend objects, no props

B. Symbolic play roles

    1. Roles assumed in representational play:

    2. Direction of pretend actions *(circle those that apply)*:

        a. Self   b. Object or toy   c. Adult

    3. Demonstration of behaviors with roles:

    4. Ability to direct play with action figures:

    5. Understanding of behaviors of characters when directing play:

    6. Level of role interaction:

V. Imitation

A. Level of imitation

    1. Simple visible gestures:

    2. Simple invisible gestures:

    3. Single-scheme imitations using objects:

    4. Complex imitations:

    5. Imitation of problem-solving approaches:

    6. Imitation of dramatic play sequences *(circle those that apply)*:

        a. Familiar   b. Unfamiliar

    7. Imitation of drawing *(circle those that apply)*:

        a. Within child's repertoire   b. Novel

OBSERVATION GUIDELINES FOR COGNITIVE DEVELOPMENT: PROBLEM-SOLVING APPROACHES

VI. Problem-Solving Approaches
   A. What interest does the child show in cause-and-effect objects and events?
      1. Does the child use physical "procedures" or bodily movement to make events recur?
      2. What behaviors were observed where the child uses the adult as an agent to make something recur?
      3. What behaviors were observed where the child acted as the agent to make something recur?
      4. What behaviors were observed where the child used an object as a tool to solve a problem?
   B. What means does the child use to accomplish goals? How does he or she figure out challenging tasks?
      1. Does the child use a repetitive approach, doing the same act over and over to cause something to happen (continually bangs box to get it open)?
      2. What evidence was observed of trial-and-error problem-solving using alternative approaches to achieve a goal?
      3. What evidence is observed of advance planning in problem-solving?
         a. The child uses physical searching behaviors in selecting an approach
         b. The child uses visual scanning to select an approach
         c. The child uses verbal mediation (talking to self) or questioning of another to select a problem-solving approach

From Linder, T.W. (1993). *Transdisciplinary play-based intervention: Guidelines for developing a meaningful curriculum for young children,* p. 152. Baltimore: Paul H. Brookes Publishing Co.; reprinted by permission.

Uzgiris and Hunt Infant Psychological Development Scale (IPDS): Dunst Revision

Author(s):   C.S. Dunst
Year: 1980
Publisher: PRO-ED
Address: 5341 Industrial Oaks Boulevard, Austin, Texas 78735
Phone: 512-892-3142
Cost: $40+

Assessment type: Curriculum compatible; norm /developmental process based; description of stage of cognitive competence or sensorimotor development.

Age/focus group: Birth to 30 months.

Domains/content: Sensorimotor abilities in seven subscales: object permanence, means–end relationships, vocal imitation, gestural imitation, operational causality, spatial relationships, and scheme actions.

Special needs options: Qualitative scoring procedures and flexible tasks accommodate the behavior patterns of children with various disabilities.

Curricular links: Developmental programming accomplished when linked with *Infant Learning* (Dunst, 1982), a program that matches assessed levels with goals and intervention strategies.

Authenticity: Emphasizes play-based, applied, problem-solving tasks using Piagetian framework; focuses on observation of natural behaviors with structured probes; links to an activity-based curriculum that stresses transactional development.

Family involvement: Incorporates parent reports.

Scoring/sample: Seven scoring categories for developmental ages: + (elicited behavior), √ (demonstration needed), ±

(emerging), − (absent), O (omitted), R (reported), and M (mistrial); age placements and concurrent validity in a sample of 36 infants and toddlers who are at risk for or who have disabilities in Washington, D.C.

Validation: Concurrent and construct validity data are adequate; widely field-tested with children who have various disabilities (however, samples are small).

Training needed: Supervised administration by an infant diagnostic specialist.

Comments:
- *Detects qualitative features of infant's interaction with the environment*
- *Provides flexible procedures to accommodate some special needs*
- *Offers intervention linkages when used with parallel curriculum*
- *Norm group is limited*
- *Requires more concurrent and predictive validity studies*

LINK Index			
Authentic	1	②	3
Convergent	1	②	3
Collaborative	1	②	3
Equitable	1	2	③
Sensitive	1	2	③
Congruent	1	2	③
Total Index	☐ +	6 +	9 ÷ 6 = 2.5
Overall quality: high			

3.0, exemplary; 2.5, high; 2.0, acceptable; 1.5, low; 1.0, negligible.

Uzgiris and Hunt Infant Psychological Development Scale (IPDS): Dunst Revision

In the child development field, Piagetian scales have been used extensively for research purposes. Diagnostic specialists have attempted to use such instruments as the Infant Psychological Development Scale (IPDS) (Uzgiris & Hunt, 1975) to assess the competencies of infants with special needs. One of the shortcomings of the IPDS and similar instruments, however, has been the lack of a structured scoring manual, profile forms, and procedures that would foster precision. Furthermore, the IPDS is not organized to release prescriptive information for treatment planning. *Clinical and Educational Manual for Use with the Uzgiris and Hunt Scales of Infant Psychological Development*, designed by Dunst (1980), superbly eliminates these shortcomings and strengthens the IPDS for prescriptive assessment purposes.

The revised IPDS has numerous features that support its use with young children, from birth to 30 months of age, who have disabilities. Although the norming is inadequate, the revised IPDS was normed on 36 infants. The derived developmental ages, therefore, have both theoretical and research bases. In addition, the revised IPDS is one of the few instruments that has been field-tested with infants and toddlers with varying developmental disabilities, including mental retardation requiring extensive supports, Down syndrome, and cerebral palsy.

The revised IPDS uses a flexible, multidimensional scoring system to determine the nature of an infant's interaction with people and objects in the environment. For example, in addition to recording emergent skills, the assessor records whether demonstrations or prompting was needed to elicit a behavior. This feature adds to program relevancy.

Developmental competencies across several developmental processes in cognition, social communication, and motor exploration are sampled by the revised IPDS. Flexible scoring, administration procedures, and multidomain coverage highlight the scale's adaptive use for young children with special needs. This broad survey, although Piagetian in orientation, appraises competencies that are targeted in most early intervention programs. For prescriptive curriculum-based practices, the revised IPDS can be linked with its treatment package, *Infant Learning: A Cognitive-Linguistic Intervention Strategy* (Dunst, 1981). The revised IPDS may be used with other curricula as well.

Dunst's revision of the IPDS effectively systematizes the assessment process. The accompanying forms allow diagnosticians to profile discrepancies in levels of functioning among processes, derive developmental ages, and determine important behaviors for intervention. The forms operationally define the critical behaviors that exemplify each task.

The Dunst revision of the IPDS is a much-needed and very pragmatic tool. Its clinical application of a Piagetian approach is a model for other instruments, and its linkage to an existing curriculum with the same theoretical base greatly enhances its worth to practitioners. The IPDS's potential can be fully realized if the inadequate normative base for the instrument is expanded to make it a true hybrid measure; that is, a norm-, curriculum-, and adaptive/process-based measure.

Sample from the Uzgiris and Hunt Infant Psychological Development Scale (IPDS): Dunst Revision

Child's Name _____ Date of Birth _____ Date of Test _____

I. VISUAL PURSUIT AND THE PERMANENCE OF OBJECTS

SCALE STEP	AGE PLACEMENT (Months)	DEVELOP-MENTAL STAGE	ELICITING CONTEXT	CRITICAL ACTION CODE	CRITICAL BEHAVIORS	SCORING 1	2	3	4	5	OBSERVATIONS
E₁	1	I	Visual Fixation	—	Fixates on object held 8 to 10 inches above the eyes						
1	2	II	Visual Tracking	1d	Tracks object through a 180° arc						
2	3	II	Visual Tracking	2c	Lingers at point of object's disappearance—child in supine position or in an infant seat						
E₂	4	III	Visual Tracking	—	Searches for object at point of disappearance—child seated on parent's lap						
3	5	III	Visible Displacement	3c	Secures partially hidden object						
4	6	III	Visual Tracking	2d	Returns glance to position above the head after object moves out of visual field						
E₃	7	IV	Visual Tracking	—	Reverses searching for object in anticipation of reappearance—child seated on parent's lap						
E₄	7	IV	Visible Displacement	—	Withdraws object held in hand following covering of hand and object with cloth						
5	8	IV	Visible Displacement	4d	Secures object hidden under a single screen						
E₅	9	IV	Visible Displacement	5b	Secures object hidden with two screens (A & B)—hidden under A twice then B—searches under A only						
6	9	V	Visible Displacement	6c	Secures object hidden under one of two screens—hidden alternately						
7	9	V	Visible Displacement	7c	Secures object hidden under one of three screens—hidden alternately						
E₆	10	V	Successive Visible Displacement	8e	Secures object hidden through a series of successive visible displacements with three screens						
8	10	V	Superimposed Screens	9c	Secures object under three superimposed screens						
9	13	V	Invisible Displacement	10d 10e	Secures object hidden with a single screen						
10	14	VI	Invisible Displacement	11c	Secures object hidden with two screens (A & B)—hidden under A twice then B						
11	14	VI	Invisible Displacement	12c	Secures object hidden under one of two screens—hidden alternately						
12	15	VI	Invisible Displacement	13c	Secures object hidden under one of three screens—hidden alternately						
13	18	VI	Successive Invisible Displacement	14c	Secures object hidden with three screens—object left under last screen—child searches along pathway						
E₇	22	VI	Successive Invisible Displacement	14d	Secures object hidden with three screens—object left under last screen—child searches directly under last screen						
14	23	VI	Successive Invisible Displacement	15c	Secures object hidden with three screens—object left under first screen—child searches in reverse order						

From Dunst, C. (1980). *Uzgiris-Hunt Scales for Infant Psychological Development Development Scale (IPDS)*, p. 1. Austin, TX: PRO-ED; reprinted by permission of the author.

Vulpe Assessment Battery, Revised Edition (VAB–R)

Author(s):	S.G. Vulpe
Year:	1994
Publisher:	Slosson Educational Publications
Address:	Post Office Box 280, East Aurora, New York 14052
Phone:	800-828-4800
Cost:	$75+

Assessment type: Process-oriented, curriculum-compatible, developmental assessment emphasizing children's functional abilities; used to gather information for early intervention.

Age/focus group: Birth to 8 years.

Domains/content: Six domains of developmental behaviors: gross motor, fine motor, language, cognitive processes, adaptive behaviors, and activities of daily living; 60 skill sequences, including breathing, balance, stairs, scissors, expressive and receptive language, attention, time, and social interaction.

Special needs options: "Appropriate for children with atypical developmental patterns related to medical or social conditions"; graduated scoring enables recording of the degree of instructional/behavioral assistance required and performance under various conditions.

Curricular links: Curriculum-compatible scales provide a practical basis for individualizing treatment, including task analysis and descriptions of acquired, emergent, and absent capabilities of the child. Direct link to teaching via a treatment instructional focus, a method to modify/adapt tasks, prescriptive information about the teaching-learning process, and a method to monitor a child's response to learning.

Authenticity: Graduated scoring of functional skills; performance is rated on the basis of multiple data sources; focus is on child capabilities, instructional strategies, and family/environmental supports.

Family involvement: Integrates parent priorities in goal setting.

Scoring/sample: Analysis scale on a 7-point continuum to determine level of assistance required for improved performance (i.e., maximum, moderate, minimum, stand by).

Validation: Strong field validation in numerous efficacy studies performed over 15 years; important research with disability groups.

Training needed: Can be administered by any person who is familiar with the child or professionally trained in child development.

Comments:

- *One of the few comprehensive measures for use from birth to 8 years*
- *More dense task analysis than most developmental scales*
- *Clear and often detailed curricular links by specific task*
- *Exemplar of the graduated scoring system approach for charting progress*
- *Excellent for assessing low functional levels although somewhat cumbersome*
- *Arguably the most "curriculum-like" instrument available; often surpasses the features of dedicated curricula*

LINK Index			
Authentic	1	②	3
Convergent	1	2	③
Collaborative	①	2	3
Equitable	1	2	③
Sensitive	1	2	③
Congruent	1	2	③
Total Index	$\boxed{1}$ +	$\boxed{2}$ +	$\boxed{12}$ ÷ 6 = $\boxed{2.5}$
Overall quality: high			

3.0, exemplary; 2.5, high; 2.0, acceptable; 1.5, low; 1.0, negligible.

Vulpe Assessment Battery, Revised Edition (VAB–R)

One of the most unique characteristics of the early intervention field has been its practitioners' self-reliant and resourceful attitude toward the development of materials and methods that work. Curriculum-based developmental assessment systems are the most obvious example of self-reliance. Numerous curriculum-based assessment instruments have a long history in early intervention but none more so than the various incarnations of Vulpe Assessment Battery, which has been revised and updated for commercial publication (Vulpe Assessment Battery–Revised [VAB–R]).

VAB–R is a functional and criterion-referenced assessment system that contains developmental sequences of moderate density and can be administered in a flexible manner to combine observation, parent report, and direct assessment sources of information. Unique to the system are assessments of the early intervention program environment and the caregiving styles of staff. VAB–R is one of the few published instruments to gauge performance by using a 7-point, graduated scoring system that details the type of assistance needed for the child to demonstrate capabilities and for professionals and parents to detect small increments of change. Although VAB–R contains many traditional developmental tasks (e.g., shape discrimination), many items are more authentic tasks that require observation of natural, daily activities (e.g., sustained attention in play for 5 minutes).

VAB–R will be a welcome addition for programs that enroll young children with more severe disabilities. Its adaptive qualities, use of sensory and response modifications, team-oriented approach, reliance on convergent data sources, and flexible procedures incorporate most principles of recommended practice.

Sample from the Vulpe Assessment Battery, Revised Edition (VAB–R)

PERFORMANCE ANALYSIS/DEVELOPMENTAL ASSESSMENT

Date: _____

Name: _____   Birthdate: _____

Developmental Area: **ADAPTIVE BEHAVIORS**
Attention And Goal Orientation

Age	Activity & References	Equipment & Directions	SCALE SCORE No / Attention / Phys. Assis. / Soc./Emot. Assis. / Verbal Assis. / I. Sometimes / Transfer (1 2 3 4 5 6 7)	COMMENTS — INFORMATION PROCESSING AND ACTIVITY ANALYSIS
0 - 6 m o.	1. Attention to visual stimuli. 12, 32, 67, 106, 107, 131, 176.	Colorful object or toy: Observe the child's response when colorful object or toy is held in view. The child looks at the object. (The response may vary considerably in quality, immediacy, duration, etc.)		1. Analyze activities considering component parts of each and relationship to: Basic Senses & Functions / Adaptive Behaviors / Cognitive Processes & Specific Concepts / Language / Gross & Fine Motor 2. Information Processing — Consider: Input / Processing / Output
	2. Attention to auditory stimuli. 31, 32, 67, 106, 107, 131, 176. RL-1,3.	Observe the child's response to noises in the environment. The child attends to individual sounds. (Responses may vary considerably in quality, immediacy, duration, etc.)		
	3. Attention to tactile stimuli. 17, 31, 32, 67. 176.	Observe the child's response when touched by another person, object, or material. The child responds appropriately, for example, with pleasure, displeasure, etc. (The response may vary considerably in quality, immediacy, duration, etc.)		
	4. Attention to olfactory stimuli. 31, 32, 67, 107. 176.	Observe the child's response to a variety of odors. The child responds visibly in most cases. (The response may vary considerably in quality, immediacy, duration, etc.)		
	5. Attention to vestibular stimuli. 31, 32, 67, 107. 176.	Observe the child's response to being rocked rhythmically by a familiar person. The child responds visibly, usually by quieting or indicating pleasure. (The response may vary considerably in quality, immediacy, duration, etc.)		

Work Sampling System (WSS)

Author(s): J.R. Jablon, D.B. Marsden, S.J. Meisels, & M.L. Dichtelmeiller
Year: 1994
Publisher: Rebus Planning Associates
Address: 317 South Division Street, Suite 155, Ann Arbor, Michigan 48104
Phone: 800-435-3085
Cost: $120

Assessment type: Curriculum-compatible, authentic performance assessment for portfolio development.

Age range: Preschool (3–5 years old) through fifth grade.

Domains/content: Personal and social, language and literacy, mathematical thinking, scientific thinking, social studies, the arts, and physical development.

Special needs options: Flexible design allows for individual selection of performance indicators and assessment tasks for each child on the basis of his or her strengths and limitations.

Curricular links: Performance indicators in each domain of the *Developmental Guidelines* were derived from national curriculum standards and from relevant professional research literature.

Authenticity: Assessment focuses on developmentally appropriate curricular tasks by means of performance assessment in the natural environment and the use of Developmental Checklists and student portfolios.

Scoring/sample: The Developmental Checklist for each level involves rating the student as "proficient," "in process," or "not yet" on each performance indicator. This information is synthesized by completing a Summary Report that rates the child's overall performance as "developing as expected" or "needs development."

Technical support: Research findings support the internal reliability of the Developmental Checklist and Summary Report and the criterion validity as a predictor of performance on norm-referenced measures.

Training needed: Teacher's manual includes a section titled "Getting Started," and training workshops are conducted at locations across the United States.

Comments:
- *Well organized and easy to implement*
- *Flexible design of system facilitates adaptations for children with developmental delays*
- *Provides an excellent link between assessment and instruction*
- *Portfolio and checklist provide ongoing documentation of child's progress*

📖 ↔

LINK Index			
Authentic	1	2	③
Convergent	1	2	③
Collaborative	1	2	③
Equitable	1	②	3
Sensitive	1	②	3
Congruent	1	②	3
Total Index	☐ +	6 +	9 ÷ 6 = 2.5
Overall quality: high			

3.0, exemplary; 2.5, high; 2.0, acceptable; 1.5, low; 1.0, negligible.

Work Sampling System (WSS)

Work Sampling System (WSS) provides an excellent structure for implementing developmentally appropriate programs for young children of all developmental levels. This system mirrors the NAEYC's (1996) guidelines that state that curricula should reflect integrated themes and be flexible in regard to the unique patterns of development in individual children. The authentic assessment component of WSS clearly reflects the NAEYC recommendation that young children be evaluated through observation of performance and not be assigned letter grades for passing or failing. WSS's developmental guidelines for each age/grade level include specific descriptions of "performance indicators" to guide the professional's assessment of a child's demonstrated proficiency in each domain skill. Assessment frequently occurs on the basis of actual samples of children's work, which are collected for portfolios in very creative ways (e.g., written samples; audiotapes and/or videotapes; photographs; creations in visual arts, music, or drama).

The Developmental Checklist and Summary Report are completed three times each year (i.e., fall, winter, spring) and are an excellent method for evaluating the child's progress through the curriculum. These WSS components facilitate communication with parents as to whether a child is progressing "as expected" or "other than expected." (The latter categorization indicates a rating of "needs development.") This feature is particularly helpful for children with specific learning and behavior needs in that the choice of indicators in each domain and the selection of performance indicators from different age and/or grade levels for inclusion in the IEP are entirely flexible.

WSS is a powerful tool for use in the process of transition to kindergarten programs. The portfolio of children's work samples and the accompanying developmental checklists provide an ongoing scenario of specific competencies demonstrated in domains that are relevant to kindergarten curricula. The portfolio also chronicles those instructional strategies and materials that are particularly effective for a given child. This information, combined with the child's IEP, will clearly reflect that child's strengths and areas of concern and will guide the family and receiving program staff in making decisions regarding appropriate goals, strategies, materials, and evaluation procedures.

Sample from the Work Sampling System (WSS) Kindergarten Developmental Guidelines

 I **Personal and Social Development**

This domain has a dual focus. First, it refers to children's feelings about themselves. The teacher can learn about these feelings by observing children, listening to their comments, and hearing families talk about their children. Included in this focus are indicators that refer to children's views of themselves as learners, and their sense of responsibility to themselves and others. The second focus concerns their social development, including children's interactions with peers, adults, and family members. Particularly important are the skills children show they are acquiring while making friends, solving conflicts, and functioning effectively in groups.

A   Self concept

1   Shows comfort and confidence with self.

Self-awareness and positive self image grow through interactions with others and through experiences of being effective. Five year olds display a positive sense of self by:

- entering established groups confident they will be accepted;
- suggesting roles for themselves in dramatic play or blocks;
- coping well with personal awkwardness or mistakes when trying new tasks;
- entering the classroom in the morning with the assurance they are expected and accepted;
- enjoying the creative process and expecting that their accomplishments will be appreciated by others;
- explaining their disabilities and coping strategies to able-bodied children.

2   Shows initiative and self-direction in actions.

Independence in thinking and action enables children to be creative and take responsibility for their lives. Children often need help from adults as they begin to expand their independence. Some examples of independence are:

- originating projects and working on them without extensive direction from the teacher;
- finding materials for projects, such as scissors and tape to build a house out of a cardboard box;
- finding their outdoor clothes and dressing without extensive supervision;
- assuming classroom chores without being asked (for example, sweeping sand from the floor, watering the plants, helping to clean up spilled juice);
- knowing how and where to stack blocks at clean-up time.

B   Self control

1   Follows classroom rules and routines.

Children who are successful within a group know and accept the rules established for that particular group. Five year olds are learning this skill and can be quite dogmatic with their peers, insisting on adherence to the rules. They are comfortable when they know the routines and can plan their activities around the daily schedule. Ways that children show this ability are:

- knowing that only three people can be at the work bench at one time and choosing another activity until space is available;
- recognizing that because it is almost time for snack, there isn't enough time to take out a new toy or build something new;
- waiting until everyone is dressed before going out on the playground;

From Marsden, D.B., Meisels, S.J., Jablon, J.R., & Dichtelmiller, M.L. (1994). *Work Sampling System: Kindergarten developmental guidelines,* p. 2. Ann Arbor, MI: Rebus Planning Associates; reprinted by permission.

Sample from the Work Sampling System (WSS)

I Personal and Social Development

A Self concept
F W S

1 Shows comfort and confidence with self (p.1)
Not Yet ☐☐☐
In Process ☐☐☐
Proficient ☐☐☐

2 Shows initiative and self-direction in actions (p.1)
Not Yet ☐☐☐
In Process ☐☐☐
Proficient ☐☐☐

B Self control
F W S

1 Follows classroom rules and routines (p.1)
Not Yet ☐☐☐
In Process ☐☐☐
Proficient ☐☐☐

2 Uses classroom materials purposefully and respectfully (p.2)
Not Yet ☐☐☐
In Process ☐☐☐
Proficient ☐☐☐

3 Manages transitions and adapts to changes in routine (p.2)
Not Yet ☐☐☐
In Process ☐☐☐
Proficient ☐☐☐

C Approach to learning
F W S

1 Shows eagerness and curiosity as a learner (p.2)
Not Yet ☐☐☐
In Process ☐☐☐
Proficient ☐☐☐

2 Chooses new as well as a variety of familiar classroom activities (p.2)
Not Yet ☐☐☐
In Process ☐☐☐
Proficient ☐☐☐

3 Approaches tasks with flexibility and inventiveness (p.3)
Not Yet ☐☐☐
In Process ☐☐☐
Proficient ☐☐☐

4 Sustains attention to a task over a period of time, even after encountering problems (p.3)
Not Yet ☐☐☐
In Process ☐☐☐
Proficient ☐☐☐

D Interactions with others
F W S

1 Interacts easily with one or more children when playing or working cooperatively (p.3)
Not Yet ☐☐☐
In Process ☐☐☐
Proficient ☐☐☐

2 Interacts easily with familiar adults (p.3)
Not Yet ☐☐☐
In Process ☐☐☐
Proficient ☐☐☐

3 Participates in the group life of the class (p.4)
Not Yet ☐☐☐
In Process ☐☐☐
Proficient ☐☐☐

4 Participates and follows rules in group activities (p.4)
Not Yet ☐☐☐
In Process ☐☐☐
Proficient ☐☐☐

5 Shows empathy and caring for others (p.4)
Not Yet ☐☐☐
In Process ☐☐☐
Proficient ☐☐☐

E Conflict resolution
F W S

1 Seeks adult help when needed to resolve conflicts (p.4)
Not Yet ☐☐☐
In Process ☐☐☐
Proficient ☐☐☐

2 Uses words to resolve conflicts (p.5)
Not Yet ☐☐☐
In Process ☐☐☐
Proficient ☐☐☐

II Language & Literacy

A Listening
F W S

1 Listens for meaning in discussions and conversations (p.6)
Not Yet ☐☐☐
In Process ☐☐☐
Proficient ☐☐☐

2 Follows directions that involve a series of actions (p.6)
Not Yet ☐☐☐
In Process ☐☐☐
Proficient ☐☐☐

B Speaking
F W S

1 Speaks clearly, conveying ideas in discussions and conversations (p.6)
Not Yet ☐☐☐
In Process ☐☐☐
Proficient ☐☐☐

2 Uses language for a variety of purposes (p.7)
Not Yet ☐☐☐
In Process ☐☐☐
Proficient ☐☐☐

C Literature and reading
F W S

1 Listens with interest to stories read aloud (p.7)
Not Yet ☐☐☐
In Process ☐☐☐
Proficient ☐☐☐

2 Shows independent interest in reading-related activities (p.7)
Not Yet ☐☐☐
In Process ☐☐☐
Proficient ☐☐☐

3 Predicts what will happen next using pictures and content for guides (p.7)
Not Yet ☐☐☐
In Process ☐☐☐
Proficient ☐☐☐

4 Retells information from a story (p.8)
Not Yet ☐☐☐
In Process ☐☐☐
Proficient ☐☐☐

5 Recognizes the association between spoken and written words (p.8)
Not Yet ☐☐☐
In Process ☐☐☐
Proficient ☐☐☐

D Writing
F W S

1 Uses letter-like shapes or letters to depict words or ideas (p.8)
Not Yet ☐☐☐
In Process ☐☐☐
Proficient ☐☐☐

2 Copies or writes words needed for work or play (p.8)
Not Yet ☐☐☐
In Process ☐☐☐
Proficient ☐☐☐

III Mathematical Thinking

A Approach to mathematical thinking
F W S

1 Shows interest in solving mathematical problems (p.10)
Not Yet ☐☐☐
In Process ☐☐☐
Proficient ☐☐☐

2 Uses words to describe mathematical ideas (p.10)
Not Yet ☐☐☐
In Process ☐☐☐
Proficient ☐☐☐

B Patterns and relationships
F W S

1 Recognizes patterns and duplicates or extends them (p.10)
Not Yet ☐☐☐
In Process ☐☐☐
Proficient ☐☐☐

2 Sorts objects into subgroups, classifying and comparing according to a rule (p.11)
Not Yet ☐☐☐
In Process ☐☐☐
Proficient ☐☐☐

3 Orders or seriates a variety of objects on the basis of several attributes (p.11)
Not Yet ☐☐☐
In Process ☐☐☐
Proficient ☐☐☐

C Number concept and operations
F W S

1 Shows understanding of the concept of number and quantity (p.11)
Not Yet ☐☐☐
In Process ☐☐☐
Proficient ☐☐☐

2 Begins to understand relationships between quantities (p.12)
Not Yet ☐☐☐
In Process ☐☐☐
Proficient ☐☐☐

D Geometry and spatial relations
F W S

1 Identifies, labels, and creates a variety of shapes (p.12)
Not Yet ☐☐☐
In Process ☐☐☐
Proficient ☐☐☐

2 Shows understanding of and uses positional words (p.12)
Not Yet ☐☐☐
In Process ☐☐☐
Proficient ☐☐☐

From Marsden, D.B., Meisels, S.J., Jablon, J.R., & Dichtelmiller, M.L. (1994). *Work Sampling System: Kindergarten developmental guidelines*, p. 3. Ann Arbor, MI: Rebus Planning Associates; reprinted by permission.

Sample from the Work Sampling System (WSS)

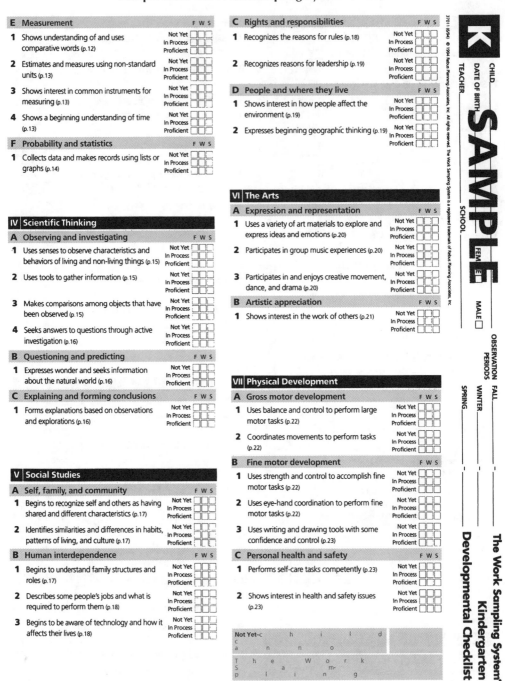

E Measurement F W S

1 Shows understanding of and uses comparative words (p.12)
Not Yet ☐☐☐
In Process ☐☐☐
Proficient ☐☐☐

2 Estimates and measures using non-standard units (p.13)
Not Yet ☐☐☐
In Process ☐☐☐
Proficient ☐☐☐

3 Shows interest in common instruments for measuring (p.13)
Not Yet ☐☐☐
In Process ☐☐☐
Proficient ☐☐☐

4 Shows a beginning understanding of time (p.13)
Not Yet ☐☐☐
In Process ☐☐☐
Proficient ☐☐☐

F Probability and statistics F W S

1 Collects data and makes records using lists or graphs (p.14)
Not Yet ☐☐☐
In Process ☐☐☐
Proficient ☐☐☐

IV | Scientific Thinking

A Observing and investigating F W S

1 Uses senses to observe characteristics and behaviors of living and non-living things (p.15)
Not Yet ☐☐☐
In Process ☐☐☐
Proficient ☐☐☐

2 Uses tools to gather information (p.15)
Not Yet ☐☐☐
In Process ☐☐☐
Proficient ☐☐☐

3 Makes comparisons among objects that have been observed (p.15)
Not Yet ☐☐☐
In Process ☐☐☐
Proficient ☐☐☐

4 Seeks answers to questions through active investigation (p.16)
Not Yet ☐☐☐
In Process ☐☐☐
Proficient ☐☐☐

B Questioning and predicting F W S

1 Expresses wonder and seeks information about the natural world (p.16)
Not Yet ☐☐☐
In Process ☐☐☐
Proficient ☐☐☐

C Explaining and forming conclusions F W S

1 Forms explanations based on observations and explorations (p.16)
Not Yet ☐☐☐
In Process ☐☐☐
Proficient ☐☐☐

V | Social Studies

A Self, family, and community F W S

1 Begins to recognize self and others as having shared and different characteristics (p.17)
Not Yet ☐☐☐
In Process ☐☐☐
Proficient ☐☐☐

2 Identifies similarities and differences in habits, patterns of living, and culture (p.17)
Not Yet ☐☐☐
In Process ☐☐☐
Proficient ☐☐☐

B Human interdependence F W S

1 Begins to understand family structures and roles (p.17)
Not Yet ☐☐☐
In Process ☐☐☐
Proficient ☐☐☐

2 Describes some people's jobs and what is required to perform them (p.18)
Not Yet ☐☐☐
In Process ☐☐☐
Proficient ☐☐☐

3 Begins to be aware of technology and how it affects their lives (p.18)
Not Yet ☐☐☐
In Process ☐☐☐
Proficient ☐☐☐

C Rights and responsibilities F W S

1 Recognizes the reasons for rules (p.18)
Not Yet ☐☐☐
In Process ☐☐☐
Proficient ☐☐☐

2 Recognizes reasons for leadership (p.19)
Not Yet ☐☐☐
In Process ☐☐☐
Proficient ☐☐☐

D People and where they live F W S

1 Shows interest in how people affect the environment (p.19)
Not Yet ☐☐☐
In Process ☐☐☐
Proficient ☐☐☐

2 Expresses beginning geographic thinking (p.19)
Not Yet ☐☐☐
In Process ☐☐☐
Proficient ☐☐☐

VI | The Arts

A Expression and representation F W S

1 Uses a variety of art materials to explore and express ideas and emotions (p.20)
Not Yet ☐☐☐
In Process ☐☐☐
Proficient ☐☐☐

2 Participates in group music experiences (p.20)
Not Yet ☐☐☐
In Process ☐☐☐
Proficient ☐☐☐

3 Participates in and enjoys creative movement, dance, and drama (p.20)
Not Yet ☐☐☐
In Process ☐☐☐
Proficient ☐☐☐

B Artistic appreciation F W S

1 Shows interest in the work of others (p.21)
Not Yet ☐☐☐
In Process ☐☐☐
Proficient ☐☐☐

VII | Physical Development

A Gross motor development F W S

1 Uses balance and control to perform large motor tasks (p.22)
Not Yet ☐☐☐
In Process ☐☐☐
Proficient ☐☐☐

2 Coordinates movements to perform tasks (p.22)
Not Yet ☐☐☐
In Process ☐☐☐
Proficient ☐☐☐

B Fine motor development F W S

1 Uses strength and control to accomplish fine motor tasks (p.22)
Not Yet ☐☐☐
In Process ☐☐☐
Proficient ☐☐☐

2 Uses eye-hand coordination to perform fine motor tasks (p.22)
Not Yet ☐☐☐
In Process ☐☐☐
Proficient ☐☐☐

3 Uses writing and drawing tools with some confidence and control (p.23)
Not Yet ☐☐☐
In Process ☐☐☐
Proficient ☐☐☐

C Personal health and safety F W S

1 Performs self-care tasks competently (p.23)
Not Yet ☐☐☐
In Process ☐☐☐
Proficient ☐☐☐

2 Shows interest in health and safety issues (p.23)
Not Yet ☐☐☐
In Process ☐☐☐
Proficient ☐☐☐

CHILD _____
DATE OF BIRTH _____
TEACHER _____
SCHOOL _____

K

SAMPLE

FEMALE ☐ MALE ☐

OBSERVATION PERIODS
FALL _____
WINTER _____
SPRING _____

The Work Sampling System®
Kindergarten
Developmental Checklist

From Marsden, D.B., Meisels, S.J., Jablon, J.R., & Dichtelmiller, M.L. (1994). *Work Sampling System: Kindergarten developmental guidelines*, p. 4. Ann Arbor, MI: Rebus Planning Associates; reprinted by permission.

5

Forging and Evaluating an Authentic Assessment/Curriculum LINK

LINK, as discussed in Chapters 1, 2, 3, and 4, is a process and set of standards and procedures that help early intervention teams implement authentic curriculum-based evaluations. LINK enables teams to collect functional, goal-oriented information about a child's capabilities on the basis of real-life examples of behavior derived by using natural settings and techniques. An example of such LINK-obtained information is curricular goals that highlight cause–effect problem-solving skills that are observed naturally or reported by parents and professionals at home and in child care settings (e.g., turning on the VCR); such information about a child's capabilities can be recorded and corroborated by observations, ratings, critical incident records, and videotaped episodes.

The LINK model evolved from and incorporates the strengths of the six alternative assessment models (see Chapters 1, 2, and 3) to link assessment and intervention; LINK represents a significant advance toward an authentic approach to assessment. Those instruments and materials that are designated curriculum embedded and curriculum compatible in Chapter 4 represent the best scales available for use by early intervention teams to implement LINK.

This chapter is a how-to primer for combining any of the curriculum-based instruments reviewed in Chapter 4 to use LINK to conduct an authentic curriculum-based evaluation. LINK fulfills the several interrelated missions and purposes of early intervention and is in keeping with recommended practice mandates.

CENTRAL PURPOSES OF EARLY INTERVENTION

Recall that LINK is founded on the developmental hierarchy of goals set in developmental curricula but incorporates the strengths

327

of the six alternative assessment models to guide the style of assessment, ensure that a range of data are collected, and tailor the process to each child and family. Because of its solid field-validation, LINK fulfills several missions, or purposes, of early intervention. The seven central missions of early intervention are 1) family–professional teamwork, 2) eligibility determination, 3) authentic and adaptive-to-disability assessments, 4) IFSP/IEP development, 5) curricular progress monitoring, 6) evaluation of program outcomes and impact, and 7) longitudinal profiles to define developmental diagnosis. In this chapter, we discuss each of these missions; explain steps in the LINK process that accomplish these missions; and present a vignette that illustrates the LINK steps that synchronize assessment, intervention, and progress evaluation through authentic curriculum-based evaluation.

Family–Professional Teamwork

Few assessment approaches invite and foster collaborative teamwork among parents and professionals. The exception is curriculum-based developmental assessment systems, most of which were created by interdisciplinary professionals for use within team formats. Several features of LINK promote teamwork; these include flexibility, use of functional/developmental tasks, domain organization, and treatment and social validities.

LINK is best used with curriculum-based assessment systems that are organized by functional domains that encompass hierarchical sequences of functional skills. These domains (e.g., cognitive, language, gross motor, perceptual/fine motor, social-emotional, adaptive), when contained within a common instrument, encourage interactions among several parties (e.g., psychologist, parent, teacher, speech-language pathologist, occupational therapist, physical therapist) working together to determine a child's capabilities by using the style of teaming that is deemed most appropriate (i.e., multidisciplinary, interdisciplinary, transdisciplinary). One of the hallmarks of LINK's curriculum-based methods is flexibility in collecting data, gauging performance, and staging the assessment. Parents and professionals together can choose the most effective environmental arrangement, or staging (e.g., at home, during play, at a table, in the preschool classroom), to gain the truest picture of a child's development and behavior. Information about the child's capabilities is collected through multiple and convergent sources (e.g., parent observations and reports, direct child assessment, assessment under prompting conditions).

The use of LINK procedures entails gathering authentic information from multiple sources, settings, occasions, and methods. In addition, collaborative decision making about child capabilities and family strengths and needs relies on the capacity of parent–professional teams to synthesize diverse information and facilitate consensus judgments, curricular goals, and strategies for service de-

livery. This process of converging information from observations, interviews, child performance, and other sources during curriculum-based assessment and resolving differences through consensus building is known as convergent assessment (see Chapter 1).

Eligibility Determination

Parents and professionals in the early intervention community advocate the use of assessment methods that have greater treatment and social validities. Notable examples of such methods include play-based arrangements, team decision-making formats, and dynamic and other natural assessment strategies that provide more direct links between assessment of real-life capabilities and intervention and that rely on parent–professional collaboration.

Within this movement for change, family-centered perspectives should influence how programs determine a child's eligibility to receive early intervention services. More direct links among the family's concerns and priorities, the child's demonstrated needs, and the intensity of program services are central to such change. Most eligibility definitions are based on normative standard score deviations and/or percentage delay criteria. LINK and its curriculum-based systems offer practical advantages in that they allow us to choose from several metrics to define a child's status and needs.

These metrics, or measurements, include 1) easily understood DA scores, 2) calculable ratio developmental rate indices (DA/CA × 100) (average rate is 100), and 3) a more precise and functional curriculum-based metric; that is, the number or percentage of expected authentic curricular objectives achieved that are contained within the sequence of the curriculum's developmental objectives. Curricular criteria (e.g., number or percentage of goals achieved) directly relate a child's capabilities and family-identified priorities to goals emphasized within a specific program's curriculum as opposed to relating them to performance on nationally norm-referenced measures that sample skills that are often unrelated or only globally related to program goals. In addition, it is possible to construct longitudinal learning curves or curricular trajectories on the basis of the number of curricular objectives achieved by groups of children who are typically developing and those who have developmental delays; these curves provide a more representative and valid portrayal of the progress of young children with mild to severe developmental disabilities.

Authentic and Adaptive-to-Disability Assessments

Increasingly, curriculum-based instruments, such as those we use in LINK, contain authentic tasks and methods that reflect real-life skills that are adaptive to children with various sensory, neuromotor, language, and behavioral differences. In contrast with traditional norm-referenced scales, authentic curriculum-based scales fulfill two important purposes in the early intervention process: 1) providing low-inference estimates of the child's competencies in everyday settings and 2) determining the degree of current functional limitations when appropriate adaptations are applied to accommodate children with impairments or disabilities.

First, authentic curricular developmental tasks, such as recognizing the McDonald's sign, finding a requested favorite toy hidden in the bottom of the toy box, and initiating a social interaction with an adult or peer, all share the aspect of requiring no inference about a child's competency. In contrast, pointing to a picture of a requested object on a easel at a table requires inferences about whether the child can demonstrate the same skill at home or at a mall because the task is contrived and attempts to provide a structured sample of behavior in a controlled setting.

Second, LINK assessments are adaptive and ensure flexibility in accommodating the functional needs of children with various impairments. Interventionists can, therefore, change the toys and materials used or the response mode available to the child to reflect each child's individual needs, thereby resulting in optimal child performance. Authentic tasks to which appropriate modifications have been made go hand-in-hand with the creation of activity-based intervention plans in the IFSP/IEP that stress the performance of functional skills in natural settings and during everyday routines (Bricker & Cripe, 1992).

IFSP/IEP Development

Authentic curriculum-based assessment translates directly into goals for individualized program planning in the major developmental, behavior, and family domains; that is, the tasks contained in the developmental task analysis are interrelated and linked with field-tested strategies for instructional and therapeutic intervention contained in the curricular package of materials. *Inside HELP: Administration and Reference Manual* (Parks, 1992b) and AEPS are two strong examples of this linkage among authentic assessment tasks, goals, and intervention strategies tailored to individual children and families with various needs; examples of ways in which materials may be tailored include use with infants who were born prematurely, use with parents who have mental retardation, and inclusion of home-based suggestions for play. Linked systems enable parents and professionals to create collaborative, relevant IFSPs/IEPs.

Curricular Progress Monitoring

Linked assessment–intervention–evaluation systems provide simple, tangible, and readily understood evidence of a child's progress in acquiring specific developmental competencies through the use of practical metrics, such as the number of curriculum objectives achieved in each developmental domain. The curriculum, itself, rather than a strict and inappropriate normative comparison, provides evidence of each child's individual progress on objectives that are typically acquired within 6- or 12-month time frames by typical peers. Curricular progress is also charted according to which goals are targeted as priorities by the parents and professionals in the IFSP/IEP.

Evaluation of Program Outcomes and Impact

The authentic curriculum-based assessments central to LINK serve the larger administrative purpose of informing program supervisors about the probable efficacy of their interventions for individual children and for groups enrolled in both inclusive and specialized settings. Curricular metrics also enable staff to document changes across children within and between programs using both developmental scores (e.g., DA, developmental quotient [DQ]) and curricular metrics (e.g., number of curriculum objectives achieved by both typical and atypical children). Moreover, meager evidence of change by children in certain developmental domains (e.g., social skills, social communication, self-regulatory behavior) informs administrators of those areas of their programs that require rethinking and modifications. LINK, therefore, can also serve a quality control purpose for early intervention programs.

Longitudinal Profiles to Define Developmental Diagnosis

We firmly believe that prediction of developmental diagnosis and outcome is impossible and unethical in the absence of intervention.

Simply put, professionals can reliably determine neither an accurate diagnosis nor a future status for a child until that child's response to individualized teaching and therapy has been systematically documented. We believe that authentic curriculum-based evaluation provides the best way to link progress monitoring and eventual developmental diagnosis. By repeating LINK curricular assessments over time (e.g., 3- or 6-month intervals) while a child participates in an early intervention program, professionals and parents can generate a "longitudinal profile" of the child's plateaus, regressions, and accelerations in acquiring authentic developmental competencies in the major functional domains. A portrait of functional progress emerges through the use of multiple metrics (e.g., ratings, developmental scores, frequencies of objectives achieved, videotaped segments), so that past presumptions about likely capabilities can be revised, the slope of gains can be determined, and the likelihood of permanent future disabilities can be determined. The importance of the longitudinal profile is highlighted by the following two salient examples of premature diagnosis in the absence of intervention: 1) misdiagnosing mental retardation in a 2-year-old child when language skills are absent and 2) misdiagnosing autism when a child has a severe communication disorder that distorts behavior and social interactions.

LINK STAGING, ORGANIZATION, AND PROCEDURES

Authentic curriculum-based assessments, unlike traditional, standardized, norm-referenced tests, which require rigid adherence to administration regimens, are flexible and adaptable to child characteristics. In general, LINK standardizes, or operationalizes, the behaviors under examination rather than the conditions under which the child must demonstrate his or her skills. This flexibility allows parents and professionals to adapt assessment to a child's characteristics and needs and a family's preferences. Although most assessment systems include administration procedures in their manuals, LINK gives professionals wide latitude to modify those procedures to meld testing and teaching behaviors and to create a flexible and responsive process of authentic assessment and collaborative decision making.

Where Does LINK Occur?

For infants and preschoolers with developmental delays, it is important that assessment be conducted in as natural a setting and under as authentic circumstances as possible. The preferred setting for LINK is in the child's home and involves the close physical participation of parents. Families must be given the choice of selecting from a "menu" of possible settings and arrangements that they believe will best enable their children to show their capabilities. Setting must be viewed by professionals as the most important variable influencing a child's performance. If assessment in the home is not feasible, then professionals must create, or stage, physical surroundings that are naturalistic and that closely approximate the comfort of the home. Such setting "comfort" factors include wall pictures, rugs, couches and chairs, a television set, and lamps. A family should be encouraged to bring the child's toys or other familiar objects to this setting to increase the likelihood of the child's participation in the assessment activities.

Despite the centrality of assessment in home settings for young children, it is important that assessment within the LINK model be conducted across multiple settings and occasions to offer the most representative sample of child capabilities. Early intervention professionals must, therefore, ensure that assessment data are gathered from home, preschool, and community settings for each child. Samples of critical functional competencies, such as initiating social interactions, indicating wants to others, playing with toys, waiting, sharing, taking turns, and following directions, can be gained from a trial 2-hour placement in the preschool classroom or child care environment or at the playground and from complementary observations in, for example, the grocery store.

What Constitutes LINK Data?

LINK data comprise the curriculum and its task analysis, as well as the sequence and hierarchy of teachable, functional skills, goals, and objectives. The primary aim of professionals and parents working in partnership is to gain real-life examples of these data across as many people, settings, and occasions as possible. It is not always possible to physically sample each behavior in every setting, so reports of others are included in the LINK database. Most LINK curricular systems allow professionals to collect data from multiple sources. Multiple, convergent sources of data (i.e., multiple people, multiple measurements) provide a broader, richer, and more complete sample of behavior that generates a truer picture of each child's capabilities, limitations, and needs. LINK data sources should include systematic observations, videotaped episodes, work samples (e.g., portfolios), play-based observations, interviews/reports, direct assessments, trial teaching, and ratings.

How Are LINK Data Reported and Displayed?

LINK emphasizes the synthesis of qualitative and quantitative information. Quantitative data on the acquisition of authentic curricular competencies or goals can be profiled and graphed in various ways within and across the major functional developmental domains; these include the use of developmental scores (e.g., DA, DQ), the graduated scoring of degree of skill acquisition (i.e., fully acquired, emerging, conditional, absent), the comparison of curricular objectives achieved with expectancies, and the determination of the percentage of curriculum objectives achieved. Similarly, qualitative data on the acquisition and change in authentic curricular competencies should be collected and portrayed in various creative ways, such as episodes videotaped before and after intervention; critical incident reports (or vignettes) of the child's changing "standout" (i.e., most outstanding) and "stick out" (i.e., most problematic) behaviors (Schwartz & Olswang, 1996); multisource ratings of status and change in various functional capabilities; audiotapes of language use; and portfolios of the child's drawings, constructions, and computer work.

How Are LINK Competencies Elicited?

Authentic curriculum-based evaluations are best conducted through a combination of structured and unstructured circumstances. Professionals and parents can work together to initiate semistructured play-based routines on the floor and about the room so that the child's interests suggest which toys and activities to choose. In this way, activity-based assessments (i.e., play routines that elicit several competencies simultaneously [e.g., social, language, motor, thinking]) allow professionals to blend flexibly structured and unstructured tasks. Once the child is comfortable, more structured tasks that require more traditional preschool skills (e.g., pointing to picture cards, completing puzzles, repeating words/phrases from memory) can be introduced.

What Materials Does LINK Require?

The toys and materials required for use with most traditional norm-referenced scales fail to interest and motivate young children; lack important developmental attributes; and require operational skills that children with sensory, language, affective/behavioral, and neuromotor impairments are incapable of demonstrating.

In contrast, the toys that are most effective for authentic curriculum-based assessments include the child's personal toys as well as other toys that are selected for their adaptive qualities. Functional assessment must sample behaviors that are required in a specific child's daily life. By using toys that are familiar to the child, professionals and parents can conduct play-based, multisource observations of typical behavior across settings to determine whether and to what extent the child has acquired critical problem-solving competencies, such as means–end relationships, cause–effect relationships, object permanence, and gestural imitation. Commercially popular toys, rather than those found in test kits, should be used because, as a rule, children prefer the former. For young children with functional disorders, however, response-contingent toys available from specialty publishers, specially designed toys, or adaptive toys with electromechanical microswitches should be used. The use of computers in the assessment of young children with disabilities is not only crucial, it is recommended practice.

Common household objects are also important materials for curriculum-based assessments because they add greater ecological validity to the results obtained. Young children often show their competencies most clearly when they play with familiar objects.

Parents often provide important authentic data about criterial competencies when they report that their children can turn on the videocassette recorder, open doors with a key, use the vacuum cleaner, pretend to cook using real pots and pans, and sort eating utensils.

Who Conducts LINK Assessments?

Curriculum-based assessment systems are designed to be used by teams of parents and interdisciplinary professionals. Any mode of teaming can be selected to complete a curriculum-based team assessment: A transdisciplinary style in which the parent(s) and a "core" team member sample the child's skills in all functional domains can be used. Alternatively, an interdisciplinary style in which several different professionals and the parent(s) collaborate to simultaneously sample the child's skills can be used; for example, each specialist emphasizes his or her area of expertise (e.g., the speech-language pathologist completes the language tasks, the physical therapist completes the gross motor activities). It is even possible to use a multidisciplinary style (although this is not recommended as the primary team approach) in which different professionals complete their own assessments at different times with very limited collaboration. In the final analysis, what is most important is that professionals and parents make collaborative decisions about which style of teaming allows an optimal and representative assessment of the capabilities of the child who is being evaluated.

What Is the Primary Purpose of LINK Assessment?

As discussed, LINK has several distinct purposes, each of which fulfills a core mission of early intervention. The overarching focus of LINK, moreover, is the same as the central mission of early intervention: to promote developmental progress in infants and preschoolers with special needs.

In fact, all forms of appraisal in the early intervention field must be aligned with this central mission. Because curriculum-based assessment is the premier form of evaluation for early intervention, it fulfills this purpose most effectively by offering sensible and sequential assessment information that is authentic, functional, adaptive, and teachable. Early intervention eschews normative assessment data that purport to be diagnostic and predictive; rather, it requires intraindividual assessment data that describe current capabilities and prioritize those instructional and therapeutic needs and complementary goals that are most responsive to treatment and, ultimately, developmental progress. In this way, early intervention effectively eradicates premature and, too often, erroneous diagnoses.

PERFORMING AN AUTHENTIC
CURRICULUM-BASED EVALUATION THROUGH LINK

Three characteristics of curriculum-based evaluation render it the premier form of assessment for early intervention. The three attributes are 1) a developmental sequence or hierarchy of competencies, 2) direct links between assessed skills and functional goals that have treatment and social validities (i.e., they are teachable and acceptable to others), and 3) repeated assessments of child gains in acquiring specific developmental competencies over time.

The three above-cited attributes describe the assessment–intervention–evaluation model, which was previously characterized as the test–teach–test approach or developmental assessment/curriculum linkage (Bagnato et al., 1989). This model advances the concept that accurate evidence of an individual child's progress is based, not on comparative appraisals with typically developing children (i.e., interindividual profile), but on comparisons with that individual child's previous levels of competence (i.e., intraindividual profile) and on an emphasis on higher-level competencies in the hierarchy as criteria to be mastered. Too often, interindividual, normative comparisons inaccurately portray young children with disabilities as failing to show important developmental progress. The use of the curricular goals/competencies themselves as the intraindividual mastery criteria for progress assessments enables parents and professionals to detect even small increments of change in a child's capabilities. Direct curricular data disprove limited normative data about child progress.

An initial comprehensive assessment of capabilities across several developmental domains establishes a baseline profile of current skills and limitations or needs. On the basis of this baseline assessment, early intervention teams set priority goals along the development sequence; these goals become the focus of instruction and therapy set out in the IFSP or IEP. Finally, with these goals as benchmarks, the early intervention team can first provide services and then reassess the impact of those services at some predetermined time(s) to detect and document evidence of progress. As the child gains competencies, more challenging clusters of related skills are then selected to amplify the child's program and to set new mastery criteria. This process is demonstrated by the case vignette that follows. It presents Vanessa, a young girl with cerebral palsy and developmental delays.

∞∞∞∞∞∞ VANESSA ∞∞∞∞∞∞

Age 41 marked a turning point for Mrs. Burns. She had always wanted a child, but the years had passed quickly, and the possibility of having a child had begun to seem remote. Now, she was pregnant. Her uneasy mixture of excitement and apprehension grew. Although her prenatal exams were fine, Mrs. Burns had previously had a miscarriage, so she was worried.

In her seventh month of pregnancy, complications arose. Because of a double-footing breech presentation, Vanessa was delivered by cesarean section at 26 weeks of gestational age; she weighed 2 pounds, 1 ounce. Her Apgar scores were 4 and 7 at 1 and 5 minutes, respectively. In addition, her condition was complicated by mild chronic lung disease, intraventricular hemorrhage, and patent ductus arteriosis. Vanessa progressed relatively well, however, in the neonatal intensive care unit of the regional university's children's hospital and was discharged to home after 3 months.

Despite Vanessa's problems, it was easy to take care of her because she cried little and slept often. She did, however, have some difficulty feeding from a bottle because she could not suck very well. As Vanessa grew, her parents became worried about the unusual posturing of her legs and back. Her pediatricians were sensitive to these concerns but cautioned Mr. and Mrs. Burns to wait until Vanessa was about 1 year old to see if things changed. This advice did not lessen their concerns, so Vanessa's parents sought another evaluation. This time, the pediatric diagnostic team at the local children's rehabilitation center confirmed their worries. Because of her difficulties at birth, Vanessa had experienced a brain insult that now showed itself as spastic quadriplegic cerebral palsy. Mr. and Mrs. Burns were devastated, but they were also relieved that their suspicions had finally been confirmed.

At 8 months of age, Vanessa was enrolled in a home-based infant intervention program. Because the Burns family lived in a rural area, center-based, coordinated services had been hard to obtain. A cooperative effort between the local Easter Seals program and a nursery school at the local college provided Vanessa specialized services as well as weekly interactions with friends who did not have disabilities. Everyone believed that Vanessa understood nearly everything said to her, but her speech-language difficulties, poor head control, and inability to use her hands functionally complicated their ability to assess her accurately. When Vanessa began to use a consistent yes–no response, things changed dramatically. The team began to concentrate on concept development and language understanding and use in their program for Vanessa.

It was becoming clearer that Vanessa had severe physical disabilities, near-average intellectual abilities, and significant language and motor problems. On the basis of this diagnosis, she was enrolled in the local early intervention program operated by the public school district; an initial evaluation was necessary to make this transition occur successfully for Vanessa and her parents. Mr. and Mrs. Burns had been under great stress as a result of Vanessa's physical needs and their continuing search to find coordinated services for her. They had strong concerns about her speech difficulties, but her recent progress has made them hopeful. They viewed the opportunity to enroll Vanessa in the school district's program as a new plateau in their lives.

THE SIX STEPS OF AN AUTHENTIC CURRICULUM-BASED EVALUATION THROUGH LINK

Six steps illustrate the LINK procedures used to link authentic curriculum-based assessment, intervention, and progress evaluation for Vanessa and to accomplish the central early intervention purposes. The six steps are

1. Select an authentic curriculum-embedded assessment system and battery of curriculum-compatible scales.
2. Appraise comprehensive developmental status using a convergent approach to determine eligibility and to identify curricular levels.
3. Determine functional authentic competencies.
4. Highlight authentic "transitional competencies."
5. Link authentic competencies to curricular goals and instructional/therapeutic strategies within the IFSP/IEP and teach to mastery.
6. Reevaluate comprehensive developmental status and profile progress on authentic competencies by using convergent methods.

These steps are explained in detail below.

Step 1. Select an authentic curriculum-embedded assessment system and battery of curriculum-compatible scales. The first priority for an effective and responsible early intervention team is to select a developmental curriculum and its embedded scale as well as other compatible scales. The selection of such a linked assessment/intervention system must be based on several factors (reviewed in Chapters 1–3). Perhaps the most important of these factors is how well the content of the selected system and that of compatible instruments match the developmental needs, functional levels, or simply individual differences of the range of children enrolled in the program. In most cases, early intervention professionals can select one curricular system to accommodate the diverse needs of approximately 80% of the young children in their

Table 5.1. The four curriculum-based systems used most widely in the United States

1. *Inside HELP: Administration and Reference Manual* (Parks, 1992b) and *HELP for Preschoolers: Assessment and Curriculum Guide* (VORT, 1995)
2. The Carolina Curriculum for Infants and Toddlers with Special Needs (2nd ed.) (Johnson-Martin et al., 1991) and The Carolina Curriculum for Preschoolers with Special Needs (Johnson-Martin et al., 1990)
3. Developmental Programming for Infants and Young Children (DPIYC) (0–36 Months) (Rev. ed.; Rogers & D'Eugenio, 1981) and Developmental Programming for Infants and Young Children (DPIYC) (3–6 Years) (Brown et al., 1981)
4. Assessment, Evaluation, and Programming System (AEPS) for Infants and Children (Volumes 1–4; series edited by D. Bricker)

programs. The four linked assessment/curricular systems in Table 5.1 are the most widely used in early intervention programs in the United States precisely because they do accommodate diverse needs.

For the other approximately 20% of children, early intervention program staff must select a companion (i.e., supplement to the program's primary curriculum) specialized curriculum that has unique content and more detailed developmental sequences to accommodate the needs of young children with more challenging functional disabilities (e.g., children with severe communication disorders, autism, acquired brain injury, severe physical and neuromotor impairments, mental retardation requiring extensive supports). Table 5.2 lists examples of dedicated, or disability-specific, curricula for low-incidence disabilities.

Table 5.3 summarizes the LINK convergent assessment battery chosen for Vanessa on the basis of her functional needs. The foundational authentic curriculum-based system chosen for Vanessa was Developmental Programming for Infants and Young Children (0–36 Months): Volume 2, Early Intervention Developmental Profile (EIDP) (Rogers & D'Eugenio, 1981). This system contains clear links between assessment tasks and curricular objectives and instructional/therapeutic activities. Moreover, EIDP was sensitive to Vanessa's neurological impairments and responsive to the adaptations required to enable Vanessa to demonstrate her capabilities through various response modes. As an adjunct to EIDP, the early

Table 5.2. Examples of disability-specific curricula

1. Every Move Counts (EMC; Korsten et al., 1989)
2. Individualized Assessment and Treatment for Autistic and Developmentally Disabled Children (Schopler, Reichler, Bashford, Lansing, & Marcus, 1979)
3. Developmental Communication Curriculum (Hanna, Lippert, & Harris, 1982)
4. Therapeutic Education for the Child with Traumatic Brain Injury: From Coma to Kindergarten (McKerns & Motchkovitz, 1993)

Table 5.3. LINK convergent assessment battery for Vanessa

Scale type	Measure
Curriculum embedded	EIDP
Curriculum compatible	BDI
	SPECS

intervention team and Vanessa's parents chose BDI as a curriculum-compatible measure that would enable them to collect corroborative data about Vanessa's capabilities and needs from multiple sources to link assessment and curricular goals and to provide broader data about her eligibility for services. Finally, the team chose SPECS to facilitate parent–professional consensus about Vanessa's capabilities and needs and to focus collaborative decisions on the intensity of intervention required to promote developmental progress.

Step 2. Appraise comprehensive developmental status using a convergent approach to determine eligibility and to identify curricular levels. Once an appropriate curriculum-embedded assessment system and curriculum-compatible instruments have been selected for a particular child, the early intervention team can complete a comprehensive developmental assessment by using convergent assessment strategies. This approach involves collecting data from multiple information sources across multiple settings and occasions to identify the child's skills and impairments in multiple developmental and behavioral domains (e.g., cognitive, language, perceptual/fine motor, gross motor, social-emotional, adaptive skills, self-regulation). Such an approach to assessment enables parent–professional collaboration to estimate, for each developmental domain, a child's DA in months (e.g., 32 months) and DQ or to determine a simple ratio between the child's CA and DA (DA/CA × 100).

This convergent curriculum-based assessment meets state standards in those states in which percentage delay criteria are used to establish early intervention program eligibility. We argue, however, that misplaced precision in assessment often stands as a barrier to gaining access to services for many children because of the inherent limitations and inappropriateness of early intervention program eligibility standards that are based on standard score criteria determined by norm-referenced assessment (e.g., standard deviation scores of 1.5–2.0). We believe strongly that the use of ratio DQs that are based on intraindividual, disability-sensitive, curriculum-based assessments rather than on interindividual, norm-referenced, traditional instruments provide a more accurate portrayal of child status and needs—not to mention a direct link between assessment and intervention that does not require the redundant and faulty intervening first step of conducting a standardized norm-referenced assessment.

Nevertheless, if a particular state's standards mandate the use of a traditional norm-referenced measure to document program eligibility, then it is important for the team to champion the use of curriculum-compatible measures that are norm referenced but that survey content that is linked with the program's base curriculum to offer general curriculum entry points. The most widely used curriculum-compatible measure is BDI, which generates DA and standard deviation developmental quotients based on norms for 800 children from birth to 7 years.

Figure 5.1 shows that Vanessa clearly meets eligibility criteria for entry into and services in an early intervention program (although her severe neurological impairment [i.e., spastic quadriplegic cerebral palsy] alone should qualify her in most states). Her summative child progress sheet shows that, in the language, perceptual/fine motor, gross motor, and adaptive domains (for the first quarter), her functional capabilities range from approximately 30% to 67% of those expected for her age (greater than 25% delay and more than 2 standard deviations below the average). Moreover, Figure 5.2 from EIDP shows that Vanessa's acquisition of developmental competencies and curricular objectives is significantly below expectations for her age. Data from both BDI and EIDP converge to support her need for services and, equally important, emphasize her strong cognitive and social-emotional skills despite her severe neuromotor difficulties; these strengths can become compensatory goals to foster within Vanessa's IEP/IFSP and her individual curricular plan.

Step 3.   Determine functional authentic competencies.   Comprehensive developmental assessments first establish a child's current functional levels and ranges in each developmental domain and identify the curriculum entry level that is most appropriate given the child's general competencies. Next, the early intervention team can analyze each competency (item or task) within the developmental sequence or task analysis at that particular developmental level (e.g., 30–36 months) to determine the extent to which the child has acquired a particular skill and its behavioral components. Developmental task analysis involves an appraisal of which specific skills in each developmental domain are fully acquired (+ or pass [P]); which are absent from the child's repertoire (− or fail [F]), and which are emerging (± or PF). A child's full functional range (i.e., widely scattered skills across the 24- to 42-month range) can, therefore, be ascertained to guide individualized curriculum goal planning in the IEP.

Figures 5.2, 5.3, and 5.4 show a selected portion of Vanessa's developmental task analysis from EIDP curricular objectives and BDI. Her functional ranges are wide, as evidenced by her first-quarter DA ranges. For example, because of her neuromotor limitations, Vanessa's functional ranges extend from 6- to 30-month level skills across the major domains: In the cognitive domain, her functional range is from 18 to 30 months, whereas in the perceptual/fine motor domain, it is from 9 to 12 months. These functional ranges reveal Vanessa's widely variable functional capabilities—both her

EARLY INTERVENTION PROGRESS PROFILE

Child: **Vanessa Burns**   B.D.: **82-5-22**

Disability: **Cerebral Palsy** Preschool: **Wilkins**   Curriculum: **DPIYC**

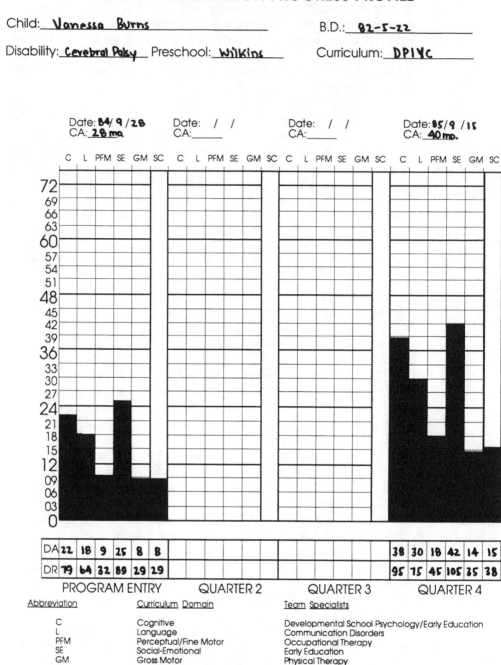

Figure 5.1.   Vanessa's developmental levels graphed on EIDP.

6–8 months

56	Attains partially hidden object	+			
57	Looks to the floor when something falls	+			
58	Uncovers face	+			
59	Bangs object	+			
60	Rotates a bottle inverted less than 180° to drink	±			
61	Imitates hand movements already in his/her repertoire	+			

9–11 months

62	Attains completely hidden object	+			
63	Pulls string to secure ring and succeeds	+			
64	Shows knowledge of toy hidden behind a screen	±			
65	Imitates facial movements inexactly	±			
66	Imperfectly imitates movements never performed before	—			
67	Rotates a bottle inverted 180° to drink	—			
68	Reacts to novel features of an object	±			

Developmental Programming for Infants and Young Children
Volume 2: Early Intervention Developmental Profile

ITEM NUMBER	*DEVELOPMENTAL LEVELS AND ITEMS*	DATE	DATE	DATE	DATE

12–15 months

69	Imitates body action on a doll	±			
70	Repeatedly finds toy when hidden under one of several covers	+			
71	Lifts a ½-inch cube off a 1-inch cube	O			
72	Balances nine 1-inch cubes in a coffee cup	O			

16–19 months

73	Repeatedly finds toy when hidden under multiple covers	±			
74	Uses a stick to try to attain an object out of reach (**Adp**)	±			
75	Retrieves raisin by inverting small vial	±			
76	Corrects imitations of new movements	—			
77	Deduces location of hidden object, single displacement	±			
78	Pulls cloth to reach object	—			

Figure 5.2.   Illustration of Vanessa's current skills on BDI transferred to congruent EIDP curriculum tasks. (From Rogers, S.J., & D'Eugenio, D.B. [1981]. *Developmental Programming for Infants and Young Children: Vol. 2. Early Intervention Developmental Profile*, pp. 6–7. Ann Arbor: University of Michigan Press; reprinted by permission.)

Subdomain: Memory

CG 11	0–5	Follows auditory stimulus	2
CG 12		Follows visual stimulus	2
CG 13	6–11	Uncovers hidden toy (adapted)	2
CG 14		Searches for removed object	2
CG 15	24–35	Repeats two-digit sequences	0
CG 16		Selects hand hiding toy ✱	1
CG 17	36–47	Recalls familiar objects ✱	1
CG 18	72–83	Repeats four-digit sequences	0
CG 19		Recalls facts from story presented orally	0
CG 20	84–95	Repeats six-digit sequences	0

Subdomain Score | 10 |

Subdomain: Reasoning and Academic Skills

CG 21	6–11	Pulls string to obtain toy or ring (adapted)	2
CG 22	12–23	Reaches around barrier to obtain toy	2
CG 23	36–47	Responds to *one* and *one more* ✱	1
CG 24	48–59	Identifies sources of common actions	0
CG 25		Gives three objects on request	0
CG 26		Answers simple logic questions	0
CG 27		Completes opposite analogies	0
CG 28		Identifies larger of two numbers	0
CG 29	60–71	Selects single words from visual presentation	0
CG 30		Identifies missing parts of objects	0
CG 31		Recognizes picture absurdities	0

Figure 5.3. Analysis of Vanessa's performance on selected BDI tasks. (From Newborg et al. [1988]. *Battelle Developmental Inventory*, p. 31. Chicago: Riverside Publishing; reprinted by permission.)

solid strengths and her severe limitations. The EIDP curricular objectives show the specific authentic functional competencies that compose these functional ranges. For example, Vanessa has acquired the cause–effect and object permanence competencies (e.g., attains a completed hidden object, imitates hand movements) expected at the 6- to 11-month age levels, as demonstrated by the predominance of fully acquired (+) skills in her developmental task

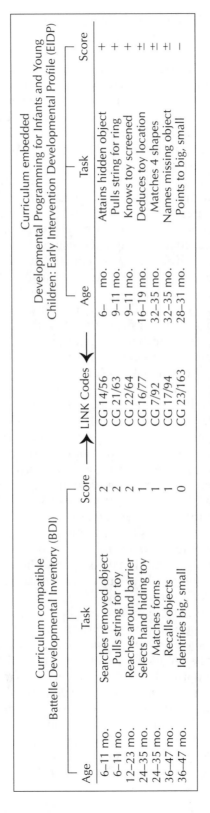

Curriculum compatible Battelle Developmental Inventory (BDI)				Curriculum embedded Developmental Programming for Infants and Young Children: Early Intervention Developmental Profile (EIDP)		
Age	Task	Score	LINK Codes →	Age	Task	Score
6–11 mo.	Searches removed object	2	CG 14/56	6– mo.	Attains hidden object	+
6–11 mo.	Pulls string for toy	2	CG 21/63	9–11 mo.	Pulls string for ring	+
12–23 mo.	Reaches around barrier	2	CG 22/64	9–11 mo.	Knows toy screened	+
24–35 mo.	Selects hand hiding toy	1	CG 16/77	16–19 mo.	Deduces toy location	±
24–35 mo.	Matches forms	1	CG 7/92	32–35 mo.	Matches 4 shapes	±
36–47 mo.	Recalls objects	1	CG 17/94	32–35 mo.	Names missing object	±
36–47 mo.	Identifies big, small	0	CG 23/163	28–31 mo.	Points to big, small	–

Figure 5.4.   The linkages between Vanessa's performance on BDI tasks and similar EIDP curriculum objectives.

analysis. When more sophisticated competencies from the 12- to 30-month age levels are examined, however, Vanessa shows a denser array of emergent (±) and absent competencies in her repertoire of skills (e.g., finds a hidden object with a single displacement, corrects imitations of new movements).

Step 4. Highlight authentic "transitional competencies." Figure 5.4 illustrates the important clinical process of linking the results from curriculum-compatible scales with the primary goals in the curriculum-embedded system used in a program. We have termed this process *developmental assessment/curriculum linkage* (Bagnato et al., 1989). For Vanessa, the team's convergent assessment battery consisted primarily of BDI and EIDP. Figure 5.4 demonstrates the clear linkages between BDI tasks and EIDP goals. The psychologist on the team, who used BDI, needed only to match tasks with goals through the use of a flexible clinical procedure. Matches, or linkages, were constructed according to the degree to which items on the two curriculum-based instruments were—on the basis of data collected from multiple sources, settings, people, and occasions—similar in 1) wording, 2) responses required from the child, 3) level of difficulty, and 4) approximate age-level placements within the two scales. Note that link codes fused the two compatible tasks to denote a common transitional competency. For example, the BDI task, "searches for removed object," and the EIDP goal, "attains hidden object," were similarly scored, placed at similar age levels, and matched by BDI code CG 14 and EIDP item number 56. Professionals can follow a comparable procedure to ensure that the results from other curriculum-compatible scales are translated into curriculum entry points of the curriculum-embedded systems that are used. In this way, the program's curriculum and its integrated instrument and goal sequence become the primary framework for assessment, goal setting, and progress/program evaluation in the subsequent steps of the LINK model.

The next step is for early interventionists and parents to isolate those specific skills that are partially acquired, or emerging (±). Emergent, or transitional, skills are those authentic competencies that the young child seems to be ready to master next because he or she can demonstrate some of the behavioral components of the required skill, can demonstrate the skill inconsistently (e.g., 50% of the time), or can demonstrate the skill under certain instructional conditions (e.g., when physical or verbal prompts are used). Transitional skills are ideal instructional objectives because they usually are at the optimal "challenge level" for the child—not too difficult, not too easy. We have termed such transitional competencies *authentic curricular linkages*. These offer specific curriculum entry points for individualized curriculum planning and sensitive benchmarks for monitoring child progress and the impact of intervention.

Table 5.4 highlights examples of particular authentic transitional, or building-block, skills that match Vanessa's current functional capabilities and that the team has identified as the cross-situational competencies that will best promote Vanessa's developmental progress and increasing independence and self-efficacy. (Evidence of Vanessa's progress is presented in detail in the expanded discussion of Step 6 on pp. 349–359.)

Step 5. Link authentic competencies to curricular goals and instructional/therapeutic strategies within the IFSP/IEP and teach to mastery. The transitional skills identified in Step 4 provide the basis for planning IFSP or IEP goals that have been determined through collaborative parent–professional decision making. The team can match intervention strategies to transitional skills/goals

Table 5.4. LINK authentic curriculum competencies for Vanessa

Domains/goals	Progress index score (0, 1, 2)	
	Time 1	Time 2
Cognitive		
Finds hidden toys in toy box	1	2
Matches correct foods or toys	0	2
Knows number/amount	1	2
Total	**2**	**6**
Social-emotional		
Starts social interactions	1	2
Plays and shares toys with others	1	2
Indicates need for help	0	2
Total	**2**	**6**
Language		
Gives objects on request	1	2
Follows 2+ verbal commands	0	2
Associates words with objects	1	2
Total	**2**	**6**
Perceptual/fine motor		
Opens drawers at home	0	2
Operates switches on toys/appliances	0	2
Gives toy to adult with help	0	2
Total	**0**	**6**
Gross motor		
Moves from lying to sitting position	0	1
Sits without support on floor/chair	0	2
Gets about the room on floor	1	1
Total	**1**	**4**
Adaptive		
Drinks from cup with help	0	2
Feeds with spoon with help	0	2
Coordinates suck/swallow/breathe process	1	2
Total	**1**	**6**
Authentic competencies totals	**8**	**34**
Preintervention = 20% acquisition level		
Postintervention (12 months) = 94% acquisition level		

in the context of activity-based lessons or modules, in which clusters of related skills across multiple functional domains are targeted simultaneously in purposeful and natural tasks (Bricker & Cripe, 1992). For example, play activities using a house, dolls, telephone, appliances, and kitchen utensils enable young children (with teacher guidance) to communicate reciprocally, share, take turns, practice different social roles, follow routines, and coordinate their motor movements. The most valid criterion for mastery and generalization of trained skills occurs when skills are displayed repeatedly with different people, in different settings, using different materials, and under environmental circumstances that are distinct from the training conditions. In this approach, behavior change and learning can be charted in increments; the rating of skill attainment by using the transitional skills/goals as benchmarks is not a simple question of whether a child displays (P) or does not display (F) a particular behavior but, rather, whether the child can show components of the target skill under various conditions.

Step 6. Reevaluate comprehensive developmental status and profile progress on authentic competencies by using convergent methods. Periodic formative appraisals are needed to track changes in developmental competencies during early intervention and to provide staff with feedback about effective and ineffective instructional arrangements. Program personnel chart behavior changes on a daily, weekly, or monthly basis by using applied behavior analysis methods. Evidence of child progress made on curriculum-based developmental measures is most effectively documented by the early intervention team on a quarterly, 6-month, or 12-month basis. Longitudinal assessments are the only responsible method for documenting developmental gains, venturing developmental diagnoses, and forecasting levels of disabilities.

The curriculum-based developmental assessment instrument and its embedded developmental task analysis are used again to measure gains within the major curricular areas (i.e., cognitive, language, social-emotional, gross motor, perceptual/fine motor, adaptive skills). Diagnosticians must not emphasize rote, isolated completion of splinter skills but, instead, should focus on the functional and purposeful use of skills in a child's natural daily routines. When completed, this reassessment generates an intraindividual profile of changes in the fully acquired (+), emergent (±), and absent (−) skills in the child's repertoire. This profile compares present performance with the child's preintervention, or formative, skill levels by using each child as his or her own control. Again, the previous pattern of DAs, DQs, functional ranges, and sequence of absent-emerging-acquired skills yields the tangible and discrete benchmarks for monitoring developmental progress. The synchrony between developmental curriculum-based assessment and developmental instruction is the key to contemporary early intervention. The specifics of Step 6 are expanded in the section that follows and are illustrated and summarized in Figure 5.5.

SUMMATIVE CHILD PROGRESS/PROGRAM EVALUATION SHEET

Child: __Vanessa Burns__   C.A. __40 months__   Date: __85-9-18__

Developmental/ Curricular Domain	1ST Quarter			4th Quarter							
	DA	DA Range	DQ	DA	DA Range	DQ	DA Gain	IEI	CEI	M%	P%
COGNITIVE	22	18-30	79	38	36-45	95	16 mo.	1.3	1.5	59%	41%
LANGUAGE	18	8-26	64	30	22-34	75	12 mo.	1.0	.92	64%	36%
SOCIAL-EMOTIONAL	25	21-32	89	42	36-48	105	17 mo.	1.4	1.8	63%	37%
PERCEPTUAL/ FINE MOTOR	9	9-12	32	18	12-20	45	9 mo.	.75	.75	42%	58%
GROSS MOTOR	8	6-10	29	14	10-16	35	6 mo.	.50	.41	58%	42%
SELF-CARE	8	8-10	29	15	10-18	38	7 mo.	.58	.67	50%	50%
DEVELOPMENTAL AVERAGE	15		54	27		65	12 mo.	1.0	1.01	54%	46%

Figure 5.5.   Analysis of Vanessa's developmental progress and her program's therapeutic impact.

LINK METRICS TO MONITOR AND
PROFILE CURRICULAR PROGRESS: STEP 6 EXPANDED

Two of the most important but generally neglected phases of early intervention are the evaluation and monitoring of both child progress and program effectiveness. Preschool program personnel frequently report that they are too understaffed to "retest" children or that program evaluation is too difficult and removed from everyday services to be important. The stark reality is that, without a progress/program evaluation system that enables staff to document the benefits of their services and efforts, early interventionists may be engaging in unethical and experimental practices with children. Assessment and intervention must be linked through program evaluation. Given the linkages between managed health care and early intervention services, accountability and program outcomes have become paramount to retain funding.

The child progress/program evaluation phase brings the LINK sequence full circle. The complete assessment–intervention–evaluation process enables professionals to determine both effective and ineffective intervention practices and to modify practices periodically for the benefit of children and families. As children make gains on the curriculum entry goals identified in Step 4 and through the intervention plans and methods implemented during

Step 5, program evaluation focuses on these goals as criteria, or benchmarks of progress. In this way, assessment, intervention, and evaluation maintain a consistent focus and underlying foundation: authentic curriculum goals.

Various methods are available to evaluate child progress (i.e., changes in development and behavior) during intervention. Each method has its own technical advantages and disadvantages; when several are combined, however, they can provide valuable data regarding child gain and program impact. *Acquisition of curriculum competencies is the primary index of change.* Changes in various curriculum-compatible measures (i.e., norm based, judgment based, ecological) provide important corroborative evidence.

Two types of program evaluation methods are noteworthy: formative evaluation and summative evaluation. *Formative evaluation* occurs on a regular basis throughout the early intervention process. It involves the systematic observation of child behavior and adult–child and child–child interactions and the monitoring of attainment of curricular goals on a per-session or a daily, weekly, monthly, and/or quarterly basis, depending on the program's needs and resources. *Summative evaluation* involves comparisons of baseline or preintervention functioning with follow-up, or post-intervention, functioning. In general, summative evaluation uses norm-based data to compare beginning-of-the-year functioning with end-of-the-year functioning. As a rule, summative evaluation is usually based on global data comparisons, such as comparisons of DAs and DQs, whereas formative evaluation is usually based on specific and discrete data comparisons, such as those of frequency and duration of behaviors and/or the number of curriculum goals attained within a specified time period, supplemented by other, more global, data. Nevertheless, developmental curricula, when used for both summative and formative evaluation purposes, enable the early intervention team to track and chart both general (e.g., DA, DQ, percentiles) and discrete (e.g., number of curricular goals attained, time on task) units of change.

Figure 5.5 presents Vanessa's LINK Summative Child Progress/ Program Evaluation Form. This form is organized by the six curricular domains cross-referenced with various evaluation indices. First-quarter and fourth-quarter data are compared through the use of various scores, including DAs and DQs, gain scores, efficiency indices, maturation–intervention comparisons, and curricular indices. Each of these types of scores is reviewed in the following sections.

Developmental Scores

For performance on both norm- and curriculum-based measures, a child's acquisition of skills can be converted into indices of age functioning and developmental rate. These "standard scores" can be calculated by using either normative tables, if a hybrid norm-referenced scale (e.g., BDI) is used, or the old ratio methods (DA/CA × 100).

DAs and DQs indicate the child's comparable age-equivalent functioning in each developmental domain and the child's rate or quotient of progress, respectively, with 100 being the average from which deviations are calculated. For example, a DQ of 75 indicates a functioning rate that is approximately 75% of that expected from a typically developing child. With a 40-month-old child such as Vanessa, this rate converts to a DA equivalent of only 30 months in the language area, which indicates a mild impairment.

In addition, for all young children with disabilities, it is important to determine the child's DA *range* of functioning from basal to ceiling levels; that is, the scattering of developmental capabilities. For example, at the fourth-quarter evaluation, although Vanessa was functioning at the 30-month level in language skills, her skills were widely scattered in this area (from a low of 22 months in expressive skills to a high of 34 months in identifying and recalling pictures, objects, and concepts from memory). This range may later narrow or widen on the basis of therapeutic gains; it also may reflect both purposeful and isolated splinter skills. EIDP and BDI were used to derive these progress indices for Vanessa, just as they were used previously to determine parent–professional consensus as to curriculum entry goals.

DA gain is calculated over a specific period of intervention (e.g., 6 or 12 months) by subtracting DA at program entry from DA at the end of that period. Vanessa's gains during the 12-month intervention period were 16 months in the cognitive area and 9 months in the perceptual/fine motor area.

Intervention Efficiency Indices

Controversy has surrounded the use of efficiency indices in early childhood special education (Bagnato & Neisworth, 1980; Jellnek, 1985; Simeonsson & Weigerink, 1975). When such indices are coupled pragmatically with other progress measures, however, they can provide useful administrative evidence of child change and program impact.

We proposed the intervention efficiency index (IEI) (Bagnato & Neisworth, 1980) to document how much developmental change (e.g., gain in age scores) was evident during the specific period of intervention. The IEI documents change during instruction and therapy. For example, Vanessa's gain of 16 months in the cognitive area during a 12-month period of structured intervention suggested a rate of growth that was 1.3 times that expected in normal child development (i.e., 1 month of development for each month of life).

We devised another invaluable efficiency measure, the curricular efficiency index (CEI) (Bagnato & Neisworth, 1983), but it is not widely known. The CEI compares the number of curriculum objectives that a child achieves during a 1-month period with the number achieved either by a sample of typically developing children or, for a child in a special program, by a preschooler with disabilities. In essence, a "local program norm," or limited comparative sample, is used to determine a child's relative standing for curriculum skill acquisition. For example, Vanessa achieved 12 cognitive objectives, whereas the norm group achieved 8 objectives in the same 12-month period. This ratio (12:8) suggested a curricular efficiency rate that was 1.5 times the rate expected for Vanessa's peers.

IEI, CEI, and DAs and DQs can be used to "triangulate" consistent evidence of a child's progress and a program's impact. Formulas to calculate the IEI and CEI follow.

The IEI is the ratio of a child's developmental gain in months to the number of months that the child has received program intervention. The IEI is calculated for each developmental domain as follows:

$$IEI = \frac{\text{Number of months developmental gain (DA2 $-$ DA1)}}{\text{Number of months receiving program intervention}}$$

The CEI is the ratio of the average number of curriculum objectives achieved by a child per month to the average number of curriculum objectives achieved by either a local sample of typically developing children or other children in the child's program (when the child has special needs). The CEI is calculated for each developmental domain as follows:

$$CEI = \frac{\begin{array}{c}\text{Number of curriculum objectives} \\ \text{achieved by the child per month}\end{array}}{\begin{array}{c}\text{Number of curriculum objectives} \\ \text{achieved by a group per month}\end{array}}$$

A variation of the CEI that is specific to each curriculum and its curriculum-embedded assessment instrument is the curricular efficiency index–age referenced (CEI–AR). CEI–AR involves the use of age reference points, or internal curriculum age norms, to determine the number of developmental competencies (i.e., curricular objectives) that a typically developing child can be expected to achieve within a given time period. Figure 5.6 shows a cross section of Vanessa's curricular goals in the cognitive domain of EIDP. Note that this cross section outlines the sequence of cognitive competencies that are expected to be achieved by a typically developing child beginning at 12 months of age and continuing through 42–48 months of age. To use the CEI–AR metric here, you would simply follow these steps:

1. Calculate the child's DA at the preintervention assessment.
2. Calculate the child's DA at the postintervention assessment (usually after 12 months of intervention).
3. Count the curricular objectives that the specific curriculum-embedded scale in use identifies as those that a typically developing child could achieve between the pre- and postintervention assessments.
4. Count the objectives that the child being assessed actually achieved between the pre- and postintervention assessments (e.g., assign 1 point to a fully acquired skill, 0.5 points to a partially acquired skill).

ITEM NUMBER	DEVELOPMENTAL LEVELS AND ITEMS	DATE	DATE	DATE	DATE
	12–15 months	*Pre*	*Post*		
69	Imitates body action on a doll	+	+		
70	Repeatedly finds toy when hidden under one of several covers	+	+		
71	Lifts a ½-inch cube off a 1-inch cube	+	+		
72	Balances nine 1-inch cubes in a coffee cup	+	+		
	16–19 months				
73	Repeatedly finds toy when hidden under multiple covers	+	+		
74	Uses a stick to try to attain an object out of reach	+	+		
75	Retrieves raisin by inverting small vial	+	+		
76	Corrects imitations of new movements	+	+		
77	Deduces location of hidden object, single displacement	+	+		
78	Pulls cloth to reach object	+	+		
	20–23 months				
79	Imitates unseen body movements immediately and exactly	−	+		
80	Attempts to activate flashlight	−	+		
81	Deduces location of hidden object, multiple displacements	−	+		
82	Anticipates path of rolling ball by detouring around object	+	+		
83	Matches two sets of objects by item	−	+		
	24–27 months				
84	Imitates a model from memory	−	+		
85	Matches two sets of objects by color	−	+		
86	Assembles three-piece body puzzle correctly	−	+		
87	Recognizes four pictures from reduced cues	+	+		

(continued)

Figure 5.6. CEI–AR of a cross-section of Vanessa's curricular goals in the EIDP cognitive domain.

Figure 5.6. *(continued)*

ITEM NUMBER	*DEVELOPMENTAL LEVELS AND ITEMS*	DATE	DATE	DATE	DATE
	28–31 months	*Pre*	*Post*		
88	Matches colored cubes (red, yellow, blue, green, black)	−	+		
89	Understands concept of one	−	+		
90	Identifies three objects by their use (car, penny, bottle)	±	+		
	32–35 months				
91	Repeats two digits	−	+		
92	Matches four shapes (circle, square, star, cross)	−	+		
93	Inverts a picture	−	+		
94	Names a missing object	−	+		
Classification **3–3½ years *(36–42 months)***					
36	Tells whether pictures are the same or different	−	+		
37	Points to picture that doesn't belong	−	+		
	3½–4 years *(42–48 months)*				
38	Names things asked for by use	−	+		
39	Groups identical pictures	−	+		
40	Names two things that are round	−	−		

5. Calculate the score according to the following formula:

$$\text{CEI–AR} = \frac{\text{Number of curriculum objectives achieved}}{\text{Number of curriculum objectives possible}}$$

6. Multiply this score by 100 to determine a curricular efficiency rate, or developmental learning curve, for the intervention period.

When the CEI–AR was used by Vanessa's team, they determined her preintervention DA to be 22 months (range, 18–30 months) and her postintervention DA to be 38 months (range, 36–45 months). EIDP identifies 21 developmental curricular competencies that can presumably be learned by a typically developing child during the period between 20 months and 48 months of age. During a 12-month period of intervention, Vanessa actually achieved 19.5 curricular objectives; this achievement represents a curricular efficiency rate, or developmental learning trajectory, of 93% (19.5/21 = 0.93 × 100 = 93%). Note that this metric yields a result that is in line with both the acquisition rate for authentic curricular competencies of 94% displayed in Table 5.4 and the ratio DQ of 95 graphed in Figure 5.1. If, however, we had predicted Vanessa's achievement solely on the basis of her preintervention DQ of 79 (see Figure 5.1), then we would have anticipated that she would achieve only 15 or 16 objectives. Vanessa's actual developmental trajectory is approximately 15% higher than that expected—the difference between having a mild impairment and average cognitive capabilities! Vanessa's experience is another strong argument for allowing a child's response to early intervention to be the deciding factor when predicting progress and making diagnoses.

Maturation/Intervention Percentages

Few programs use procedures that attempt to estimate the amount of relative gain that can be attributed to maturation effects versus intervention (i.e., treatment) effects (Bagnato & Mayes, 1986; Irwin & Wong, 1974). For young children with congenital disabilities— that is, presumably constant or static disabilities and DQs (e.g., cerebral palsy, mental retardation, autism)—maturation/intervention comparisons are justifiable and practical.

Maturation percentages (M%) and intervention percentages (I%) are calculated with reference to the child's own preintervention levels and rates of functioning. The use of such percentages assumes that children with static disabilities will maintain relatively constant rates of development and behavior in the absence of intervention or major environmental changes. Preintervention rates, therefore, are used as reference points to project the level at which the child will most probably function in the future; this projection is made on the basis of the historical reference point, presumes linearity of skill acquisition, and describes the child's maturation rate as a percentage. When the child is enrolled in a treatment program, the child's DQ is reevaluated after a period of intervention. If the child's postintervention rate of progress exceeds the maturation rate, the amount of gain is attributed to treatment and characterized as the intervention rate or percentage.

To compare the proportion of developmental gain that may be attributable to the effects of the child's maturation (M%) with that resulting from the effects of the program's intervention (I%), the following formulas are used:

$$M\% = \frac{\text{Expected maturational gain in months}}{\text{Actual developmental gain in months}}$$

$$I\% = \frac{\text{Actual developmental gain in months} - \text{maturational gain expected}}{\text{Actual developmental gain in months}}$$

For Vanessa, DA (and range and gain) and DQ, IEI and CEI, and M% and I% were calculated for each developmental/curricular domain (see Figure 5.5). In the cognitive area, the amount of maturational gain expected in a 12-month period of intervention was calculated, presuming Vanessa continued to progress at a preintervention DQ rate of 0.79. Multiplying 12 months by 0.79 results in an expected maturational gain of 9.5 months. This expected gain of 9.5 months is then divided by the actual developmental gain, which is 16 months, resulting in an M% of 59%. In other words, 59% of Vanessa's developmental gain of 16 months in the cognitive domain could reasonably be attributed to the effects of maturation; the remainder of the total percentage of gain could reasonably be attributed to the effects of intervention. Accordingly, the expected maturational gain was subtracted from the actual developmental gain (16.0 − 9.5 = 6.5 [months]), and this number was divided by the actual developmental gain (16 months) to determine an I% of 41%. Thus, 41% of Vanessa's progress in acquiring cognitive skills likely is attributable to the impact of the program's plan of instruction and therapy. (Figure 5.5 indicates that Vanessa showed significant intervention effects in all developmental areas, despite her congenital neuromotor impairments.) In theory, if a child continues to progress at the initial preintervention developmental rate and no faster, the maturation effect would be 100% and the intervention percentage would be 0%. Therefore, any I% that exceeds 0% suggests an intervention effect.

Another method for charting curricular progress on a select array of goals is to focus on the authentic competencies that were derived through parent–professional consensus as a focus of the IFSP/IEP (see Table 5.4). These goals are isolated from the array of developmental competencies within the developmental task sequence of the EIDP for each functional domain. Again, Table 5.4 summarizes Vanessa's progress on these authentic competencies during 12 months of instruction, therapy, and family support. Progress indices are based on graduated scoring using a 0, 1, or 2 scoring system (in which 0 denotes the absence of a skill; 1 indicates a partially acquired skill; and 2 denotes a fully acquired, consistently displayed competency across situations). Note that, when Vanessa entered the early intervention program at a chronological age of 28 months, she had acquired only 20% of the authentic criterial competencies prioritized by the team. However, after 12 months of intensive intervention, Vanessa had fully acquired 94% of the prioritized authentic goals. These progress data corroborate further Vanessa's other progress data using the metrics in Step 6 and portray more fully the slope of Vanessa's developmental gain.

Functional Behavior Ratings and Program Data

The final program evaluation strategy applies data for both clinical and administrative purposes. In the LINK system, judgment-based and ecological sources of data are used to enhance assessments of a child's status, progress, and therapeutic impact. In Vanessa's case, data obtained from the observations of interdisciplinary team members and parents were recorded on the SPECS scale.

As noted, SPECS functionally rates a behavior according to its maturity or problem severity on the basis of observation and clinical judgment. A rating of 5 indicates normal functioning, 4 indicates borderline functioning, 3 indicates a mild impairment, 2 indicates a moderate impairment, and 1 indicates a severe functional impairment. This rating scale provides a shorthand method of characterizing functional levels after intervention.

Figure 5.7 shows Vanessa's progress, as determined by team consensus of her scores on the SPECS scale. After 12 months of intervention, she had generally progressed from a severe (1) to a mild (3) level of overall disability, which corroborated the curriculum results.

Permanent product data can be another rich source of progress information. Characteristics such as grouping pattern, behavior management strategies, days per week in programming, adaptive aids, auxiliary therapies, and medical involvement are all examples of program product information that indicates specific service delivery options implemented as a result of the program. At the end of the intervention period, the team can reconsider each area and determine whether the intensity of each service delivery need has decreased—a clear, practical index of child change.

Functional Scoring and Metrics

Only a few researchers (e.g., Cole, Swisher, Thompson, & Fewell, 1985) have advocated the use of more functional and graduated scoring systems with young children. Graduated scoring systems have four distinct advantages: 1) they enable professionals to track

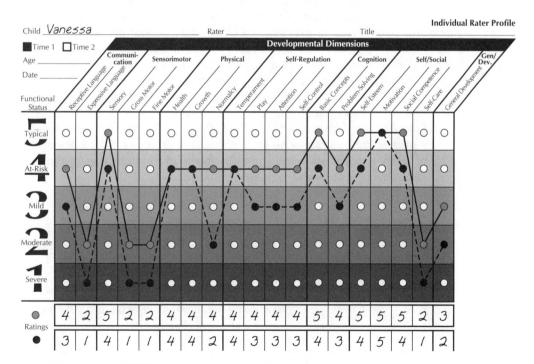

Figure 5.7.   Vanessa's SPECS ratings, as determined by team consensus.

small increments of skill attainment for young children with disabilities; 2) they match the score applied to the degree of instructional help that the child needs; 3) program staff can set their own operational criteria for each level of a graduated scoring system to fit the approaches used in the program; and 4) graduated systems can be applied to any curriculum and the skills in its developmental sequence.

Professionals can chart changes in behavior as a function of a hierarchy of instructional strategies proceeding from the absence of the behavior in the child's repertoire to the independent display of the behavior. For example, a common functional developmental skill contained in several curricula is operating a simple, mechanical, or electronic toy. Table 5.5 presents a 4-point graduated scoring system that uses a variation of the typical binary system (i.e., 0 = absent, 1 = present); this 4-point system could be applied to monitor status and progress more sensitively.

By using such a scoring system, professionals can count, or score, smaller units of behavior change to better determine the type of instructional help that the child needs to show a particular functional skill. As a result, scoring does not merely rate a skill as passed or failed; rather, it shows actual progress that is linked to instructional strategies.

Goal Attainment Scaling

A more individualized and functional method for monitoring a child's unique needs and patterns of progress is *goal attainment scaling* (GAS) (Kiresuk, Smith, & Cardillo, 1994; Simeonsson, Huntingdon, & Short, 1982). GAS is simple and precise in that it enables parents and professionals to collaborate to set goals for both children and families that reflect their individual priorities and capabilities. GAS allows parents and professionals to establish a sequence of goals that plot varying degrees of favorable and unfavorable outcomes across numerous domains of functioning or concern. Outcomes are plotted on a -2, -1, 0, $+1$, $+2$ scale that converts to a normalized t-score with an average of 50 and a standard deviation of 10 by using a goal attainment formula. Individuals can assign different weights to various goals or domains.

Table 5.5. Graduated scoring criteria

Graduated score	Functional level
1.00	Independent display of behavior
0.75	Display with verbal prompt; 2 of 3 trials
0.50	Display with verbal and physical prompts; 2 of 3 trials
0.25	Display with physical prompt
0.00	Absence of behavior in repertoire

Table 5.6 shows a sample GAS profile of a 3-year-old child who, like Vanessa, has neurodevelopmental disabilities. The GAS scale establishes various possible outcomes over five domains: expressive communication, social orientation, attention span, play behavior, and response to frustration.

CONCLUSIONS

The process and procedures that compose the LINK system help to operationalize the important relationships among assessment, intervention, and child progress/program evaluation that must become the foundation of all early intervention programs. This foundation is especially important because continued funding for early intervention programs, which are considered a developmental health care service, hinges on programmatic evidence of clear accountability, consumer satisfaction, and treatment outcomes (i.e., efficacy).

We have argued that the authentic curriculum-based evaluation of the LINK system provides the most appropriate mix of rigor and individualized options. LINK demonstrates that service delivery guided by an understanding of the needs and goals that are unique to each child and family effectively promotes the developmental and behavioral progress of young children with special

Table 5.6.   GAS profile of a child with a severe disability

Scale attainment levels	Scale 1: expresses, communicates (w 1–5)	Scale 2: social orientation (w 2–2)	Scale 3: attention span (w 3–3)	Scale 4: play behavior (w 4–4)	Scale 5: frustration response (w 5–5)
–2: Most unfavorable treatment outcome thought likely	Communicates needs/wants by use of upper extremities, reaches for/pushes away with hands (I)	Turns away from social approach, no response to people who are present (I)	Attends to tasks for less than 30 seconds (I)	Plays with toy/object less than 30 seconds, throws it when finished (I)	Gives up when only slightly frustrated (1 or 2 attempts), cries when urged (I)
–1: Poorer-than-expected success with treatment	Has command of 10 signs, difficult to elicit use	Intermittent response to social approach and people who are present less than 50% of the time	Attends to task for 1 minute when reward and social reinforcement are received	Plays with toy/object for 30 seconds, puts it down when finished 50% of the time	Gives up when only slightly frustrated, will try again without crying when urged
0: Expected level of treatment success	Has command of 10 signs and uses them when reminded	Consistently responds to social approach, shows awareness of others present less than 50% of the time (A)	Attends to task for 1 minute when much social reinforcement is received (A)	Plays with toy/object for 30 seconds, puts it down when finished 100% of the time	Gives up only after several attempts (5–6) (A)
1: Better-than-expected success with treatment	Has command of 10 signs and uses them consistently whenever appropriate (A)	Consistently responds to social approach, shows appropriate awareness of others present	Attends to task for 1 minute with little or no reinforcement needed	Plays with toy/object for up to 1 minute	Persists through a good number of tries (8–10) before giving up
2: Best anticipated success with treatment	Has command and consistent use of 15–20 signs	Consistently responds to social approach, initiates social interaction with familiar others	Attends to task for as long as is appropriate in situation, switches to new task as presented	Plays with toy/object for as long as 3 minutes	Uses varied and imaginative ways to achieve the end before giving up

Abbreviations: w, weights; I, initial performance; A, attained level.

360

needs. To accomplish this overarching objective, we recommend that early intervention teams of parents and professionals

- Select an authentic curriculum-embedded assessment system and battery of curriculum-compatible scales.
- Appraise the child's comprehensive developmental status by using a convergent approach to determine eligibility for services and identify curricular levels.
- Determine functional authentic competencies as goals.
- Highlight authentic transitional competencies within a curriculum.
- Link authentic competencies to both curricular goals and instructional/therapeutic strategies within the IEP/IFSP and teach to mastery.
- Reevaluate the child's comprehensive developmental status and profile his or her progress on authentic competencies by using convergent methods.

This final point, the last step in the LINK system, calls for us to use varied metrics to determine a child's response to intervention. The resultant fusion of quantitative and qualitative data paints a rich, real-life portrait of the benefit of early intervention for young children with special needs and their families.

6

LINK Vignettes

Early intervention interdisciplinary teams are challenged by the complex needs of families and young children with various neurodevelopmental disabilities. Professionals routinely report that they need guidance as to the most effective combinations of instruments and procedures to link assessment and intervention for infants and preschoolers with specific disabilities. The LINK system for conducting authentic curriculum-based evaluation is an easily understood and efficient framework to use to profile a child's capabilities and needs, identify individual goals and adaptive options, and chart progress and program impact.

Vignettes that present case studies of young children are most often effective in illustrating assessment–intervention–evaluation links because they present *authentic* problems that require *authentic* and pragmatic solutions. This chapter offers vignettes that demonstrate how the LINK model is used to plan goals and profile status and progress during early intervention programming for individual children with specific disabilities. The final case vignette shows the unique application of LINK on a statewide basis to compare both individual and group progress of typically developing children and children with disabilities enrolled in inclusive early childhood education programs.

∞∞∞∞∞∞ LINK VIGNETTE 1: AUTISM ∞∞∞∞∞∞

Derek had always been a puzzle. When he was a newborn, he was very difficult to feed, and he did not seem to enjoy cuddling or playing games such as peekaboo. In fact, his parents reported that he seemed to "look through" them when he was on his back, on the floor, or in the crib. He walked at an earlier age than did their older child and, at one point, seemed to begin to understand how to play with toys and with adults purposefully. By the time Derek was 2½ years old, however, it was clear that something was very wrong with his behavior. He had learned several words but rarely used them for their objects; more important, he did not seem to understand that

words should be used to tell people what he wanted. Derek resisted eye contact with adults and refused to be held; he spent much of his time alone and would wander about the room twirling in circles, looking at his fingers, and echoing words and phrases that he had heard on television. In his bed, at night, he would often rock repetitively so hard that he would bang his head on the wall, but he never seemed to get hurt. Finally, Derek often appeared to be afraid of various sounds and would cup his ears, roam the room, and make rhythmic sounds when a loud car passed or a siren sounded.

Derek and his parents lived in a very rural area. It took Derek's parents several years to believe friends and relatives who said that Derek's behavior was not normal for a child of any age. In particular, friends and relatives were concerned about his lack of language skills and his inability to play with the toys they bought him. Derek's mother began to read about special children. When she read about autism, she thought it described Derek's behavior, but Derek's father insisted that Derek was just stubborn and would outgrow "his little world." She did, however, convince her husband that Derek needed to be evaluated by specialists so that they could understand him and help him. She approached the local school district for guidance because Derek had never before received services.

SCREEN/IDENTIFY PHASE

At Derek's mother's request, a social worker and an itinerant teacher from the school district's pupil appraisal center visited Derek at home. Through observation and interview, they gathered developmental information. At the close of their first session, they asked Derek's parents if they would be willing to bring him to the center for a more detailed evaluation.

The next day, the social worker and teacher presented their initial impressions to their program supervisor at a team meeting. Their initial judgments are profiled on the D–Specs (Figure 6.1). In the profile, they indicated that Derek had moderate to severe impairments in several areas, in particular, communication and social interaction skills. Given these limitations and Derek's atypical behaviors, they were concerned about the possibility that he had autism. In addition, they were concerned about the presence of mental retardation that would require extensive supports. The team members concluded their meeting by deciding to recommend that Derek's parents enroll him in the center's preschool-kindergarten diagnostic program, because Derek had recently turned 6 but had never been involved in a classroom experience, except for participation in Sunday school. The team wanted to analyze more fully Derek's developmental competencies using both structured and unstructured methods because he was difficult to keep on task. They chose a flexible diagnostic battery that would allow them to assess Derek's adaptive behaviors and atypical behavior patterns.

ASSESS/LINK PHASE

Table 6.1 outlines the convergent assessment battery that the team selected for Derek. The scales were chosen for their flexible qualities and their ability to guide the team in assessing Derek's cognitive, communication, and social competencies, while defining the severity of his atypical behavior patterns. The assessment was designed to lead to goals for curriculum planning or skill building, reducing atypical behaviors, and increasing appropriate interactive and play behaviors.

Figure 6.2 graphs Derek's developmental levels when he entered the program. The team's assessment indicated that Derek was functioning at a level of mental retardation requiring intermittent to limited supports, with the most significant impairments being seen in the social and expressive communication domains.

Social and Behavioral Observations

Derek's attention difficulties and overactivity required that the psychologist kneel beside his seat and place one arm gently about his shoulders until he became engaged in activities. Then, the structure was reduced somewhat. To maintain Derek's attention, motivation, and performance on tasks, it was necessary to intersperse more focused, high-demand tasks with active toys as reinforcers. He also needed constant physical and verbal–visual prompts to maintain his performance because he showed poor visual scanning skills on discrimination tasks.

Derek's limit on discrimination tasks remained a three- to four-choice task; approximately 1 year after the home intervention, his eye contact and sustained attention had, however, improved dramatically. Derek now showed longer periods of face-to-face gazing with smiling and laughing. He often hugged on request and sought greater emotional contact with others. He also showed greater participation in verbal and fine motor imitation

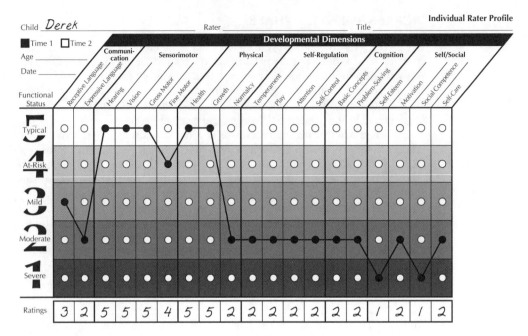

Figure 6.1. Derek's D-Specs.

games. He still displayed some echolalic behavior, but this had decreased significantly in the previous 3 months. He showed some hand flapping and twirling behavior when he was excited; when he was engaged in tasks, however, he exhibited fewer instances of these sterotypies.

Conceptual

Derek's least-developed cognitive skills were in the conceptual area. He knew some colors, shapes, and positional and size concepts. He showed limitations, however, in understanding opposites, number concepts, and spatial concepts and in performing memory tasks that required attention. His strongest cognitive skills were in remembering and recalling pictures presented visually, defining basic words (e.g., coat, towel, car), grouping words into generic categories (e.g., things to eat), and identifying missing details in pictures. Derek's performance on nonverbal problem-solving tasks was limited by poor visual scanning and attention, although he showed conceptual knowledge at the 5-year level. For example, he was able to match clothes to appropriate people on a discrimination task. When his attention was focused, he was capable of good visual problem solving, as

Table 6.1. Derek's convergent assessment battery

Type	Scale
Curriculum compatible	BDI Autism Screening Instrument for Educational Planning (ASIEP)
Curriculum embedded	Psychoeducational Profile (PEP) from IATA
Judgment based	D–Specs
Ecologically based	Childhood Autism Rating Scale (CARS)

EARLY INTERVENTION PROGRESS PROFILE

Child: **Derek Webster**   B.D.: **81-1-3**

Disability: **Autism**   Preschool: **Franklin**   Curriculum: **IATA**

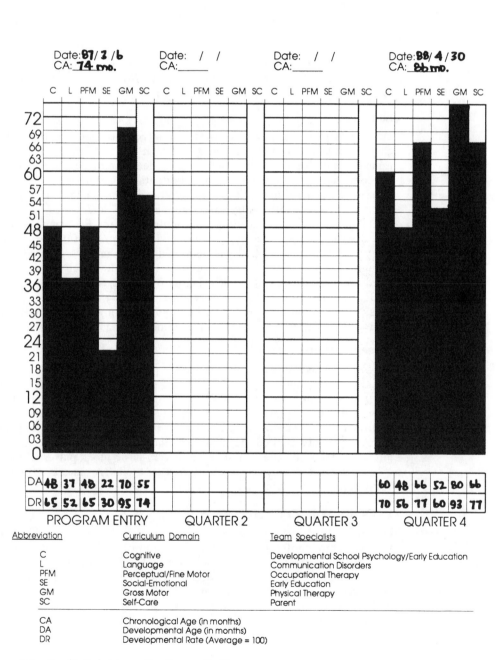

| DA | 48 | 37 | 48 | 22 | 70 | 55 | | | | | | | | | | | | | 60 | 48 | 66 | 52 | 80 | 66 |
| DR | 65 | 52 | 65 | 30 | 95 | 74 | | | | | | | | | | | | | 70 | 56 | 77 | 60 | 93 | 77 |

PROGRAM ENTRY   QUARTER 2   QUARTER 3   QUARTER 4

Abbreviation	Curriculum Domain	Team Specialists
C	Cognitive	Developmental School Psychology/Early Education
L	Language	Communication Disorders
PFM	Perceptual/Fine Motor	Occupational Therapy
SE	Social-Emotional	Early Education
GM	Gross Motor	Physical Therapy
SC	Self-Care	Parent
CA	Chronological Age (in months)	
DA	Developmental Age (in months)	
DR	Developmental Rate (Average = 100)	

Figure 6.2.   Derek's Early Intervention Progress Profile.

shown in his completion of a missing parts task (e.g., wagon—the wheel broke off).

Attention

Derek's selective and sustained attention skills at age 6 were comparable with those expected of children at the 18- to 24-month level. His impulsivity and distractibility hindered his understanding and performance on tasks. He seemed to be able to learn through visual cues, modeling, and guided performance with physical prompts; and he could repeat actions. His attention to auditorially presented material, in contrast, was significantly limited. As a result, he had difficulty remembering numbers and unrelated words presented in a series and had great difficulty attending to a story and recalling details, even in short eight-word forms or descriptive sentences. Careful visual scanning and comparing tasks that had three to four choices were areas of particular concern.

Language

Derek's pattern of capabilities showed a large discrepancy between language understanding and use. Derek had great difficulty expressing definitions beyond objects and functions; even when he may have understood a concept, he could not express his thoughts in coherent sentences or phrases. He showed many of the word-retrieval impairments displayed by children with neurologically based language disorders; for example, because he had difficulty recalling a particular word for a concept, he often gave associative responses, such as identifying a horn as a tune or a lock as a key. Finally, he had difficulty remembering more than two or three words or elements presented in an instruction. He would usually say the last word that was presented quickly, before it disintegrated in his memory. With more meaningful forms (short sentences), he tried to repeat the details in telegraphic fashion before he forgot. He showed strong improvements, however, in his ability to imitate fine motor actions and gestures.

Perceptual/Fine Motor

One of the areas that was of greatest concern was Derek's ability to express perceptual/fine motor skills (shown in tasks such as drawing, block building, puzzle completion, and other coordinated activities); his ability in these skills was comparable to that expected in a child between 24 and 36 months of age. Tracing forms and imitating (as compared with copying) were his primary methods. He had particular difficulty with three-part disjointed puzzles and the reproduction of very basic block patterns. Figure 6.3 presents the authentic goals for Derek on the IATA materials from the TEACH program curriculum.

PROGRAM/INTERVENE PHASE

On the basis of the authentic curriculum-based evaluation, the early intervention team wanted Derek to have as many typical social interactions with his friends as possible. Appropriate social and language models would be crucial. In addition, he would need to learn prerequisite behaviors, such as paying attention during conversation and using language to initiate social exchanges, waiting, sharing, and turn taking. The team planned to promote the selective use of a computer as a learning aid for Derek, so that he could

NAME Derek Webster   AGE 74 months

CURRICULUM Individualized Assessment and Treatment for Autistic and Developmentally
                     Disabled Children (IATA)

LINK AUTHENTIC CURRICULUM COMPETENCIES		
Domains/Goals	Progress Index (0,1,2)	
	Time 1 Score	Time 2 Score
Cognitive		
◆ Recalls familiar objects	0	1
◆ Gives three objects on request	0	1
◆ Engages in puppet story play	0	1
COG TOTAL	0	③
Social-Emotional		
◆ Attends to activity for 1 min +	0	2
◆ Takes turns in simple game	0	2
◆ Plays with friends	0	2
SE TOTAL	0	⑥
Language		
◆ Responds to position commands	0	1
◆ Answers "wh" questions	0	1
◆ Uses 2-3 word phrases	0	2
LNG TOTAL	0	④
Perceptual/Fine Motor		
◆ Opens padlock with key	1	2
◆ Holds paper while drawing	0	1
◆ Copies clay model of animal	0	2
PFM TOTAL	1	⑤
Gross Motor		
◆ Alternates feet down stairs	0	2
◆ Catches ball	0	1
◆ Balances on jungle gym	1	1
GM TOTAL	1	④
Self-Care		
◆ Washes-dries hands assisted	0	2
◆ Buttons with little assistance	0	1
◆ Puts on shoes with little assist	0	1
SC TOTAL	0	④
AUTHENTIC COMPETENCIES TOTALS Preintervention 6% acquisition level Postintervention 72% acquisition level	2/36	26/36

Figure 6.3.   LINK authentic goals for Derek.

receive immediate reinforcement for learning and work more independently on preacademic tasks. The individual dimensions of Derek's program are shown in the Early Childhood Program Prescription form (Figure 6.4).

EVALUATE/MONITOR PHASE

After Derek had spent 12 months in the school district's preschool-kindergarten diagnostic program, he demonstrated some important functional gains. Analysis of the progress data showed that, in three of six areas, the structured intervention program designed for Derek was responsible for his dramatically exceeding the rate of progress attributable to maturation. Gains in the perceptual/fine motor and adaptive skills areas were notable, but the greatest generalizable gains were evident in the social-emotional area (see Figure 6.5).

Affective, Social, and Behavioral Characteristics

The areas in which Derek demonstrated the most dramatic changes were in his style of behavior with peers and adults and his orientation to structured tasks. It was clear that the program and Derek's parents deserved much credit for promoting these gains. Quantitatively, on Childhood Autism Rating Scale (CARS) (Scholpler, 1984), Derek's atypical behavior had previously met criteria for a moderate autistic disorder; in this progress evaluation, his atypical behavior was indicative of a mild autistic disorder.

It was clear that Derek had learned to adapt and respond to a structured routine. He smiled at success, was motivated by novel activities, and indicated that he wanted to continue rather than end activities. He stayed at tabletop tasks for long periods of time; listened to and followed directions; and took cues, prompts, and redirections (e.g., "look at all of the pictures with your eyes," "look before pointing," "wait until I am done saying all of the words").

Derek's performance on the attention subtest of the BDI and IATA goals suggested significant gains in duration and selection when completing activities. He took longer to compare pictures on receptive language and concept tasks and made fewer errors. In addition, Derek now initiated social verbal exchanges with others by asking questions (e.g., "Is that your tie?"). He called people by name. Similarly, he showed a much wider and more appropriate range of emotions. He smiled at his successes, showed frustration with harder tasks, and laughed openly at funny situations. At times, however, his laughing became silly and too loud and escalated, as if he were still learning to regulate his own behavior and emotions. Simple directions, such as "use your little voice" and "we have to stop laughing before we can work some more," were, however, usually sufficient to help him manage himself.

Derek had also made gains on individual skills in the cognitive domain; however, these were not as apparent as his behavioral progress. Although he had gained in important language skills, his rate of progress had remained the same in overall cognitive skills since his previous evaluation.

As noted, Derek was more competent at solving problems nonverbally and less competent when verbal reasoning was required. Preacademically, he recognized letters (i.e., *D, C, K, R, I*), counted with one-to-one correspondence, recognized some colors consistently, and had begun to print the letters of his name. The team recommended that, the following year, Derek be enrolled in a specialized program for children with autism and have regular integrated experiences for nonacademic subjects.

EARLY CHILDHOOD PROGRAM PRESCRIPTIONS

Child: **Derek Webster** CA: **74 mo.** Date: **87-3-15**

DEVELOPMENTAL ASSESSMENT SUMMARY: Derek's overall performance on play, conceptual, and fine motor tasks was most like that of a 48 month old child. His greatest needs are apparent on prerequisites such as attention, task orientation, social interaction, and purposeful use of language. Derek shows less severe atypical behaviors than reported in the past. Language acquisition & social competence will be the best predictors for the future.

DEVELOPMENTAL PROGRAM GUIDELINES:

FEATURES	OPTIONS	COMMENTS
Instructional Setting	☐ Home-based ☒ Center-based ☐ Combo ☐ Hospital-based	Consider specialized SED or Autism class @ mainstreaming for non-academics
Instructional Methods	☒ Verbal prompts ☒ Physical prompts ☐ Shaping	Focus on behavioral prerequisites; pair, then fade manual cues
Grouping Pattern	☐ 1:1 ☒ 1:1 & small group ☐ 1:1, small/large groups	Start @ 1-1 on focused task; pair @ peer; groups of 6 only
Adaptive Arrangements	☒ Special toys ☒ Communication system ☐ Wheelchair ☐ Room arrangement	Response-contingent toys; computer lessons Word Skill program + pictures
Auxiliary Therapies	☒ Speech ☐ PT/OT ☒ Psychologist ☐ Pediatrician ☐ Sensory	1-1 speech/language therapy & classroom teacher consultation structured behavior plan
Behavioral Strategies	☐ Primary reinforcement ☒ Token economy ☐ Behavioral contract ☒ Social praise ☒ Time out ☐ Planned ignoring	Stickers, tokens Timers for start-stop activities Social praise paired with other reinforcers
Parent Participation	☐ Conference only ☒ Parent education/training ☒ Counseling/therapy	Parent participation in class; support groups

Figure 6.4. Derek's Early Childhood Program Prescriptions Profile.

SUMMATIVE CHILD PROGRESS/PROGRAM EVALUATION SHEET

Child: _Derek Webster_   C.A. _86 months_   Date: _88-4-30_

Developmental/ Curricular Domain	1ST Quarter			4TH Quarter			DA Gain	IEI	CEI	M%	I%
	DA	DA Range	DQ	DA	DA Range	DQ					
COGNITIVE	48	(28-52)	65	60	(48-66)	70	12 mo.	1.00	.89	65%	35%
LANGUAGE	37	(21-40)	52	48	(36-52)	56	11 mo.	.92	.96	57%	43%
SOCIAL-EMOTIONAL	22	(18-24)	30	52	(48-54)	60	30 mo.	2.50	1.89	12%	88%
PERCEPTUAL/ FINE MOTOR	48	(30-50)	65	66	(52-68)	77	18 mo.	1.50	1.45	43%	57%
GROSS MOTOR	70	(54-72)	95	80	(78-85)	93	10 mo.	.83	.75	100%	0
SELF-CARE	55	(48-60)	74	66	(52-66)	77	19 mo.	1.58	1.36	47%	53%
DEVELOPMENTAL AVERAGE	46.7		63	62.0		72	15.3 mo.	1.28	1.18	49%	51%

Figure 6.5. Evaluation of Derek's authentic curricular progress.

Derek shows substantial global progress in social-emotional, language, and cognitive capabilities. An analysis of his acquisition of specific authentic curricular competencies that had been targeted for intervention (see Figure 6.3) underscores his specific response to early intervention. Before intervention, Derek's acquisition rate of age-appropriate, real-life skills was 6% for those targeted for intervention. After intervention, his acquisition rate was 72%. His program emphasized important criterial competencies in the social communication areas involving skills such as attention, task orientation, sharing and turn taking in social games, making friends, answering questions, and using language for communication.

∞∞∞∞∞∞ **LINK VIGNETTE 2:** ∞∞∞∞∞∞
VISUAL IMPAIRMENT

Although visual impairment ran in Sara's family, no one suspected that Sara had also been affected. Sara's older brother was born with Leber optic atrophy, a hereditary disorder that causes cortical blindness and is often associated with mental retardation and neuromotor impairments. When Sara was born, the doctors and the family believed that she was fine because her mother's pregnancy, labor, and delivery had been uncomplicated. Sara was an easy baby for whom to care. She slept often and showed no signs of being upset, even when she was hungry. During Sara's second month, however, her mother began to worry because Sara's eyes began to show roving, jerky movements, she seemed uninterested in faces and toys, and she was floppy. A visit to the pediatrician confirmed her parents' worst fears: A neurophysiological examination and visually evoked response assessment showed that Sara was blind. Despite this diagnosis, the pediatrician indicated that he believed Sara was too young to be involved in any programming. The parents became worried and contacted their local mental health/mental retardation center, which agreed to provide only home-based services to Sara, beginning at 8 months of age, because the family lived in a rural area.

When Sara was almost 3½ years old, she showed slow but important progress in gross motor, social communication, and play skills. She also, however, seemed to be increasingly frustrated and moody; she often threw tantrums when she did not get her way or when demands were made upon her, especially during physical therapy. Because Sara was still being educated at home, her mother wanted her to be able to go to a center and be involved with other children and adults. The mother was beginning to feel overwhelmed by Sara's needs and the needs of her older son. A recent divorce had left her alone with the children, and she was under a great deal of stress. After an initial home visit, the early intervention team from the local school district met to discuss Sara's and her mother's involvement in a center-based program.

SCREEN/IDENTIFY PHASE

The team members talked with Sara's mother and observed Sara informally; on the basis of a consensus of their judgments and assessments derived from Sara's previous home-based program and their observations, they converted their initial impressions and screening information into data on D–Specs (Figure 6.6). On the basis of these functional ratings, the team began to make some decisions about Sara's assessment and possible

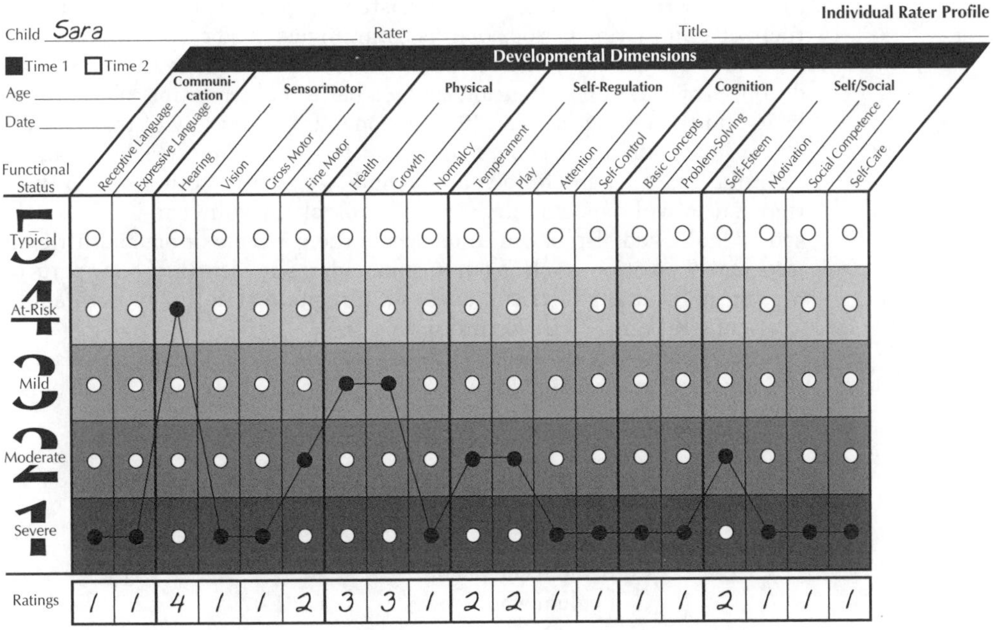

Figure 6.6.   Sara's D–Specs.

programming needs. The profile demonstrated that, despite her progress during home-based treatment, Sara displayed significant impairments in numerous areas, especially sensory, gross motor, communication, self-regulation, cognitive, and social skills. It was clear that adaptive assessment strategies were required to determine both specific levels of attainment in these areas and purposeful goals that could integrate therapies for Sara in her new preschool program.

ASSESS/LINK PHASE

The team decided that the best initial approach would be to use a convergent battery of specialized scales for young children with visual impairments that also included norms for children who are blind. Table 6.2 lists the ecological and norm-, curriculum-, and judgment-based measures that were selected for Sara. Reynell-Zinkin Developmental Scales for Young Visually Handicapped Children (RZS) (Reynell & Zinkin, 1979) and Oregon Project Curriculum (OPC) for Visually Impaired and Blind Preschool Children (Brown, Simmons, & Methwin, 1994) offered the most effective basis for program planning. In addition, Parenting Stress Index (Abidin, 1995) allowed the team to determine the degree of stress that Sara's mother was experiencing and to tailor counseling and therapy so that they targeted the dynamics of the interaction between Sara and her mother.

The Early Intervention Progress Profile (see Figure 6.7) shows Sara's performance in the major developmental domains. In general, the results confirmed the screening indications; it was, however, apparent that Sara had made substantial progress since her last evaluation in the home-based program 3 months previously, when she was 37 months old. Gains in the cognitive and social areas were most evident.

Sara's strongest skills on the RZS and OPC scales were shown on various tasks that required her to search for and identify objects tactilely and to follow directions. She displayed consistently well-developed skills in tactilely discriminating various objects commingled in a bowl or sequenced in front of her (e.g., rabbit, fish, elephant, shoe, spoon, ball, rattle, bell). In addition, Sara's auditory attention enabled her to hold a sample object in her hand and then "find one just like this one" from an array of three to four objects (e.g., holding a spoon; matching it to spoon, cup, shoe, bell, ball). In a similar manner, she followed one- and two-part directions, even those that had novel aspects (e.g., "put the block in your ear," "sit on the spoon"). She had also begun to recognize the concepts of big and little objects and of position, such as on, in, and under. She identified body parts on herself, dolls, and adults and engaged in reciprocal doll play with adults (e.g., "hug Kermit," "kiss Kermit").

In problem-solving tasks, Sara was capable of completing basic activities involved in searching for an object. She located toys that made noises

Table 6.2. Sara's convergent assessment battery

Type	Scale
Curriculum compatible	RZS
Curriculum embedded	OPC
Judgment based	D–Specs
Ecologically based	PSI

EARLY INTERVENTION PROGRESS PROFILE

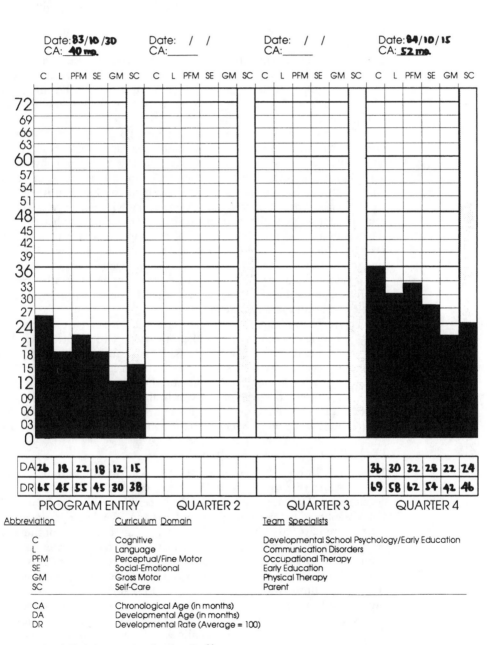

Child: **Sara Hauser**   B.D.: **80-6-21**

Disability: **Visual/MR**   Preschool: **IU# 19**   Curriculum: **Oregon**

| | Date: **83/10/30** CA: **40 mo.** | Date: / / CA: | Date: / / CA: | Date: **84/10/15** CA: **52 mo.** |

	DA																								
DA	26	18	22	18	12	15													36	30	32	28	22	24
DR	65	45	55	45	30	38													69	58	62	54	42	46

PROGRAM ENTRY   QUARTER 2   QUARTER 3   QUARTER 4

Abbreviation	Curriculum Domain	Team Specialists
C	Cognitive	Developmental School Psychology/Early Education
L	Language	Communication Disorders
PFM	Perceptual/Fine Motor	Occupational Therapy
SE	Social-Emotional	Early Education
GM	Gross Motor	Physical Therapy
SC	Self-Care	Parent
CA	Chronological Age (in months)	
DA	Developmental Age (in months)	
DR	Developmental Rate (Average = 100)	

Figure 6.7.   Sara's Early Intervention Progress Profile.

when they were hidden in containers and under cloths, and she could build two-block towers using oversize blocks. Finally, Sara showed emergent skills in completing basic three-hole, form board, shape-matching tasks; however, she used a very haphazard, trial-and-error approach, which allowed her to match only the circle with its recess.

The following three major impairments seemed to have a significant impact on Sara's cognitive problem-solving skills: 1) her inability to use single words consistently for communication and object labeling; 2) her inability to use, and the resistance she displayed to using, her right hand as a tactile exploratory guide in object manipulation; and 3) her haphazard, trial-and-error style of completing structured problem-solving tasks.

Sara's behavior is typical of 1½- to 2-year-olds: She showed definite preferences for toys and situations. Abrupt changes in situations or physical demands that were placed on her, such as those involved in physical and occupational therapy, often resulted in tantrums and screaming. In addition, Sara often stubbornly shook her head "no" in the middle of an activity to assert her independence.

The best approach to working with Sara, given her temperament and visual impairments, seemed to be a flexible play approach that emphasized using novel tasks and toys and giving Sara definite verbal and physical cues and preparatory statements (e.g., "now, we're going to find toys in a bowl"). She understood contingencies and could respond to some limits (e.g., "first, we will play with the puzzle, then we can play with your toy"). The team thought that a clock with a timer might serve to give Sara a better sense of the beginnings and ends of segments of a therapy session or of a structured task and reduce her tantrums to some degree. Finally, Sara was very sensitive to position changes; she needed to sit in a wedge seat that stabilized her at the trunk, facing a table elevated to her hand level, to allow more efficient manipulation of objects; otherwise, she would become afraid and irritable and begin to throw tantrums.

The form in Figure 6.8 matches Sara's developmental competencies with authentic objectives in the OPC that were used for interdisciplinary instruction and therapy. For example, Sara had begun to show greater selective attention and memory skills in searching for hidden objects with cues (i.e., toys that made noises). In addition, her functional communication skills were targeted to the use of words and other means to convey her wants and to initiate interactions with adults and peers. A parallel goal was to promote a wider range of emotional reactions.

PROGRAM/INTERVENE PHASE

The Early Childhood Program Prescriptions form in Figure 6.9 outlines those features that the team believed were essential to Sara's center-based developmental program. Increased time in center-based programming (versus home-based programming) was required to give Sara opportunities to learn more naturally about real-life events (e.g., play and conflicts with peers, field trips to zoos and parks). In addition, increased center-based programming would address Sara's mother's needs to reduce her stress and adjust her interactions with Sara. Behavior management programming would concentrate on methods of rewarding and managing Sara's responses to rules and limits and to the demands of others. It was agreed that respite care would be made available to Sara's mother to ease her separation from Sara, foster her independence, and allow her time to cope emotionally. Fi-

NAME Sara Hauser   AGE 40 months

CURRICULUM Oregon Project Curriculum & Reynell-Zinkin Scales

LINK AUTHENTIC CURRICULUM COMPETENCIES		
Domains/Goals	Progress Index (0,1,2)	
	Time 1 Score	Time 2 Score
Cognitive ♦ Gets object in box with lid ♦ Sorts big-little objects ♦ Pairs common objects	0 0 0	1 1 0
COG TOTAL	0	②
Social-Emotional ♦ Attends to speaker ♦ Demands personal attention ♦ Seeks comfort from familiar people	0 0 1	0 1 1
SE TOTAL	1	②
Language ♦ Gives object on request ♦ Uses "more" appropriately ♦ Names common toys/objects	0 0 0	1 1 1
LNG TOTAL	0	③
Perceptual/Fine Motor ♦ Gets objects from toy box ♦ Explores moving toy parts ♦ Adaptive use of spoon	0 0 0	1 1 1
PFM TOTAL	0	③
Gross Motor ♦ Reaches-moves to sounds/voice ♦ Finds door of room & stands ♦ Gets about using physical cues	0 0 0	2 2 2
GM TOTAL	0	⑥
Self-Care ♦ Holds cup while drinking ♦ Feeds self with spoon ♦ Pulls off socks-shoes	0 0 0	1 1 1
SC TOTAL	0	③
AUTHENTIC COMPETENCIES TOTALS **Preintervention** 3% acquisition level **Postintervention** 53% acquisition level	1/36	19/36

Figure 6.8.   LINK authentic goals for Sara.

EARLY CHILDHOOD PROGRAM PRESCRIPTIONS

Child: _Sara Hauser_   CA: _40 months_   Date: _83-10-30_

DEVELOPMENTAL ASSESSMENT SUMMARY: Sara has shown progress since her involvement in home-based programming, yet, important additional areas must be emphasized, particularly social, language, and behavioral. She has begun to "make sense" out of her world since learning to move out to sound sources. Her play with toys is more purposeful. Yet, she shows little emotional reactions to success on tasks and is often irritable with tantrums. She typically uses her body and behavior rather than language to communicate. Give-and-take social games are beginning.

DEVELOPMENTAL PROGRAM GUIDELINES:

FEATURES	OPTIONS	COMMENTS
Instructional Setting	☐ Home-based ☒ Center-based ☐ Combo ☐ Hospital-based	Learning about real life events in natural settings (parks, etc.) Low distraction settings
Instructional Methods	☒ Verbal prompts ☒ Physical prompts ☒ Shaping	Needs physical cues Stress direction following Stress facial orientation
Grouping Pattern	☒ 1:1 ☒ 1:1 & small group ☐ 1:1, small/large groups	One-one-for instruction Peer-pairing for games not large groups
Adaptive Arrangements	☒ Special toys ☐ Communication system ☐ Wheelchair ☒ Room arrangement	Toys with levers; tactile & auditory cues Corner chair for support Setting: high pile rug
Auxiliary Therapies	☒ Speech ☒ PT/OT ☒ Psychologist ☐ Pediatrician ☒ Sensory	Integrated goals thru consultation, not separate sessions Behavior plan
Behavioral Strategies	☐ Primary reinforcement ☐ Token economy ☐ Behavioral contract ☒ Social praise ☒ Time out ☒ Planned ignoring	Thrives on adult attention Loves physical play Discipline by withd. attention
Parent Participation	☐ Conference only ☒ Parent education/training ☒ Counseling/therapy	Vision specialist with mother; reduce stress respite care

Figure 6.9. Sara's Early Childhood Program Prescriptions Profile.

nally, the team decided to introduce special response-contingent toys and computer programs in an effort to increase Sara's ability to be a responsive learner, to teach her task orientation and attention without constant adult guidance, and to provide immediate reinforcement for her problem-solving behaviors and communication skills.

PHASE 4: EVALUATE/MONITOR

At the end of the year, program personnel evaluated Sara's progress on the curricular goals highlighted during her prescriptive assessment at entry into the program. Figure 6.10 summarizes the progress data. A comparison with the D–Specs profile sheet in Figure 6.6 reveals how consistent Sara's gains were across various dimensions. In general, she demonstrated very significant functional gains in the center-based program—an overall gain of 10 months over a 12-month period. All of the progress indices suggested that the individualized program designed for her had had a significant impact on her rate of gain, which was, in general, higher than that observed at program entry.

Sara had begun to use words, instead of misbehavior or global gestures, for communication. Her tantrums had stopped both at home and at the preschool center. She responded better to directions and faced a person who spoke to her. She was much more expressive, both socially and emotionally, and she smiled and clapped her hands when she was successful on

SUMMATIVE CHILD PROGRESS/PROGRAM EVALUATION SHEET

Child: Sara Hauser   C.A. 52 months   Date: 84-10-18

Developmental/ Curricular Domain	1ST Quarter			4th Quarter			DA Gain	IEI	CEI	M%	P%
	DA	DA Range	DQ	DA	DA Range	DQ					
COGNITIVE	26	(20–34)	65	36	(28–40)	69	10 mo.	.83	.75	78%	22%
LANGUAGE	18	(12–21)	45	30	(18–32)	58	12 mo.	1.00	.95	45%	55%
SOCIAL-EMOTIONAL	18	(15–24)	45	28	(21–30)	54	10 mo.	.83	.80	54%	46%
PERCEPTUAL/ FINE MOTOR	22	(18–30)	55	32	(24–36)	62	10 mo.	.83	.82	66%	34%
GROSS MOTOR	12	(9–14)	30	22	(15–26)	42	10 mo.	.83	.74	36%	64%
SELF-CARE	15	(12–16)	38	24	(18–28)	46	9 mo.	.75	.75	51%	49%
DEVELOPMENTAL AVERAGE	18.5		46	28.7		55	10.2 mo.	.85	.82	54%	46%

Figure 6.10. Evaluation of Sara's authentic curricular progress.

tasks. She actively initiated social games with others and had started to tease in play. She showed particular gains in using her hands more precisely to explore and play with toys; she also used her hands to guide her in attending to the parts or features of objects to identify them.

Sara's mother had become a true partner in Sara's classroom programming; she felt much more confident and comfortable in being separated from Sara, in disciplining her when necessary, and in encouraging her to become more independent in work and play. The mother reported that, because of Sara's gains, and because she had recognized the benefits of using respite care and "refueling" herself emotionally, she felt much less stress than she had previously. She had joined a parents' group and had begun to socialize with several friends. Because her son was presently being educated in a part-time residential school elsewhere in the state, she felt that she had much more control over her life and could now help Sara with new-found energy.

In summary, because of her visual impairment, Sara experienced a barrier to learning in all major developmental domains. Figure 6.8 shows that her preintervention repertoire of expected authentic curricular competencies was only 3% of that expected for her age and developmental level. As a result of intervention, Sara's acquisition rate increased to 53%. Important gains in real-life skills were observed in Sara's moving out toward sound and voice cues, using language for naming and following simple directions, getting and exploring objects appropriately, and basic eating and drinking skills.

∞∞∞∞∞∞∞   LINK VIGNETTE 3:   ∞∞∞∞∞∞∞
TRAUMATIC BRAIN INJURY

Nicki was having so much fun with her friends in the yard that she never saw the car coming. The driver of the car swerved just as Nicki bolted into the street. Nicki, age 33 months, was admitted to the local university's children's hospital with a closed brain injury. In addition, she suffered numerous fractures, contusions, and lacerations because she was dragged 50 feet by the car that hit her. When she arrived in the emergency room, she was comatose with evidence of brain trauma, fractures, and possible abdominal injuries. As a result, a shunt was placed in her brain to relieve the pressure of the cerebral spinal fluid. She had sustained a subdural hematoma to the right parietal area of her brain.

Nicki's next 2 months, which were spent in an acute care hospital, were filled with further complications. Her shunt became infected, resulting in encephalitis, a brain inflammation. Recurrent bouts of encephalitis necessitated two brain operations to revise her shunt. Furthermore, during her first 3 weeks of acute care hospitalization, she was responsive only to pain. Ophthalmological evaluation revealed bilateral optic atrophy. As Nicki emerged from coma, she was functionally blind in her left eye and showed significant visual impairment in the right. A computed tomography scan revealed evidence of pressure on her brain as well as some cortical atrophy. Clinically, she showed a left hemiparesis.

After approximately 3 months in the acute care hospital, Nicki was well enough to be transferred to a pediatric rehabilitation facility for intensive interdisciplinary intervention. At first, she was responsive mostly to specific tactile and auditory stimulation. Gradually, over the first month in the rehabilitation hospital, Nicki began to recover. She began to use her right hand to reach toward people in a halting manner; the vision in her right eye also began to resolve. Nicki's mother, who was only 17 years old, was encouraged by these changes but was afraid and overwhelmed by what had happened to her daughter. In addition, the staff had begun to observe recurrent seizures; minor episodes of sensitivity to sights, sounds, and position changes; and some staring, or "tuning out," behavior.

SCREEN/IDENTIFY PHASE

The rehabilitation team decided that Nicki's recent gains in the acute care hospital setting indicated that she was ready for a full program of rehabilitation services to support her developmental progress and recovery. The team consisted of specialists in occupational therapy, physical therapy, speech-language pathology, early childhood special education, developmental school psychology, pediatrics, social work, nursing, and therapeutic recreation. The team had experience in planning services that would be sensitive to Nicki's temperamental/behavior style, sensorimotor limitations, and neurophysiological status. After observing Nicki in several situations, the team members independently completed the D–Specs rating scales and then met to reach a consensus about her functional needs.

Figure 6.11 profiles Nicki's degree of functional impairments as judged by the team. Her impairments in most areas were severe; the team members consistently agreed, however, that Nicki's social interaction skills and affective responses, such as smiling and vocalizing to gain adult attention, were her strongest capabilities and needed to be fostered early. It was decided that Nicki's mother would be the focal point of the therapies; she would be counseled regarding her own needs and would receive practical coaching on how best to encourage Nicki's recovery.

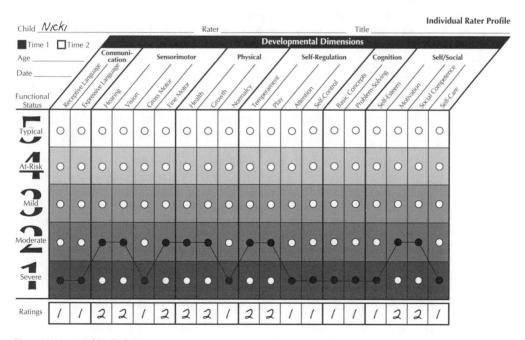

Figure 6.11.   Nicki's D–Specs.

ASSESS/LINK PHASE

It was clear that Nicki would remain in the rehabilitation hospital for some time, until she could make the transition to a community early intervention program. Her ongoing health concerns and her emergent recovery of skills dictated hospital-based services. The team chose a convergent assessment battery that would guide them in more comprehensively assessing Nicki's status and progress (see Table 6.3). Pediatric Evaluation of Disability Inventory (PEDI) (Haley et al., 1992), EIDP, and Carolina Record of Individual Behavior (CRIB) (Simeonsson, 1985) were selected because they were all sensitive to Nicki's neurodevelopmental and neurobehavioral patterns and included adaptations for her visual and neuromotor impairments. The central instrument was EIDP, which was selected because of its adaptations, sensitivity, and field-testing for children with neurological impairments.

Nicki's Progress Profile (Figure 6.12) showed that many of her adaptive behaviors were very similar to those observed for a 1-month-old infant, although she was 33 months of age at the time of the accident. Her social interactions approximated those of a 3-month-old infant. The team observed that Nicki had begun to "spurt" developmentally in the 2 weeks after the initial evaluation, which probably reflected the phenomenon of spontaneous recovery that is characteristic of the early stages of a brain injury. The team decided, therefore, to wait to design a detailed intervention plan. The next month, at a CA of 35 months, Nicki showed dramatic gains, to the extent that many of her social, play, and language skills were much like those expected of an 18-month-old. At this point the team reevaluated Nicki and began to plan her program. Figure 6.13 shows the authentic curricular goals in Nicki's program for the 2 months spent at the rehabilitation hospital.

PROGRAM/INTERVENE PHASE

The team members planned specific strategies that would enable them to implement their classroom-based and individual therapies with Nicki, as shown on the Early Childhood Program Prescriptions form in Figure 6.14. Note the emphases on the use of technology, such as response-contingent toys and computers, and the use of peer pairing during instructional sessions. The team placed special emphasis on the pressing demands made on Nicki's mother as a single, adolescent mother who was depressed, anxious, and unsure of her ability to care for her daughter's ongoing, multiple impairments. The issue of possibly placing Nicki in foster care needed to be explored.

Nicki's mother reported great stress on the PSI; she felt the need for more social support and counseling, as indicated in interviews with the social worker and by her responses on Family Needs Survey (Bailey & Simeonsson, 1990). The team observed that mother–daughter interactions were strained and anxious. Unfortunately, the mother felt incapable of interacting

Table 6.3.   Nicki's convergent assessment battery

Type	Scale
Curriculum compatible	PEDI
Curriculum embedded	EIDP
Judgment based	CRIB
Ecologically based	D–Specs

EARLY INTERVENTION PROGRESS PROFILE

Child: **Nicki Colter**　　　　　　　　　　　B.D.: **85-5-30**

Disability: **Brain injury**　Preschool: **Hospital**　　　Curriculum: **DPIYC**

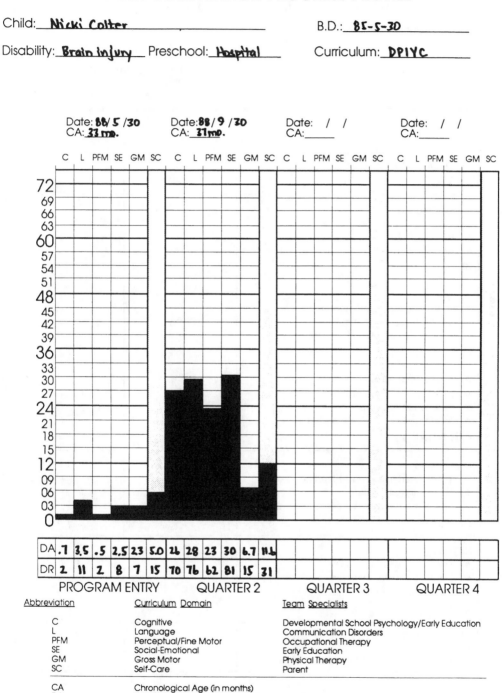

Figure 6.12.　Nicki's Early Intervention Progress Profile.

NAME Nicki Colter   AGE 35 months

CURRICULUM Developmental Programming for Infants & Young Children: EIDP and Pediatric
            Evaluation of Disability Inventory (PEDI)

LINK AUTHENTIC CURRICULUM COMPETENCIES		
Domains/Goals	Progress Index (0,1,2)	
	Time 1 Score	Time 2 Score
Cognitive		
◆ Reaches around barrier for toy	0	2
◆ Selects hand hiding toy	0	2
◆ Finds right toy in toy box	0	2
COG TOTAL	0	⑥
Social-Emotional		
◆ Initiates social interactions	1	2
◆ Plays with toys appropriately	0	2
◆ Plays alongside friend	0	2
SE TOTAL	1	⑥
Language		
◆ Follows simple commands	0	2
◆ Gives object on request	0	2
◆ Associates spoken words/pictures	0	2
LNG TOTAL	0	⑥
Perceptual/Fine Motor		
◆ Releases toy from grasp	0	2
◆ Pulls open drawers	0	2
◆ Attempts to coordinate both hands	0	1
PFM TOTAL	0	⑤
Gross Motor		
◆ Turns head in supported sitting	0	1
◆ Moves lying to sitting	0	1
◆ Sits without support-5 secs.	0	1
GM TOTAL	0	③
Self-Care		
◆ Feeds self with spoon	0	1
◆ Drinks from cup assisted	0	2
◆ Coordinates suck-swallow	0	2
SC TOTAL	0	⑤
AUTHENTIC COMPETENCIES TOTALS **Preintervention** *3% acquisition level* **Postintervention** *85% acquisition level*	1/36	31/36

Figure 6.13.   LINK authentic goals for Nicki.

EARLY CHILDHOOD PROGRAM PRESCRIPTIONS

Child: **Nicki Colter**   CA: **35 months**   Date: **88-6-5**

DEVELOPMENTAL ASSESSMENT SUMMARY: Nicki has shown remarkable gains in play, language, and social skills. Her revised program must capitalize on these gains to help her use the skills functionally across people and situations. We must pair her with 1-2 other children to model social and language behaviors; use electromechanical toys to prompt attention & cause-effect play. Mother needs our help to decide on the foster care issue.

DEVELOPMENTAL PROGRAM GUIDELINES:

FEATURES	OPTIONS	COMMENTS
Instructional Setting	☐ Home-based ☒ Center-based ☐ Combo ☐ Hospital-based	5-½ days/week to increase endurance Integrated therapies
Instructional Methods	☒ Verbal prompts ☒ Physical prompts ☐ Shaping	Must learn to respond to verbal cues only
Grouping Pattern	☐ 1:1 ☒ 1:1 & small group ☐ 1:1, small/large groups	1-1 for therapy Peer-pairing to practice skills
Adaptive Arrangements	☒ Special toys ☒ Communication system ☒ Wheelchair ☐ Room arrangement	Switch toys Computer – light pointer Adapted pogon buggy
Auxiliary Therapies	☒ Speech ☒ PT/OT ☒ Psychologist ☒ Pediatrician ☒ Sensory	Integrate PT/OT, speech @ preschool Behavior plan Seizures Check left eye vision
Behavioral Strategies	☐ Primary reinforcement ☐ Token economy ☐ Behavioral contract ☒ Social praise ☒ Time out ☒ Planned ignoring	Social praise & preferred activities as reinforcers Time-out & ignoring
Parent Participation	☐ Conference only ☒ Parent education/training ☒ Counseling/therapy	Help for mother's anxiety & depression; check foster care

Figure 6.14.   Nicki's Early Childhood Program Prescriptions Profile.

with Nicki; Nicki's irritability with her, contrasted with the calm, organized behavior she displayed with other team members, exacerbated the problem. Individual counseling with the mother had been only slightly successful.

EVALUATE/MONITOR PHASE

After 4 months of intensive rehabilitation, Nicki was ready to be transferred to a community-based Easter Seals program. At this point, the mother had made a firm decision to transfer Nicki to a specialized foster care family. Nicki had demonstrated significant developmental and behavioral gains as the result of a combination of factors, including her resolving physical conditions, her body and brain's somewhat spontaneous recovery, and the impact of intensive team instruction and therapy (see Figure 6.15). Overall, she had progressed at the accelerated rate of a 6-month average developmental gain for each month of treatment/therapy, or six times the expected rate in normal child development. Although significant intervention gains exceeding 90% were apparent, these numbers were somewhat inflated as a result of the element of spontaneous recovery.

Nicki's strongest functional gains were in the acquisition of language, social, and cognitive skills. She also showed strong increases in perceptual/fine motor skills, but these were tempered by her visual impairments and left hemiparesis, which appeared to be a permanent disability. Her least well-developed skills were in the gross motor and adaptive skills domains.

SUMMATIVE CHILD PROGRESS/PROGRAM EVALUATION SHEET

Child: __Nicki Cotter__   C.A. __31 months__   Date: __88-9-30__

Developmental/ Curricular Domain	1ST Quarter			2ND Quarter			DA Gain	IEI	CEI	M%	I%
	DA	DA Range	DQ	DA	DA Range	DQ					
COGNITIVE	.7	Newborn	2	26.0	(21–32)	70	25.3	6.0	5.8	1%	99%
LANGUAGE	3.5	(0–3.5)	11	28.0	(12–28)	76	24.5	6.0	6.8	2%	98%
SOCIAL-EMOTIONAL	2.5	(0–3.5)	8	30.0	(24–34)	81	27.5	7.0	4.6	1%	99%
PERCEPTUAL/ FINE MOTOR	.5	Newborn	2	23.0	(18–26)	62	22.5	6.0	5.5	1%	99%
GROSS MOTOR	2.3	(0–2.5)	7	6.7	(3–8)	15	4.4	1.0	1.9	7%	93%
SELF-CARE	5.0	(0–5.0)	15	11.6	(7–12)	31	6.6	2.0	3.4	9%	91%
DEVELOPMENTAL AVERAGE	2.4		7	20.9		56	18.5	4.5	7.4	4%	96%

Figure 6.15. Evaluation of Nicki's authentic curricular progress.

Nicki showed marked improvements in various behavior areas that involve social communication skills; on CRIB, however, she continued to show enduring impairments in various self-regulatory areas, such as hyperactivity, inattention, memory impairments, low tolerance for frustration, widely changeable moods, and high sensitivity to changes in stimulation. Overall, in 4 months, Nicki had progressed from a severe to a moderate/ mild level of developmental disability in cognitive, language, and social areas, as shown in her DQ of 70 and her D–Specs ratings of 3 and 4. It was decided that the hospital team would work with the Easter Seals personnel in transferring Nicki's program, in consultation with the pediatrician and nurses regarding care for her ongoing health concerns (in particular, her seizures).

Nicki's accident and resultant brain injury caused a major loss of functional developmental skills in all domains. Nicki's left hemiparesis and resolving blindness in her left eye made learning difficult. Nevertheless, her overall progress was dramatic in all areas, although enduring impairments are evident in gross and fine motor areas. A review of her gains in acquiring specific authentic curricular competencies (see Figure 6.13) supports the striking nature of her response to rehabilitation and early intervention. Pre- and postintervention learning rates are 3% and 86%, respectively. Nicki acquired important functional skills in areas such as visual memory, initiating and maintaining social interactions, playing with others, following commands, associating words and pictures, using her right hand adaptively, and basic eating and drinking skills.

∞∞∞∞∞∞ LINK VIGNETTE 4: ∞∞∞∞∞∞
KINDERGARTEN TRANSITION

Charlie was identified as having a developmental delay in the area of communication with particular difficulties in the development of receptive language skills and auditory skills such as sequencing, discrimination, and memory. He had received preschool services in an inclusive prekindergarten program, and support was provided by the speech-language pathologist and the preschool special education teacher. In November of the year before Charlie's proposed transition to a kindergarten program, all of the children in his class took the Metropolitan Readiness Test (MRT), which was intended to assess their readiness for kindergarten. The administrators of the receiving school district believed that scores from this test would predict children's success in their kindergarten program. Charlie completed the testing over a full week in November.

Charlie's teachers were concerned by his low MRT scores, but they seemed to disregard the discrepancy between the scores and his actual classroom performance in forming their judgments of his future success. The results of Charlie's MRT were presented to his parents with a message that his preschool teachers were concerned about his future success because of his "weaknesses" on the auditory skill (10th percentile) and language skill (15th percentile) subtests, which involved skills such as listening for sequence and beginning consonant sounds and following directions. Charlie's parents were aware that the scores on this test did not provide a clear picture of their son's skill level and that he had, in fact, begun to master some of the letters and their sounds, as evidenced in his performance of classroom and home-based activities. After several discussions with Charlie's parents regarding the discrepancy between the format and content of items on the MRT and the type of rich, authentic tasks included in the program's curriculum activities, the preschool staff decided to incorporate an authentic performance assessment approach using student work portfolios and a curriculum-based skills checklist. Charlie's parents participated with the preschool teacher in administering subtests of BRIGANCE® Prescriptive Readiness: Strategies and Practice (Brigance, 1985) and BRIGANCE® Diagnostic Inventory of Early Development (Rev. ed.; Brigance, 1991).

On these curriculum-based measures, Charlie was able to auditorally discriminate between same and different word pairs on the basis of the initial and final consonant sounds of the words. He also demonstrated emergent skill in identifying the initial consonant sounds of words and produced associated sounds for three consonants (Figure 6.16).

In planning for Charlie's transition, his parents and preschool teachers reviewed his progress in the curriculum and took particular note of his progress in developing auditory skills. The work samples collected for Charlie's portfolio revealed a much different picture of Charlie's development of these skills than that initially indicated by his scores on the MRT: He was able to print the letters representing the consonant sounds of words studied in thematic units (e.g., fruits and vegetables) and, in some cases, was able to write the letters in the correct sequence of beginning, medial, and final sounds in words (Figure 6.16). His work included delightful pictures of each word that he attempted to spell (Figure 6.17), and he was able to verbally relate all of the information that he had learned about each concept in the units.

The use of a norm-referenced measure (e.g., MRT) that is disconnected from a program's curriculum, the classroom teacher's teaching methods, and the child's actual classroom work very often gives a negative portrayal of the child as having a problem. This vignette is a stark testament of how,

NAME Charlie Beulah   **AGE** 66 months

CURRICULUM BRIGANCE Prescriptive Readiness: Strategies and Practice

LINK AUTHENTIC CURRICULUM COMPETENCIES		
Domains/Goals	**Progress Index (0,1,2)**	
	Time 1 Score	**Time 2 Score**
<u>Cognitive</u> ◆ **Distinguishes same-different consonant sounds**	1	2
◆ **Produces sounds for 3 consonants**	1	2
◆ **Prints letters of consonants**	0	2
◆ **Spells words to match drawings**	1	2
◆ **Groups concepts in thematic units**	1	2
COG TOTAL	4	(10)
AUTHENTIC COMPETENCIES TOTALS **Preintervention** *40% acquisition level* **Postintervention** *100% acquisition level*	4/10	10/10

Figure 6.16.   LINK authentic goals for Charlie.

Figure 6.17.   Charlie's drawings of fruits and vegetables.

through the use of such a measure, Charlie was erroneously viewed as having a developmental delay or being at risk for learning disabilities. Charlie's performance on the authentic tasks and activities of the BRIGANCE® Diagnostic Inventory of Early Development and his own drawings and spelling attempts underscore the fact that he has age-appropriate skills and is progressing as expected (see Figure 6.18). Moreover, his response to teaching that emphasizes prereading skills through a natural, activity-based approach is apparent in Figure 6.17. Before goal-directed teaching, Charlie had acquired 40% of the prereading skills expected; after intervention, he had acquired 100%, or all 5 of the major categories of reading skills expected at kindergarten transition. His attainment of authentic practical skills in response to what he had learned in the classroom provides the only true test of his abilities.

At this point, both parents and teachers were very optimistic regarding Charlie's potential to make a smooth transition to the inclusive kindergarten program in his home school district. When preparing Charlie's transition plan and IEP, the team decided to continue to provide speech and language support and consultation from the special education teacher to ensure his success in the new program. Authentic performance assessment in this case played a critical role in demonstrating that Charlie clearly had developed the requisite auditory skills for success in kindergarten, which was a job that a narrow-focus, norm-referenced readiness test could not perform. Charlie turned out to be one of the strongest readers in his kindergarten/first-grade class.

∽∽∽∽∽∽∽ LINK VIGNETTE 5: ∽∽∽∽∽∽∽
HEARING IMPAIRMENT

Andrea Hughes was a healthy 5-pound, 8-ounce baby; no complications or risks had been evident during her mother's pregnancy or delivery, except for a mild episode of jaundice, which did not require treatment. Andrea was discharged after only 3 days in the hospital. She slept and nursed well during her first few months and, in general, seemed to be content and interested in the world around her. Nevertheless, Mrs. Hughes was worried about her daughter's hearing because the baby seemed to be "too" content; her friends and relatives tried to reassure her and suggested that such fears were typical of first-time mothers. Even Andrea's pediatrician discounted Mrs. Hughes doubts and indicated that Andrea was most likely a "visual learner."

However, when Andrea was 13 months old, Mrs. Hughes became convinced that Andrea had a hearing problem because she did not turn to sounds and was unusually interested in vibrations of the washing machine on the floor. In addition, Andrea seemed to have stopped "talking" and never learned any words after learning to babble and coo. To add to her worries, Mrs. Hughes remembered that her mother's father, his two sisters, and a cousin all either were deaf or had hearing impairments.

At this point, Mrs. Hughes insisted that her pediatrician refer her to the speech and audiology clinic at the hospital in her city. After a series of tests, it was determined that Mrs. Hughes had been correct all along; Andrea was diagnosed as having severe congenital sensorineural hearing loss in both ears. The clinic counseled Mrs. Hughes about Andrea's needs and referred her to a specialized school for children who were deaf; the school operated a center-based early intervention program for children from birth to 5 years of age. Mrs. Hughes's feelings of relief at having received a diag-

I. Basic Reading Skills (continued)

Assessment	Page	
		Auditory Discrimination:
1-6	205	5-3 1.(b) 2.(b) 3.(s) 4.(m) 5.(w) 6.(f) 7.(l) 8.(l) 9.(c/k) 10.(d) 11.(p) 12.(n) 13.(r) 14.(g) 15.(y) 16.(k) 17.(j) 6.0
		Notes: *12-2-94 Recognized same & different word pairs in initial & final positions*
		Matches Initial Consonants with Pictures: *had to find 2 pictures to match with consonant.*
1-7	207	**Page C-207** **Page C-208** **Page C-209**
		6-3 1.(b) 2. h 3.(s) 4.(m) 5. w 6.(f) 7. l 8. t 9. c/k/ 10. d 11. p 12. n 13. r 14. g 15. y 16. k 17. j 7.0
		Notes: *I picture (1) picture*
		12-2-94 able to produce consonant sound for b, d, k
		Substitutes Initial Consonant Sounds:
1-8	210	**Page C-210** **Page C-211** **Page C-212**
		6-3 1. b 2. h 3. s 4. m 5. w 6. f 7. l 8. t 9. c/k/ 10. d 11. p 12. n 13. r 14. g 15. y 16. k 17. j 7.0
		Notes:
		Substitutes Short-Vowel Sounds:
1-9	214	6-3 1. a 2. e 3. i 4. o 5. u 7.0
		Notes:
		Substitutes Long-Vowel Sounds:
1-10	217	6-3 1. a 2. e 3. i 4. o 5. u 8.0
		Notes:

Figure 6.18. Charlie's performance on the BRIGANCE® goals and materials.

nosis were mixed with anger and confusion that her doubts had not been taken more seriously and that the problem had not been diagnosed earlier. She worried whether it was too late to help Andrea.

SCREEN/IDENTIFY PHASE

The home visit by the speech-language pathologist from the school reduced Mrs. Hughes's anxieties considerably. Andrea warmed up to the her immediately and was able to play well with the toys she had brought. This provided the team and Mrs. Hughes with some estimate of Andrea's relative strengths and weaknesses.

The speech-language pathologist's impressions, as she presented them to the team, are profiled on the D–Specs graph (Figure 6.19). It was clear that, despite her hearing impairment, Andrea had many strong capabilities, especially in the play, motor, and social areas. On the basis of this screening, the team decided to move Andrea directly into the classroom-based program.

ASSESS/LINK PHASE

The team selected the convergent assessment battery in Table 6.4 to prescribe initial goals for Andrea's IEP and therapeutic program. The scales were chosen because they included adaptations or accommodations for children with hearing impairments and because they identified authentic goals that are important in the development of social orientation, gestural language, and total communication for young children who are deaf.

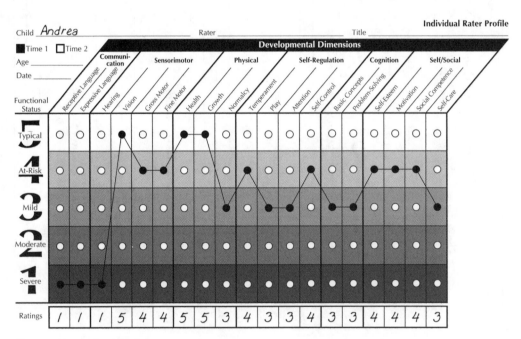

Figure 6.19. Andrea's D–Specs.

Table 6.4. Andrea's convergent assessment battery

Type	Scale
Curriculum compatible	BDI
Curriculum embedded	DCC
Judgment based	Kendall Preschool Curriculum
	D–Specs

Affective and Behavioral Characteristics

Andrea was an extremely socially responsive girl. Her activity level was typical for her age. She was engaging, playful, and cooperative throughout the evaluation, and the team found it to be a true joy to work with her. In the evaluation setting, she explored her environment and was interested in the toys and new people. Her attention to tasks and people was fairly age appropriate. It was easy to get her interested in new items and fairly easy to get her to relinquish objects no longer needed in the assessment. She was fairly persistent in her efforts and aware of her successes. At times, she would clap for herself when she successfully completed a task. She would then look to the adults in the room for added positive reinforcement.

Cognitive and Adaptive Skills

Andrea's cognitive performance on various developmental tasks, excluding language, revealed a rather consistent performance level of approximately 16–20 months, as profiled in Figure 6.20. Her style of playing with toys was primarily manipulative and relational, and she showed some emergent symbolic play capacity.

Communication Skills

On the basis of reports and observation, Andrea appeared to have developed some alternative forms of communication. She pointed, used hand gestures, and made noises to indicate her wants and needs. She differentiated sounds such as screaming, yelling, laughing, and other excited noises. She engaged in eye contact readily and used her facial expressions and body in a communicative fashion.

Andrea had independently developed specific gestures for activities; she had a hand-to-mouth gesture for EAT and a hand gesture for GIVE ME. In addition, she and her mother had created a play activity in which the mother would gently blow air on her face. Andrea had developed a symbol for this activity—she made a circular movement in the air with her hand to generate a breeze, and she consistently used this symbol to demonstrate that she wanted her mother to continue playing the game. Furthermore, when the examiner showed her the sign for MORE during play, it seemed to be meaningful to her and was incorporated into play with the examiner.

Figure 6.21 highlights those authentic curricular competencies that best indicate Andrea's current needs and her curriculum entry points. Note the emphases on social interaction, signing, and gesturing responses. Vocal/ verbal expression, self-regulation for attention, and occupying herself at a task for increasing periods of time were also highlighted.

EARLY INTERVENTION PROGRESS PROFILE

Child:__**Andrea Hughes**_____　　B.D.:__**86-10-2**_____

Disability:__**Deaf**_____ Preschool:__**Lansdale**__　Curriculum:__**DCC**_____

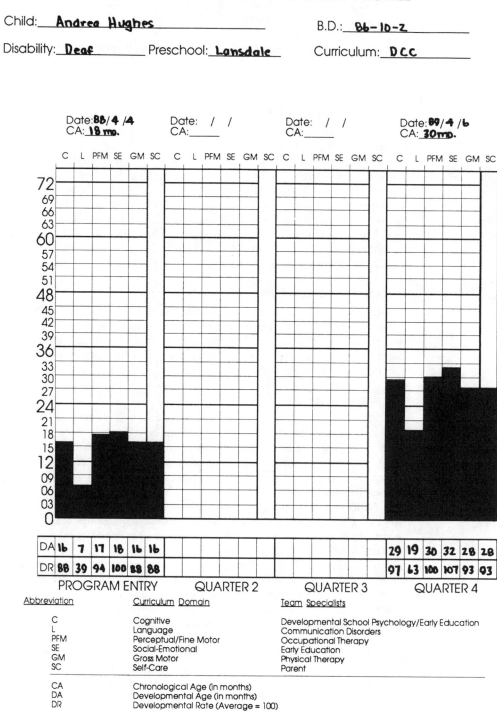

	C	L	PFM	SE	GM	SC
DA	16	7	17	18	16	16
DR	88	39	94	100	88	88

PROGRAM ENTRY

	C	L	PFM	SE	GM	SC
DA	29	19	30	32	28	28
DR	97	63	100	107	93	93

QUARTER 2　　QUARTER 3　　QUARTER 4

Abbreviation	Curriculum Domain	Team Specialists
C	Cognitive	Developmental School Psychology/Early Education
L	Language	Communication Disorders
PFM	Perceptual/Fine Motor	Occupational Therapy
SE	Social-Emotional	Early Education
GM	Gross Motor	Physical Therapy
SC	Self-Care	Parent
CA	Chronological Age (in months)	
DA	Developmental Age (in months)	
DR	Developmental Rate (Average = 100)	

Figure 6.20.　Andrea's Early Intervention Progress Profile.

NAME Andrea Hughes _____   AGE 18 months _____

CURRICULUM Developmental Communication Curriculum & Kendall Preschool Curriculum

LINK AUTHENTIC CURRICULUM COMPETENCIES		
Domains/Goals	**Progress Index (0,1,2)**	
	Time 1 Score	**Time 2 Score**
Cognitive ◆ Reaches around barrier for toy ◆ Knows object by use/function ◆ Pairs common objects in play COG TOTAL	*1* *1* *0* *2*	*2* *2* *2* *(6)*
Social-Emotional ◆ Responds to social praise ◆ Enjoys play with friends ◆ Identifies self in mirror SE TOTAL	*1* *1* *1* *3*	*2* *2* *2* *(6)*
Language ◆ Associates signs with objects ◆ Uses gestures for wants ◆ Attends to speaker LNG TOTAL	*0* *0* *0* *0*	*2* *2* *2* *(6)*
Perceptual/Fine Motor ◆ Removes samll toys in boxes ◆ Releases grasp on toy ◆ Shows neat pincer grasp PFM TOTAL	*1* *1* *1* *3*	*2* *2* *2* *(6)*
Gross Motor ◆ Moves about little assistance ◆ Stoops, squats, stands up ◆ Kicks ball in play GM TOTAL	*1* *1* *0* *2*	*2* *2* *2* *(6)*
Self-Care ◆ Feeds self with spoon ◆ Helps in dressing self ◆ Plays by self 10 + SC TOTAL	*1* *1* *0* *2*	*2* *2* *2* *(6)*
AUTHENTIC COMPETENCIES TOTALS **Preintervention** *33% acquisition level* **Postintervention** *100% acquisition level*	*12/36*	*36/36*

Figure 6.21.   LINK authentic goals for Andrea.

PROGRAM/INTERVENE PHASE

A total communication program was judged by the team to be the best approach to promote Andrea's development and learning (see Figure 6.22). Given her near-average cognitive abilities, it was thought that signing paired with words would prove to be the best option. The team believed strongly that Andrea, at her early age, needed to be integrated with typically developing toddlers and preschoolers so that she would readily model appropriate social, communication, and self-regulatory behaviors. The program also emphasized Mrs. Hughes's close involvement in the classroom as a means of learning effective behavior management techniques and teaching behaviors.

EVALUATE/MONITOR PHASE

After 12 months in the center-based program, Andrea showed important functional gains in several developmental and behavior areas (see Figure 6.23). During the same time, Mrs. Hughes had become a much more effective teacher and manager of Andrea's behavior; she was strongly motivated and created highly interactive learning opportunities for Andrea. The staff members were very impressed with Mrs. Hughes's quick ability to understand and use the strategies demonstrated.

A review of Andrea's progress chart showed that the total communication program seemed to be well-matched with Andrea's needs; her language progress had increased from 39% to 63% of the expected rate. In fact, during the 1-year program in the communication area, her language gain was maintained at a normal rate; that is, 1 month of gain for each month of programming. It was decided that Andrea would be integrated increasingly with her typically developing peers as she continued to thrive in the program.

The true measure of Andrea's progress is that she learned the critical authentic curricular competencies that formed the basis for her intervention plan (see Figure 6.21). Before intervention, Andrea had acquired only 33% of the competencies expected; after intervention, she had acquired 100% of those competencies. By using a total communication approach, the team helped Andrea make dramatic gains in social, gestural language, play, and cognitive skills.

∞∞∞∞∞∞ LINK VIGNETTE 6: ∞∞∞∞∞∞
INCLUSIVE PRESCHOOLS FOR CHILDREN WITH
MILD DEVELOPMENTAL DELAYS

Authentic curriculum-based assessment procedures are also valuable for comparative evaluations of the progress of groups of young children in early childhood programs and their longitudinal responses to intervention. From 1991 to 1992, the Bureau of Special Education of the Commonwealth of Pennsylvania instituted the Pennsylvania Preschool Integration Initiative (PAPII). PAPII provided funding and technical support for 23 school districts and three special education intermediate unit programs to establish and operate inclusive early childhood programs for young children with and without developmental delays or disabilities. In conjunction with PAPII, the Bureau of Special Education instituted a program evaluation effort that was designed to monitor the responses to intervention and the progress of young children who met the state's standards for developmental delay; that is, a 25% delay from CA in at least one developmental domain or a standard score of 1.5 standard deviations below the mean (a DQ of 78 or below).

EARLY CHILDHOOD PROGRAM PRESCRIPTIONS

Child: _Andrea Hughes_ CA: _18 months_ Date: _88-4-6_

DEVELOPMENTAL ASSESSMENT SUMMARY: Andrea has many well-developed play, social, motor, and symbolic skills despite her severe hearing impairment. Unlike some other such young children, she has acquired a sense of the value of communicating and has even developed some creative signs on their own. A Total Communication program is vital to foster her range of competencies with mother as a "partner" in the classroom.

DEVELOPMENTAL PROGRAM GUIDELINES:

FEATURES	OPTIONS	COMMENTS
Instructional Setting	☐ Home-based ☒ Center-based ☐ Combo ☐ Hospital-based	_Arrange opportunities with normal toddlers regularly_
Instructional Methods	☒ Verbal prompts ☒ Physical prompts ☐ Shaping	_Andrea already attends expecting manual cues & signs_
Grouping Pattern	☐ 1:1 ☒ 1:1 & small group ☐ 1:1, small/large groups	_Couple some 1-1 language therapy (s) class routines_
Adaptive Arrangements	☐ Special toys ☒ Communication system ☐ Wheelchair ☐ Room arrangement	_Total communication approach_
Auxiliary Therapies	☒ Speech ☐ PT/OT ☒ Psychologist ☐ Pediatrician ☒ Sensory	_Integrate in classroom_ _Focus on preventing behavior problems_ _Consultant on materials_
Behavioral Strategies	☐ Primary reinforcement ☐ Token economy ☐ Behavioral contract ☒ Social praise ☐ Time out ☐ Planned ignoring	_Highly motivated by activities themselves_ _Is motivated by stickers on harder tasks despite young age; great attention_
Parent Participation	☐ Conference only ☒ Parent education/training ☐ Counseling/therapy	_Use TSI to promote mand skills_

Figure 6.22. Andrea's Early Childhood Program Prescriptions Profile.

SUMMATIVE CHILD PROGRESS/PROGRAM EVALUATION SHEET

Child: __Andrea Hughes__　　　　C.A. __30 months__　　　　　　Date: __89-4-6__

Developmental/ Curricular Domain	1ST Quarter			4th Quarter			DA Gain	IEI	CEI	M%	I%
	DA	DA Range	DQ	DA	DA Range	DQ					
COGNITIVE	16	(12-20)	88	29	(24-32)	97	13 mo.	1.08	1.00	81%	19%
LANGUAGE	7	(6-10)	39	19	(12-21)	63	12 mo.	1.00	1.02	39%	61%
SOCIAL-EMOTIONAL	18	(16-24)	100	32	(24-34)	107	14 mo.	1.17	1.08	86%	14%
PERCEPTUAL/ FINE MOTOR	17	(15-19)	94	30	(27-32)	100	13 mo.	1.08	1.00	87%	13%
GROSS MOTOR	16	(15-18)	88	28	(24-30)	93	12 mo.	1.00	1.00	88%	12%
SELF-CARE	16	(12-17)	88	28	(21-28)	93	12 mo.	1.00	.96	88%	12%
DEVELOPMENTAL AVERAGE	15	(6-24)	83	27.7	(12-34)	92	12.7 mo.	1.06	1.02	78%	22%

Figure 6.23.　Evaluation of Andrea's authentic curricular progress.

Within the inclusive classroom programs created by PAPII, 1,112 children (620 with developmental delays and 492 without developmental delays; average CA, 4 years, 3 months), received early childhood education with modifications to accommodate individual differences. A convergent assessment model was used to monitor the children's progress, and various authentic curriculum-based evaluation metrics were used to document learning and evaluate program outcomes and impact (see Table 6.5).

Figure 6.24 shows the authentic curricular goal targets that were most frequently set for young children with developmental delays; these targets were outcomes of the baseline assessments (preintervention) on BDI and 2 to 6 (Bos, Vaugh, & Levine, 1992). Note the focus on curricular competencies that were embedded within integrated instructional activities that em-

Table 6.5.　Authentic curriculum-based assessment and curricular targets for children with developmental delays in PAPII

Type	Scale
Curriculum compatible	BDI
Curriculum embedded	2 to 6 High/Scope
Ecologically based	Preschool Behavior Questionnaire SPECS D–Specs P–Specs

NAME <u>Pennsylvania Preschool Integration Initiative</u>   AGE <u>Average = 51 months</u>

CURRICULUM <u>2-6 Instructional Activities for Children At-Risk and High/Scope</u>

LINK AUTHENTIC CURRICULUM COMPETENCIES		
Domains/Goals	**Progress Index (0,1,2)**	
	Time 1 Score	**Time 2 Score**
<u>Cognitive</u>		
◆ Identifies objects by touch	0	2
◆ Make and compare clay shapes	0	2
◆ Distinguish size and number	1	2
◆ Compare size of familiar objects from memory	0	1
◆ Identifies missing objects	0	1
COG TOTAL	1	(8)
<u>Social-Emotional</u>		
◆ Initiates socal contact-adult	0	2
◆ Initiates social contact-peer	0	1
◆ Attends to stories	1	2
◆ Identifies feelings	0	2
◆ Shares and takes turns in games	0	2
SE TOTAL	1	(9)
<u>Language</u>		
◆ Communicates in social play	0	2
◆ Uses 3-5 word sentences	0	2
◆ Tells personal experiences	0	1
◆ Recalls story details	0	1
LNG TOTAL	0	(6)
AUTHENTIC COMPETENCIES TOTALS **Preintervention** *7% acquisition level* **Postintervention** *82% acquisition level*	2/28	23/28

Figure 6.24.   LINK authentic goals for children participating in PAPII.

phasized survival skills for kindergarten transition in the personal-social, language, and cognitive domains, including turn taking, task orientation and attention, following social rules, interactions with peers and adults, social communication, and readiness in prereading and math.

DEVELOPMENTAL STATUS AND PROGRESS

In this section, we examine the performance of children enrolled in these programs on all nine areas of BDI and 2 to 6. Because BDI is both norm based and curriculum compatible, each child's status at program entry, as well as progress throughout the program, could be age referenced to provide normative comparisons. Comparisons were made with average expecta-

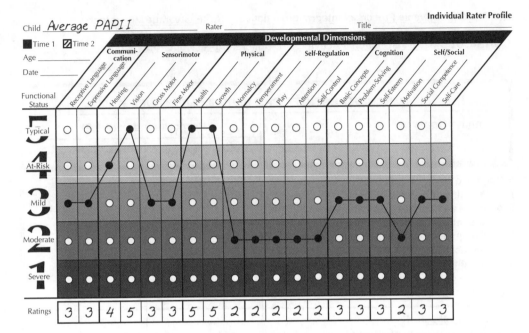

Figure 6.25. Average D–Specs domain ratings (by parents and teachers) for children participating in PAPII.

tions and between groups of children who were nondevelopmentally delayed (NDD) and groups of children without developmental delays (DD). Furthermore, because BDI and 2 to 6 items, themselves, are curricular goals commonly included in early childhood programs, this process is also useful for appraising curriculum-based progress; analyses of progress and differences on developmental curricular objectives were made for each group. Figure 6.25 shows parents' and teachers' convergent average D–Specs ratings of the children. Preintervention functional capabilities reveal that most skills are mildly to moderately delayed.

DD Group ($n = 373$)

Table 6.6 shows that children in the DD group do, indeed, exhibit clear (mild) impairments in all nine BDI areas and meet Pennsylvania standards

Table 6.6. Developmental status and progress of DD group

BDI subdomains (Overall years 1+2)	DD (time 1)		DD (time 2)		$p < 0.05$
	DA	DQ	DA	DQ	
Personal-social	36	64	45	71.4	$p = 0.000$
Adaptive	43.5	77.4	49.5	78.6	$p = 0.000$
Motor	40.5	72	50.5	80.2	$p = 0.000$
Gross motor	43.5	77.4	49	77.8	$p = 0.000$
Fine motor	36	64	46	73	$p = 0.000$
Communication	35	62.2	45.5	72.2	$p = 0.000$
Receptive language	39	69.4	50	79.4	$p = 0.000$
Expressive language	35	62.2	45	71.4	$p = 0.000$
Cognitive	39.5	70.2	49.5	78.6	$p = 0.000$

for early intervention. The average CA in the DD group was 53 months, and the average DA was 43 months. The DQ range was 61–77, and the mean DQ was 69. There is, therefore, no question that these children would be considered eligible for and in need of special early education. It seemed important to examine and make definitive the special needs status of the children in the DD group so that progress might better be appreciated.

The progress of the DD group is clear and encouraging. Statistically significant progress was manifested in all nine BDI areas over the 2-year period (i.e., from the beginning of year 2 to the end of year 3) when DA was the dependent variable. The greatest gains, in order from largest to smallest, were shown in the personal-social, motor, cognitive, and communication domains. Despite these noteworthy gains, it is clear that, at end of year 3, the children in the DD group still met the standards for special education and required some support services—in particular, in the personal-social, fine motor, and expressive language domains. In summary, the children's progress was great, but their developmental lag remained.

NDD Group (*n* = 214)

Table 6.7 shows that children in the NDD group seem typical of Head Start participants. The NDD group displayed no significant impairments on the BDI, although, like Head Start children, they had some immaturities/lack of experiences (DQ range, 76–100; mean, 85) with some problems in speech and language and in school readiness. The NDD group is, therefore, typical of children who can benefit from professional attention but who do not meet Pennsylvania standards for early intervention.

The NDD group showed significant improvement in all nine BDI areas, with more marked progress being displayed in personal-social, motor, and language areas. Both the DD and NDD groups, therefore, displayed satisfactory or better progress while participating in PAPII inclusive programs.

Comparative Curricular Gains of DD and NDD Groups

Table 6.8 displays the comparisons of BDI gains in terms of curricular goals achieved (rather than norm-referenced comparisons). For these comparisons, we use *effect size* to portray more meaningfully the practical significance of the gains and differences. Effect size reflects the statistical strength of a relationship independent of sample size and is increasingly

Table 6.7.   Developmental status and progress of NDD group

BDI subdomains (Overall years 1+2)	NDD (time 1)		NDD (time 2)		$p < 0.05$
	DA	DQ	DA	DQ	
Personal-social	45	80.8	55	88.1	$p = 0.000$
Adaptive	49.5	88.9	58.5	93.7	$p = 0.000$
Motor	45	80.8	56	89.7	$p = 0.000$
Gross motor	46	82.6	55.5	88.9	$p = 0.000$
Fine motor	46	82.6	56	89.7	$p = 0.000$
Communication	47.5	85.3	51.5	82.5	$p = 0.000$
Receptive language	50	89.6	62.5	100	$p = 0.000$
Expressive language	45	80.8	56.5	90.5	$p = 0.000$
Cognitive	51.5	92.4	61	97.7	$p = 0.000$

Table 6.8.   Developmental curricular progress for DD and NDD groups for years 2 and 3 combined

BDI domains	DD (n = 373)			NDD (n = 214)			CEI
	Time 1	Time 2	Differ- ence	Time 1	Time 2	Differ- ence	
Personal- social	27.1	32.1	+5.0	32.1	35.5	+3.4	1.47
Adaptive	26.9	30.0	+3.1	30.0	32.9	+2.9	1.07
Motor	25.1	29.5	+4.4	28.0	32.0	+4.0	1.10
Gross motor	11.9	14.0	+2.1	13.2	15.3	+2.1	1.00
Fine motor	13.0	15.4	+2.4	14.9	16.8	+1.9	1.26
Communi- cation	20.3	23.9	+3.6	24.8	27.5	+2.7	1.33
Receptive language	10.0	11.8	+1.8	12.3	13.7	+1.4	1.29
Expressive language	9.9	12.2	+2.3	12.4	13.9	+1.5	1.53
Cognitive	21.4	25.4	+4.0	26.0	28.2	+2.2	1.82
Total	165.6	194.3	+28.7	193.7	215.8	+22.1	
Mean	18.4	21.6	+3.2	21.5	24.0	+2.5	1.30

used to appraise the practical *functional* significance of intervention or treatment outcomes; that is, the educational validity of these results.

For both year 2 and year 3, it is clear that the developmental trajectory of the DD group is greater than that of the NDD group in all nine areas. This greater rate of improvement might be interpreted as a catching-up phenomenon and/or at least as a partial regression effect, wherein lower-scoring children show greater percentages of improvement. In any event, it is encouraging to see that the children in the DD group do, indeed, display improvements at a greater pace than they had previously and that they are "closing the gap" between themselves and the children in the NDD group. (Effect sizes are −0.03–0.61 with corresponding percentiles of 49–73.)

The NDD group progressed at expected (norm) or *better* rates in all BDI areas; in comparison, the DD group's progress is all the more impressive.

Figure 6.26 illustrates the overall curricular progress of the DD group for years 2 and 3 combined by using the NDD group as a "local norm." The CEI was used to examine progress within the program's curriculum and adjust for time in the program. The DD group's progress was, therefore, divided by time-in-program. Then, to compare the DD group's progress with the program's expected impact on typically developing children (i.e., the NDD group), the DD group's progress/time-in-program was divided by the progress rate of the NDD group. This procedure allows for meaningful comparisons within a given program, class, or teacher's unit.

Because the children in the NDD group showed expected or better progress, they serve as a standard against which the children in the DD group may be compared to permit interpretations even beyond the local level. With the "typical" contrast group, therefore, comparisons were made over a 10-month period. Remember that the BDI instrument was used as a curriculum to design IEP/IFSP goals. Therefore, we measured *acquisition of actual functional skills* that are the basis of IEP, IFSP, and program activ-

Comparative Goal Attainment During Inclusive Education

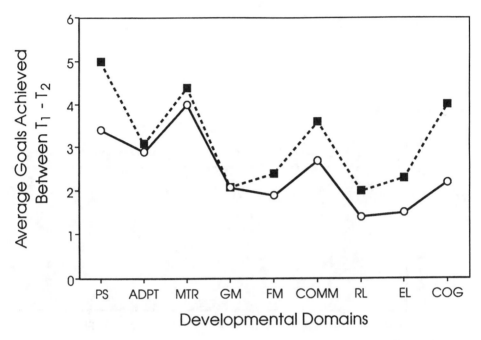

Figure 6.26. Comparative goal attainment of children in the DD and NDD groups during inclusive education. (--■-- = DD; –O– = NDD.)

ities to make the following comparisons: 1) the NDD group, on average, achieved a total of 22 goals, or 2.5 annual goals in each BDI area; and 2) the DD group attained 29 goals, or 3.2 annual goals in each area.

Dividing the CEI of the DD group by that of the NDD group provides an additional comparison (see Figure 6.27): the DD children show an average CEI of 1.30 with a range of 1.1–1.82, depending on BDI area. In other words, DD group progress is 130% of NDD group progress; that is, 130% of local or normal expectation in terms of number of curricular goals achieved!

The greatest curricular progress was observed in the personal-social, expressive/receptive, cognitive, and fine motor areas. These findings are consistent with the norm-referenced results but are of direct relevance to the intervention efforts in the programs.

Figure 6.24 portrays the types of specific real-life curricular competencies that formed the basis for inclusive early education for the children in the DD group and quantifies the group's curricular gains on specific instructional skills.

The progress of children on the BDI tasks and 2 to 6 curriculum showed the accelerated learning curve for the DD group. Figure 6.24 also reveals that, before inclusive intervention, the children had acquired only 7% of the expected cognitive, social-emotional, and language skills. After intervention, the DD group had acquired 82% of these authentic curricular competencies. As a group, the most frequent skill acquisitions occurred in distinguishing size and number, initiating social contacts, increasing atten-

Curriculum Goal Acquisition Rates for DD Group Compared to NDD Group Norms (1989 to 1992)

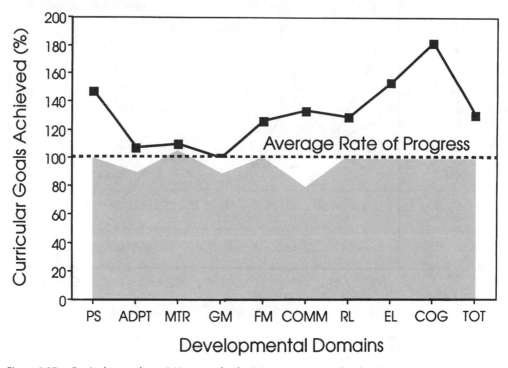

Figure 6.27. Curriculum goal acquisition rates for the DD group compared with NDD group norms for the period for 1989 to 1992. (–■– = DD; ■■ = NDD.)

tion to tasks, sharing and taking turns, social communication, and using longer sentences.

CONCLUSIONS

The LINK vignettes of Derek, Sara, Nicki, Andrea, Charlie, and the PAPII research groups offer real-life applications to the real-life issues faced by young children and their families, teachers, program administrators, and other professionals. The LINK vignettes combine descriptive information, quantitative assessment data, critical instances of child progress, and child work and performance to illustrate the use of a convergent assessment approach within a curriculum-based model of authentic evaluation. These vignettes demonstrate that such an approach provides the most unique, most defensible, and richest strategy for linking assessment and curricular outcomes and for evaluating a child's developmental progress and a program's impact.

References

Abidin, R. (1995). *Parenting Stress Index (PSI)*. Odessa, FL: Psychological Assessment Resources, Inc.

Alpern, G., Boll, T., & Shearer, M. (1986). *Developmental Profile II (DP II)*. Los Angeles: Western Psychological Services.

Arndorfer, R., & Miltenberger, R. (1993). Functional assessment and treatment of challenging behavior: A review with implications for early childhood. *Topics in Early Childhood Special Education, 13*(1), 82–105.

Ausubel, D.P., & Sullivan, E.V. (1970). The nature of developmental processes. In D.P. Ausubel & E.V. Sullivan (Eds.), *Theory and problems of child development* (2nd ed., pp. 98–132). New York: Grune & Stratton.

Bagnato, S.J. (1980). Developmental scales and developmental curricula: Forging a linkage for early intervention. *Topics in Early Childhood Special Education, 1*(2), 1–8.

Bagnato, S.J., & Hofkosh, D. (1990). Curriculum-based developmental assessment for infants with special needs: Synchronizing the pediatric early intervention team. In E.D. Gibbs & D.M. Teti (Eds.), *Interdisciplinary assessment of infants: A guide for early intervention professionals* (pp. 161–175). Baltimore: Paul H. Brookes Publishing Co.

Bagnato, S.J., & Neisworth, J.T. (1979). Between assessment and intervention: Forging an assessment/curriculum linkage for the handicapped preschooler. *Child Care Quarterly, 8*(3), 179–195.

Bagnato, S.J., & Neisworth, J.T. (1980). The Intervention Efficiency Index (IEI): An approach to preschool program accountability. *Exceptional Children, 46*(4), 264–269.

Bagnato, S.J., & Neisworth, J.T. (1983). Monitoring developmental progress of young exceptional children: The Curricular Efficiency Index (CEI). *Journal of Special Education, 17*(2), 189–193.

Bagnato, S.J., & Neisworth, J.T. (1990). *System to Plan Early Childhood Services (SPECS)*. Circle Pines, MN: American Guidance Service.

Bagnato, S.J., & Neisworth, J.T. (1991a). *Assessment for early intervention: Best practices for professionals*. New York: Guilford Press.

Bagnato, S.J., & Neisworth, J.T. (1991b). How can teamwork be effective: In S.J. Bagnato & J.T. Neisworth (Eds.), *Assessment for early intervention: Best practices for professionals* (pp. 14–35). New York: Guilford Press.

Bagnato, S.J., & Neisworth, J.T. (1994). A national study of the social and treatment "invalidity" of intelligence testing for early intervention. *School Psychology Quarterly, 9*(2), 81–102.

Bagnato, S.J., Neisworth, J.T., & Capone, A. (1986). Curriculum-based assessment for the young exceptional child: Rationale and review. *Topics in Early Childhood Special Education, 6*(2), 97–110.

Bagnato, S.J., Neisworth, J.T., & Munson, S.M. (1989). *Linking developmental assessment and early intervention: Curriculum-based prescriptions.* Rockville, MD: Aspen Publishers.

Bagnato, S.J., Neisworth, J.T., & Munson, S.M. (1993). Sensible assessment. In D. Bryant & M. Graham (Eds.), *Implementing early intervention* (pp. 148–155). New York: Guilford Press.

Bailey, D.B., Clifford, R.M., & Harms, T. (1982). Comparison of preschool environments for handicapped and nonhandicapped children. *Topics in Early Childhood Special Education, 2*(1), 9–20.

Bailey, D.B., & Henderson, L. (1993). Traditions in family assessment: Toward a reflective, inquiry-oriented approach. In D.M. Bryant & M. Graham (Eds.), *Implementing early intervention: From research to best practice* (pp. 124–147). New York: Guilford Press.

Bailey, D.B., & Simeonsson, R.J. (1988a). Assessing needs of families with handicapped infants. *Journal of Special Education, 22*(1), 117–127.

Bailey, D.B., & Simeonsson, R.J. (1988b). *Family assessment in early intervention.* Columbus, OH: Charles E. Merrill.

Bailey, D.B., & Simeonsson, R.J. (1990). *Family Needs Survey (FNS).* Chapel Hill, NC: Frank Porter Graham Child Development Center.

Bailey, D.B., & Wolery, M. (1989). *Assessing infants and preschoolers with handicaps.* Columbus, OH: Charles E. Merrill.

Bailey, D.B., & Wolery, M. (1992). *Teaching infants and preschoolers with handicaps.* Columbus, OH: Charles E. Merrill.

Bayley, N. (1969). *Bayley Scales of Infant Development.* New York: Psychological Corporation.

Bayley, N. (1993). *Bayley Scales of Infant Development–Second edition.* New York: Psychological Corporation.

Bell, R.Q. (1979). Parent, child, and reciprocal influences. *American Psychologist, 34,* 821–826.

Bell, R.Q., & Harper, L.V. (1977). *Child effects on adults.* Hillsdale, NJ: Lawrence Erlbaum Associates.

Bos, C., Vaughn, S., & Levine, L. (1992). *2 to 6: Instructional activities for children at risk.* De Soto, TX: Science Research Associates.

Brazelton, T.B. (1973). *Neonatal Behavioral Assessment Scale.* London: Spastics International Medical Publications.

Bricker, D. (1988). *Early intervention with at-risk and handicapped infants.* Glenview, IL: Scott-Foresman & Co.

Bricker, D. (Ed.). (1993). *Assessment, Evaluation, and Programming System for infants and children: Vol. 1. AEPS measurement for birth to three years.* Baltimore: Paul H. Brookes Publishing Co.

Bricker, D., & Cripe, J.J.W. (1992). *An activity-based approach to early intervention.* Baltimore: Paul H. Brookes Publishing Co.

Bricker, D., & Pretti-Frontczak, K. (Eds.). (1996). *Assessment, Evaluation, and Programming System (AEPS) for infants and children: Vol. 3. AEPS measurement for three to six years.* Baltimore: Paul H. Brookes Publishing Co.

Bricker, D., & Squires, J. (1989). The effectiveness of parental screening of at-risk infants: The infant monitoring questionnaires. *Topics in Early Childhood Special Education, 9,* 67–85.

Bricker, D., Squires, J., & Mounts, L., Potter, L., Nickel, B., & Farrell, J. (1995). *Ages & Stages Questionnaires (ASQ): A parent-completed, child-monitoring system.* Baltimore: Paul H. Brookes Publishing Co.

Bricker, D., & Waddell, M. (Eds.). (1996). *Assessment, Evaluation, and Programming System for infants and children: Vol. 4. AEPS curriculum for three to six years.* Baltimore: Paul H. Brookes Publishing Co.

Brigance, A.H. (1985). *BRIGANCE prescriptive readiness: Strategies and practice.* N. Billerica, MA: Curriculum Associates.

Brigance, A.H. (1991). *BRIGANCE Diagnostic Inventory of Early Development–Revised (BDIED–R).* N. Billerica, MA: Curriculum Associates.

Bromwich, A. J. (1981). *Working with parents and infants: An interactional approach.* Baltimore: University Park Press.

Bronfenbrenner, U. (1979). *The ecology of human development.* Cambridge, MA: Harvard University Press.

Brown, L.B., Simmons, J.C., & Methwin, E. (1994). *Oregon Project Curriculum for Visually Impaired and Blind Preschool Children.* Medford, OR: Jackson County Education Service District.

Bruder, M.B. (Ed.). (1993a). *A model for statewide faculty training.* Philadelphia: Temple University, Northeastern Early Intervention Faculty Training Institute.

Caldwell, B., & Bradley, R.A. (1978). *Home Observation for Measurement of the Environment (HOME).* Little Rock: University of Arkansas.

Cohen, L.J., & Spenciner, L.G. (1994). *Assessment of young children.* New York: Longman.

Cole, M., & Cole, S. (1989). *The development of children.* New York: Scientific American Books.

Cole, K.N., Swisher, M.V., Thompson, M.D., & Fewell, R.R. (1985). Enhancing the sensitivity of assessment instruments for children: Graded multidimensional scoring. *Journal of The Association for Persons with Severe Handicaps, 10*(4), 209–213.

Cone, J.D., Bourland, G., & Woods-Shuman, S. (1986). Template matching: An objective approach to placing clients in appropriate residential services. *Journal of The Association for Persons with Severe Handicaps, 85*(2), 110–117.

Coster, W.J., & Haley, S.M. (1992). Conceptualization and measurement of disablement in infants and young children. *Infants and Young Children, 4,* 11–22.

Coutinho, L.P., & Malouf, L. (1992). Performance assessment and children with disabilities: Issues and possibilities. *Teaching Exceptional Children, 25*(4), 62–67.

Cripe, J., Slentz, K., & Bricker, D. (1993). *Assessment, Evaluation, and Programming System (AEPS) for infants and children: Vol. 2. AEPS curriculum for birth to three years.* Baltimore: Paul H. Brookes Publishing Co.

Cronbach, L. (1988). Five perspectives on validity argument. In H. Wainer (Ed.), *Test validity* (pp. 3–17). Hillsdale, NJ: Lawrence Erlbaum Associates.

Diamond, K., & Squires, J. (1993). The role of parental report in the screening and assessment of young children. *Journal of Early Intervention, 17*(2), 107–115.

Division for Early Childhood Task Force on Recommended Practices. (1993). *Recommended practices: Indicators of quality in programs for infants and young children with special needs and their families.* Reston, VA: Council for Exceptional Children, Division for Early Childhood.

Dodge, D.T., & Colker, L. (1992). *Creative Curriculum for Early Childhood* (3rd ed.). Washington, DC: Teaching Strategies.

Dunst, C. (1980). *Uzgiris-Hunt Scales of Infant Psychological Development Scale (IPDS).* Pittsburgh, PA: Allegheny-Singer Research Institute.

Dunst, C.J. (1981). *Infant learning: A cognitive-linguistic intervention strategy.* Austin, TX: PRO-ED.

Dunst, C.J. (1991, January). *Symposium on family-centered care—From principles to practices.* Paper presented at the Leadership Training Institute for Faculty Involved in the Preparation of Family-Centered Early Interventionists, Center for Developmental Disabilities, University Affiliated Program of Vermont and Parent to Parent of Vermont, Burlington, VT.

Dunst, C.J., Jenkins, V., & Trivette, C.M. (1984). Family support scale: Reliability and validity. *Journal of Individual, Family and Community Wellness, 1*(4), 45–52.

Dunst, C.J., & McWilliam, R.A. (1988). Cognitive assessment of multiply handicapped young children. In T.D. Wachs & R. Sheehan (Eds.), *Assessment of developmentally disabled children* (pp. 213–238). New York: Plenum.

Education for All Handicapped Children Act of 1975, PL 94-142, 20 U.S.C. § 1400 *et seq.*

Education of the Handicapped Act Amendments of 1986, PL 99-457, 20 U.S.C. § 1400 *et seq.*

Elliot, S.N. (1991). Authentic assessment: An introduction to a neobehavioral approach to classroom assessment. *School Psychology Quarterly, 6,* 273–278.

Elliot, S.N. (1994). *Creating meaningful performance assessments: Fundamental concepts.* Reston, VA: Council for Exceptional Children.

Ensher, G.L., Bobish, T.P., Gardner, E.F., Michaels, C.A., Butler, K.G., Foertsch, D., & Cooper, C. (1996). *Syracuse Scales of Infant and Toddler Development (SSITD).* Syracuse, NY: Applied Symbolix.

Ensher, G.L., Bobish, T.P., Meller, P.J., Gardner, E.F., Michaels, C.A., & Butler, K.G. (in press). *Developmental scoring form: Syracuse Scales of Infant Development.* Syracuse, NY: Applied Symbolix.

Feuerstein, R. (1979). *Dynamic assessment of retarded performers.* Baltimore: University Park Press.

Feuerstein, R. (1980). *Instructional enrichment.* Baltimore: University Park Press.

Fuchs, D., Fuchs, L.S., Benowitz, S., & Barringer, K. (1987). Norm referenced tests: Are they valid for use with handicapped students? *Exceptional Children, 54*(3), 263–271.

Gesell, A. (1923). *The preschool child: From the standpoint of public hygiene and education.* Boston: Houghton Mifflin.

Gesell, A. (1949). *Gesell Developmental Schedules.* New York: Psychological Corporation.

Glascoe, F., MacLean, W., & Stone, W. (1991). The importance of parents' concerns about their child's behavior. *Clinical Pediatrics, 30,* 8–11.

Glover, E., Preminger, J., & Sanford, A. (1995). *Early Learning Accomplishment Profile (E–LAP).* Chapel Hill, NC: Chapel Hill Training–Outreach Project.

Glover, E., Preminger, J., Sanford, A., & Zelman, J. (1995). *Learning Accomplishment Profile–Revised (LAP–R).* Chapel Hill, NC: Chapel Hill Training–Outreach Project.

Goodman, J.F. (1990). Infant intelligence: Do we, can we, should we assess it? In C. Reynolds & R. Kamphaus (Eds.), *Handbook of psychological and educational measurement of children* (pp. 183–208). New York: Guilford Press.

Goodwin, W.L., & Goodwin, L.D. (1995). Young children measurement: Standardized and nonstandardized instruments in early childhood education. In *Research strategies for early childhood education.* Washington, DC: National Association for the Education of Young Children.

Greenspan, S., & Meisels, S. (1994). Toward a new vision for the developmental assessment of infants and young children. *ZERO TO THREE, 14*(6), 1–8.

Gresham, F., & Elliott, S.R. (1990). *Social Skills Rating System.* Circle Pines, MN: American Guidance Service.

Haley, S.M., Coster, W.J., Ludlow, L.H., Haltwanger, J.T., & Andrellos, P.J. (1992). *Pediatric Evaluation of Disability Inventory (PEDI): Development, standardization, and administration manual.* Boston: PEDI Research Group and New England Medical Center Hospital.

Haley, S.M., Hallenborg, S.C., & Gans, B.M. (1989). Functional assessment in young children with neurological impairments. *Topics in Early Childhood Special Education, 9*(1), 106–126.

Hanline, M.F., & Knowlton, A. (1988). A collaborative model for providing support to parents during their child's transition from infant intervention to preschool special education public school programs. *Journal of the Division for Early Childhood, 12*(2), 116–125.

Hanna, R.P., Lippert, E.A., & Harris, A.B. (1982). *Developmental Communications Curriculum.* San Antonio, TX: Psychological Corporation.

Hanson, M.J. (1987). *Teaching the infant with Down syndrome: A guide for parents and professionals* (2nd ed.). Austin, TX: PRO-ED.

Harms, T., & Clifford, R.M. (1980). *Early Childhood Environment Rating Scale (ECERS).* New York: Teachers College Press.

Harms, T., & Clifford, R.M. (1989). *Family Day Care Rating Scale (FDRS).* New York: Teachers College Press.

Harms, T., Cryer, D., & Clifford, R.M. (1990). *Infant/Toddler Environment Rating Scale (ITERS).* New York: Teachers College Press.

Hassett, V.B., & Herson, M. (Eds.). (1987). *Psychological evaluation of the developmentally and physically disabled.* New York: Plenum.

Havinghurst, R. (Ed.). (1958). *Education of the gifted: 57th Yearbook of the National Society for the Study of Education, Part 2.* Chicago: University of Chicago Press.

Hayes, S.C., Nelson, R.O., & Jarrett, R.B. (1987). The treatment utility of assessment: A functional approach to evaluating assessment quality. *American Psychologist, 42,* 963–974.

High/Scope Staff. (1992). *High/Scope Child Observation Record (COR).* Ypsilanti, MI: High/Scope Press.

Hresko, W., Miguel, S., Sherbenou, R., & Burton, S. (1994). *Developmental Observation Checklist System (DOCS).* Austin, TX: PRO-ED.

Individuals with Disabilities Education Act Amendments of 1991, PL 102-119, 20 U.S.C. § 1400 *et seq.*

Irwin, J.V., & Wong, S.P. (1974). Compensation for maturity in long-range intervention studies. *Acta Symbolica, 5*(4), 33–45.

Jellnek, J.A. (1985). Documentation of child progress revisited: An analysis method for outreach or local programs. *Journal of Division for Early Childhood, 9*(2), 175–182.

Johnson-Martin, N.M., Attermeier, S.M., & Hacker, B.J. (1990). *The Carolina Curriculum for Preschoolers with Special Needs.* Baltimore: Paul H. Brookes Publishing Co.

Johnson-Martin, N.M., Jens, K.G., Attermeier, S.M., & Hacker, B.J. (1991). *The Carolina Curriculum for Infants and Toddlers with Special Needs* (2nd ed.). Baltimore: Paul H. Brookes Publishing Co.

Kiresuk, T.J., Smith, A.S., & Cardillo, J.E., (1994). *Goal Attainment Scaling: Applications, theory, measurement.* Hillsdale, NJ: Lawrence Erlbaum Associates.

Knobloch, H., Stevens, F., & Malone, A.F. (1980). *Gesell Developmental Schedules: Manual of developmental diagnosis* (rev. ed.). New York: Harper & Row.

Korsten, J.E., Dunn, D.D., Foss, T.V., & Francke, M.K. (1993). *Every Move Counts.* San Antonio, TX: Therapy Skill Builders/Psychological Corporation.

Krug, D., Arick, J., & Almond, P. (1980). *Autism Screening Instrument for Educational Planning, second edition (ASIEP–2).* Austin, TX: PRO-ED.

Langley, B. (1980). *Teachable moment and the handicapped infant.* Reston, VA: Council for Exceptional Children.

LeVan, R. (1990). Clinical sampling in the assessment of young, handicapped children: Shopping for skills. *Topics in Early Childhood Special Education, 10*(3), 65–79.

Lewis, V. (1987). *Development and handicap.* New York: Basil Blackwell.

Lidz, C.S. (1991). *Practitioner's guide to dynamic assessment.* New York: Guilford Press.

Lillie, D.L. (1975). *Carolina Developmental Profile.* Winston-Salem, NC: Kaplan Press.

Lincoln, Y.S., & Guba, E.G. (1985). *Naturalistic inquiry.* Beverly Hills, CA: Sage Publications.

Linder, T.W. (1993a). *Transdisciplinary Play-Based Assessment: A functional approach to working with young children* (Rev. ed.). Baltimore: Paul H. Brookes Publishing Co.

Linder, T.W. (1993b). *Transdisciplinary Play-Based Intervention: Guidelines for developing a meaningful curriculum for young children.* Baltimore: Paul H. Brookes Publishing Co.

Mahoney, G.J., & Powell, A. (1986). *The transactional intervention program: Teacher's guide.* Farmington: University of Connecticut Health Center Pediatric Research and Training Center.

Marsden, D.B., Meisels, S.J., Jablon, J.R., & Dichtelmiller, M.L. (1994). *Work Sampling System: Kindergarten developmental guidelines.* Ann Arbor, MI: Rebus Planning Associates.

Martin, R.P. (1988). *Temperament Assessment Battery for Children (TABC)*. Austin, TX: PRO-ED.

McAllister, J. (1994). *Instrument for Measuring Progress (IMP)*. Pittsburgh, PA: Children's Hospital of Pittsburgh.

McKerns, D., & Motchkavitz, L.M. (1993). *Therapeutic Education for the Child with Traumatic Brain Injury: From Coma to Kindergarten*. San Antonio, TX: Psychological Corporation.

McLaughlin, R., & Warren, S.M. (1995). *Performance assessment and students with disabilities: Usage in outcomes-based accountability systems*. Reston, VA: Council for Exceptional Children.

Meisels, S. (1989). High stakes testing in kindergarten. *Educational Leadership, 49*(7), 16–22.

Meisels, S.J., Jablon, J.R., Marsden, D.B., Dichtelmiller, M.L., Dorfman, A.B., & Steele, D.M. (1994). *Work Sampling System: An overview* (3rd ed.). Ann Arbor, MI: Rebus Planning Associates.

Merrell, K.W. (1994). *Preschool and Kindergarten Behavior Scales (PKBS)*. Austin, TX: PRO-ED.

Messick, S. (1988). The once and future issues of validity: Assessing the meaning and consequence of measurement. In H. Wainer (Ed.), *Test validity* (pp. 33–45). Hillsdale, NJ: Lawrence Erlbaum Associates.

Messick, S. (1989). Meaning and values in test validation: The science and ethics of assessment. *Educational Researcher, 18*(2), 5–11.

Meyer, C. (1992). What's the difference between *authentic* and *performance* assessment? *Educational Leadership, 49*(8), 39–40.

Mittler, P. (Ed.). (1981). *Frontiers of knowledge in mental retardation*. Baltimore: University Park Press.

Moog, J., & Geers, A. (1975). *Scales of Early Communication Skills for hearing impaired children (SECS)*. St. Louis, MO: Central Institute for the Deaf.

Mori, A.A., & Neisworth, J.T. (1983). Curricula in early childhood education: Some generic and special considerations. *Topics in Early Childhood Special Education, 2*(4), 1–8.

Moss, P. (1992). Shifting conceptions of validity in educational measurement: Implications for performance assessment. *Review of Educational Research, 62*(3), 229–258.

Mott, S.E., Fewell, R.R., Lewis, M., Meisels, S., Shonkoff, J., & Simeonsson, R.J. (1986). Methods for assessing child and family outcomes in early childhood special education programs: Some views from the field. *Topics in Early Childhood Special Education, 6*(2), 1–15.

National Association for the Education of Young Children. (1991). *Developmentally appropriate practice*. Washington, DC: Author.

National Association for the Education of Young Children. (1996). *Guidelines for preparation of early childhood professionals*. Washington, DC: Author.

National Association for the Education of Young Children & National Association of Early Childhood Specialists in State Departments of Education. (1991). Guidelines for appropriate curriculum content and assessment in programs serving children ages 3 through 8. *Young Children, 46*(3), 21–38.

National Association of School Psychologists. (1990). *Statement on assessment in early childhood*. Rockville, MD: Author.

Nehring, A.D., Nehring, E.F., Bruni, J.R., & Randolph P.L. (1992). *Learning Accomplishment Profile–Diagnostic Standardized Assessment (LAP–D)*. Lewisville, NC: Kaplan School Supply & Chapel Hill Training–Outreach Project.

Neilsen, S., van den Pol, R., Guidry, J., Keeley, E., & Honzel, R. (1994). *On Track: A comprehensive system for early childhood intervention*. Longmont, CO: Sopris West.

Neisworth, J.T., & Bagnato, S.J. (1988). Assessment in early childhood special education: A typology of dependent measures. In S.L. Odom & M.B. Karnes (Eds.), *Early intervention for infants and children with handicaps: An empirical base* (pp. 23–49). Baltimore: Paul H. Brookes Publishing Co.

Neisworth, J.T., & Bagnato, S.J. (1992). The case against intelligence testing in early intervention. *Topics in Early Childhood Special Education, 12*(1), 1–20.

Neisworth, J.T., & Bagnato, S.J. (1996). Recommended practices in assessment for early intervention. In S. Odom & M. McLean (Eds.), *Early intervention/early childhood–special education: Recommended practices.* Austin, TX: PRO-ED.

Neisworth, J.T., Bagnato, S.J., & Salvia, J. (1995). Neurobehavioral markers for early regulatory disorders. *Infants and Young Children, 8*(1) 8–17.

Newborg, J., Stock, J.R., Wnek, L., Guidubaldi, J., & Svinicki, J.S. (1988). *Battelle Developmental Inventory (BDI).* Chicago: Riverside.

Newland, T.E. (1973). The psychological assessment of exceptional children and youth. In W.M. Cruickshank (Ed.), *Psychology of exceptional children and youth* (3rd ed.). Englewood Cliffs, NJ: Prentice Hall.

Nurse, J.R., & McGauvran, M.E. (1986). *Metropolitan Readiness Tests.* San Antonio, TX: Psychological Corporation.

Odom, S., & McLean, M. (Eds.). (1996). *Early intervention/early childhood–special education: Recommended practices.* Austin, TX: PRO-ED.

Odom, S., & Shuster, S. (1986). Naturalistic inquiry and the assessment of young handicapped children and their families. *Topics in Early Childhood Special Education, 4*(4), 1–19.

Parks, S. (1992a). *HELP strands: Curriculum-based developmental assessment birth to three years.* Palo Alto, CA: VORT Corporation.

Parks, S. (1992b). *Inside HELP: Hawaii Early Learning Profile administration and reference manual.* Palo Alto, CA: VORT Corporation.

Pellegrini, A.D., & Dresden, J. (1991). The concept of development in the early childhood curriculum. In B. Spodek & O.N. Saracho (Eds.), *Issues in early childhood curriculum* (pp. 46–63). New York: Teachers College Press.

Perrone, V. (1991, Spring). On standardized testing: A position paper of the Association for Childhood Education International. *Childhood Education,* 132–142.

Peterson, N.L. (1987). *Early intervention for handicapped and at-risk children: An introduction to early childhood special education.* Denver, CO: Love Publishing Co.

Piaget, J. (1952). *The origins of intelligence in children.* New York: International Universities Press.

Piaget, J. (1987). *Possibility and necessity: The role of necessity in cognitive development.* Minneapolis: University of Minnesota Press.

Pike, K., & Salend, S.J. (1995, Fall). Authentic assessment strategies: Alternatives to norm-referenced testing. *Teaching Exceptional Children,* 15–20.

Pre-College Programs, Gallaudet University. (1989). *Kendall Demonstration Elementary School (KDES) preschool curriculum guide.* Washington, DC: Pre-College Outreach Services, Kendall Demonstration Elementary School.

Provence, S., Erikson, J., Vater, S., & Palmeri, S. (1995). *Infant-Toddler Developmental Assessment.* Chicago, IL: Riverside.

Reuter, J., & Bickett, L. (1985). *The Kent Infant Development Scale (KIDS).* Kent, OH: Developmental Metrics.

Reynell, J., & Zinkin, K. (1979). *Reynell-Zinkin Developmental Scales for Young Visually Handicapped Children (RZS).* Wood Dale, IL: Stoelting Company.

Rogers, S.J., & D'Eugenio, D.B. (1981). *Developmental Programming for Infants and Young Children (DPIYC): Vol. 2. Early Intervention Developmental Profile (EIDP).* Ann Arbor: University of Michigan Press.

Rosenkoetter, S.E., Hains, A.H., & Fowler, S.A. (1994). *Bridging early services for children with special needs and their families: A practical guide for transition planning.* Baltimore: Paul H. Brookes Publishing Co.

Salvia, J., & Ysseldyke, J.E. (1995). *Assessment in special and remedial education* (6th ed.). Boston: Houghton Mifflin.

Sameroff, A.J., & Chandler, M. (1975). Reproductive risk and the continuum of caretaking casualty. In F.D. Horowitz, M. Hetherington, S. Scarr-Salapatek, & G. Siegle (Eds.), *Review of child development research* (Vol. 4). Chicago: University of Chicago Press.

Scholpler, E., Reichler, R., Bashford, A., Lansing, M., Marcus, L., & Waters, L. (1979). *Individualized Assessment and Treatment for Autistic and Developmentally Disabled Children (IATA).* Austin, TX: PRO-ED.

Schwartz, I.S., & Olswang, L.B. (1996). Evaluating child behavior change in natural settings. *Topics in Early Childhood Special Education, 16*(1), 82–101.

Shonkoff, J.P. (1981). The limitations of normative assessments of high-risk infants. *Topics in Early Childhood Special Education, 3*(1), 29–41.

Simeonssen, R.J. (1985). *Carolina Record of Individual Behavior.* Chapel Hill, NC: Author.

Simeonsson, R.J., Huntington, G.S., & Parse, S.A. (1980). Expanding the developmental assessment of young exceptional children. In J. Gallagher (Ed.), *New directions for exceptional children* (pp. 51–74). San Francisco: Jossey-Bass.

Simeonsson, R.J., Huntington, G.S., & Short, R.J. (1982). Individual differences and goals: An approach to the evaluation of child progress. *Topics in Early Childhood Special Education, 1*(4), 71–80.

Simeonsson, R.J., Huntington, G.S., Short, R.J., & Ware, T. (1982). Carolina Record of Individual Behavior: Characteristics of handicapped infants and children. *Topics in Early Childhood Special Education, 2*(2), 43–55.

Simeonsson, R.J., & Weigerink, R. (1975, April). Accountability: A dilemma in infant intervention. *Exceptional Children,* 474–480.

Slentz, K., & Bricker, D. (1992). Family-guided assessment for IFSP development: Jumping off the family assessment bandwagon. *Journal of Early Intervention, 16*(1), 11–19.

Snell, M. (Ed.). (1987). *Systematic instruction for persons with severe handicaps* (3rd ed.). Columbus, OH: Charles E. Merrill.

Spodek, B., & Saracho, O.N. (1994). *Dealing with individual differences in the early childhood classroom.* New York: Longman.

Sternberg, R.J., Wagner, R.K., Williams, W.M., & Horvath, J.A. (1995). Testing common sense. *American Psychologist, 50*(11), 912–927.

Stillman, R. (1974). *Callier-Azusa Scale: Assessment of Deaf-Blind Children (CAS).* Reston, VA: Council for Exceptional Children.

Suen, H.K., Logan, C.R., Neisworth, J.T., & Bagnato, S.J. (1995). Parent–professional congruence: Is it necessary? *Journal of Early Intervention, 19*(3), 243–252.

Suen, H.K., Lu, C.H., Neisworth, J.T., & Bagnato, S.J. (1993). Measurement of team decision-making through generalizability theory. *Journal of Psychoeducational Assessment, 11,* 120–132.

Terman, L., & Merrill, M. (1960). *Stanford-Binet Intelligence Scale.* Newton, MA: Houghton Mifflin.

Uzgiris, I., & Hunt, J. (1975). *Assessment in infancy: Ordinal scales of psychological development.* Urbana: University of Illinois Press.

VORT Corporation. (1995). *HELP for preschoolers.* Palo Alto, CA: Author.

Vulpe, S. (1994). *Vulpe Assessment Battery–Revised (VAB–R).* East Aurora, NY: Slosson Educational Publications.

Wachs, T.D., & Sheehan, R. (1988). Issues in the linkage of assessment to intervention. In T.D. Wachs & R. Sheehan (Eds.), *Assessment of young developmentally disabled children* (pp. 397–406). New York: Plenum.

Wechsler, D. (1989). *Wechsler Preschool and Primary Scale of Intelligence–Revised.* San Antonio, TX: Psychological Corporation.

Wetherby, A.M., & Prizant, B.M. (1993). *Communication and Symbolic Behavior Scales (CSBS), normed edition.* Chicago: Riverside.

Wiggins, G. (1989). A true test: Toward more authentic and equitable assessment. *Phi Delta Kappan, 70,* 703–713.

Will, M. (1984). *Bridges from school to working life: OSERS programming for the transition of youth with disabilities.* Washington, DC: U.S. Department of Education, Office of Special Education and Rehabilitative Services.

Willoughby-Herb, S.J., & Neisworth, J.T. (1983). *The HICOMP curriculum.* San Antonio, TX: Psychological Corporation.

Wolfe, M.M. (1978). Social validity: The case for subjective measurement or how applied behavior analysis is finding its heart. *Journal of Applied Behavior Analysis, 11,* 203–214.

Woodruff, G., & Hanson, C. (1987). *Project KAI.* Brighton, MA: Handicapped Children's Early Education Program.

World Health Organization. (1980). International classification of impairments, disabilities, and handicaps (ICIDH). Geneva, Switzerland: Author.

Zeitlin, S., & Williamson, G.G. (1994). *Coping in young children: Early intervention practices to enhance adaptive behavior and resilience.* Baltimore: Paul H. Brookes Publishing Co.

Zeitlin, S., Williamson, G.G., & Szczepanski, M. (1988). *Early Coping Inventory (ECI).* Bensenville, IL: Scholastic Testing Service.

Zelazo, P.R., & Barr, R.G. (Eds.). (1989). *Challenges to developmental paradigms: Implications for theory, assessment, and treatment.* Hillsdale, NJ: Lawrence Erlbaum Associates.

Author Index

Subject Index

~~~~~~

Page numbers followed by "f" indicate figures; those followed by "t" indicate tables.